AWAKE IN AMERICA

Other Books by Daniel Tobin

POETRY

Where the World Is Made

Double Life

The Narrows

Second Things

Belated Heavens

CRITICISM

Passage to the Center:
Imagination and the Sacred in the Poetry of Seamus Heaney

AS EDITOR

The Book of Irish American Poetry
from the Eighteenth Century to the Present

Light in Hand: Selected Early Poems of Lola Ridge

Poet's Work, Poet's Play: Essays on the Practice and the Art
(with Pimone Triplett)

Awake in America

ON IRISH AMERICAN POETRY

Daniel Tobin

UNIVERSITY OF NOTRE DAME PRESS
NOTRE DAME, INDIANA

Copyright © 2011 by University of Notre Dame
Notre Dame, Indiana 46556
www.undpress.nd.edu
All Rights Reserved

Published in the United States of America

Library of Congress Cataloging-in-Publication Data

Tobin, Daniel.
  Awake in America : on Irish American poetry / Daniel Tobin.
       p. cm.
  "Portions of many of these essays were given as papers over the years at regional, national, and international meetings of the American Conference for Irish Studies"—Pref.
  Includes bibliographical references and index.
  ISBN-13: 978-0-268-04237-0 (pbk. : alk. paper)
  ISBN-10: 0-268-04237-3 (pbk. : alk. paper)
  1. American poetry—Irish American authors—History and criticism. 2. Irish Americans in literature. 3. National characteristics, Irish, in literature. I. Title. II. Title: Irish American poetry.
  PS153.I78T63 2011
  811.009'89162—dc23
                                                              2011025683

For Ben and Emily

Contents

Preface   ix

"Double Life"   xv

I. DOUBLE LIVES

ONE
Dinner at the Café Marliave   1

"Near Hag's Head"   57

II. READINGS

TWO
Modernism, Leftism, and the Spirit:
The Poetry of Lola Ridge   61

THREE
The Westwardness of Everything:
Irishness in the Poetry of Wallace Stevens   87

FOUR
Lines of Leaving, Lines of Returning:
John Montague's Double Vision   113

FIVE
Starting from Wexford, Ending in the Sublime:
The Poetry of James Liddy   136

SIX
Two for the Road:
The New Irish Routes of Eamonn Wall and Greg Delanty   158

SEVEN
The Parish and Lost America:
The Witness of Michael Coady's *All Souls*   196

EIGHT
Back Through Distance: Currents of Tradition in
the Poetry of Louise Bogan and Thomas McGrath   217

"Crossings"   245

III. CROSSINGS

NINE
The Need for Routes:
Genealogy in Irish American Poetry   249

TEN
From Crispus Attucks to Mr. Bones:
Race in Irish American Poetry   279

ELEVEN
Over There: Irish American Poets Return   322

"A Green Road in Clare"   363

IV. THE WAKE OF EVERYTHING GONE

TWELVE
Soundings and Erasures:
An Irish American Poet Digs Up His Past   367

"The Line"   401

Notes   403
Works Cited   433
Index   445

Preface

The title of this book presents a double entendre to the reader. On the one hand it alludes to the oft-performed ritual of the American wake, that sad and raucous gathering experienced in so many nineteenth-century townlands in which families unable to sustain any more members at home feted their emigrant sons and daughters before they departed for the New World, likely never to come back again. On the other hand, it suggests an awakening in magical lands to the west, Tir na nÓg, the Country of the Young, the far end of those legendary journeys, the *immrama* of Celtic legend. Though perhaps the title poses a triple entendre, for it also aims to affirm a creative and critical awareness of the presence and extent of Irish American poetry within the American literary tradition and also within the traditions of Irish poetry, more broadly conceived and considered. This last may prompt objections from scholars, critics, and poets who prefer to keep their ideas about tradition within long-established boundaries, though one of the central intentions of the inquiry is to explore where such well-worn boundaries become permeable even if they do not entirely break down.

Likewise, the essays that form the chapters of *Awake in America* at times blur the boundaries between literary criticism and the personal essay, or what I would prefer to call the poet's essay. As a poet and critic who happens to be Irish American by circumstance of history—really Irish *and* American since I hold two passports—I have made an effort over the years to comprehend my own creative and critical preoccupations in light of that complex history, that convergence and divergence of lives and cultures. From such a vantage this book constitutes a poet's critical musings in pursuit of self-definition, though the trajectory of this pursuit intends by and large to be more exploratory and outwardly directed than entirely retrospective to the poet's lived experience and creative aspirations. For this reason the reader will also find a degree of recursive progression in some chapters, an overlap of themes and reference that intends to place certain considerations of the subject in somewhat different contexts, following the example of Eavan Boland's *Object Lessons*.

The first section of *Awake in America* presents a reconsideration of the dual tradition of Irish poetry through discussions ranging from the significance of nineteenth-century poets John Boyle O'Reilly, Louise Imogen Guiney, and James Jeffrey Roche to twentieth-century figures Robinson Jeffers, Marianne Moore, Padriac Colum, and Oliver St. John Gogarty; contemporary "New Irish" poets Eamonn Wall and Greg Delanty; Irish American Famine poetry; and the work of noted contemporary Irish American poet Brendan Galvin. The aim of the chapter is to question and expand both scholarly and "writerly" considerations of the relationship between Irish and Irish American poetry.

"Readings," the second section, comprises a series of shorter chapters on poets "over here" in an America born substantially out of tides of diaspora. The first of these essays discusses the significance of the largely forgotten Irish American poet Lola Ridge, whose work during the first half of the twentieth century presented a leftist alternative to modernism. The essay that follows examines "Irishness" as a shaping theme in the work of Wallace Stevens and provides a sustained example of how "Irish America" as a category limited to genetic ancestry is insufficient to the reality, a concern that surfaces by passing example in some of the other essays. Conversely, in the succeeding chapter, I regard Brooklyn-born John Montague's poetry from an American perspective in order to highlight the Irish American component of his work. In turn, I examine James Liddy's poetry from the vantage of the Whitman tradition and the category of the sublime in order to examine the confluence of the Irish parochial and Beat poetics in his hybrid Irish and American poems. The chapter that follows concentrates on the two most important poets of the "New Irish" diaspora to America in the 1980s, Greg Delanty and Eamonn Wall. The focus shifts in the next chapter to Michael Coady's *All Souls*, in which he defines his idea of "presequence" in light of his concern with family, emigration, and genealogy, a discussion that I expand on in the next section. Before turning in that direction, however, the last chapter in this section offers a comparative look at two important American poets with close ties to Ireland in their work—

Louise Bogan and Thomas McGrath—whose contrary aesthetics nonetheless exemplify the persistence of the Irish heritage in the context of American poetry.

The long essays that compose the third section turn their attention to the theme of "Crossings." The first of these engages the impact and importance of genealogy head on and examines how genealogy has influenced Irish American poets from Robinson Jeffers to contemporary women writers such as Mary Swander, Maura Stanton, and Kathryn Stripling Byer. The essay that follows explores the complex convergences and fraught history of Irish America and African America as they are represented in the work of John Boyle O'Reilly, Charles G. Halpine, Ernest Walsh, Gwendolyn Brooks, and others, and most significantly in John Berryman's *The Dream Songs*. A major figure in his time, John Boyle O'Reilly wrote a substantial ode in homage to Crispus Attucks, the first casualty of the American Revolution, in whom he saw a figure similar to Irish revolutionaries like himself. O'Reilly campaigned vigorously on behalf of African American rights, so much so that Paul Laurence Dunbar, in turn, wrote a moving elegy to O'Reilly. In the chapter I also discuss *Avenia,* a largely forgotten abolitionist epic written by Thomas Branagan in the early nineteenth century. It is fair to say Irish American and African American relations have been tension-filled through the course of American history, though this chapter aims to uncover some lesser-known mutually generative figures. The final essay in this section focuses, in turn, on poets living in Ireland and seeks to bring these writers to greater visibility by exploring the role of Irish and American senses of place in their work, the role of parody, and the growing transnational emphasis of younger poets like Chris Agee, the late Michael Donaghy, and Julie O'Callaghan.

In the fourth section, in what constitutes something of a compositional memoir, I follow the example of African American poet Elizabeth Alexander in her essay "The Negro Digs Up Her Past: 'Amistad'" and explore the role of hidden history in my own long poem, *The Narrows*. Collectively the book intends to range over poets both prominent and lesser-known and does not presume to exhaust its subject, but hopes rather to serve as a catalyst for future critical and scholarly inquiry in the field. If anything, I have favored giving the lion's share of attention to lesser-known poets, though surely more substantive attention to the likes of Paul Muldoon, Eavan Boland, and Derek Mahon from the perspective of Irish American writing would be a welcome development in the critical reception of their work.

Finally, I want to thank the editors of the following journals and books where essays or portion of essays appeared for the first time, many in earlier versions: *New Hibernia Review*, *The Wallace Stevens Journal*, *Well Dreams* (Creighton University Press, 2003), *The North Dakota Quarterly*, *An Sionnach,* and *Etudes Irlandais*. An earlier version of "Irish American Poetry and the Question of Tradition" appeared in *The Encyclopedia of the Irish in America* (University of Notre Dame Press, 1999), and a revised version served as the introduction for *The Book of Irish American Poetry from the Eighteenth Century to the Present* (University of Notre Dame Press, 2007). The present chapter substantially extends the discussion of tradition treated in the previous two incarnations. In addition to appearing in *New Hibernia Review,* a version of "Modernism, Leftism, and the Spirit: The Poetry of Lola Ridge" served as the introduction for *Light in Hand: Selected Early Poems of Lola Ridge* (Quale Press, 2007).

Portions of many of these essays were given as papers over the years at regional, national, and international meetings of the American Conference for Irish Studies. A condensed version of "Shades, Minstrel and Majestic" in chapter 10 was given as a paper at the Affecting Irishness Conference in Dublin, January 2006, and subsequently published in *Affecting Irishness* (Peter Lang, 2009). Portions of "Soundings and Erasures: An Irish American Poet Digs Up His Past" were given as talks at the Thirty Year Anniversary of the Program for Writers at Warren Wilson College in July 2006 and at the Crossroads Irish American Festival in San Francisco in March 2008 under the title "Notes Toward the Story Behind a Poem." Portions of chapters treating the work of Robinson Jeffers were given as a keynote address at the Institute for Ulster Scots Studies, the University of Ulster, Magee Campus, in October 2009, for the conference From Ulster to America: Ulster Diaspora Literature in North America.

Finally, "The Line," which serves as the coda poem to the book, first appeared in the *Sewanee Review* along with "A Green Road in Clare." The poems that serve as section markers—"Double Life," "Near Hag's Head," and "Crossings"—appeared in my book-length sequence, *The Narrows* (Four Way Books, 2005), and are reprinted with the permission of the publisher.

I also thank the many members of the American Conference for Irish Studies who over the years have been vital in their rigor and collective intelligence as well as supportive in their inclusiveness and all-around good cheer. In addition, gratitude goes to two of my colleagues at Emerson College: Wendy Walters, who alerted me to the important work of Eric Lott and Matthew Frye Jacobson for my discussion of race in Irish American poetry, and Kim McLarin, who alerted me to Elizabeth Alexander's "The Negro Digs Up Her Past: 'Amistad.'" I especially want to extend my gratitude to Thomas Dillon Redshaw and James Silas Rodgers of *New Hibernia Review* for their helpful suggestions and support, as well as Chris Agee, Greg Delanty, Charles Fanning, Joseph Lennon, and Eamonn Wall for the inspiration and example of their work and friendship, encouragement, and more than a few helpful leads and insights over the years. Finally, I want to commend Beth Wright of Trio Bookworks for her careful editorial eye.

DOUBLE LIFE

The Sky Road

To have been born on the very edge of things
in a whitewashed hut with blonde bangs of thatch
and an unlatched gate that leads into the open,
sky and sky beyond the window onto land's end,
everything blending and the ocean shattered with light

and not to be this strange face peering through a hedge
your dead once walked beside, earrings of fuchsia
astride the rock wall: it is no nostalgia,
but the plain air of things, the very curb of exile,
this dwelling on the edge where you are born.

Headlands

To have driven along blue levitating roads
this far into land's end, golden, rumpled,
these humps that could be the goddess's bedclothes,
and that red broach of a bridge pinning the continent
together; it is all ample and errant

like this wind and the garrulous ocean below
bellowing on in the voice of Whitman
Death, Death, Death, Death, Death on the wrong shore,
the horizon as much behind us as before,
always our eyes rising to the sky's imprint on tar.

I

Double Lives

ONE

Dinner at the Café Marliave

John Boyle O'Reilly and the Dual Tradition

Emerging from the busy underground of the Park Street T stop at the corner of Tremont and Winter, where the green fan of the Boston Common flares out between Downtown Crossing and Beacon Hill toward Boylston Street, Chinatown, and the Back Bay, you can join those stepping from a motorized trolley or one of the neon pink amphibious Duck Tours and, like Dorothy toeing the origin of the yellow brick road, take your first steps on the Freedom Trail. The alternating redbrick and scarlet-painted line angles continuously through downtown Boston's warren of streets—paved, prerevolutionary cow paths that laid out the pattern for what is arguably America's first and most history-obsessed city. You might choose to head straight up the esplanade toward the capitol's golden dome and spend time at St. Gauden's famous bronze bas relief of Robert Gould Shaw on horseback leading his "bell-checked Negro Infantry" into Civil War battle and civic immortality, into Robert Lowell's great poem "For the Union Dead" and the "glory" of several academy awards. Or you might head north toward the Park Street Church and the Old Granary Burial Ground on your way to the Old Statehouse and the Old North Church with a stop along the way at one of the chowder bars at Fanuiel Hall and Quincy Market. If you go that way, as you come to the Burial Ground filled with tombstones from before the Revolution—like rows of chipped brown teeth—leave the trail and cross the street toward the glittering show-sign of the Beantown Pub, and keep walking down the narrow street that looks almost like an alley—Bosworth Street—behind the Parker House Hotel, famous for its rolls, where Malcolm X once worked as a bellhop. Keep walking still under the half-lowered fire escapes of old print shops toward the tall metal grill at the dead end, and stop there, just before the stone stairs at the stone building on the right, where hangs a black sign with gold, cursive, nineteenth-century lettering that reads "Café Marliave."

Navigating though Boston by foot and certainly by car can be like making your way through a Maurice Escher print—first you're in the basement, then you're on the roof, and there's no telling how you got there—but arriving at the Marliave, and going inside, is fortuitous. If the café doesn't throw you wholly back to the nineteenth century, it at least conjures the kind of bygone restaurant one might remember from the mid-twentieth, itself a holdover from ragtime days—tin ceiling, high straight-backed wooden booths packed back-to-back and closely together. If you ask for the "Brief History" with the menu as you're led to your booth by one of the wait staff, you can read about how Henry Marliave, who, after emigrating from Paris, founded his first small restaurant in 1868, which burned in the great Boston fire of 1872; how he moved to Hot Springs, Arkansas, for his health but returned in 1882 to open the present establishment; and how after his death in 1895 the café continued under his wife's management until 1904, then under his nephew's, and finally under the management of just two succeeding owners who have dedicated themselves to the "traditions of the Marliave." One of those traditions that does not appear even in the brief, photocopied history and will not be proffered this evening by our waiter entails the booth in back—easily the most cramped of all the booths in the dining room—presided over by the portrait of a large, dignified-looking man with intense eyes, a broad, drooping moustache, and a neat cravat, who might be a politician or a civic leader, certainly a famous man in his day. And he was: "John Boyle O'Reilly" the frame reads, but the portrait does not hang there to commemorate the civic contributions of this mostly forgotten figure, for we have arrived, as the gold-plated plaque tacked to the wall just below the portrait tells us, at The Poet's Corner.

In his day, John Boyle O'Reilly was a man of considerable national and international renown, one in a long line of Irish rebels and exiles banished from his home by the British colonial authorities whose exploits, writing, and public accomplishments made him one of the keynote figures during the last half of the nineteenth century. Born in 1844, the same year as Gerard Manley Hopkins, in the village of Dowth, County Meath, near the Boyne River, in the looming shadow of the Great Famine, O'Reilly would seem destined as a poet to draw his creative resources from a singular place deeply resonant with Irish history back to Neolithic times—the passage graves at Newgrange; Patrick's arrival at the Boyne's mouth; the rise of Celtic monasticism; the final, hope-crushing defeat of Ireland at the Battle of the Boyne in 1690; and all the fraught history that followed. Instead, as A. G. Evans's biography *Fanatic Heart* describes, O'Reilly's life reads like the perfect epic vehicle for a film staring Russell Crowe.

It began in the parish fields of Dowth, where he wrote his first poems. After his apprenticeship as a journalist for the *Drogheda Arms,* his emigration to England to advance his opportunities like so many young Irish of his time, his enlistment in the Tenth Hussars of the English army, and his clandestine swearing of the Fenian oath while still a soldier to join the Irish Republican Brotherhood, he was court-marshaled as traitor to the crown and confined behind the Dickensian walls of Dartmoor Prison in the Devon moorlands before being banished to Freemantle in Western Australia. He then attempted suicide, had a doomed love affair with the warder's daughter, and made a spectacular escape through the bush and the sand dunes at Australind. From there he paddled out into the Indian Ocean in a makeshift dory to meet the whaling boat *Gazelle,* which would convey him to Java, through the Southern Seas, around the Cape of Good Hope—with some periodic delays for expeditions, including one in which he barely survived after a harpooned whale splintered his whaleboat with one of its flukes—and onward, still in disguise from the colonial authorities, to Liverpool. There he boarded the S.S. *Bombay* to Philadelphia, arriving to huge acclaim as a heroic figure and a life in America as the preeminent Irish American literary figure of his time, editor of the *Boston Pilot,* embodiment of the gradual acceptance of the Catholic Irish into the status quo of Protestant America, as well as a vocal and tireless advocate for African American rights when Jim Crow minstrelsy prevailed and shaped the attitudes of what he saw as his own historically distressed people. He died at the ripe age of forty-six in 1890, one year after Hopkins's death and two years before Whitman's, possibly by a last suicide attempt, though more likely by accidental overdose of sleeping pills for his chronic insomnia.[1]

As one looks up at the picture above the table in the Poet's Corner of the Marliave, it seems impossible to plumb the complex life and history behind the inevitable mask of portraiture. One would have to know the story behind the portrait and recognize that other elaborate stone monuments commemorate the man inside the frame not far away at Boston's Fenway and in Holyhood Cemetery in Roxbury, and farther away also in Dowth Churchyard in Ireland and among the dunes of Australind in Western Australia—a man whose image is enshrined on three continents but whose writing is all but entirely neglected by literary historians and anthologists.

Reading most of O'Reilly's poetry, one is not surprised to see at first why such an art of the purely occasional and public-minded, and bound to the technical conventions of the day, might quickly fall out of favor at the brink of the twentieth century while Hopkins's poetry—so individually tuned and formally idiosyncratic—obtained greater and greater currency and influence despite the relative obscurity of the poet. One could, perhaps, picture O'Reilly as a kind of Irish American version of Whitman writing the epic "Song" of the great European migration to America, or at least the Irish version of it—that diasporic "open road" across the Atlantic with its still more brutal parallel in the Middle Passage, a wake parting the waves behind a coffin ship, an American wake. That missing epic of America he never wrote, perhaps in part because of his public position, and perhaps for more complex reasons of the poet being unable to carry the full imaginative weight of the historical circumstance of which he was so centrally a part.

Of O'Reilly's literary meetings at the Marliave, Evans writes, "There is little doubt O'Reilly was proud of his position as editor and he enjoyed the companionship of the Boston literary set. He dined in their company on formal occasions and lunched with them less formally at the Marliave Restaurant on the corner of Bosworth Street, a short distance from the *Pilot* offices. The tables were divided by wooden partitions and set around the walls so that small groups of like-minded friends could meet without distraction from neighbors."[2] One can imagine O'Reilly, perhaps during the same week of similar close literary gatherings at the Papyrus Club (later the St. Botolph Club), animatedly discussing poetry with his fellow Irish American poets James Jeffrey Roche and Louise Imogen Guiney within the intimate surroundings of the Marliave. On any given day, Longfellow, Oliver Wendell Holmes, John Greenleaf Whittier, William Dean Howells, and Ralph Waldo Emerson might have been gathering at other literary salons and clubs, and surely O'Reilly would have been welcome among the Brahmin literary set by the time he had established himself sufficiently to host Oscar Wilde on his visit to Boston in 1882. As A. G. Evans observes, O'Reilly had indeed "constructed a bridge" between "Yankee Boston" and the Boston Irish, in part one might say by emulating the kind of popular and declamatory poetry written by Longfellow, whose death in 1882 deeply affected him.[3] His long patriotic ode, "America," has the ring of a uniquely American brand of optimism but is all the more startlingly prescient for its vision of Europe's future that seems to predict the formation of the European Union, which occurred a little more than a century after his death:

> O, this thy work, Republic! This thy health,
> To prove man's birthright to a commonwealth;
> To teach the peoples to be strong and wise,
> Till armies, nations, nobles, royalties,
> Are laid to rest with all their fears and hates;
> Till Europe's thirteen monarchies are States,
> Without a barrier and without a throne,
> Of one grand Federation like our own![4]

It is O'Reilly's backward look to Europe from his New World vantage in the rousing rhetoric of these lines that most suggests the kind of deeply seated historical, cultural, and retrospective pressures that were ultimately subversive of his prospects as a poet of singular voice and accomplishment, despite all the visionary heraldry. For all the rhapsodic sentiment of poems like "America," "At Fredericksburg," and "Crispus Attucks," steeped as they are in the turbulent milieu of American history, John Boyle O'Reilly is not just another would-be American bard left in the dust on Whitman's open road in the predawn of modernism.

He is perhaps the last, misbegotten heir of an older Irish bardic tradition, the *file,* so thoroughly displaced into his life and literary ambitions as to be little more than a trace asserting itself across the spectrum of his varied civic and literary passions.

Reflecting on the quality of nineteenth-century English poetry in Ireland, Thomas Kinsella comes to the judgment that such verse is "of general dullness, a great supply of bad verse" but for individual poems by James Clarence Mangan, Samuel Ferguson, William Allingham, Thomas Davis, and Thomas Moore.[5] Of course, the same might be said for verse generally in any time and place, but certainly none of these figures matches the achievements of the great English Romantic and post-Romantic poets. For Kinsella, of these, Mangan's poetry commands the highest stature, if only for those few "exceptional poems" of which "The Nameless One," "Siberia," and "Dark Rosaleen" are the quintessential examples.[6] What characterizes Mangan's work is its psychic intensity, its willingness to turn inward while at the same time situating itself in the social and cultural context of an Ireland divorced from the shaping literary traditions of a lost language. Mangan's best poetry manifests the collective psyche, individually pitched, of an imploded bardic tradition centuries removed from sustaining social conditions. As such, his work is a pivot point between an eclipsed ancient tradition and the advent of a modern world characterized, as Edward Said remarked, by exile. As Said further reflects, exile "is predicated on the existence of, love for, and real bond with one's native place; the universal truth of exile is not that one has lost that love or home, but that inherent in each is an unexpected, unwelcome loss.... No one today is purely one thing."[7]

Perhaps it is an internal hybridity not yet fully assimilated into the poet's identity that drove James Clarence Mangan ever deeper into idiosyncrasy and madness within the limits of his long-colonized native place. Perhaps also it is the irreconcilable loss, his permanent exile from his native place, that drove John Boyle O'Reilly to embrace a hybrid identity in nineteenth-century America well in advance of its currency in the latter half of the twentieth century and today. At the same time, O'Reilly's understanding of himself as a poet and civic leader harkens back to what Declan Kiberd calls "the strong sense of social vocation and the public tone"[8] of the Irish bardic ideal without testing it against the kind of individual, personal urgency that has shaped the most permanent poetry of the past two hundred years.

As his personal history of imprisonment, exile, and emigration testifies, John Boyle O'Reilly's life was nothing if not tumultuous. He embodied the emigrant experience—the experience of exile from Ireland in its harrowing extreme—but his poetry remains opaque to that ordeal except in the most general public way. Here is the opening of "The Exile of the Gael":

> "What have ye brought to our Nation-building, sons of the Gael?
> What is your burden or guerdon from old Innisfail?"
>
> "No treason we bring from Erin—nor bring we shame or guilt!
> The sword we hold may be broken, but we have not dropped
>   the hilt!
> The wreath we bear to Columbia is twisted of thorns, not bays,
> And the songs we sing are saddened by thoughts of the desolate
>   days.
> But the hearts we bring for Freedom are washed in the surge
>   of tears,
> And we claim our right by a People's fight outliving a thousand
>   years!"[9]

The poem begins with a question posed by what could easily be the voice of Columbia herself, torch in hand above New York harbor, if not an atypically liberal-minded Know Nothing willing to at least entertain Irish emigration and enfranchisement in the American democracy. In addition to making a passionate rhetorical argument for the Irish joining the ranks of America and its national, imperial future, O'Reilly's eponymous speaker harkens back to "the desolate days" of cultural and linguistic loss under a thousand years of colonial rule, as well as "the surge of tears" of displacement, exile, and emigration. Needless to say, as unique and yet emblematic as O'Reilly's experience must have been in the wrenching details of his life, the stock images that populate "The Exile of the Gael" carry none of the gravitas of his hard-won experience. His unique diasporic narrative of loss and crossing is submerged beneath a bardic directive that eschews the individual for what Stephanie Rains calls "the macro-narrative" of emigration.[10] O'Reilly leaves his own "micro-narrative"—the narrative that is irreducibly closer to the bone of experience—undocumented in the poetry. It is an act of self-exclusion that largely recurs in Irish American poetry well into the twentieth century.

Nevertheless, in "The Exile of the Gael" O'Reilly intends to sing the collective experience of his tribe in true bardic fashion, though in Kinsella's words "the native aristocracy" that formed "the basis" for the *file*'s "social—virtually administrative function in society" has long since vanished.[11] What he would sing instead of the lore of place names (*dinnseanchas*), or the praises and satires supportive of a lost order, are the odes that would redress a still further dispossession from the native place experienced by millions who left their homes often under social, cultural, economic, and political duress. In this light, it is not outlandish to see O'Reilly in the line of latter-day bards, dispossessed, nostalgic for the vanished order, singing brutally out of their hopelessness. For O'Reilly his place in that line might have been at most only a half-conscious thought. Beyond this subliminal link, his work differs from the likes of Dáibhí Ó Bruadair and Aogán Ó Rathaille in its optimism—showing American influence—though it is an optimism achieved without admission into the poetry of the raw edge of experience, a circumstance that left his work at once belated and immature, for all its ambition and largesse of feeling.

As one early commentator wrote, O'Reilly "might have been the Dickens or even the Tolstoy of Ireland's mass migrations and national agitations" had he been able to achieve a "systematic and realistic depiction of either."[12] Or perhaps in his poetry, instead of his fiction, he might have been able to represent those same harsh realities in work that heralded twentieth-century poetics, instead of harkening back to an outmoded bardic calling through received models of declamatory verse. Because he was not able to make that transition, his poetry stands preeminently alongside the popular nineteenth-century Irish American poems that memorialize the exile's loss of the native place or invoke in purely political terms Ireland's long travail under British colonial rule.[13]

Interestingly, in *The Dual Tradition*, Thomas Kinsella identifies similar flaws in the preponderance of Irish poetry written in the English language during roughly the same period. The inadequacies of Irish poetry at the time, he observes, "have something to do with the loss of a working Irish literary tradition" while simultaneously having even more to do with "the related colonial impulse to present the home literature to a 'senior' outside audience for its amusement and instruction."[14] In turn, the weakness of Irish American poetry during roughly the same historical moment may have something to do with the exile's need to remain connected to his Irish homeland while simultaneously proving his mettle in his new country. In both instances, Irish and Irish American poets had to inflect their work largely away from inner experience—from what Yeats would later call "passionate, normal speech"[15]—and either toward an audience whose communal support for the poet's artistic growth had been abrogated by historical circumstance through the loss of the Irish language or, in the case of Irish America, toward an audience that was as yet nascent in the emigrant's painful but gradual enfranchisement within the American cultural order. In either case the historical and cultural forces at work were very nearly crushing; certainly they were inimical to the making of great poetry.

For Kinsella the root of the problem for Irish poetry in the nineteenth century lies in the loss of the Irish language as a "possible sustaining force."[16] What could be more devastating to a poet's inner creative resources than the loss of his or her native language and the cultural community it perforce implies? In Ireland, "the virtual absence of good writers in both languages during the whole nineteenth century, when the people were painfully shedding one language and slowly acquiring another," likewise symbolizes for Declan Kiberd the fundamental division of Irish literature from which it is still seeking to recover.[17] Kinsella states it succinctly: "Irish literature is a dual entity," and it is so because one language had to be "abandoned for another" through a centuries-long process of dispossession "reducing energies of every kind, undermining individual confidence, lessening quality of thought."[18] In his essay "The Divided Mind," Kinsella's seminal reflections on his separation from a thousand-year-old tradition of Irish-language poetry are deeply moving:

> The inheritance is certainly mine but only at two enormous removes—across a century's silence and through an exchange of worlds. The

greatness of the loss is measured not only by the substance of Irish literature itself, but also by the intensity with which we know it is shared; it has an air of continuity and shared history which is precisely what is missing from Irish literature, in English or Irish; in the nineteenth century and today. I recognize that I stand on one side of a great rift, and can feel the discontinuity in myself. It is a matter of people and places as well as writing—of coming from a broken and uprooted family, of being drawn to those who share my origins and finding that we cannot share our lives.[19]

Both Declan Kiberd and Richard Kearney regard Kinsella's "double vision" as shaping his insightful assessment of the trauma underlying Irish literary intelligence.[20] The great rift Kinsella laments likewise haunts O'Reilly's poetry; he is another of its stillborn literary heirs, only further removed by forced emigration from his native ground. What is so striking in Kinsella's lament, however, is that this Irish poet's classic statement on "the divided mind" of the Irish writer might just as well have been written by any Irish American poet conscious enough to recognize that the legacy of emigration and exile constitutes not only a divided mind but a mind doubly divided by being uprooted from those people and places and writing from which he or she is dispossessed by distance and not only by time. If we add to the traumatic loss of the Irish language the further traumatic loss of native place experienced by millions of Irish in the nineteenth and early twentieth centuries, and acknowledge as we should that emigration is as much a part of the Irish experience as the Irish American experience, and in turn situate the burgeoning of Irish American poetry in the twentieth century after O'Reilly in the context of both losses, then what we have before us is not simply "a dual tradition" but a tradition further displaced through the historical, cultural, and psychic trauma of emigration and exile. It is as if Irish American poetry has raised the dual tradition Kinsella articulated so astutely to yet another power.

Dialectics of Home and Abroad

What does this mean for how we understand the continuities and discontinuities of Irish poetry? For one thing, it suggests that to speak merely of a dual tradition is not adequate, unless one is willing either to elide or to minimize the impact of mass emigration on Irish identity. To do so would constitute the most thoroughgoing denial of historical fact. This is very nearly what Patrick Ward claims in *Exile, Emigration, and Irish Writing,* in which he notes that even in this time of intellectual sensitivity to matters of cultural diaspora, Irish journals "reveal a noticeable neglect of exile and emigration in spite of the fact that it has been and remains a central fact of Irish experience for writers as well as the population as a whole."[21] Yet even in Ward's urgent assessment his objection remains focused on what might be called "insular Ireland"—the writers he speaks of are "Irish" construed narrowly, as is the population to which he refers. It is one thing to consider the self-elected emigration of Joyce and Beckett as insufficiently examined through the lens of exile; it is another to bring attention to the work of those who left under more grave duress than artistic choice, or who are, as members of the succeeding generations, the heirs of that legacy of exile and emigration.

This leads, naturally, to a second admission of substantial importance relative to how we understand the traditions of Irish poetry: it means Irish American poetry has not yet been sufficiently acknowledged or explored either for its continuities with the poetry of the homeland or for its own continuities and discontinuities or for its potent affinities with other diaspora literatures. The result is a greater rift, a larger gulf, than Thomas Kinsella's dual tradition wholly acknowledges. It also means the "quarantine" between Irish and Anglo Irish that Declan Kiberd saw as dividing "Irish schoolrooms"[22] in the late seventies has hardly begun to be admitted even to exist between Irish and Irish American poetry, except in those cases where the "Irishness" of the poet is not in question. In those cases the more centrifugal complexities of identity hardly matter where the centripetal identifier "Irish" trumps the hybrid-making realities of history.

This is not to say, of course, that emigrant and expatriate writers, and poets in particular, do not populate the Irish literary landscape. From the early twentieth century onward, poets like Padraic Colum and Brian Coffey register limited but important responses to the experience of migration out of Ireland, if only for a time. Here is Colum's "A Rann of Exile":

Nor right, nor left, nor any road I see a comrade face
Nor word to lift the heart in me I hear in any place;
They leave me, who pass by me, to my loneliness and care,
Without a house to draw my step nor a fire that I might share!

Ochone, before our people knew the scatt'ring of the dearth,
Before they saw potatoes rot and melt black in the earth,
I might have stood in Connacht, on top of Cruchmaelinn,
And all around me I would see the hundreds of my kin.[23]

Padraic Colum's lyric assumes a moving eponymous voice born of the Irish post-famine diaspora, and one suspects that his many years of living and traveling outside of Ireland in America and as far a field as Hawaii fostered his imaginative access to the experience of forced emigration. At the same time, to adopt Andrew Gurr's useful distinction, Colum might best be identified as an "expatriate" Irish poet rather than an exile, since he could and did return to Ireland.[24] The like is true for Brian Coffey, who wrote his long poem, "Missouri Sequence," during his time teaching philosophy in St. Louis from 1947 to 1952. Here are lines from "Nightfall, Midwinter, Missouri":

We live far away from where
my mother grows very old.
Five miles away, at Byrnesville,
the cemetery is filled with Irish graves,
the priest an old man born near Cork,
his bloss like the day he left the land.

People drifted in here from the river,
Irish, German, Bohemians,
more than one hundred years ago,
come to make homes.

Many Irish souls have gone back to God from Byrnesville,
many are Irish here today
where cedars stand like milestones
on worn Ozark hills

and houses white on bluegrass lawns
house people honest, practical and kind.

All shows a long love
yet I am charmed
by the hills behind Dublin,
those white stone cottages,
grass green as no other grass is green,
my mother's people, their ways.[25]

What is so striking in these lines is how the poet's affirmation of continuity with the diasporic Irish who populated Byrnesville—even the name inscribing a founding Irish identity—suddenly elides to the recognition of difference. The hills behind Dublin are not the Ozark hills, and the stone cottages of Ireland are not those of this Midwestern town despite its Irish cemetery. For Coffey, what finally makes the Irish of Byrnesville not Irish in the fullest sense is the simple fact that they no longer live in Ireland where "grass is green as no other grass is green" and as such where "the ways" of his mother's people manifest an unbreached continuity. In their unguarded honesty Coffey's lines perform a paradigmatic slippage—the remarkable erasure of Irish identity from Irish America based on the absence of Irish Americans from the native place. They likewise exemplify perfectly Patrick Ward's judgment that "the dialectics of 'home' and 'abroad,' consciously or unconsciously, pervaded the cultural and artistic consciousness of those who stayed, and those who left."[26] Yet if "the fact of emigration and expatriation covertly permeated all aspects of national life, for all Irish people, one way or another,"[27] then how is it possible the very reality that so defined consciousness and culture in Ireland for hundreds of years is the same reality that asserts itself as a marker of difference rather than identity, and as such between Irish and Irish American poetry?

One centrally important contemporary Irish poet for whom the "dialectic of home and abroad" becomes the vital substance of the work, explored consciously and embodied in poems imbued with an unflagging awareness of both Irish and American history and culture, is Eamonn Wall. Born in Enniscorthy, County Wexford, Wall emigrated to America with the other so-called New Irish during the 1980s, before the

Celtic Tiger changed Ireland from one of the weakest economies in Europe to the economic player it became before the recession and the debt crisis of 2010. Throughout his five books of poems Wall dives persistently and deeply into the gulf of discontinuity and displacement articulated in Coffey's "Missouri Sequence." "The Wexford Container Tragedy" in *Refuge at DeSoto Bend* can be read as an answering sequence to Coffey's in which the experience of migration is the identifying thread uniting diasporic peoples from different cultures. The sequence begins in the New York Holocaust Museum and ranges broadly from the poet's native place of Wexford to Ellis Island to St. Louis, Missouri, where he presently lives, in an effort to reconcile the tragic discovery of eight dead African stowaways in the Wexford Business Park on December 8, 2001. Their death in the ship container, as Wall implies, makes the boat on which they traveled the twenty-first-century version of a coffin ship. Yet as the poem "From St. Louis, Missouri" suggests, the heart-rupturing tragedy belies a deeper continuity among emigrant peoples:

> These words are whispered from St. Louis
> where last night children in green gathered
> at the Sheldon Concert Hall to play music,
> dance jigs, sing in the ancient languages of
> monks, navigators, saints, sinners, builders,
> homesteaders, nuns, bakers, bankers, all
> peoples of a scattered cast called Irish:
> Catholic, Protestant, Muslim and Jew,
> piled merrily to applaud dancers on a stage.
> Adults and pumped-up relatives had fought
> the dismal early December night—city workers
> in warm canteens drinking hot chocolate,
> playing five card stud—streets and highways
> uncleared, cars and semis in the ditch, a rolled
> mini van upside down, wedged between the
> guard rail and storm drain on I-44 between
> the Hampton & Kingshighway exits. Of
> German, French, Swiss, Nigerian, and Irish
> ancestry, these performers in hard shoes
> gathered in our bright French city to dance
> a steady narrative of removal and survival.[28]

In contrast to Coffey's "Nightfall, Midwinter, Missouri," Wall's "From St. Louis, Missouri" describes a contrary arc of consciousness in which the Irish are identified as a "scattered cast" that includes Irish America. For all its empathy toward its American setting, Coffey's poem reasserts the idea of the Irish as an insular people. To be really Irish is to be native in one's native place. In Wall's poem, on the contrary, to be Irish is to be scattered, a wandering tribe. Paradoxically, the status of the Irish as a diasporic people is what most defines them and, in turn, binds them to other diasporic peoples in Wall's "steady narrative of removal and survival."

Thus Wall shifts the concept of identity away from nativist constructions and toward a more complex web of relations both cultural and historical—a common experience of passage rather than a common ground. Within that web, to be Irish cannot be separated from being Irish American—or Jewish, Swiss, or African, for that matter. Implicitly, Eamonn Wall's poem redresses what James Byrne has observed to be the Irish American struggle "to locate itself along the lines of other, more successful, ethnic minorities, by striving to imbue itself with a sense of ethnic authenticity."[29] Wall's poem does so not by assuming an equivalency in the magnitude of racial and ethnic discrimination, but by furthering the insight that the experience of diaspora inherently composes a nexus of stories that need not at this historical moment compete for recognition and validation at another's expense. Within the related narratives of diaspora we become more ourselves in every sense by becoming more "other" than what we might initially deem ourselves to be.

Wall's poetry is potently significant, for to understand "emigration, immigration, and migration"[30] requires us to recognize how these related experiences ultimately converge in a kind of subtending narrative of loss and endurance that unites people from different cultures and histories. It is a more capacious understanding of diaspora that brings together all the "othered" others. Nevertheless, when he reflects on his own experience as an expatriate Irish poet in his groundbreaking study *From the Sin-é Café to the Black Hills,* Wall affirms the double nature of his life as an Irish immigrant in America:

If I wish to define myself in the future, I would have to begin
With two huge words: Irish and American. But over the years

I have revered both terms while at the same time seeking to
Understand them better. But the two can never be separated.
I have double vision; I am doubled in every way.³¹

Whether or not he intends to do so, Wall's affirmation of his own doubleness underscores the need to enlarge Kinsella's "dual tradition." It requires the dual tradition to acknowledge that the rift the older poet rightly identifies deepens still further in the experience of "removal and survival" outside the homeland of Ireland. Not surprisingly, Wall implicitly sees the connection when he reflects: "Being an Irish exile is a heavy business because it is so tied up with mythology, pain and history. When I left Ireland I thought I was getting away from history; little did I know I was walking right into the middle of an historical web from which there would be no escape."³² The sentiment is underscored powerfully in his poem "Leaving Boise" from his most recent book, *A Tour of Your Country:*

> Last night, you drank
> at the Ha' Penny Bridge in Boise to come-all-ye roars
> of local balladeers
> as Irish miners heard ringing in saloons rollicking songs
> of home, thinking as we must,
> all of us across time, of many destinies we had managed
> to escape. Not one of us
> willing to put America behind us so intent were
> we to learn what we did
> not know. . . .³³

Even as "Leaving Boise" wittily and cunningly portrays the bar life of this Montana town as a kind of wry simulacrum of Dublin—a Ha' Penny Bridge pub instead of a Ha' Penny Bridge—the poem simultaneously extends a metaphorical bridge to "all of us across time." Thus Wall's poem modulates quietly from physical place to metaphysical condition. America is one destiny of many possible destinies, though its very presence in the moment as the destiny actually encountered and lived calls for the poet's assent, his intention to embrace the vast "unknowing" of America. Through this assessment, hard-won, both the poet's fate and the importance of Irish American experience for Ireland and Irish history gains purchase in the landscape of Irish and Irish American literature.

Of course, Eamonn Wall is not the first Irish poet to venture into that historical web. O'Reilly found himself in it, as did Padraic Colum and Brian Coffey to far lesser extents, as well as many others in their day. Wall's contemporary Greg Delanty, also a New Irish poet, has likewise produced a sustained body of work through five books of poems, as well as a recent *Collected*. He and Wall have been established as the two Irish poets of their generation who have given themselves the task of bringing the emigrant experience to the fore in Irish poetry, an experience that was until recently all but entirely ignored. Like Wall's poetry, Delanty's work reflects the double vision of the expatriate Irish writer living in America. Though they live much of the year in the United States and hold posts at American institutions of higher education, both have strong ties to Ireland and spend significant time there for personal and professional reasons. They exemplify the transnational lifestyle of many contemporary Irish living in the United States, who return often to their native place. At the same time, both poets have American families as well as American jobs. The experience of being "doubled" pervades the poems of each, yet their work reveals important differences in the way each evokes the emigrant relationship to his adopted country.

To read through Eamonn Wall's growing body of work is in large part to follow the poet's venture ever deeper into the continent, into the West in the historical as well as the metaphorical sense. As a poet who found academic work in Nebraska and Missouri, Wall made a literal journey that was the rehearsal for his poetry's imaginative venture. Even the lineation of his poetry shows the open-form influences of American poets like James Schuyler and Frank O'Hara.

In contrast, Delanty's poems reveal the emigrant's awareness of a fascinating and significant difference from his new home. His early poem "America" begins with the declaration "I'm buffaloed / by this landscape / without voice / or memory."[34] The shock expressed in these lines at once demonstrates the poet's consciousness of his own "otherness" in the midst of the American landscape and rehearses the myth of America as a land without a past. The poet might as well be a Pilgrim arriving at Plymouth Rock or any European explorer from the Age of

Exploration who projected on the American landscape the status of a historical and metaphysical blank slate. At the same time the verb "buffaloed" is an American idiom, not an Irish one, so from the beginning the poem inscribes the poet's veiled equivocation—he has already been taken in linguistically by the landscape and its history. By the poem's third word the landscape has already altered the identity of the poet—I am buffaloed; I am become that which I am not, and that is surely not Irish. As such, the landscape is hardly without voice but is voiced by the poet, hardly without memory since the poem's trope reiterates the history of "discovery" by which Europeans assumed the New World as at once an otherworld to be feared and, perhaps more significantly, an opportunity—again the empty slate on which they might imprint a new version of the long-standing nexus of Western tradition.

Delanty is clearly aware of these tensions and countercurrents, for in the lines that follow he floats an analogy that potentially fuses American and Irish histories in what is nothing less than an archetypal pattern of oppression, victimization, and survival, or at least a palimpsest of such:

> Perhaps it pow-wows
> with surviving Abenaki
> the way Iveragha or Beara
> parleys with us.

In this poem's analogical conceit the Irish are like the Abenaki, the American landscape like the wild West of the west of Ireland. What saves the analogy from being strident to the point of confusion, a forced equation, is, again, the poet's equivocation—"perhaps." As before, the verbs carry the metaphor. "Pow-wow" and "parley" define parallel actions of verbal exchange between the landscapes and their inhabitants. "Pow-wow," like "buffaloed," brings Native American culture into the poem, while "parley" inscribes an entire history of Irish conquest into one word, since the verb "parley" arrives in Middle English through the Middle French *parlee,* which in turn originates in the late Latin *parabolare,* which is related to "parable" and "parabola." This brief excursion into the etymology is worth the effort, since Delanty's poem is hyperconscious of its own parabolic parallels between identities, landscapes, and cultures, while at the same time questioning the very parallels it asserts, the final one reiterating a pre-Columbian journey to the New World from Irish legend:

> Yet I can't help but feel
> I'm one of Brendan's crew,
> oblivious to the nature
> of the fishy shore
>
> they settled
> before the whale
> beneath their feet
> surged to life.

The poem's final parallel is to assert a parable of the emigrant's inevitable slippage of identity, at once firm in the archetypal pattern of legendary passage and fundamentally unsettled since the archetype itself is founded on the undermining of firm ground, both native and adopted, through the parabolic journey away from home that will inevitably alter one's consciousness of home, wherever it is. As Delanty observes in "We Will Not Play the Harp Backward Now, No," "many of us learned the trick / of turning ourselves into ourselves, / free in the *fé fiada* anonymity of America."[35] Here, playing on the Irish legend of Earl Gerald, who turned himself into a stag, the poet affirms his emigrant identity as bound neither to the native place with its "all-seeing" small towns, nor to the ideal of American assimilation, but rather to the idea of the emigrant as artist whose freedom is enabled by America's *fé fiada,* its cloak of invisibility, an art made possible by America's sheer immensity relative to Ireland.

Marianne Moore alludes to the same legend in "Spenser's Ireland," and Delanty's poem in turn alludes to Moore's formally as well. Delanty's poem, however, supplies an additional intertextual nuance by transplanting Earl Gerald's transformation into an American context. Moreover, in Delanty's poem the use of Irish to describe an American phenomenon underscores the poet's equivocation about even his artistic identity—as artist he would be neither one thing nor the other, and perhaps both Irish and American at the same time, and/or as needed by the particular poem, or even at a particular moment in a particular poem. Such poems are about the shifting, essentially hybrid nature of the emigrant's sense of identity, as well as the cultural gaps and allegiances the emigrant must negotiate, and the poet negotiates through language. As such, a poem like Delanty's "Tagging the Stealer" uses baseball to track the shift from scoffing ignorance at the American pastime to seeing the game as an art that, like poetry, has its own complex "sign language" through which the game is made possible.

Such poems in turn track the emigrant experience somewhat differently than does Eamonn Wall's work. His poetry feels rather more at ease in the emigrant encounter with the "otherness" of America, with that defining openness, whereas Delanty's poetry equivocates and thereby charts an emigrant's resistance to redefinition and assimilation in the image of the immigrant's new world. Nevertheless, both poets render apparent what Richard Kearney calls in *Navigations* a transnational paradigm that underlies the history of Irish culture, and they suggest the extension of that paradigm to the Irish American context and to Irish American poetry specifically.

A Traveling Tradition

Eamonn Wall and Greg Delanty are the most prominent poets of their generation who explore the Irish experience of emigration to America, though they have their progenitors as well in a few key figures who, like the prototypical John Boyle O'Reilly, stayed and made lives in America. The work of the late James Liddy, born in Wexford in 1934, stands as a bridge between Patrick Kavanagh's Dublin and Ginsberg's Haight-Ashbury—and gives a winking nod to John Ashbery along the way. Born in Dublin in 1941, Eamon Grennan established his career entirely in America and through American presses, garnering a substantial number of American awards. Born in 1951 in County Armagh, Paul Muldoon moved to the United States in 1987 and has since become an American citizen; he won a Pulitzer Prize for his book *Moy Sand and Gravel* in 2004.

Like O'Reilly, each of these poets is an Irish poet by virtue of his birth on the island; still, American models, culture, and history have influenced their work pervasively. Could one consider them Irish American poets, as John Boyle O'Reilly is? (While he may be seen only as a minor poet, his work certainly has resonance for the expressly Irish experience of emigration and exile.) Again, as Eamonn Wall reminds us, after Dermot Bolger, many Irish writers now are not exiles at all but "commuters."[36] This is true to some extent for each of these poets, since each has easy access to frequent flyer miles as well as friends and family back in the home country, along with families, jobs, and publishers in the United States. But to see such writers as only identifiably Irish—that is, Irish by birth and therefore inextricably bound to the native place—is once again to cover with a kind of *fe fiada* cloak of invisibility the undeniable fact that emigration, as the novelist Joseph O'Connor observed, "is as Irish as Cathleen Ni Houlihan's harp."[37] Beyond O'Connor's rueful barb, to miss the American impact on these writers and its place in the history of Ireland and America—or to treat it as merely ancillary—is to avoid confronting the complex and perhaps challenging fact that the divided tree of Kinsella's dual tradition has another transnational limb.

That there are few poems expressly treating emigration and exile in so defining a literary and cultural resource as *The Field Day Anthology of Irish Writing* is significant. A quick track of such poems in the first volume notes Haicead's seventeenth-century "The Emigrant's Love for Ireland" and James Orr's eighteenth-century "Song, Composed on the Banks of Newfoundland." One has to wait until the third volume to find Brian Coffey's "Missouri Sequence." The third volume also includes work by John Montague and Eamon Grennan, both poets with strong ties to the United States, though none of Montague's poems from *The Dead Kingdom*—his work that most directly treats the experience of exile—is represented. We do, however, find his classic poem of emigrant longing, "All Legendary Obstacles." Still, it is a telling omission that none of Montague's poems engaging his family's emigration to America or his father's decision to stay in his adopted country find admission to this definitive collection. Thank goodness Eavan Boland's "The Emigrant Irish" appears with its stern reproach—"What they survived we could not even live"—though the poem's admonition might just as well be turned against a definition of tradition that appears to prune much of the poetry of emigration from the canon.

There are no poems by John Boyle O'Reilly in the anthology (examples of his more purple poetry appear in others), though a poem like "At Fredericksburg" commemorating the Irish soldiers who died in the American Civil War is certainly worthy of inclusion. Also missing is Padraig O'Heigeartaigh's "My Sorrow, Donncha," an exile's lament for his lost daughter written in Irish, though it does appear in Kinsella's *Oxford Anthology of Irish Verse*. Nor are there any poems by Lola Ridge, a prominent but neglected literary and political figure during the 1920s and 1930s, poetry editor of the *Dial,* and contemporary of William Carlos Williams, Wallace Stevens, and Hart Crane, whose work gained substantial notice during her lifetime. Nor do we find Louis MacNeice's "Last Before America," again one of the few Irish poems that speak to the experience of exile and emigration.

Future anthologies of Irish writing might seek to include more poems that explore this central theme of Irish history. Among them should be Michael Coady's poem "The Letter," which together with his essay "The Use of Memory" form a classic exploration of how the experience of emigration takes a personal toll on the lives of Irish families for generations. Coady himself forcefully addresses the fundamental problem in "The Sea-Divided Silence," in which he identifies at the heart of the Irish literary tradition a denial of the magnitude of the diaspora for Irish literature. What we have, in his estimate, is "a tragic history of the unsaid, an evasive and disabling mode of response based upon the twin stereotypes which conspire to conceal rather than reveal—on the one hand the streets-paved-with-gold-vista of America from Ireland and on the other the sentimentalised idealisation of the homeland among exiles, each curiously reinforcing the other, though in seeming contradiction." The result, he judges, is a "lacuna in the national discourse" and in the literature.[38] The point here, without sounding shrilly critical, is to identify a significant blind spot in the Irish literary tradition, one that appears to manifest pervasively in the world of cultural memory the words of Boland's lament for the emigrant Irish—"Like oil lamps we put them out the back, // of our houses, of our minds."[39]

The growing significance of this historical and cultural lacuna becomes even more apparent when one considers Irish American poetry from the standpoint of those poets who are not Irish-born but who by ancestry deserve to have their work considered within a more encompassing formulation of tradition. From such a widened perspective, however, would Irish American poets merely be appropriating an Irishness lost to them by history? Then again, is the tradition of Irish poetry complete without some measure of recognition given those works and poets who embody Ireland's history of emigration? Or does assimilation over just one generation into the American cultural milieu preclude such considerations? Eamonn Wall broaches the subject implicitly when he writes: "Irish culture has become so widely disseminated and influential in the United States, and travel has become so easy, that Americans bypass Irish America and come straight to Ireland. Similarly, many of the young Irish who go to America nowadays go straight to the Lower East Side of Manhattan and steer clear of an Irish American world they consider having ground to a halt, wallowing in a time warp." Wall's intention here is to argue for definitions of Irish and American to be "enlarged, inclusive, and allow both for fluidity and for a changed world," particularly regarding the "migrant" Irish poets who move between both shores.[40] One might ask, What of first-, second-, and third-generation Irish American poets? Are they also to be considered part of an Irish American world that has ground to a halt? Such a judgment would be inconsistent with the remarkable burgeoning of Irish American poetry over the course of the last century or so since John Boyle O'Reilly's death.

Moreover, the idea that assimilation into America should preclude the Irish American poet from being considered within an expanded understanding of Irish literary tradition is inconsistent with Irish history. Kinsella himself speaks of "the way of assimilation" as essential to the development of "the dual tradition" of Irish and Anglo Irish literature and culture. Likewise, to envision being born on the island as the litmus test for Irishness is likewise inconsistent with Irish history. Is John Montague not an Irish poet because he was born in Brooklyn? Is Eva Bourke not an Irish poet because she was born in Germany, though she lives and teaches in Galway and publishes with Dedalus Press in Ireland? Assimilation is part of Ireland's history, as is the history of migration—emigrant, exile, or contemporary "commuter." Irish assimilation to America was born of the forces of the Irish diaspora and is a part of the story of the Irish people. To further neglect that story would be to persist in what Declan Kiberd has called "a revivalist culture," a culture trapped by the need to define itself against a colonizer,[41] though surely revivalism must be misplaced when it is levied against one's own historically and culturally extended community abroad. Given Ireland's inevitable and increasing confrontation with multiculturalism through the European Union, as well as the growing recognition of its own multicultural past, vestiges of revivalism should give way to broader views on the conception and formation of tradition. This means taking fuller account of the poetic legacy of the emigrant Irish in America and thereby bringing Irish American poets out of the poet's corner for a long-awaited place at the larger banquet.

Such a revised understanding of tradition would embrace Richard Kearney's insight that "tradition is not just a homogenous totality; it is a multi-layered manuscript with each layer recording some new crisis, rupture or spasm that has altered the course of history."[42] To shift metaphors, however, Irish tradition has also been a culture en route, given the exigencies of history, and that conception at times pulls strongly against the more deeply ingrained conception of being rooted to place—despite the long experience of peregrination that informs Irish culture and literature. Irish tradition is a traveling tradition, to adapt Paul Gilroy's use of the concept of traveling cultures from his book *The Black Atlantic: Modernity and Double Consciousness*. Surely Irish American poetry is a part of that tradition and provides a unique vantage on the crisis or rupture of diaspora as well as on the idea of a tradition that remains fruitfully en route despite the spasms of history. To deny as much would be an impoverishment both of that tradition and of our understanding of tradition.

Here, again, Richard Kearney is illuminating on the subject, particularly in his objection to what he sees as the nature of T. S. Eliot's view of tradition as a static totality of monuments. In contrast, as I underscore in "Irish American Poetry and the Question of Tradition," Eliot's conception of tradition is not as static or as reified as it has been portrayed, and it may in fact be useful to the idea of a traveling tradition.[43] For Richard Kearney, an authentic understanding of tradition remains "wary of the Eliotic view of tradition as a pantheon of eternal monuments that 'form an ideal order among themselves,' an order that is 'complete before any new work arrives.'" Instead, he sees tradition as "a seedbed of multiple readings that subvert any pretension to univocal self-identity or self-completion."⁴⁴ While certainly a compelling and needed corrective, the problem with such a view is that it undermines the aesthetic directive at the root of Eliot's understanding of tradition. Without the aesthetic directive we are reduced to an idea of tradition beholden entirely to what Yeats called in his "General Introduction to My Work" the poetry of the point of view. As such, supremely achieved works of art with their technical sufficiency and innate surplus of meaning—their capacity to translate beyond their own times and cultures and hence their ability to enlarge our collective and ideally communal understanding of our selves and our world—become reduced to solely political and cultural surrogates. Part of the problem rests in Eliot's tendency—a common one—to conflate the formation of tradition, which is the process of "handing over" (*tradere*), with the formation of a canon, the process by which works of art are determined to "measure up" (*kanon,* from the Greek *kana* or "cane"). Eliot affirms that no artist has "complete meaning alone" but can be valued only when set "for contrast and comparison, among the dead."⁴⁵ This speaks to the complexities of canon formation quite honestly and indubitably from the artist's perspective as one who would not only make art but seek to make great art.

Tradition, however, is more encompassing than canon. Where canon asserts the aesthetic sense as the predominating category of judgment, tradition requires a broader field of inclusion; it requires receptivity to the new, even in the most bounded circumstances. That is why, though Eliot asserts "the existing order is complete before the new work arrives," he also avers that "for order to persist after the supervention of novelty, the *whole* existing order must be, if ever so slightly, altered." Eliot's "eternal order" is not "eternal" at all, if by "eternal" we mean unchanging; rather, tradition requires "a sense of the timeless as well as of the temporal." What makes a writer traditional for Eliot is a historical sense that holds both together. Imbedded in this notion of the traditional is the canonical, although, as Eliot continues in his explication, we discern the thread of the canonical giving way to the wider, evolving weave of tradition:

> To proceed to a more intelligible exposition of the *relation* of the poet to the past . . . The poet must be very conscious of the main current,

which does not at all flow invariably through the most distinguished reputations. He must be quite aware of the obvious fact that art never improves, but that the material of art is never quite the same. He must be aware that the mind of Europe—the mind of his own country—a mind which he learns in time to be much more important than his own private mind—is a mind which changes, *and that this change is a development which abandons nothing en route.*[46]

Taken in relief of its own relational and developmental processes, Eliot's conception of tradition is far from a cold pantheon of eternal monuments. It is an organic body composed of artistic minds, both living and dead, that not only can change but does change. Certainly Eliot's own proclivities toward "the mind of Europe" and "the main current" manifest themselves here, but the direction of Eliot's thought is distinctly forward, or perhaps we should say recursive—a gathering up of the past in the consciousness of the present as tradition grows, a living embodiment, at once fundamentally and radically en route.

Eliot's idea of tradition may yet survive both the tidal wave of politicized criticism and his own narrow views, provided such an understanding of tradition can become recognized as resilient beyond its canonical intent and Western inflections in order to become even more encompassing and en route—a "traveling tradition." Such a tradition not only rides the "main current" of a single history but recognizes that it evolves through confluences of lives, cultures, and artistic expressions. This concept also affirms that, rather than being simply a palimpsest of multiple, segregated narratives or traces from the ruptures of history, tradition tends optimally toward an interfusion of expressions, all of which have the potential to enrich our self-understanding and some of which may be sufficiently distinguished as to enlarge our artistic as well as our critical resources. Tradition is a monumental configuration of history in the multifarious life of art; moreover, it is always a reconfiguration of that history in the present through the evolving amplitude of the past, with the aim, however fraught and imperfect, of providing a more humanly available future. Given a twenty-first-century global nexus shaped so pervasively by social, cultural, and economic interfusion, all would do well to keep mindful of how traditions evolve by acknowledging and assimilating what once might have been inadmissible. The like is true for Ireland, America, and Irish America.

The Way of Assimilation: The Great Famine as Example

One important arena of Irish history and tradition that Irish American poetry appears to have acknowledged and engaged more substantively than has Irish poetry—at least those Irish poems written in English—is the Great Famine. By now there have been so many studies on the Great Famine and its catastrophic effects on Irish society from the early 1840s to the early 1850s that an extensive treatment in this context would be redundant. Suffice it to say that it stands in Irish history as a profound cultural and historical negation, with more than a million dying of starvation and millions emigrating on "coffin ships" in the most appalling conditions of crowding and disease to escape the effects brought on by the total collapse of the potato crop in Ireland. It is impossible to say how many more died at sea or in the lazar houses of Grosse Isle and Partridge Island. All the while, the British Empire pursued its policies of Malthusian neglect, the colonial authorities evicted peasants to workhouses or to death on the roads and enforced banishments, and corn and grain were exported from the country while the native Irish starved.

Given the profundity of the experience and the near obliteration of a language and way of life that had already been under severe cultural stress for centuries, it is remarkable that so few poems of genuine literary intent and merit have been written about the Famine, either by the Irish or by Irish Americans. Patrick Kavanagh's "The Great Hunger" alludes to the famine in its title but really employs the historical catastrophe as an analogy for the spiritual, social, and sexual starvation of the Irish peasantry. Eavan Boland, in her early poem "Famine Road," likewise uses the Famine as an analogy, this time for female barrenness—the poem juxtaposes Charles Trevelyan's decision to employ the starving Irish to build roads to nowhere in order to earn their bread with a doctor diagnosing a woman's infertility. "What is your body but a famine road," the poem concludes. Seamus Heaney's early poems "At a Potato Digging" and "For the Commander of the 'Eliza'" confront the historical gravity of the famine head-on and movingly, as well as the phenomenon of cultural amnesia about the Famine. His contemporary potato diggers "spill libations of tea" and "scatter crusts" at the end of "At a Potato Digging," as if innocent of the images of death and waste ("live skulls, blind-eyed") evoked in the poem's second section. None of these poems confront the brutal conditions of eviction and emigration, or the effect of the Famine on the emigrants, the coffins ships, and the brutal conditions forced on them in the New World.

Irish poetry's nearly collective amnesia relative to the Famine and in particular to the Famine emigrant's experience begins to be redressed in Eamonn Wall's "The Class of 1845"—"Those who were broken / crawled by brown ditches / into coffin ships // In the new world / they were known as / filth, disease, and silence." In those scant six blunt summary lines Wall says more about the emigrant's experience of the Famine than virtually any Irish poet of note since the Famine itself. Greg Delanty's "The Heritage Center, Cobh 1993" evokes the specter of coffins ships in the sanitized aura of "papier-mâché emigrants" and dioramas.

A few Irish American poets have written poems that seek to plumb the theme of the Great Famine in substantive ways. James McMichael's "The Begotten" in his recent book *Capacity* is a poem of nearly four hundred lines that draws the reader gradually into the historical circumstances that led to the Famine, as well as its repercussions for Irish emigration. The poem reads as a kind of extemporizing of Eamonn Wall's terse reflection; it places the Famine in philosophical perspective:

>   Until given out as what has been
> risen from,
>
> origin has not happened.
> It cannot be returned to, having
> never yet been.
> Able to be longed-for
>
> rearward through forgottenness are
>
> kin willed whole.[47]

Here the idea of origin in relation to Irish American identity emerges as a matter of communal, historical, and metaphysical will, and one that positively demands an engagement with difficult historical fact. Yet origin itself is recognized as a matter of construction on the part of the poet's generational consciousness, removed as it is from the world portrayed and lost through the actual events leading to the past's unfathomable loss.

Brendan Galvin approaches the subject somewhat less philosophically and more dramatically in "1847." Galvin's poem is a short sequence of three parts that, while retrospective, nevertheless places the reader in the historical scene. As such the poem collapses temporal distance. The first poem places us in the perspective of a man from Adare in County Limerick who fired a pistol, unsuccessfully, at Queen Victoria during her visit to Ireland during the worst year of the Famine. Galvin's poem is laudable for its ability to place us in the mind of the desperate man, or at least to create that illusion, an approach that stands in marked contrast to McMichael's. The latter's intent is to highlight historical distance rather than collapse it into dramatic fiction:

> Shoveled out, improved off the hand
> too poor to be ballast for
> a Black Star packet, his fate in
> the failed potato, maybe he survived
> the season of blackberries
> while his children stared
> like storybook rabbits
> from under a scalpeen. . .[48]

Galvin's manipulation of perspective here—we are both inside and outside of the man's point of view—heightens the reader's empathy toward the figure. In the section that follows, Galvin fictionalizes a real report from the Board of Potato Commissioners that instructs the starving in how to derive nourishment from the rotted potatoes by mixing the soaked pulp with other ingredients—as if there were any—to make bread: "All true Irishmen, / we are confident, will exert themselves / to all we recommend." The poet's bitter irony is palpable and reminiscent of Heaney's tone in "For the Commander of the 'Eliza.'" Galvin's sequence ends not in Ireland but in Grosse Isle, and thus affirms continuity with origin precisely through the searing breakage between the Old World and the New caused by the Famine. "Everywhere you step / into the indentations under grass,"[49] Galvin reflects, thereby acknowledging the presence—or absence—of the thousands who died in the New World from the brutal social and historical machinery at work in the Old.

In both James McMichael's "The Begotten" and Brendan Galvin's "1847" the huge historical, communal, and metaphysical gulf that is the Great Famine emerges from the unspoken of history in a manner that faces up to the whole of the event, including the emigrant experience, from the standpoint of Irish American poets removed from the horror of the experience by the space of the Atlantic as well as a couple of generations. Jewish theologian Arthur Cohen adapts the term *tremendum* (from Rudolf Otto's *mysterium tremendum*) to describe an event that totally shatters human meaning with the enormity of death on a scale that demolishes ontological assumptions about order and beneficence.[50] Cohen's historical reference point is, of course, the Holocaust, but if there is any event that approaches the magnitude of *tremendum* for the Irish it is the Great Famine. The Famine is a profound rupture in Irish history, a cultural caesura dividing modern Ireland from its past.

Something of that recognition may have spurred the writing of "After the Digging," a suite of poems by Jewish American poet Alan Shapiro. Shapiro recounts that he wrote the poems after reading Cecil Wood-Smith's *The Great Hunger* and reading journalistic accounts of the Famine in the Stanford University library. Where McMichael's poem emphasizes the constructed nature of origin in the account of transforming history into poetry, and Galvin's sequence offers three perspectives—victimized, victimizer, and belated historical witness—to mediate the subject, Shapiro's suite posits the fiction of collapsing history altogether. "After the Digging" is a narrative of the Famine told through letters. The first five of these letters evoke the brutal world of the Famine from the perspective of sympathetic members of the colonial authorities, who feel compassion for the starving even as they are required to do the bidding of the empire under Charles Trevelyan's auspices. Shapiro's achievement in these poems is to create a series of believable and sustained voices that cause the reader to encounter, despite his or her own historical remove, something of what it must have been like to witness, and be implicated in, the wholesale destruction of a society:

> Please do not think me impudent. Like you
> I feel no great affection for the Irish.
> But it is not enough that "we should tell them
> they suffer from the providence of God";
> or that "in terms of economic law
> it's beneficial that the price of grain
> should rise in proportion to the drop in wage."
> We can no longer answer cries of want
> with quoting economics, or with prayer.
> Ireland is not, and never can be, Whitehall,
> and while they starve no Englishman is safe.[51]

These lines from "Randolf Routh to Charles Trevelyan" define the fundamental moral groundwork of the Famine, and in doing so they also set forth an analogy to our own time and place. In this manner Shapiro's epistolary poems collapse history to the moment of reading—the reader is fictively speaking in the place of Charles Trevelyan—and create thereby the historical parallel in the experience of the reader.

The poet establishes the same temporal correspondence in "The Last Guest," in which an Irish driver responds to an English newspaperman after the celebrations at Cobh ("Cove" in the poem) in 1847, when Queen Victoria stood on Irish soil for the first time and Cobh was renamed Queenstown in her honor:

> Last night, in Queenstown, we may have been the hosts.
> But here today, in Cove, we are the servants
> we have always been, whose lives are but
> a getting ready for great guests, and then
> a cleaning up after the guests have gone.[52]

Shapiro's deft portrayal here owes something to his understanding that the oppressed—regardless of their ethnicity or nationality—must always communicate anger evasively if they are to avoid the repercussions. The speaker's bitterness laces through these lines and is revealed most subtly in the contrasting use of the names of the place—Queenstown and Cove (Cobh). Cobh is Queenstown when Victoria arrives, or any English dignitary, but it reverts to the Irish Cobh when they depart. Shapiro's portrayal of the psychology and politics of oppression is incisive, he creates narratives that are "negatively capable" in so far as each constructs a vivid and believable character throughout this suite of voices. The last of these is Thomas Preston, whose fictional log in "Passage Out" evokes the experience of traveling on one of the coffin ships:

> The dead are going overboard
> without prayer, and with little sorrow
> (for few have life enough for grief).
> Like spoiled meat, husbands, wives, and children
> thrown overboard into the deep—
> as if this were the last kind act
> that now they can relieve their kin
> who have at last when they lie down
> some room to change position in.[53]

In turn, Shapiro's narrative suite ends on Grosse Isle, acknowledging both the bleak future and the hatred of the dispossessed Irish who have lost their families and their world:

> After the digging, Sean McGuire,
> his skin too papery to sweat,
> drove two shovels into the ground
> making a cross, and said, "By this,
> Mary, I swear I will go back
> as soon as I earn passage
> and murder him that murdered you,
> our landlord, Palmerston."
>   And went
> like all the rest, like living refuse
> half naked, maimed, to Montreal,
> to Boston, to New York; the seeds
> of typhus already blossoming.[54]

The bitter picture painted here is the antithesis of the immigrant's ideal entry to a welcoming new world—Shapiro refuses that pretty fiction. Instead, at the poem's end, he gestures outward through the voice of Thomas Preston in a way that makes the Irish and the Irish American experience emblematic of the modern experience of exile, and not just the Irish experience isolated within its own cultural and historical reference points:

> They go
> and may God go with them who bring
> into the new world nothing else
> but epitaphs for legacies.[55]

Still, if these lines establish the Irish and Irish American experience in the extreme historical and cultural circumstances of the Great Famine as something of a model for similar experiences, at the same time they also underscore the gulf between the lost world of origin and the New World, at once defined necessarily by a divergent sense of place while yet retaining in some respects the longing for the older sense of place that has been breached by history.

Place and Displacement in Irish American Poetry

The sense of place, of course, is not only a fundamental theme in Irish poetry. As we saw in Brian Coffey's "Missouri Sequence" it is the fundamental allegiance defining Irishness as well, even when one has left the native land. Though Eamonn Wall challenges this assumption in "The Wexford Container Tragedy," the centrality of place to definitions of Irishness is incontestable—to be Irish is to be related closely to the place of Ireland and indeed, traditionally, to an even more localized sense of place than nation. One grows up in a country and townland. The north side of Dublin is not the same place as the south side. While the urgency of this localized sense of identity has surely diminished with the advent of modernity, in which differences of custom and self-definition collapse even as they heighten into at times combustible caricatures of themselves, Patrick Kavanagh's desire to distinguish the parochial from the provincial still has currency. This is even truer in our postmodern world. We live where we live, in our particular fractal portion of an ever more complex global nexus. That is why Eamonn Wall suggests changing "provincial" to "international" in Kavanagh's binary formula,[56] though he likewise cautions: "No critic of Irish writing can afford to ignore the connection between voice and place."[57] The Irish writer is stretched between the sense of place as traditionally understood—the townland, the parish, and ultimately as Heaney has observed a landscape "instinct with signs, implying a system of reality beyond the visible realities"[58]—and the sense of displacement that inevitably arises when the writer realizes that much of human history exposes the limitations of such localized systems in view of new worlds imposing themselves on the old or of their eventual destruction in the face of raw, oppressive power. Relevant again here is Kinsella's "way of assimilation," by which, he affirms, Irish literature knows the necessity of this paradigmatic negotiation and of adaptation through which it wrests some measure of continuity over the course of history—in spite of the wrenching advent of the modern world.[59]

At the same time, as might be extrapolated from Kinsella's reflections, the tension between the sense of place and the recognition of displacement forces a choice on the Irish poet—either one establishes one's voice in proximity to the "primary audience sharing the facts of experience intimately with the writer," or one constructs "an ideal audience, a projection of the self, allowing an actual audience to appear when it can." For Kinsella, "with the second choice one enters the world of modern art, an art primarily of exploration."[60] The choice is the one Yeats made against the revivalist cast of his early work, his "coat of old mythologies,"[61] and the one Joyce made to arrogate to himself the urgency of his own imagination unfettered by any allegiance to home except as chosen by his own driven and watchful consciousness. For Patrick Ward, likewise, Joyce is the paradigm of the modern and postmodern artist. Drawing on Edward Said, Ward "affiliates" Joyce "with other migratory artists . . . migratory in the literal and metaphorical modes in a loose, transnational association of highly self-conscious artists, imposing their own narrative order on culture and experience."[62]

The choice Kinsella identifies and Ward further illuminates throws light on the problem of Irish American poets and their relation to the tradition of Irish poetry. Put simply, most Irish American poems of the nineteenth century fail because they turn back in nostalgia toward the native place, toward the audience of shared native regard. In a sense, they refuse the modern directive toward exploration, toward acceptance of migration as both a historical and a metaphysical condition. Though his poems begin to move in concert with this modern directive, John Boyle O'Reilly could not fully make the transition. He lived the condition of migration to the fullest but could not bring it convincingly into his art, imprisoned as he was by two ideas of an audience, one Irish and one American.

O'Reilly's failure to transcend the conditions of his experience imaginatively finds its roots in the fraught dynamic between the sense of place and the experience of displacement. It is a dynamic that continues to inform Irish poetry, with suitable resonance for Irish American poetry as well. In his essay "Place and Displacement," Seamus Heaney memorably reflects on a passage from Wordsworth's *The Prelude,* Book 10, where the trials of witnessing the brutalities of the French Revolution undermine much more than his sense of place. "Life, where he is situated," Heaney observes, "is not where he wants to be," and he goes on to draw a connection between Wordsworth's sense of displacement and Jung's notion that "the trauma of the individual consciousness is likely to be an aspect of forces at work in the collective life."[63] Undoubtedly a similar if not more profound experience of trauma affected the consciousness of those who were forced by historical circumstance to emigrate from Ireland and to confront life anew, often facing brutal realities in the new world as in the old. Surely that trauma was nothing if not "an aspect of forces at work in the collective life."[64] Trauma of this kind certainly stifled the voices and potential of many Irish American poets during the later part of the nineteenth century. Life where they were situated was not where they wanted to be. Hence the outpourings of nostalgic verse, the volumes of displaced Irish "playing the harp backward"; hence the sentimental backward looks of many Irish Americans to this day, as well as the need for the Irish tourist industry to answer that need with package tours to Blarney. Beyond the lures of kitsch there is "a place for the genuine," to borrow a phrase from Marianne Moore, that haunts the necessary and inevitable relationship between the sense of displacement and the sense of place.

Heaney's typically and brilliantly lucid synthesis on the sense of place in poetry is worth quoting substantially here:

Irrespective of our creed or politics, irrespective of what culture or subculture may have coloured our individual sensibilities, our imaginations' assent to the stimulus of the names, our sense of the place is enhanced, our sense of ourselves as inhabitants not just of a geographical country but of a country of the mind is cemented. It is this feeling, assenting, equable marriage between the geographical country and the country of the mind, whether that country of the mind takes its tone unconsciously from a shared oral inherited culture, or from a consciously savoured literary culture, or from both, it is this marriage that constitutes the sense of place in its richest possible manifestation.[65]

More often than not Heaney's sense of place is offered, appropriately, as commentary that elucidates both his own poems and a good deal of Irish poetry, tied as it has been for centuries to specific places and the lore of place. Heaney's commentary here also may be read equally as an attempt to synthesize opposites—the geographical country and the country of the mind, or perhaps more accurately to raise both to a higher conception of consciousness about the sense of place. In Irish American poetry, the country of the mind reads back into the lost geographical country a profound sense of place displaced from the immediate present. At the same time, because the emigrant consciousness has been displaced from the geographical country, the country of the mind can be read only across a widening gap of time and space, history, and assimilation into the new world that at once displaces the old and renders it an object of longing. Though the stimulus of names calls for the imagination's assent, and the longing for the geographical place is enhanced, the marriage of the mind and the geographical place is not equable—it is broken. What informs Irish American poetry beyond the obvious gilt-edged "laments for the lost homeland" is the "unconscious ways"[66] the tone of a poem may be shaped by an inherited culture that has survived the traumatic experience of displacement, as well as the artistically astute ways in which the experience of displacement is confronted as Irish American poetry moves from O'Reilly's failed synthesis to an unforeseen and as yet largely unrecognized burgeoning in the twentieth century.

The poetry of Marianne Moore is compelling in this respect precisely because it makes no concessions whatsoever to the emigrant's longing for the lost homeland. Of course, since she was not an emigrant but a fully assimilated Irish American, it should perhaps come as no surprise that her work bears none of the obvious characteristics of the migratory artist so commensurate with modernism. Yet Marianne Moore is not only one of the most preeminent of American modernist poets who, like William Carlos Williams and Wallace Stevens, stayed on this side of the Atlantic, but also with Robinson Jeffers one of the greatest American poets who are Irish by descent. While Moore is not a migratory artist in any obvious way, from another vantage it might be said that she is, of all her contemporaries, perhaps the most "displaced" of poets. Not that her sense of displacement, at least in the historical sense, is at all apparent or even, perhaps, conscious. Instead, Moore's displacement should be understood as a matter of artistic temperament—place rarely enters her poems except as a premise for the poems' own internal textual play. Place, then, when it signifies an actual place outside the poem, becomes displaced into the poem as pure text. The same thing happens, more famously, with Moore's fabulous animals—"The Fish," The Pangolin," "The Jerboa," and so on. Of modern poets Moore is perhaps the supreme fabulist, though the poems are more fables of careful and almost obsessive artistic choices as much as they are fables that give lessons. With their minute attention to each syllable, meticulously fretted into form, they aim at a discomforting enchantment that turns the reader back to the poem, the way one might turn back toward the infinitely delicate drawings in an illuminated manuscript. The poems appear to be the epitome of the impersonal, hardly resonant with Heaney's trauma of consciousness.

On the other hand, Moore's poem "Spenser's Ireland" reveals at once her inclination to dislodge the poem as modernist artifact from history while at the same time owning however obliquely her Irish inheritance as an Irish American poet. The poem's famous opening, "Spenser's Ireland // has not altered:— / a place as kind as it is green / the greenest place I've never seen,"[67] manages at once to negate historical trauma—the very history of oppression Kinsella takes such pains to elucidate—and to confess the breach of her family's separation from their once native place. We are truly in a country of the mind rather than a real geographical country, and in this country of the mind the received ideas of the distant place carry with them a sense of the inherited culture. It is "the greenest place," and though she has never been there she knows "every name is a tune." As the poem proceeds, filled with allusions to Irish stories, various enchantments, mantles, fairies, furies, grandmothers, great-great-grandmothers, flax, fuchsia, Irish weather, Irish epigrams, and Irish legend, it becomes clear that Moore's imaginative engagement with Ireland is wholly textual—not geographical. Yet it is this very displacement into a wholly textual identification with Ireland that separates Moore's sense of connection to Ireland from the historical realities that brought her family to America, while at the same time inscribing the assimilated nature of the poet's Irish identity.

As one reads stanza by stanza the accumulation of associative details—hindered characters, fingers working a needle with care "not madness," twisted torcs and lunulae—one comes to realize that the invocations of enchantment that recur in the poem serve to draw attention to a countercurrent of hindrance, restlessness, and ultimately "discommodity." Enchantment serves the need to survive, and that is why Marianne Moore's poem is there, displaced from history in order to capture the poet and the reader with its own "supreme belief" in the efficacy of art. Still more significantly, the very details that speak to the quality of the poem as invention and artifact rather than historical commentary or reflection also perform an allegory of the process of assimilation. As the poet speaks of the poem's objects of art, its folk art weavings, its damask, its jewelry as well as its natural designs (the fuchsia, the guillemot, the hen of the heath), she confesses:

> they are to me
> > like enchanted Earl Gerald who
> > changed himself into a stag, to
> a great green-eyed cat of
> the mountain. Discommodity makes
> > them invisible; they've dis-
> appeared....[68]

As we saw earlier, Greg Delanty's "We Will Not Play the Harp Backward Now, No" wisely riffs on Moore's poem: he adapts Moore's citation of the Irish legend of Earl Gerald as a metaphor for the emigrant artist's ability to disappear into America in order to become one's own self-imagined creature in the true Joycean sense. In Moore's poem, however, the discommodity, the inconvenience of such stories, folk crafts, and geographical flora and fauna from the old country render them invisible—they disappear like the assimilated into the new world. On the other hand, it is this very recognition that prompts the poem's final declaration of identity: "The Irish say your trouble is their / trouble and your / joy their joy? I wish / I could believe it; / I am troubled, I'm dissatisfied, I'm Irish."[69] These last lines speak movingly to the poem's final awareness of an identity that is irreducibly doubled. The poet cannot believe the old Irish epithet—a bit of blarney to be sure—precisely because it cannot be tested by geographical proximity. Even the country of the mind betrays her. What she does have faith in is her dissatisfaction and hence her skepticism—a faith in the restlessness of art—and it is that which makes her by her own lights Irish. Perhaps, then, Marianne Moore is a migratory artist after all—an inner émigré, to borrow a phrase from Seamus Heaney's poem "Exposure"—whose faith in the "displacement" or the inherent making strange of poetry emerges from a sense of historical displacement that remains invisible in her work, though shapes it like the white space that defines each line on the page.

"About one million people left Ireland between 1815 and the Famine," Patrick Ward reflects, and he goes on to observe that the identity of these emigrants "was expressed in forms of sentimental attachment" to traditional customs and "paradigms of expression."[70] It is fair to say that Marianne Moore's "Spenser's Ireland" encodes such paradigms of expression only to subvert their sentimentality by owning the reality of separation from the geographical country and asserting the artist's independence over those inherited modes. At the same time, Moore's work manifests a kind of invisible Irishness. This is the case with Moore's contemporary, Robinson Jeffers, who with her stands as a preeminent figure during the time of American modernist ascendancy. Of course, unlike Moore, Jeffers's poetry exhibits an almost reactionary repugnance to the more optimistic strains of the American modernist enterprise of Williams and, later, Hart Crane. Where one feels that for Marianne Moore the object of art is primary—an imaginary garden that must admit its real toads—one realizes that for Jeffers nature is primary and far surpasses the human place entirely. We have left the tended imaginary garden for the wilds where human hubris becomes ever more diminished by nature's patience and power. Hence, while he is regarded as something of a reactionary, he also presages an environmentalist perspective on the relationship between humanity and nature that has gained greater and greater currency—and for good reason. It is a perspective he shares with his fellow Scots-Irish American poet, A. R. Ammons, though Jeffers's work is far sterner in tone and gravity than his postmodern counterpart.

Above all, Jeffers is a poet of place, and that place is the rocky shores of the California headlands around Carmel Point, where he built Tor House, his own *omphalos in extremis* on the borderline between the human and the inhuman:

> If you should look for this place after a handful of lifetimes: . . .
> Look for foundations of sea-worn granite, my fingers had the art
> To make stone love stone, you will find some remnant.
> But if you should look in your idleness after ten thousand years:
> It is the granite knoll on the granite
> And lava tongue in the midst of the bay, by the mouth of the Carmel River-valley, these four will remain
> In the change of names. . . .[71]

As these lines from the early poem "Tor House" affirm, Jeffers's identification with what he understood to be his spiritual as well as geographical home is the equal of any Irish poet's in their powerful identification with place. By the end of the poem he declares his soul will haunt the very granite of his ruined home.

Born in Pittsburgh in 1887 (the same year as Marianne Moore), son of William Hamilton Jeffers, a minister in the United Presbyterian Church and distinguished theologian, Robinson Jeffers was educated in languages and the classics in America and in schools across Europe before his family resettled in California. Jeffers began work on Tor House in 1919, on the site of a midden where Native Americans "camped for perhaps thousands of years," shortly after he and his wife, Una, moved to the Big Sur coast.[72] Of Scots-Irish ancestry like her husband, Una had a profound influence on her husband's work, and among their shared obsessions were not only the "rocky promontories called tors which they had both seen in Dartmoor, England," as Jeffers's biographer John Karman observes, but the stone towers of Ireland that they would see firsthand and tour on four extended trips to Northern Ireland and Ireland before Una's death in 1950.

Hawk Tower, which Jeffers built between 1921 and 1925 alongside Tor House overlooking the roiling immensity of the Pacific, was modeled self-consciously after the old Irish towers Una so loved, and over the years into the masonry of the tower Jeffers inserted artifacts from their many journeys to "sacred" sites, like Mount Kilauea in Hawaii, the Babylonian temple of Erich, and—most significantly perhaps for his connection to Ireland—a chip from Thoor Ballylee.[73] "And may those characters remain / when all is ruin once again," Yeats wrote in "To Be Carved on a Stone at Thoor Ballylee." A similar unflinching awareness of the transience of human aspiration characterizes Jeffers's work, as well as the heroic proclivities of a poet who looks starkly at the impending end of things. For Jeffers, unlike Yeats, however, there was no hope after the end of building again—only the vast, ultimately inhuman consciousness of a God that lives in and through all things and, beyond them, is ongoing.

Not surprisingly, Yeats was Una's favorite poet.[74] As Jeffers himself observes in his preface to *Visits to Ireland,* Una's posthumously published diary of the Jeffers family trip to Northern Ireland, Ireland, and England in 1929, his wife so loved Ireland not only for her love of its towers and her ancestry (her family comes from the village of Killinchy) but because Yeats along with George Moore "had made Ireland magical."[75] To read the diary, which is composed of entries not only by Jeffers and Una but by their twin sons, Garth and Donnan, who were young teens at the time, is to find the family driving back and forth across Ireland in search of ancient sites and round towers, visiting Coole Park and Thoor Ballylee, and once just missing Yeats himself. Una wrote of their approach: "We saw the tower at last, half a mile away, on higher ground than our road, so turned into a twisty little lane. There it stood by a small winding stream, austere, strong square tower, with the tiny cottages at its foot a walled garden in rear."[76] But for the locale in the "stoney rolling country" of central Galway, what she describes is very nearly a portrait of Tor House and Hawk Tower or Thoor Ballylee, had it been transported to the Antrim Coast to Torr Head, to Cushendall or Cushendun in the north, where the Jefferses rented a house for the duration of their time that first visit to Ireland.

Robinson Jeffers acknowledged the similarity of the coastlines of Antrim and Big Sur, both rocky and jutting out into their respective seas, though he saw himself living at the edge and "spiritual end" of Western civilization.[77] Nevertheless, it was the north of the Antrim Coast, of Cushendun, Ballycastle, the Giant's Causeway, Navan Fort, Enniskillen, and Devenish that spurred Jeffers's imagination, so he wrote *Descent to the Dead,* a series of poems written in Ireland and Great Britain, the most urgent of which express his profound sense of connection to Ulster. That urgency, a passionate declaration of ancestry and intimacy with the ancestral place, may be heard in the raw energy of his poem "Antrim" and in the last lines especially:

> The passionate flesh and nerves have flamed like pitchpine and fallen
> And lain in the earth softly dissolving.
> I have lain and have been humbled in all these graves, and mixed new flesh with the old and filled the hollow of my mouth
> With maggots and rotten dust and ages of repose. I lie here and plot the agony of resurrection.[78]

Jeffers's fierce admixture of the new flesh and the old in "Antrim" marks communion of his new world imagination at the end of the Western world with his Ulster roots, even into the graves that constitute his origins. And one can hear it, too, in Una Jeffers's more matter-of-fact reflection on the important connection for the family between California's Big Sur coast and the coast of County Antrim. "Beautiful walk to Tor Head," she writes in the diary in words that must have surely resonated with Tor House and Hawk Tower. "We felt so much at home here on the Cushendun coast near Cushleake; it is so much like our own 'down the coast.' Not so large, nor so long, but the hills very similar and beautiful, in their plunge to deep sea."[79] Antrim and California—an unlikely correspondence between two places that awakened in the poet's mind, and in his family's, a profound sense of cultural and spiritual connection despite time and distance. It is a connection audible only sporadically in Marianne Moore's work.

Like Marianne Moore, then, Jeffers is an American poet whose work can and should be read through that cultural and literary prism, though unlike Moore, Jeffers's Irish ancestry shapes his imagination more directly and pervasively, and so much so that it is not difficult to discern in Jeffers's whole imaginative enterprise a strongly Northern Irish impulse and vision, particularly after his powerful encounter with its landscape and its ruins. One can hear the influence in these lines from "Carmel Point," in which he characterizes the patience of the rock heads now defaced by "a crop of suburban houses":

> Now the spoiler has come: does it care?
> Not faintly. It has all time. It knows the people are a tide
> That swells and in time will ebb, and all
> Their works dissolve. Meanwhile the image of the pristine beauty
> Lives in the very grain of the granite,
> Safe as the endless ocean that climbs our cliff....[80]

The hard edges of Jeffers's consonants resound through these lines with a guttural terseness. His metaphor of humanity as a tide to be swept away by the wider ocean of materiality and time bespeaks the inconsequentiality of our nature, as if the God of Things had taken stern lesson from the ardent Presbyterian preacher who was Robinson Jeffers's father. Now compare these lines from "The Hebrides" by Louis MacNeice, another poet son of a Scots-Irish minister from Northern Ireland:

> On those islands
> Where no train runs on rails and the tyrant time
> Has no clock-towers to signal people to doom
> With semaphore ultimatums tick by tick,
> There is still peace though not for me and not
> Perhaps for long—still peace on the bevel hills
> For those who still can live as their fathers lived
> On those islands.[81]

Certainly Louis MacNeice has a far greater tolerance for the human presence in nature and a more forgiving vision: by living close to "the bevel hills" in harmony with nature, MacNeice's villagers appear to avoid Jeffers's judgment. They are not spoilers. On the other hand, one can hear remarkable resonance in the line cadences of "Carmel Point" and "The Hebrides," as well as in the clipped *t* and hard *c* sounds intermingling with the liquid *l* sounds, as though the sea were already subtly pervading the inlets of both poems. Jeffers visited the Hebrides on his first excursion to Ireland and the British Isles, and it is as if Jeffers's later poem "Carmel Point" had subsumed the country of the mind shaped by the geographical country of his Scots-Irish ancestry and superimposed it on the far west of the American continent—another geographical country in extremis, and one his imagination would inhabit throughout the course of his lifetime.

In poems like "Carmel Point," poems definitively of the American place, one can hear Jeffers's ear tuned to an older ancestral music. In "The Sense of Place" Heaney asserts that when John Montague writes of place he is "forced to seek a connection with a history and a heritage."[82] One could likewise say that the cumulative tone of Jeffers's poetry encodes a connection to his Irish history and heritage through subtle accruals of sonic texture and voice that resonate deeply in the work backward to the original geographical country, the original country of the mind. Still, more explicitly, Robinson Jeffers establishes the motif of the return journey of the Irish American poet. For Marianne Moore, Ireland is the greenest place she has "never seen"; for Jeffers, the haunting connection to the geographical country galvanizes his mind, his identity, in order to revitalize and strengthen the imagination:

> I also make a remembered name;
> And I shall return home to the granite stones
> On my cliff over the greatest ocean
> To be blind ashes under the butts of the stones:
> As you here under the fanged limestone columns
> Are said to lie, over the narrow north straits
> Toward Scotland, and the quick-tempered Moyle. . . .[83]

These lines from "Ossian's Grave" articulate Jeffers's desire to see his own life as an imaginative reincarnation of Óisin from the Fionn cycle of Irish myth and legend. Jeffers does not make the distinction between Ossian, the character created by James MacPherson in his eighteenth-century forgery of Scots Gaelic legends, and Óisin, the figure from Irish legend and mythology. Jeffers's poem commemorates the prehistoric monument near Cushendall in County Antrim, a monument Jeffers visited in the summer of 1929. Though only mentioned briefly in the diary, the poem's commemoration in effect recasts his life's work in the image of the Irish hero: "I shall return home . . . to be blind ashes . . . *As you* are said to lie, over the narrow north straits"[84] (my emphasis). Jeffers the American poet and Óisin of Irish legend, also a wanderer who is nonetheless bound to his sense of place, live parallel lives and die parallel deaths, both "haughtily alone," both heroic figures of the imagination. What Jeffers accomplishes in these lines is nothing less than an assimilation of Irish legend into American poetry through the pursuit of his ancestral connection to place. Jeffers's Carmel Point and Ossian's Cushendall are superimposed on each other, so that one cannot fully understand Jeffers's work without recognizing the debt of his identity, the country of his mind, to both places.

If Jeffers is the twentieth-century poet who plumbs from his perspective the impending end of human habitation on the planet, then in his identification with the North of Ireland he discovers the resonating source of his vision, a resonance to which he vividly alludes in "The Broadstone":

> Here lies the hero, more than half God,
> And nobody knows his name nor his race, in the bee-bright
>   necropolis,
> With the stone circle and his tribe around him.
> Sometimes perhaps (but who'd confess it?) in soft adolescence
> We used to wonder at the world, and have wished
> To hear some final harmony resolve the discords of life?
> —Here they are all perfectly resolved.[85]

It is nearly impossible not to hear in these lines an echo of the poet's paean to his own ghostly presence in the stones of Tor House millennia into the future, as he envisions in the earlier poem. What Jeffers discerns here is the perfect resolution of a lost past come home again into the mind of the poet.

Perhaps nowhere in Jeffers's poetry is the imaginative reciprocity between Northern Ireland and California so explicitly articulated by the poet than in his poem "Shane O'Neill's Cairn." Una Jeffers provides the occasion for the poem in her diary: "We walked to Shane O'Neill's cairn, in a high field beside the hilly cliff road to Ballycastle. It is a huge round pile of stones, marking the place where Shane of Neill was killed, three or four centuries ago. Walked back. . . . Walked on—such a glorious gorgeous day, exhilarating as California."[86] In Jeffers's poem the passing reference linking the old world and the new becomes the driving insight by which Jeffers's two worlds, the world of his lost Northern Irish landscape and the world of California at the far end of the West, inhere in a moment of stark animating vision. The poem is worth quoting in its entirety:

> When you and I on the Palos Verdes cliff
> Found life more desperate than dear,
> And when we hawked at it on the lake by Seattle
> In the west of the world, where hardly
> Anything has died yet: we'd not have been sorry, Una,
> But surprised, to foresee this gray
> Coast in our days, the gray waters of the Moyle
> Below us, and under our feet
> The heavy black stones of the cairn of the lord of Ulster.
> A man of blood who died bloodily
> Four centuries ago: but death's nothing, and life,
> From a high death-mark on a headland
> Of the dim island of burials, is nothing either.
> How beautiful are both these nothings.[87]

Appropriately dedicated and addressed to his wife, "Shane O'Neill's Cairn" does something more than memorialize an American tourist's visit to a captivating place; rather, it fuses together the geographical poles of Jeffers's imagination in a Janus-like gaze that binds together old world and new in the dual nothings of life and death to which his words bear witness like the cairn stones themselves, or the stones of Tor House. Though Jeffers baldly and culpably ignores the historical presence of Native Americans—the West of the world is a place "where hardly anything has died yet"—his tendency to hold to the myth of an ahistorical New World only serves to strengthen his connection to the old, albeit at the expense of those who arrived before the Europeans.

As such, while it might be an overstatement to call Robinson Jeffers an Irish poet—though John Montague does include his poem "Antrim" in *The Book of Irish Poetry*—it is nonetheless true that Irish poetry can only extend comprehension of its tradition by acknowledging Jeffers's work as a paradigmatic example of Irish American poetry asserting its ties to the Irish literary and geographical landscape in an effort to plumb a continuity outside the country of the mind's normal bounds of recognition.

Returns and Transmigrations: A Music of What Happened

Robinson Jeffers's "At Ossian's Grave" is important for both Irish and Irish American poetry because it not only enacts the emigrant's archetypal return to the native place but performs that return from the standpoint of one distanced from the native place by a generation. Jeffers claims his Irish identity through both a genealogical and a literary correspondence, as well as a geographical one—the parallel landscapes of California's rugged headlands and Northern Ireland's. The first-, second-, and third-generation Irish American poet's desire to claim where they "have never been" by an imagined or literal act of return defines one important aspect of the sense of place in Irish American poetry. This trope of return for Irish American poets is not inherently nostalgic, and as Irish American poetry moved into the twentieth century, the idea of the return to Ireland came to avoid the sentimental strains overheard in the poems of popular emigrant Irish verse in the nineteenth century.

Even before Jeffers and Moore one finds in the work of O'Reilly's friend and associate at the Marliave poetry soirees, Louise Imogen Guiney, an imaginative effort to return to the place of her ancestors:

> The cabin-door looks down a furze-lighted hill,
> And far as Leighlin Cross the fields are green and still;
> But once I hear the blackbird in Leighlin hedges call,
> The foolishness is on me, and the wild tears fall![88]

One hears in these lines from "In Leinster," one of her "Two Irish Peasant Songs," something of the early Yeats, but also still more deeply a tone that appears to echo from genomic memory and sounds akin to those lyrics written in the margins of manuscripts by anonymous scribes. At the same time the sense of loneliness in the lines communicates the loss someone left behind might feel after years of emigration had stripped away family and friends.

In Guiney's "Gloucester Harbor" we hear a similar tone of loss and longing, bound now to a distinctly American locale:

> The women make deep lamentation
> >   In starts and in slips;
> Here always is hope unavailing,
> Here always the dreamers are sailing
> >   After the ships!⁸⁹

Guiney's subject here is the feeling of personal loss felt by the wives of fishermen who for generations defined their lives by the dream of the sea that so shaped Gloucester's maritime history. At the same time, with little imaginative effort, one can hear the laments of those left behind after an American wake, the emigrants departing on ships across the same "pitiless sea." Guiney's rendition of place in this poem may be read as transparent to such Irish historical themes without being overtly about the Irish landscape and its people, though landscape and history clearly haunt her own imaginative engagement with place in America as in Ireland.

The like is true of Charles Olson's "Enniscorthy Suite." Written while visiting a friend's estate in Virginia, and not in Eamonn Wall's hometown, the sequence of poems commemorates the estate's name and its immediate landscape. Heaney's affirmation in "The Sense of Place" that the Irish landscape is also a text whereby we may read Ireland's conflicted history is true of Olson's Enniscorthy: the lingering historical presence of the American Civil War pervades the poem. Olson's "Enniscorthy Suite" is present to American history through the poet's awareness of place. Olson, however, does not permit the title of his sequence to remain merely incidental to Irish history, as the section "Bottom Land" demonstrates:

> The barley's bent beards shine
> the oats stand green

spring, it is the spring
green and green

The barley's bent beards shine
the oats a darker green
spring, it is the clover
love and lover

Spring, it is the barley
spring, it is the oats!
Spring, it is the one time,
Sing, springtime![90]

Reading these lines with an ear attuned to Irish as well as American history one cannot help but hear echoes of the 1798 Rebellion, of Enniscorthy in Ireland and the Croppy Boys who carried barley in their pockets for sustenance as they fought the British and died, as Heaney's poem "Requiem for the Croppies" commemorates, "waving scythes at cannon." "Bottom Land" is placed in Olson's suite between "Lower Field," which conjures the ghosts of Civil War soldiers among the wandering sheep, and "The Family Plot," which elegizes the dead of this American locale. Signifying "green" and "spring," the barley in Olson's "Enniscorthy Suite" carries the echo of those Irish soldiers into a parallel American landscape defined by the place name and by history's inherence in the landscape as a kind of text. The name "Enniscorthy" here constitutes what might be called a nominal analogy that embeds a correspondence of lives across the boundaries of time and space. In this case, the analogy is rooted in Irish and American history and developed through the Irish American poet's deep texturing of the poem by selective detail. Such detail works in concert with the place name to enact the poem's defining correspondence between the Irish dead and the American dead. As such, Olson's analogy effectively inscribes continuity across the divide history, establishing a deeper parallel. "The dead are alone / the live are alone / Alive and alone at Enniscorthy,"[91] as Olson's suite reflects in its final lines—a kind of summary consort in and through the name of the place.

The poems of Robinson Jeffers and the poems of Louise Imogen Guiney and Charles Olson broadly define the two directions of the Irish

American poet's sense of place, the first based upon the trope of return and the second on an almost psychic transmigration of an Irish sense of place into the American locale. Both seek to redress the divided nature of the Irish American poet's relationship to Ireland. After Jeffers, John Berryman makes his pilgrimage of return to face down "the majestic shades" of Yeats and his own complex and fraught sense of Irishness in the last movement of *The Dream Songs*. That pattern of return to Ireland is repeated again and again in such contemporary poets as Thomas Lynch and Michael Heffernan, while others, like Julie O'Callaghan and Chris Agee (as we shall explore later), return and remain in "the place of origin." Poets like O'Callaghan and Agee live in Ireland the way poets like Wall and Delanty live in America: they are poets with a hybrid sense of identity, and their work blurs the boundaries of what it means to be Irish or Irish American. Those boundaries are blurred even further in the work of the late Michael Donaghy, whose poems span the United States, Ireland, and Britain and absorb influences from each of these locales.

Firmly rooted in the American Northeast, in the landscape and fishing villages of Cape Cod, the poetry of Brendan Galvin embodies the Irish obsession with the local, though in a way that reveals a nearly pure transparency between Irish and American senses of place. At the same time, Galvin is as adept at absorbing and reinventing Irish legend and hagiography in his long poem *Saints in Their Ox-Hide Boat* as he is at retelling the life and work of American natural historian Loranzo Newcomb in his other major long poem, *Wampanoag Traveler*. Winner of major literary awards from the Hardison Prize to the Levinson Poetry Prize to a fellowship from the Guggenheim Foundation, and most recently a National Book Award finalist, Galvin has not received sufficient critical attention on either side of the Atlantic, though he is certainly the Irish American poet of the past thirty years whose work achieves an almost perfect imaginative commerce between Irish and American traditions and does so without strain or intellectual anxiety, but with an air of immediate reciprocity.

In Brendan Galvin's work it is as if the divided mind of the Irish American has found a vital and conducive balance between the two geographical worlds. Here are the opening lines of "Hearing Irish Spoken":

> Later I'd understand how it put
> the Atlantic west of them
> again, kept places where scraggly grass
> prevented the stones from ganging up
> the way they did in Boston. On the top
> rear porch of a triple-decker,
> it tied them to whitewashed farmsteads
> splashed with slurry, cowprints
> baked in mud by the blue summer air.[92]

As these lines demonstrate, Galvin's sense of place moves easily between the emigrant triple-deckers of Everett, Massachusetts, where he was born and grew up far from the literary gatherings of Boston to which John Boyle O'Reilly and Louise Imogen Guiney belonged, and the Irish landscape left behind by his forebears. What is so significant here is Galvin's imaginative presence in both worlds—Ireland is not "the greenest place he's never seen," but a real locale perceived in vivid detail, though not his own. What Galvin's poem envisions and embodies is continuity between worlds in spite of historical division through the traumatic loss of place achieved, paradoxically, by the poet's witness to the language he cannot speak:

> All through the distant thwack and roar
> of baseball at Glendale Park,
> the Saccos voluble at their supper
> next door, it ran like water
> steady a thousand years from a limestone
> lip, plaited itself through bogs
> that absorbed roadsigns in English,
> ran with watery sunlight after days
> of rain. . . .[93]

The wonderfully modulated flow of Galvin's lines trace at once a counterpoint and equipoise between immigrant America with all its volubility, as well as the "thwack" and "roar" of baseball, that most American of games, and the world opened up to the child by listening to the language of his deeper past and hence to a sense of place that likewise traces a deeper history of displacement. "I stood at the twilit / meeting of their knees and voices," Galvin recounts at the poem's end, "wondering if it meant some failing in me." I do not know of a more truthful and tender rendering of the first- or second-generation Irish American experience than is found in this scene, speaking at once to the sense of wonder and strangeness before the loss of what might have been one's linguistic birthright and the sense of otherness from one's own family. Irish is a language in exile in Galvin's poem, having had to endure despite its usurpation by English, though it is also the stream that bears the undertow of the poet's deeper sense of identity. He lives in both worlds, the vital cacophony of America and an Ireland "plaited" like DNA into the fabric of his sense of self and sense of place. The "code" of Irish, then, is at once the cipher of Ireland as lost world and the conveyor of continuity for the poet's connection to that world. It is as if Kinsella's subtending continuity through division and the near culture-leveling catastrophe of the Famine had traveled with the emigrants and exiles to the New World, and that rift and nexus of meaning and identity are now made manifest in Galvin's moving poem.

"Plaited" is the perfect verb in Galvin's "Hearing Irish Spoken" to communicate both the intimacy of the Irish language with place and the encoding of the sense of being at once Irish and American for this Irish American poet. His mindfulness of Irish America's continuity with Ireland is maintained despite the disruptive passages of exile and emigration, but without denying the force of that disruption. As he reflects in his poem "Donegal," "Now I understand / why treelessness and / bog that keeps brown water / are in me like a code, Grandfather."[94] In these important lines Galvin raises to consciousness the circumstance not only of being an Irish American poet but of being Irish American, and more than this—of being anyone for whom the encounter with place awakens an almost unspeakable sense of connection. The sense of place is encoded in the sense of identity. At the same time, Galvin's poem registers the feeling of incompleteness experienced by the loss of place that is perceived to be the "ground" of one's identity:

> But to say how the world began
> where sheep lie down for
> the journey into quartzite,

> I will have to learn that single
> jog of the head
> men use to speak paragraphs
> on the weather and the hard road
> around here, where a lark
> goes up each morning,
> singing to penetrate the sun.⁹⁵

Unlike Jeffers's "Ossian's Grave," Galvin's "Donegal" refuses to affirm a perfect analogy between the poet's sense of identity and his sense of Ireland as the place of origin. Rather, though the code is inside him, it is not entirely readable—he will have to learn other codes or the subtler nuances of the code he knows has shaped his entire being. As such, Galvin's awareness of the discontinuity between his sense of being Irish and his sense of being American is equally vital for his poetry. The sense of displacement as well as place explicitly shapes his identity and his poetry. The lark will not penetrate the sun, but the vital effort to do so is what enables the lark to sing, and so too the poet. As his recent poem "Blackthorn and Ash" articulates, incompleteness, the sense of displacement, provides the vantage that enables the poet to read and evoke the breakages of history behind his encounter with Ireland as native place:

> So this is the source,
> obscured by the ash trees and black thorns
> growing through rooms my grandfather's
> mother and father grew their children in,
> before the boys caught rides to Moville and took
> the lighter out to the Glasgow-Boston steamer
> anchored on Lough Foyle, with ash twigs
> in their pockets, charms against drowning,
> that tree possessing the power resident in water.⁹⁶

It is important that as Galvin comes to the source, the perceived place of origin, his consciousness pivots forward to the journey endured by his family in leaving the source rather than sentimentalizing the passage of return. This ability to balance, to counterpoint, to stand imaginatively on the pivot between affirming his Irish identity and recognizing its loss through historical displacement is what makes Brendan Galvin's poetry so significant—and not only for Irish America. Irish poetry should take stock of Galvin's vantage on what is a characteristically Irish experience, as it should take stock of other Irish American poets exploring such themes.

Even when Galvin writes about the environs of his home in Truro on Cape Cod, one hears unmistakable echoes from the older tradition:

> The first anonymous baying
> from those backlit hills petitions a single
> greeny-blue winter star.
> It silvers as I watch, tuning its sharpness.
> Deep January in the natural dark,
> and now another to the south is yelping
> Sladesville trying to talk with Prince Valley,
> or Corn Hill calling Pond Village across
> the cold. This is their time, who have
> no heaven unless they create it
> with their fierce singing from hogsbacks
> and down in the evergreen-lined
> pockets of the dark. . . .[97]

As "Dogs of Truro" continues, Galvin summons the names of towns and townlands with a sense of place and connection to the indigenous locale as vital as any Irish hermit's. He does not need to make the passage of return to the Irish source for the source to live in him or in his singing. By the poem's end, even the stars draw nearer and a planet turns to listen in a kind of vocally generated communion of various places— "sociable," as Galvin puts it understatedly—as though through these canine proclamations and affirmations of presence, this "fierce singing," Truro had become a nexus of the finest music felt, as it must be, in the ordinary, or as Fionn said to Óisin, in "the music of what happens."

If we read back from Brendan Galvin's success in singing out of the Irish American awareness of historical displacement and equally out of a sense of place as vivid as Kavanagh's parish within its own indigenous

American locale, it throws into sharp relief the evolution of Irish American poetry from John Boyle O'Reilly's time to the present. One senses in O'Reilly's work a kind of straining anxiety, a desire to produce poetry at once emphatically in tune with the retrospective tradition he was forced to leave behind and responsible to his new American prospect. It manifests, in Edward Said's words, "the unhealable rift forced between a human being and a native place, between the self and its true home."[98] The work of other Irish poets who came to America, in the nineteenth century until today, have had to negotiate a similar sense of double allegiance and have done so in their own individual idioms while recognizing their connection to the tradition of Irish poetry.

For those poets whose immediate connection to Ireland has been broken by a generation or more, there has been a slow but evident passage of embracing their dual inheritance, of realizing the significance of the Irish diaspora for their sense of identity. As Stephanie Rains observes, "for diasporic communities whose ancestors made these journeys . . . the process was a single and indivisible event, albeit open to multiple meanings" as well as "a foundational narrative for the communities of these emigrants' descendants."[99] For Irish American poets it has taken generations for that "foundational narrative" to find its voice through many voices and sensibilities scattered across the wide and varied landscape of American poetry. Just as Patrick Ward affirms a "subterranean continuity within native Irish culture that survived the demise of the formal literary tradition and preserved the modified concerns of the *file* in the folk tradition," so too there is what I call a submerged continuity between the dual Irish tradition as defined by Thomas Kinsella and the poetry produced by Irish Americans that, though modified, nonetheless preserves an identification and connection with what was once the native place.

It would be liberating for the Irish tradition, doubled as it already is, to acknowledge and examine these identifications and connections "plaited" and "encoded" into and through the further breach of tradition caused by the Irish diaspora in America. If so, we might have to envision Robinson Jeffers's Tor House at the edge of the Pacific as a sixth tower to add to Heaney's "quincunx" of Irish keeps—the round tower of prior Irelandness, Spenser's Kilcolman Castle with its tower symbolizing English conquest, Yeats' Norman tower at Thoor Ballylee, Joyce's

Martello Tower on Dublin Bay, and MacNeice's Carrickfergus Castle in the North—together configuring a still more encompassing nexus of Irish identity and tradition.[100] If so, we would have to invite the poets from the back corner of the Marliave, or at least lower the high-backed booths so the various parties might converse across the dining room in something akin to Brendan Galvin's Truro dogs at once announcing their existence and awaiting a reply. We might have to open a space for a suitably large table in the center of the old café where the whole crowd might sit down—Irish, Irish American, American Irish, and all the poets of diaspora from other traveling traditions—palavering on through the long night until the planet started to listen.

NEAR HAG'S HEAD

(Cliffs of Moher, Ireland)

This headland is the battered prow
of a ship my silent father rides
into the Atlantic. Gust after gust
buffets the raw crag of his face,
his windbreaker flapping like a sail.

He could be his own father's grandfather
the way he stands before the rail
as others stood before the hold, the blind
journey before them, and nods to me
in recognition despite the ocean between us.

Even he knows on these cliffs the dead
are reading aloud from the book of the wind.

11

Readings

TWO

Modernism, Leftism, and the Spirit
The Poetry of Lola Ridge

Making a Religion of It

Born Rose Emily Ridge in Dublin on December 12, 1873, the woman who would reinvent herself to become perhaps the most impassioned and certainly the most authentic of the proletarian poets of the New York modernist avant-garde emigrated with her mother as a child to New Zealand, where she would marry the manager of a gold mine at the age of twenty-one. To look ahead thirty years from the life she chose in 1895 is to gain some measure of insight into the transformation she underwent. In 1927, Alfred Kreymborg—one of the leading avant-garde poets of the day—describes her as "the frailest of humans physically and the poorest financially"; nevertheless, as Peter Quartermain remarks, she was a "woman on the spiritual barricade fighting with her pen against tyranny."[1]

After her marriage to Peter Webster failed and her mother died, Lola Ridge immigrated to the United States in 1907, stayed for a brief time in California, and then settled in Manhattan's Greenwich Village. So began her life as one of the leading left-wing literary and political figures of the day, one of the multitudes of left-wing reformers and artists—among them Kay Boyle, John Dos Passos, Harold Loeb, and Emma Goldman—who moved to lower Manhattan and contributed to its hotbed of activism. Indeed, throughout the nineteenth century lower

Manhattan had filled with poor immigrants and workers supportive of leftist causes. As an activist of revolutionary fervor, over the next three decades, until her death in Brooklyn in 1941, Ridge composed some of the most politically conscious poems of her day. At the same time, her presence among New York's avant-garde places her work within the context of such luminaries of modernist American poetry as Marianne Moore, William Carlos Williams, and Hart Crane. The peripatetic literary and cultural sojourns of the Lost Generation, to whom Ridge had strong if contentious ties, also provide an evocative counterpoint to both the literary and the civic life she decided to lead, as do both the right-wing modernist programs of expatriate mandarins Ezra Pound and T. S. Eliot and the pure poetries of the Dadaists. From this perspective, Ridge appears to be a notable lone figure standing amid the crowds of our American literary history, at once recognizable in the aesthetic and wider cultural currents of her time, and curiously otherwise—a vivid original whose life and work embody the tumultuous confluence of forces that shaped the twentieth century.

To picture Lola Ridge as a defiant and heroic loner is not to engage in a kind of romanticism that she herself would refuse to embrace. Like Yeats, but without the imaginative infrastructure of a spiritual system, Ridge had already invented an "idealized version of herself" by the time she arrived in San Francisco or at least by the time she moved to Greenwich Village.[2] "Rose Emily" had become "Lola," ten years younger than her actual age, as well as a poet, artist, and revolutionary. In this regard she reminds one of another Lola—Lola Montez, born Maria Delores Eliza Rosanna Gilbert in Limerick in 1824 before recreating herself as the Spanish "Spider Dancer" and nineteenth-century America's embodiment of immodesty. Both women were Irish emigrants who were forced to rely on their own powers of self-imagination to establish places for themselves in their respective worlds; both became famous in their time; both turned to religion and embraced the plight of the poor and the outcast.

Unlike Montez, however, whose beauty and sensuality were legendary, Ridge assumed the visage of a saint and ascetic. She was tall and thin, "frail enough to be blown away like a leaf"[3] according to Kay Boyle; blood-drained, her body was slowly wasted with pulmonary tuberculosis. Lola Ridge emerges as an impassioned and even saintly idealist in Katherine Anne Porter's description of the protest on August 22, 1927, outside Boston's Charlestown Prison, where Sacco and Vanzetti, a shoemaker and a fish peddler, both avowed anarchists, were to be executed for a payroll robbery and murder committed seven years earlier. Many believed them innocent and that execution would be martyrdom for their political beliefs. As the police at the protest galloped about on horseback, "bearing down" as Porter tells us "on anyone who ventured beyond the edge of the crowd . . . one tall, thin figure of a woman stepped out alone, a good distance into the empty square, and when the police came down on her and the horse's hoofs beat over her head, she did not move, but stood with her shoulders slightly bowed, entirely still."[4] The woman was Lola Ridge.

So dramatic a commitment to her political and social ideals was not uncommon, nor was it alien to her artistic temperament. Horace Gregory, like Kay Boyle another Irish American with a substantial literary future, described their mutual friend as legendary in her "austere devotion to her talents." Indeed, beyond linking the intensity of Ridge's verve for social justice to her poetry, Gregory declares, "Lola Ridge was possessed of a Celtic imagination whose insights gave life and color to her convictions." He goes still further to portray Ridge as "unworldly," a "vision-haunted Irish heroine" whose wind-swept, cold-water loft in the Village "was like some neatly, frugally kept cold-water flat in Dublin."[5]

While one ought to take both Gregory's perhaps overly romanticized portrayal of Ridge and his presuppositions about a Celtic imagination with a grain of salt, the fervency of Ridge's embrace of a life of deliberate poverty and her devotion to making poems both artistically vital and mindful of the poor and oppressed no doubt have their origins at least in part in her sense of identity as someone born Irish and therefore the inheritor of a particularly passionate and tragic cultural experience. Her passion for social justice finds an explicitly Irish expression in her poems dedicated to James Larkin, the Irish labor organizer and socialist who orchestrated the Dublin Walkout of 1913 and shortly after joined the Socialist Party of America, and Kevin Barry, whom Ridge saw as a model of idealism in the face of force and a martyr to British oppression after his execution at the age of eighteen for his participation in the Easter Rising. Her devotion to Ireland comes nearest to

Gregory's belief in a Celtic imagination in her poem "The Tidings," written on the occasion of the Easter Rising. With a longing reminiscent and perhaps derivative of Irish poet Francis Ledwidge's in the trenches of France, she writes, "My heart is like a lover foiled / By a broken stair— / They are fighting tonight in Sackville Street, and I am not there!"[6]

She broaches the subject of Ireland again, now symbolically, in the poem "Incompatibility" from her third book, *Red Flag*:

> Bull's-hide white under red wrath
> And a curt tone of blue. . .
> By a gold harp on a green cloth—
> How should they blend, these two?[7]

Though long departed from Ireland, Ridge's poem places her concern with the country of her birth and its continued dominance by John Bull's Union Jack in a volume that promotes its leftist sensibility in its title. At the same time, given the image of Ridge's willingness to undergo a potential martyrdom under the horse's hooves at Charlestown Prison, and the increasingly mystical tenor of her poetry in the books that followed *Red Flag*, her work comes to echo the spiritual radicalism of Padraic Pearse: "O King that was born / To set bondsmen free / In the coming battle / Help the Gael!"[8] Ridge would write her own poem, the epic *Firehead*, to dramatize the life of that king. Moreover, as the poet and novelist Kay Boyle recounts, Lola Ridge's advocacy of suffering as a means to achieve redemption—not merely of the individual soul but of the world—greatly influenced Boyle during the formative years of her own artistic and imagination growth.

"Lola's causes became mine," Boyle writes,

> and when I wrote my poems now I borrowed from her conscience and her poetic vocabulary. She gave to my rebellion a wider and, at the same time, a more indigenous setting. For a long time my heart had bled with the Irish insurgents, and I had carried everywhere with me a copy of Terrence MacSwiney's letter to Cathal Brugha, a letter which he . . . had written after forty-six days of hunger striking. . . . The reason for MacSwiney's death had defined for me in clearest terms the

rebellion of the flesh against organized authority. . . . But now it was Lola who spoke the vocabulary I wanted to hear, and all I had cherished vicariously took on the shadowy dimensions of another country's history.[9]

For the young Kay Boyle, Lola Ridge had become the embodiment of a specifically Irish dedication to a rebellion against injustice that was at once spiritual and worldly, as well as a mother figure at once associated with her own mother and with the Virgin.[10] Still more significantly, as the daughter of Irish immigrants Boyle envisions the spiritually fueled "rebellion of the flesh against authority" as an ideal to put into practice in the New World, a legacy to be carried over from "another country's history."

Ridge surely envisioned her connection to this tradition along similar lines, though at the same time the uniquely American context displayed in the majority of her poems reveals the forward-looking heading of her work. Her imagination is not merely Celtic, as Horace Gregory would have it, but emigrant in its character. One need only read her long poem "The Ghetto," a sustained portrait of life in the Jewish American ghetto, or the ironic "Lullaby," in which an African American baby is thrown into a burning house by a white woman, to recognize that Ridge harbors no nostalgia either for "Innisfail" or "The Land Paved with Gold." Indeed, her implicit affirmation of an Irish American poetic consciousness in poems like "Crucible," written in praise of Robinson Jeffers, as well as in her affiliation with and support of such younger poets as Horace Gregory and especially Kay Boyle, bears witness to her desire to forge both a life and a body of work resonant with Irish traditions though nonetheless cast in the American grain.

By all accounts, the literary and artistic crucible of New York's avant-garde salons in the 1920s created a striking mix of personalities and sensibilities, and Lola Ridge quickly assumed a prominent, if often circumspect, position in that world. In February 1922 she became the American editor of *Broom*. Edited from Rome by expatriate New Yorker Harold Loeb, *Broom* sought to be the foremost journal of its day— indeed, *the* journal of cultural note, publishing work by the likes of the poet, novelist, and editor Alfred Kreymborg; philosopher Kenneth Burke; expatriate, "lost-generation" poets and writers Robert McAlmon,

Ernest Walsh, Gertrude Stein, and Malcolm Cowley; as well as a host of others, a few of whom—like Marianne Moore, William Carlos Williams, and the young Hart Crane—would eventually enter the canon of American literature.

Part of Ridge's duties as editor was to host a literary salon on Thursday afternoons with her second husband, David Lawson. There the likes of Kay Boyle, John Dos Passos, Mina Loy, Glenway Wescott, Jean Toomer, Edward Arlington Robinson, Marianne Moore, and William Carlos Williams would read their work and discuss artistic and literary trends. "We had arguments over cubism that would fill an afternoon," William Carlos Williams recounts in his *Autobiography*.[11] For her part, Kay Boyle observes in *Being Geniuses Together* that Ridge inspired sharply divided responses among those attending the salon. For Boyle, Ridge was a second mother and a woman whose commitment both to the poor and to her art brought her near to sainthood. "I cherished and protected her as if she were a small bright flame," Boyle recounts. "Her work expressed a fiery awareness of social injustice as eloquently as Emanuel Carnevali's or Maxwell Bodenheim's, but it was always Lola's voice that spoke, a woman's savage voice, not theirs." In contrast, by Boyle's own admission, Robert McAlmon "had little sympathy for Lola's earnest commitment to the arts and to the working class, a commitment so dramatized that people felt the necessity of either defending or abusing her whenever her name came up."[12] William Carlos Williams sums up the manner in which Lola Ridge presided over the salon rather tersely and ironically but no doubt perceptively, given the intensity of her social, artistic, and spiritual beliefs—"She made a religion of it."[13] Matthew Josephson, a would-be poet, journalist, and associate of Harold Loeb's, dismisses her time and again in his *Life Among the Surrealists* as "difficult," and he further impugns her editorial abilities when he recounts that the European editors rejected most of the writers she recommended.[14] Harold Loeb objected to her "hair-trigger judgments and dogmatic opinions."[15]

To be sure, it appears Ridge was difficult in the way all passionate artists and social advocates are difficult when their sensibilities clash with those of others, and especially those in power. Ridge often took no salary for her work on *Broom,* and though Boyle often portrays Ridge haloed by the candle glow of sanctity, she also agrees with Italian American poet Emanuel Carnevali's remark that Ridge "suffered with the snarl of a lioness . . . flinging itself madly against the walls of the ugly city. . . . She is one of the most beautiful signs we have of women's emancipation."[16] In short, it is probably true that for all their pretenses to modernity, Josephson, McAlmon, and Loeb were afflicted by a traditional condescension toward the abilities of women—especially a woman like Lola Ridge, who, for all her modernity, clearly viewed the world of urban blight, poverty, and the progress of capitalist machine culture in a drastically different light.

In a famous phrase that has curiously come to define his own personal life more than the modern world he sought to describe, T. S. Eliot observed that our world suffered a "dissociation of sensibility," a split between intellect and emotion that the modern poet needed to overcome.[17] For Eliot, as for his fellow expatriate Ezra Pound, the modern world was a shambles. For Pound, this meant that the strong hand of Fascism became a necessary evil in order to restore an imagined golden age of Art and Culture to be appreciated, like all true art, only by the few. For Eliot, in addition to his political and cultural conservatism, it meant requiring a renunciation of "strange gods" that verged into cultural Puritanism. At the root of Pound's aesthetic elitism is the need to make a religious fetish of Art—"O bright Apollo . . . / what god, man, or hero / shall I place a tin wreath upon!"[18] Read in the light of Pound's embrace of Mussolini, these lines from *Hugh Selwyn Mauberley* are prescient in their irony in more ways than the poet first intended. For all his learned recoveries and translations from Homeric Greece, to Troubadour Provence, to T'ang China, Pound's foraging of the cultural past betrays his desire for aesthetic "purity control," an impulse that could not be further from the cultural mélange of the Lower East Side. Eliot's genius also recoils from modernity and eventually embraces an ideal of ascetic purity. In contrast, Ridge's asceticism turns her outward, toward the defining "otherness" of her world—the teeming immigrant ghetto, which is nothing if not an incipient figure for the world we've come to inhabit in the twenty-first century.

Despite being two of the defining figures of modern poetry, Pound and Eliot distrust modernity, and it is this profound distrust that separates them from poets like William Carlos Williams, who, as a futurist, embraces an art that forages lovingly among the surfaces and shattered atoms of a world tuned to the rhythms of the machine and guided by its belief in progress. It is for this reason that Williams called *The Waste Land* the great catastrophe, a claim that ironically belies the truth of his rival's insight. In contrast, for Eliot, a spiritual wound haunts the modern world, a fundamental rupture between intellect and emotion that renders Williams's embrace of modernity suspect. In turn, for Eliot, this "dissociation" is present at the heart of the West's adherence to the doctrine of perpetual progress and leads, instead, to spiritual decay. Ridge sides with Eliot's perspective on the modern world and further claims that such spiritual decay is underwritten by capitalist culture. Ridge is no futurist like Williams, or for that matter like the European editors of *Broom,* Loeb and Josephson. For Josephson, belief in the Machine Age was tantamount to a faith that could not be renounced without being labeled "retrograde."[19] Though less strident and condescending, Loeb's description of the deterioration of his editorial relationship with Lola Ridge shortly before she quit as editor of *Broom* characterizes their disagreement in terms that precisely delineate the aesthetic division between Ridge's (and Eliot's) cultural pessimism and the futurist ideals of the editors: "*Broom,* in my opinion, should favor writers who appreciated the values in the contemporary scene. This partiality soon brought me into conflict with Lola, who tended to depreciate products of the American capitalist system. To her, capitalism was corrosive, its products corrupt; I felt that capitalism was impersonal, its products magnificent. Since many an untenable religion had in the past inspired glorious artifacts, why shouldn't 'money mysticism' do likewise?"[20]

Loeb found Ridge maddeningly absolutist in her judgments, though Loeb's seemingly objective account of the rift demonstrates an equally obdurate position. Capitalism is regarded as an impersonal cultural force, not to be judged in its effects on people. The products of capitalism, to use a capitalist metaphor, are Loeb's only concern. Indeed, he invests them with a kind of fated "impersonality." At the same time as religion is deemed "untenable" and valuable only for its "glorious artifacts," capitalism becomes invested with a spiritual validity of the highest magnitude. Loeb, of course, is recounting a time when many expatriates could absorb the wealth of European life and culture by appealing to the divine economies of their trust funds. That would change after 1929, and the underside of capitalism that Ridge knew and sought to portray became more widely experienced. In any case, it is clear from such recollections that Lola Ridge not only distrusted capitalist modernity as vigorously as Eliot and Pound but also fought to overcome the spiritual decadence it fostered by seeking to fuse together in her own work and the work she championed the incompatible forces of her religious idealism with the social and materialist imperatives of her leftist convictions. That fusion, had it been successfully achieved, might have given high modernist poetry another alternative to the futurist secularism of Williams and the cultured pessimism of Pound and Eliot. Instead, Ridge's inability to adequately achieve that synthesis is itself instructive of the internal quarrel that shaped her work as well as the pressures and pitfalls she failed to negotiate in trying to attain the kind of indispensability reached by other poets of her time.

Visionary Materialism

Ridge's first published book of poems, *The Ghetto,* appeared in 1918. It is a volume at once conscious of its desired place in the tradition of American poetry, of its author's drive to innovate upon that tradition, and of its own historical and social moment. The collection begins with a poem of invocation, "To the American People," that echoes Whitman's sweeping democratic vista while at the same time waxing skeptical over the bard's infectious optimism:

> Will you feast with me American people?
> But what have I that shall seem good to you!
>
> On my board are bitter apples
> And honey served on thorns,
> And in my flagons fluid iron,
> Hot from the crucibles.
>
> How should such fare entice you![21]

Though the poem begins with an invitation, Ridge's conceit of a shared feast quickly devolves into a Blakean plate of oxymorons—bitter apples, honeyed thorns. At first the poem appears emblematic, almost allegorical, but in fact her ironic choice of metaphor instructs the reader to call to mind the brutal world of hunger and poverty that is the other America of breadlines and oppressed workers. With this deft inversion of the reader's expectations Ridge transforms a song of American innocence into a song of American experience. It is, to use her own words in describing Whitman's poetic revolution, "a grand nihilistic gesture."[22] Just as she envisioned Whitman's poetry assailing "the whole Bastille of form and thought," so she frames her own work as an effort to demolish mannerism—what she called in a review of one Georgian anthology the poetry of "a tactful hostess picking her dinner guests."[23] Instead, she would in the manner of her friend and exemplar Alfred Kreymborg "deal direct with life," to get out and make a clearing "instead of huddling in mental tenements."[24] Here is Blake's metaphor of "mind-forged manacles" updated to the twentieth century, evocative of a world akin to the stultifying cocktail parties from which Prufrock sought escape.

Real physical tenements, of course, constitute the difficult world about which she chose to write. In a review of one young poet's work she observed that he "lives and writes as one who has lived and suffered with the world's workers."[25] Perhaps nowhere is this judgment more truly applied to her own work than in the long title poem of her first book. "The Ghetto" is a poem in eight parts that depicts in intimate and vivid detail the world of the Jewish immigrants of New York's Lower East Side. Across its sections the poem moves expansively, the way a mural depicts scene after scene until, within the wider prospect of the entire structure, each individual portrayal gains in significance and intensity. Each section is alternately atmospheric and dramatic, offering a catalogue of the world beheld in the teeming streets as well as in the intimacy of domestic relationships. Throughout the poem, Ridge manages to tread the fine line between identifying herself too assertively with these immigrants and merely objectifying them. Nevertheless, since she herself is an immigrant, it is the consciousness of being "other" and nearly anonymous in this dense and vibrant urban landscape that clearly propels her imagination. Here is the poem's opening:

> Cool, inaccessible air
> Is floating in velvety blackness shot with steel-blue lights,

> But no breath stirs the heat
> Leaning its ponderous bulk upon the Ghetto
> And most on Hester Street. . .
>
> The heat. . .
> Nosing in the body's overflow,
> Like a beast pressing its great steaming belly close,
> Covering all avenues of air. . .
> . . . .
> Herring-yellow faces, spotted as with a mold,
> And moist faces of girls
> Like dank white lilies,
> And infants' faces with open parched mouths that suck at the air
>   as at empty teats.[26]

Reading Ridge's evocation of the ghetto through the lens of Eliot's "The Love Song of J. Alfred Prufrock," with its yellow fog and its streets "like an argument of insidious intent," one might be tempted to interpret the scene as one more modernist portrayal of the world's grim meaninglessness. Certainly Ridge has no illusions about the poverty of the world she depicts. Nevertheless, as the poem proceeds, Ridge looks beyond the impotent dismay of Prufrock's fraught consciousness to discover an empathy restorative of human feeling:

> Young women pass in groups,
> Converging to the forums and meeting halls,
> Surging indomitable, slow
> Through the gross underbrush of heat.
> Their heads are uncovered to the stars,
> And they call to the young men and to one another
> With a free camaraderie.
> Only their eyes are ancient and alone. . .[27]

What appalled Prufrock, among other things, was the sense of his own decadence and the world's in historical relief against what Pound called in *Mauberley* "a botched civilization." For all its poverty, severity, and ugliness, Ridge's ghetto is free of decadence. The poor young women are "surging, indomitable." The ghetto is no wasteland, and in stark contrast its vision of history is one of continuity and endurance rather than disintegration:

> Did they vision—with those eyes darkly clear,
> That looked the sun in the face and were not blinded—
> Across the centuries
> The march of their enduring flesh?
> Did they hear—
> Under the molten silence
> Of the desert like a stopped wheel—
> (And the scorpions tick-ticking on the sand. . .)
> The infinite procession of those feet?[28]

"So many, I had not thought death had undone so many"[29]: so Eliot invokes Dante in *The Waste Land,* bemoaning the modern hell of his Unreal City. In contrast, Ridge's city is filled with real people who refuse to succumb to a living death. Where Eliot sees desolation, Ridge envisions life emergent, indomitable, irreducibly various. Likewise, the poet herself refuses the crass anti-Semitism that mars some of Eliot's poems and undermines Pound's authority. Instead, for Ridge, an old scholar has "The wisdom of the Talmud stored away / In his mind's lavender."[30] Here is her portrait of a street trader:

> And he—appraising
> All who come and go
> With his amazing
> Sleight-of-mind and glance
> And nimble thought
> And nature balanced like the scales at nought—
> Looks Westward where the trade-lights glow,
> And sees his vision rise—
> A tape-ruled vision,
> Circumscribed in stone—
> Some fifty stories to the skies.[31]

Clearly the capitalist spur for profit drives Ridge's trader, though still—contrary to her own political lights—she manages to portray him in the fullness of his humanity. There are no Jews "squatting on the window sill" as we find in Eliot's "Gerontion." There is, in contrast, a profound awareness of the poet's eye seeking to encounter the other through what the French philosopher Emmanuel Lévinas would call "an epiphany of the face." In such an epiphany "I" and "other" are illuminated in a mutually sustaining relationship.

Most importantly, Ridge's ghetto is a social world where—unlike Eliot's solitary ascetic waiting and Pound's glorification of the artist as cultural *Übermensch*—the longing for transcendence involves communal as well as individual rituals. The old woman who is Ridge's neighbor lights her Sabbath candles, but far from being emblems of her loneliness or symbols of the hermit's lone pursuit of divinity,

> Her candles signal
> Infinite fine rays
> To other windows,
> Coupling other lights,
> Linking the tenements
> Like an endless prayer.[32]

Such communal rituals fill Ridge's poem, and her own patient and generous observance of them at once refuses to objectify the world it encounters and, remarkably, elaborates a promise intimated in Eliot's "Preludes"—the awareness of "some infinitely gentle, infinitely suffering thing" that would bind together the world's fragments, its fractured atoms of solitude. Ridge's perspective here is anything but impersonal in the modernist sense; rather, it is humble before the other she encounters. Indeed, as "The Ghetto" nears its crescendo, Ridge denounces "Ego" as the modern world's great ravager with the same vehemence as Pound denouncing "Usury" in *The Cantos*. Strangely enough, for the right-wing Pound and the left-wing Ridge it is the world's subservience to the economic system that breeds social injustice and misfortune, though Ridge's assertion moves beyond materialism to locate the problem in a biological and ultimately spiritual concupiscence to which the world, and in particular capitalism, gives free rein:

Egos out of the shell,
Examining, searching, devouring—

. . . .

Egos cawing,
Expanding in the mean egg. . .

. . . .

Words, words, words,
Pattering like hail,
Like hail falling without aim. . .
Egos rampant,
Screaming each other down.

. . . .

Egos yearning with the world-old want in their eyes—

. . . .

Egos crying out of unkempt deeps
And waving their dreams like flags—[33]

By the end of the poem, Ego with its acquisitive spur has blended into Life, which gives birth to "Wars, arts, discoveries, rebellions, travails, immolations, cataclysms, hates." Yet Ridge refuses the temptation to disavow life as a cruel repetition of endlessly repeated and insatiable desires, or another round of madness. For Ridge, even in the black and clotted gutters the "*electric currents of life*" (italics in original) express an indestructible creation:[34]

> *Strong flux of life,*
> *Like a bitter wine*
> *Out of the bloody stills of the world. . .*
> *Out of the Passion eternal.*[35]

The allusion to Christ's crucifixion in the final lines of "The Ghetto" may at first appear incongruous or, worse, a well-meaning condescension like Catholic theologian Karl Rahner's notion that other faiths may be forms of anonymous Christianity. What we find in these lines, however, is a primary instance of Ridge's need as an artist to fuse her own passion for the material plight of the world she encountered with a spiritual ideal. The whole world, and in particular the human struggle to attain meaningful existence, is really the material manifestation of a spiritual desire, a divine urgency that in the poet's achieved perception would confound its defining dualism and redress the demeaning fragmentation of modern life. The poet, like the revolutionary, works in history to reach this ideal; the Passion recurs, and as such Ridge's insight once again finds precedent in Pearse's sacrificial ideal. Similarly, for poetic precedent one thinks of Gerard Manley Hopkins in "As Kingfishers Catch Fire": "For Christ plays in ten thousand places, / Lovely in limbs, and lovely in eyes not his / to the Father through the features of men's faces."[36]

Objectivism, the indigenous movement in twentieth-century American poetry defined by William Carlos Williams and later by Charles Olson and George Oppen, eschews any direct appeal to the spiritual in its aesthetic formulation. Objectivism grew, in part at least, out of imagism. Ridge read Pound and Amy Lowell, who became the preeminent practitioner of imagism in the United States. As many of her poems demonstrate, Ridge found imagism a sympathetic technique. She uses it often to create atmospheric effects in "The Ghetto." More than imagism, objectivism celebrates the materials, the object itself—"No ideas but in things"—most famously exemplified in Williams's "The Red Wheelbarrow."

Nevertheless, despite her communism, Lola Ridge found pure materialism an insufficient ground for art and for life. It is for this underlying reason, perhaps, that during her American editorship of *Broom* she rejected poems by Gertrude Stein, since for Stein language is mere material, nothing more than a play of surfaces to be orchestrated. Overruled by Loeb and Josephson in Europe, Ridge quit. On the one hand, Ridge's abrupt severance might be chalked up to jealousy over Stein's accomplishment, though that is highly unlikely—she simply found her work "mostly blah."[37] Or perhaps it was the natural outcome of the degenerating relationship between Ridge and her European editors. Ridge's own editorial convictions surely fueled her break. On the other hand, in a letter to Ridge, Harold Loeb asserts that *Broom* had become "an organ with a strongly held point of view."[38] That point of view celebrated modernity and the products of modernity, particularly machine culture. In short, the side of Ridge's sensibility that needed to accommodate a dimension of life greater than life's mere materiality could not abide a point of view that obdurately negated it. The perennial conflict between spirit and flesh, to put it theologically, needed to be surpassed in a synthesis that would not deny the claims of either.

Abundant Life and the Limits of Art

For Matthew Josephson, Ridge's sensibility was "retrograde" and sentimental.[39] She was at best "an excellent woman who wrote rather dull free verse."[40] Though it is not a poem of epic magnitude and achievement, "The Ghetto" nonetheless reveals anything but a jejune imagination. Rather, it showcases Ridge's knack for simile and metaphor. Similarly, in "Flotsam," darkness crouches "like a great cat." A tired woman sprawls "like a broken beetle," and twigs rattle "like dice."[41] In "Faces"

> A late snow beats
> With cold white fists upon the tenements—
> Hurriedly drawing blinds and shutters,
> Like tall old slatterns
> Pulling aprons about their heads.[42]

In the street, beggars twitch "As though death played / with some ungainly dolls."[43] The Brooklyn Bridge, in the poem by that name, has a "pythoness body." And here is a stunning and arresting figure from "Sons of Belial" in her second book, *Sun-Up*, where she assumes the identity of a lynch mob:

> Mad nights when we make ritual
> *(Feet running before the sleuth-light...*
> *And the smell of burnt flesh*
> *By a flame-ringed hut*
> *In Missouri,*
> *Sweet as Rome's pyre....)*
> We make ropes do rigadoons
> With copper feet that jig on air....[44]

Far from being sentimental and retrograde, Ridge's poetry at its best unites what Robert Lowell (alluding to Levi-Straus) would later observe as twentieth-century poetry's tendency to divide itself between "the raw" and "the cooked." The subjects in "Sons of Belial," "The Ghetto," and "Lullaby," with its living child thrown to the flames by a white woman during a race riot, are as raw as one can ask of a poet. At the same time, her gift for metaphor coupled with her tendency to intersperse her poems with elevated diction—the ironic and perversely fanciful "rigadoons" follows "the smell of burnt flesh" in the example above—demonstrates that she can "cook" a poem quite elaborately. The ultimate failing of her work, it might be said, is that she tends to "overcook" with each successive book.

Nevertheless, while it is fair to say that in her later work Ridge's poems tend to be somewhat overcooked in their high-flown diction, there are few such moments in *The Ghetto*. When rhetoric takes over it does so in a way that manifests the poet's urgency to unify her conflicting visions:

> Lights go out...
> And the great lovers linger in little groups, still passionately debating,
> Or one may walk in silence, listening only to the still summons of
>   Life—
> Life making the great Demand...
> Calling its new Christs...
> Till tears come, blurring the stars
> That grow tender and comforting like the eyes of comrades;
> And the moon rolls behind the Battery
> Like a word molten out of the mouth of God.[45]

Reading these lines, one can see how Matthew Josephson might make his terse conclusion. They aspire to a high Romanticism worthy of Shelley, and, indeed, Lola Ridge won the Shelley Memorial Award in 1935 and 1936. On the other hand, there are passages in Crane shaped to an Elizabethan density that are no less grand in their Romantic musings than Ridge's. The real intent behind such soaring passages in "The Ghetto" is to accommodate a language of biblical and not just Romantic intensity to the circumstances of twentieth-century urban deprivation.

In her aspiration to create a communion between materialism and spirituality in her poetry, Ridge resembles another New York radical, Dorothy Day. The lines quoted above—"Life making the great Demand. . . / Calling its new Christs"—along with the poem's segue to "the eyes of comrades" articulate a sensibility profoundly attuned to that of the great social activist. Founder of the *Catholic Worker* newspaper and its houses of hospitality for the poor, Dorothy Day—even before her conversion—was not only an ardent advocate for social justice but a frequenter of the same artist and literary salons as Ridge. In her biography, *The Long Loneliness,* she recounts joining Kenneth Burke, Malcolm Cowley, and Hart Crane, among others, for the same kind of literary soirees Ridge attended and organized. Like Ridge, she was appalled at the prospect of humanity "feeding itself" to the machine. Both women had substantial literary aspirations, and they shared the same social ideology. Ridge wrote poems in praise of many leftist leaders and agitators, among them Irish American Tom Mooney, who spent years in San Quentin after being accused of setting a bomb during a labor rally in San Francisco and whom Day acknowledges in her biography. Remarkably, in describing the evolution of her own calling, Dorothy Day uses language profoundly resonant with Ridge's imaginative needs. "I wanted, though I did not know it yet," so Day remarks, "a synthesis. I wanted abundant life. I wanted it for others too."[46]

In her desire for a synthesis that would satisfy both her religious intuitions and her worldly concerns, Ridge's life and work also anticipate that other extraordinary figure who combined the most intense spiritual urgency with a stark and unflagging attention to the world, Simone Weil. After a year working in factories in the Paris suburbs, Weil wrote her essay "Factory Work," in which she sums up the circumstances of the worker in words that would have rung true for both Dorothy Day and Lola Ridge. Weil observes: "The parts circulate with labels bearing their name, material, and degree of elaboration, one could almost believe they are the persons, and the workers the interchangeable parts. . . . Things play the role of men, men the role of things. There lies the root of the evil."[47] Here is Ridge in her poem "Fuel," written sixteen years before:

What of the silence of the keys
And silvery hands? The iron sings. . .

> Though bows lie broken on the strings,
> The fly-wheels turn eternally. . .
> . . . .
> As for the common men apart,
> Who sweat to keep their common breath,
> And have no hour for books or art—
> What dreams have these to hide from death![48]

For Ridge—as for Weil after her—in a world geared toward the fulfillment of abundant life for all, both work and art ought to be spiritual disciplines no less than work and prayer. The difference is that for both of these extraordinary women, as for Dorothy Day, the contemplative cell had to be furnished among the tenements and the factories. It is this quest for abundant life, found amid the welter of life and not in the poet's solitary room nor in the hermit's cell, to which Ridge committed herself in her art.

Both imaginative poles of Ridge's sensibility—her concern with the material as well as the spiritual life—find their point of intersection in the desire for social justice. Hart Crane's early review of *The Ghetto* seems prescient, then, when he remarks that "the interpretive aspects of her work" appear to be "its most brilliant facet."[49] Though he also affirms the sometime brilliance of her figural imagination ("Over the black bridge / The line of lighted cars / Creeps like a monstrous serpent / Spooring gold. . ."[50]), he finds her sincerity all the more essential and even cautions her against devolving into "a barren cleverness." While Crane is right to suggest that the interpretive aspects of her work assume prominence over the purely aesthetic pleasure of poetry, it is her impulse to drive home the message—to provide the reader with the moral of the poem as interpreted by the poet—that infuses her poetry as it would evolve over the next twenty years. To that extent, certain poems in *The Ghetto*, like "The Song of Iron," demonstrate Ridge's tendency to indulge in rhetorical solutions in seeking to give poetic form to the clash of opposites fueling her imagination:

> Not yet hast Thou sounded
> Thy clangorous music,
> Whose strings are under the mountains. . .

> Not yet has Thou spoken
> The blooded, implacable Word...
>
> But I hear in the Iron singing—
> In the triumphant roaring of the steam and pistons pounding—
> Thy barbaric exhortation...[51]

As the poem continues, Ridge likens herself to "a cupola" poured for God's use, "a new Mary" into whom the deity might pour "thy molten, world-whelming song." Everything about "The Song of Iron"—the grandiose diction, the syntactical inversions, the hyperbolic imagery—reveals a poet who is striving for some great, definitive utterance. Though the poem intends to waken "Dictators—late Lords of the Iron" to the "blooded, implacable Word," this second coming of Christ as Divine Comrade overwhelms its phrasing and diction. The poet has lapsed into propagandist. The diction and tone are strident and bombastic. Compare the tone of this poem to these lines from "Reveille" in her second book, *Sun-Up*:

> As our forefathers stood on the prairies
> So let us stand in the ring,
> Let us tear up their prisons like grass
> And beat them to barricades—
> Let us meet the fire of their guns
> With a greater fire,
> Till the birds shall fly to the mountains
> For one safe bough.[52]

Like "The Song of Iron," "Reveille" is also a poem intended to be a call to for the workers of the world to rise up in the name of justice against their oppressors, but it accomplishes that intention with simplicity and immediacy. The difference in tone between the poems is extraordinary. Regardless of whether one agrees with Ridge's politics, "Reveille" is a far better poem than "The Song of Iron" because the poet has beaten back the temptation to assume the mantle of the transfiguring prophet. Despite her passionate convictions, or perhaps because of them, Ridge gradually substituted the hyperbole of political and religious rhetoric for the genuine quarrel with self by which a poet advances both in the craft of making and in the achievement of a sensibility that continually tests itself against its own convictions. "Pull down thy vanity I say pull down," Pound importuned himself in the "Pisan Cantos." In failing to resist this temptation, Ridge's penchant for "interpretation" leads to an equally strident indulgence in figuralism that Crane warned might transform itself into barren aestheticism. In effect, as Ridge's work evolves, more often than not it becomes overwrought in both message and medium.

In describing Lola Ridge's later work, Peter Quartermain remarks that her poems "drift toward the abstract and symbolic and toward the mystical and spiritual."[53] The mystical and spiritual, however, are not new elements in her work. They are, rather, from the outset constitutive of her imaginative proclivities. The heavy-handed symbolism and abstraction of her last three books emerge out of a spiritual urgency present in the best poems of *The Ghetto* and *Sun-Up*, as well as those instances of authentic achievement found in *Red Flag*, *Firehead*, and *Dance of Fire*. At such times, Ridge's spiritual and mystical impulses find embodiment in the material, in the hard edge of experience. In *Sun-Up*, poems like "Jaguar," "Wall Street at Night," and "East River" muster an arresting energy, though in the imagist mode. "Sons of Belial" and "Reveille" are likewise poems that refuse to sacrifice Ridge's realism to pretensions of social and religious prophecy. The long title sequence "Sun-Up," with its child's voice and swift juxtapositions, anticipates Theodore Roethke's "The Lost Son" in the same way that "The Ghetto" anticipates Galway Kinnell's "The Avenue Bearing the Initial of Christ into the New World." Moreover, throughout these two books Ridge's poems mark an advance on the portrayal of women's voices in twentieth-century poetry. As such she anticipates the explosion of women's voices in American poetry during the second half of the century; in particular the poetry of Muriel Rukeyser finds precedent in Ridge's New York of poor immigrants and workers.

One likely reason for Ridge being neglected by literary history is the time of her death: 1941, at the advent of the Second World War. Though certainly the subject of a poem like "The Ghetto" would have great resonance for the shattering events taking place under Fascism, and particularly against the backdrop of the Holocaust, her leftist views would not have endeared her to the prevailing American milieu. In the 1950s McCarthyism would have made publishing a poet of Ridge's political cast and urgency impossible. By the '60s her work was all but forgotten except as a footnote to the history of American modernist poetry. For the past fifteen years, the main reason there has not been a reexamination of Ridge's work has been the failure of her estate to produce a *Collected Works*. A more comprehensive appreciation of Ridge's contribution, and the social and cultural circumstances that helped to shape her life, remains an important if neglected prospect for American poetry.

All this more than suggests that Hart Crane's praise of Ridge's early work was not entirely misplaced. Nevertheless, after *Sun-Up* her work comes to manifest what Quartermain called an "aesthetic conservatism" that indeed often sounds "retrograde," though Ridge herself sought to forge a synthesis in her work between her materialism and her spiritualism. As Horace Gregory observed, though she desired to realize that synthesis in poems now influenced by the marriage of high and low idioms found in the poetry of Hart Crane, the younger poet's alchemy of Elizabethan texture and Jazz Age vernacular eluded her. Instead, something of Percy Shelley's least tethered flights of verbiage takes over. The poems either become baldly didactic, as in the "Red Flag" sequence that commemorates the Russian Revolution, or highly romanticized—and often both. Of course, there are poems in *Red Flag* like "Mo-Ti," "Electrocution," "Kelvin Barry," and "Street Accident" that retain the kind of fusion between realism and spiritual aspiration that characterizes Ridge at her best. The theological "Death Ray" goes some way toward finding an effective balance between rhetoric and lived experience in its attempt to capture the mystery of incarnation in the ordinary dawn light:

> a stirring at the quick
> of some white palpitating core
> of such intensity as might
> burn up Manhattan like a reed.[54]

These lines are memorable and vivid, a fusion of mystical fire and earthly embodiment. Moreover, the later poems can become increasingly "disembodied" and "curiously abstract"—to use Horace Gregory's apt phrase.⁵⁵ It is as though, rather than achieving a dynamic synthesis, the desired marriage of the materialist and the mystic in Ridge had resolved into a series of stylized gestures.

Nowhere is Lola Ridge's penchant for stylization more evident than in the long poem *Firehead,* which was to be her magnum opus. Written in response to the infamous Sacco and Vanzetti affair, Ridge's mystical "epic" recounts the crucifixion of Christ from various perspectives, among them those of Judas, the two Marys, Peter, and John. In this its intention resembles St. Ignatius's method of actively using the imagination to visualize scenes from the life of Christ in order to spur the soul to higher levels of contemplation. There is no direct mention of the trial and execution of the two anarchists, though one suspects that Ridge might have had in mind something of what Dorothy Day expresses when she remarks that the sense of solidarity felt at their executions among the poor and the workers made her "gradually understand the doctrine of the Mystical Body of Christ whereby we are members of one another."⁵⁶ Indeed, in the opening section of the poem simply titled "He," Christ, "the workman's son," is evoked as "the pivot of the world," the central point around which "the lustrous circle" of the universe takes form.⁵⁷ The poem also orchestrates images of light, fire, and the moon that recur throughout many of the poems of her first three books. In both its attempt to draw together the motifs of her early work and in the sheer audacity of its theme the poem is admirably ambitious if not successful. By the end of *Firehead,* Ridge goes so far as to place us in Christ's mind as he ascends into heaven.

Despite being deemed by Stephen Vincent Benet a work of genius, and William Rose Benet "as one of the most remarkable long poems written . . . in our time," *Firehead* is in fact an epic failure. Quartermain identifies the reason for its failure as "an abstract and incompletely formulated mysticism which makes for prolixity,"⁵⁸ though I would add that the reason for its prolixity lies in the more fundamental failure of Ridge's imagination to accommodate the materiality of human experience within her mystical vision. There are occasionally beautifully turned lines in the poem, though they often quickly and uncannily modulate into archaism and bathos. Here, first, are excerpts from Mary Magdalene's dramatic monologue:

> Even when I was a child in Magdala
> An only one; until my father died
> Imprisoned in his love as in a cell,
> I was a fire secretly burning.[59]

The simplicity and immediacy of the language carries the truth of understatement and an authenticity that continues for nearly another forty lines until we come to a passage where the monologue might have ended—Magdalene lying naked on the ground in a moment of epiphany feeling "the down-rushing arc / of heaven making no noise as it broke."[60] Then the poem goes on, its shift in diction and tone signaling Ridge's inability to discern the emotionally earned scene from the melodramatic:

> There sounded a tumultuous music.
> *Yet I was weary when I met thee, too many*
> And disparate fingers plucked upon my strings
> Vibrating to any touch, until the clear
> Theme was lost.[61]

These lines, with their forced metaphor and their shift to an antiquated mode of address, seem to bespeak the loss of the poem's theme in Ridge's visionary urgency. The bathos intensifies later in the section:

> Have I not made offering
> Before they dream whose altar is in air?
> And arrayed in glamorous fair dress
> My soul—for thy continent delight,
> For the glance, the scant word of thy praise[62]

Here, as in much of *Firehead*, the effort at transfiguration rings false because the transfiguration itself is forced, as though Magdalene ceases to be a real woman at all and becomes instead a staged oracle for the poet's visionary proclamations. It is as if the poem's individual voices are multiple personalities that modulate without warning from something akin to idiomatic speech to the operatic and hieratic.

Dance of Fire, Ridge's final book, is at times even more unabashedly florid in its diction and tone, particularly in the long sonnet sequence "Via Ignis." The twenty-eight poems composing this work combine what had become Ridge's hermetic adaptation of light and fire imagery used traditionally by such mystics as St. John of the Cross in "The Living Flame of Love" with an equally mystical vision of America created with far greater success in Hart Crane's *The Bridge.* There are also echoes of Shelley and Eliot. Not surprisingly, the two most successful poems in the book—"Crucible" and "Stone Face"—commemorate fellow Irish American poet Robinson Jeffers and fellow Irish American Socialist and labor leader Tom Mooney, respectively. Robinson Jeffers, a monumental if controversial figure of twentieth-century American poetry, espoused an antimodern vision that would have appealed to Ridge. Tom Mooney, the son of Irish emigrants who was convicted with Warren K. Billings of the Preparedness Day bombing of 1916, served more than twenty years in prison before being pardoned in 1939. Such figures, obviously, are not solely literary or merely figural but, rather, historical and committed to a contrarian vision of the future. As such these poems situate themselves in the context of those written by Ridge to celebrate Jewish and Jewish American socialists and anarchists Rosa Luxemburg, Emma Goldman, and Alexander Berkman.

Jeffers and Mooney, exemplary as they are to the world of the material to which for her any spiritual accounting must bear witness, clearly prompted Lola Ridge to reassert her allegiance to the core reality of lived experience, even at her most rhetorical:

> The promontory
> Heads are not more lone than he, forever hearing
> *The base reef, which the tides, after the torsion, hushed*
>   with their stroking,
> Mewing as in a tortured sleep, feeling all the rock-saurian
> Body of the coast arching at his touch, made solvent in this
>   heat
> Of spirit lambently playing, this audacious
> Fire that would construe to its own image all things...
>   even a world.[63]

These lines in praise of Robinson Jeffers achieve with far greater dexterity, nobility, and power Ridge's mystical intuition of divinity incarnate in the substances of matter and history—the "dynasty of fire" her later poems sought largely in vain to represent.

It is also appropriate that the late poem "Crucible" invokes another Irish American poet whose work she admired, and whose considerable presence on the American scene bears witness—along with Marianne Moore, Kay Boyle, and Horace Gregory, among others—to the contribution of Irish American poets to the cultural renaissance of which Lola Ridge was an important part. In describing the limitations of one of her friends and fellow organizers at the *Catholic Worker*, Dorothy Day remarked that those limitations were caused by the "absorption in the supernatural rather than the natural, in the unseen rather than the seen."[64] Such are the limitations of Lola Ridge's later work when she fails to forge her ideal communion between the opposing materialist and spiritualist poles of her sensibility. It is a synthesis Dorothy Day was able to achieve in her life, though she by and large gave up her artistic impulse to achieve that synthesis. At the same time, Ridge's best work, from the beginning to the end of her career, rings consonant with Simone Weil's undeniable truth: "This world into which we are cast *does* exist; we are truly flesh and blood; we have been thrown out of eternity; and we are indeed obliged to journey painfully through time, minute in and minute out."[65] It was the journey of Lola Ridge's life and work to offer just such a testimony, and her cultural and literary importance as well as her political commitment may be measured in significant part by both her passion and her persistence in staying the course.

THREE

The Westwardness of Everything
Irishness in the Poetry of Wallace Stevens

From McCarthy to MacCullough

In his centrally important essay "The Noble Rider and the Sound of Words" Wallace Stevens argues that in a world in which religious belief has declined the poet must "give to life the supreme fictions" without which the world itself is unable to be conceived.[1] In linking the poet's imaginative work to what was once the work of religion, Stevens reiterates the same concern posed by Yeats at the turn of the century: "How can the arts overcome the slow dying of men's hearts that we call the progress of the world . . . without becoming the garment of religion as in old times?"[2] Yet Stevens's reiteration of Yeats's formative insight does more than merely demonstrate an imaginative continuity between two poets' definitions of reality. While a similar "rage for order" shapes each poet's idiosyncratic vision, Stevens's use of Ireland as a metaphor in certain key poems places Ireland and Irishness at the center of the great American poet's conception of the imagination as the ordering principle of reality and, as such, of human consciousness. Though few, Stevens's "Irish poems" introduce "Irishness" as a trope for the elemental origin of reality in material forms and, ultimately, as the prototype for the emigrant nature of the human imagination. In these poems, the figure of the West in Irish myth and literature comes to resonate with the American myth of westwardness, and so these emblems of a prior culture find a new and unexpected incarnation in Stevens's work. In so doing, they also exemplify how the idea of Irish American poetry extends beyond the genetic template into the work of a major modern American poet.

From the perspective of what might be called Stevens's Irish poems, it seems a portentous coincidence that in 1900 he published his first poem, exclusive of Harvard student periodicals, in the New York magazine *East and West*.[3] Stevens's lifelong obsession with directionality, with compassing the human quest for meaning inside the charmed horizons of our earthly lives, appears nascent here. "How content shall I be in the North to which I sail," Stevens writes in "Farewell to Florida." Though in that early poem he prefers the prospect of a leafless North as sullen cure to his "sepulchral South," his imagination forever shuttles between the antipodes. Likewise, in "The Comedian as the Letter C," Crispin's neo-Romantic travelogue from the world without imagination westward to the Yucatan, then back east to a Carolina of his own invention, charts a journey in which the hero embarks on a search for a habitable world. Neither origin nor end, neither brute reality nor pure imagination is sufficient to the mind's desire to live fruitfully "as and where we live."[4] Pound's Mauberley drifting to oblivion on his hedonist's Sargasso, Shelley's Alastor sailing into the nothing of his own visionary fervor: these are the prototypical fates Crispin would avert. Instead, through his voyage, Stevens's "affectionate emigrant" comes nearer to Yeats's Óisin, "a man made vivid by the sea," who exists not only in the tradition of the nineteenth-century wanderer, but as a figure we can use to navigate much earlier literary legacies.[5]

"There is a human loneliness, a part of space and solitude," Stevens's Ulysses reminds us, which is "the inner direction on which we depend."[6] In charting that inner direction, Stevens's work seeks to align itself not only with the horizontal axis by which his voyager orients himself on the scale of earth, but with the vertical axis by which poetry might in Harold Bloom's words become "a transcendent analogue composed of the particulars of reality, created by the poet's sense of the world."[7] "Blanche McCarthy," the poem that Holly Stevens selected to open *The Palm at the End of the Mind*, despite her father's judgment that it was unworthy of inclusion in *Harmonium*,[8] elaborates its subject by using the trope of the journey to steer the gaze of the self away from the horizontal plane so it can focus itself anew on a vertical horizon:

> Look in the terrible mirror of the sky
> And not in this dead glass, which can reflect
> Only the surfaces—the bending arm,
> The leaning shoulder and the searching eye.
>
> . . . .
>
> See how the absent moon waits in the glade
> Of your dark self, and see how the wings of stars,
> Upward, from imagined coverts, fly.[9]

Bending arm, leaning shoulder, searching eye—these are the tropes, the gestures, of the quest, a quest that will inevitably require the self to turn away from the surfaces, and so turn the searching eye upward. The transposition of the principle verbs of the first stanza—to bend, to lean, to search—into the second stanza mark the literal transfiguration of the quest from an errant passage through the immanent realm of appearances into a visionary journey toward the unimagined, a region that can be traversed only through imagination: such is the significance of the absent moon waiting in the glade for the dark self. Is Blanche McCarthy the speaker of the injunction, or the self to whom these words are spoken? She is both, she is "Blanche," white, the primary self, a figure for Coleridge's primary imagination, the power of the divine endowed to all, the aspect of the imagination that Stevens would eventually claim is "part of the structure of reality."[10] She is therefore Blanche who must search into the dark of what lies beyond her superficial self, an inherently religious activity that brings one to the prospect of symbols descending and the glare of revelation.

It was appropriate for Holly Stevens to place "Blanche McCarthy" at the outset of Stevens's selected poems, since it announces her father's lifelong meditation on the relationship between imagination and reality. "It is important to see that the visible is the equivalent of the invisible," Stevens would later write in "The Figure of the Youth as Virile Poet." As the poem suggests, to "bend against the invisible" is both to explore its unimagined realms and to be wary of "the false imagination, the false conception of the imagination as some incalculable *vates* within us."[11] It is the "terrible mirror of the sky" Blanche's eye is enjoined to search, and thus the self is discovered without and not within, in a sublime where she will find herself "at once more truly and more strange."[12] She is an incipient ephebe, a nascent émigré, and in her white name blooms potentially all the colors of Stevens's tropical cosmos.

That is why she is "Blanche," but why is she "McCarthy"? It is tempting to want to hear in the oxymoron "terrible mirror" a prefiguring of Yeats's "terrible beauty," a prefiguring since Stevens's poem was written in 1915, a year before Yeats's great meditation on the Irish rebellion. After all, both poems intimate in their respective locutions the idea of terror as a revelation of some *mysterium tremendum* that presses in on the imagination. Is "Blanche McCarthy" merely a name, an invention, like Stevens's Crispin, or Chieftain Iffucan, or the Canon Aspirin—a fictive assemblage? "Blanche is a daughter, not of Mallarme and of Baudelaire, but of Emerson, Whitman, Dickinson," so Harold Bloom remarks.[13] Indeed, to see her as such is to place her, and Stevens's whole oeuvre, within the context of the Emersonian ethos so essential to Bloom's vision of "poetic crossing," his misprision—the process by which poets creatively misread their imaginative forebears. Certainly there is no absence of the transcendental in Stevens.

Yet while Stevens ought to be read within the main of the American tradition, nuances in his work suggest other influences. Fictive as it is, Blanche McCarthy's last name at the least affects an Irish origin. One can see it, as Stevens himself saw "Ramon Fernandez" in "The Idea of Order at Key West," as merely a name. Yet Ramon Fernandez was the name of a literary critic Stevens certainly would have read.[14] While as far as we know Blanche McCarthy is not a real person, the Irishness of her name, taken in concert with the other Irish references appearing in Stevens's work, reveal a spare though crucial inclusion of Irish and Irish American references within the central motifs of his poetry. In short, what is significant about the title "Blanche McCarthy" is that it *is* fictive and that its fictive character incorporates Irishness and Irish Americanness as a trope within Stevens's work.

If it is tempting to hear in the phrase "terrible mirror" an (albeit) anachronistic echo of Yeats, then it is equally tempting to see the golden, fire-fangled bird in "Of Mere Being" as a transfiguration of Yeats's Byzantine warbler. The one on its golden bough, the other in its palm tree, both sing the lineaments of their respective paradises, though where Yeats's bird sings "of what is past, or passing, or to come," Stevens's sings "a foreign song" without human meaning or feeling. Where the song of Yeats's bird inclines toward immanence despite its rarified heaven, Stevens's bird perches at the final frontier of the imaginable—a world utterly transcendent of human conception. Nevertheless, its "fire-fangled feathers dangle down," back into the "mundo" of imagination. Perched as it is at the very end of Stevens's *Palm at the End of the Mind*, we can trace the vertical axis of Stevens's work from "Blanche McCarthy" to "Of Mere Being"—that is, from first to last. The final gesture of "Blanche McCarthy" is upward into flight; the final display of "Of Mere Being" is downward into the known world. Taken together the poems inscribe the dynamic circle of Stevens's vision: neither transcendence alone nor immanence alone is sufficient to describe either reality or imagination.

Though the pigeons at the end of "Sunday Morning" sink "downward to darkness on extended wings," their undulations are ambiguous. To invert Heraclitus's famous dictum, the way down may be the way up—it depends on one's perspective. As Stevens writes in "Esthetique du Mal":

>   Perhaps,
> After death, the non-physical people, in paradise
> Itself non-physical, may, by chance, observe
> The green corn gleaming and experience
> The minor of what we feel.[15]

Just so, Stevens continues, "the adventurer / In humanity has not conceived of a race / Completely physical in a physical world."[16] He affirms this same reciprocity between transcendence and immanence theoretically in the essay "Imagination as Value" when he posits: "If the imagination is the faculty by which we import the real into the unreal, its value is the value of the way of thinking by which we project the idea of God into the idea of man."[17] It is at this point, the point of connection between transcendence and immanence, what in a more orthodox context we would call the point of incarnation, that Stevens's vertical axis tilts to the horizontal, and the adventurer in humanity becomes the fictive figure of a surpassing human excellence. It is here that the Irish preoccupation in Stevens's work finds its significance.

Though one can picture the wandering Crispin as first cousin of the wandering Óisin, such insights depend on a more generalized understanding of the voyage motif in Western literature. Crispin is also cousin to Odysseus, Aeneas, Dante, Spenser's Redcrosse Knight, Coleridge's Ancient Mariner, and the Wordsworth of *The Prelude*, among many others, and one need not appeal to archetypal criticism to see him as such. Moreover, after "Blanche McCarthy," one has to wait until 1942 for "Notes Toward a Supreme Fiction" and the figure of the MacCullough to find in Stevens's work any direct allusion to an Irish context, either literal or fictive. As Stevens stated directly in a letter to Henry Church, the man to whom "Notes Toward a Supreme Fiction" is dedicated, "your Supreme Court Justice is the MacCullough of the NOTES. They say that in Ireland God is a member of the family, and that they treat Him as one of them. For the mass of people, it is certain that humanism would do just as well as anything else.... The chief defect of humanism is that it concerns human beings. Between humanism and something else, it might be possible to create an acceptable fiction."[18]

"Notes Toward a Supreme Fiction" is, of course, Stevens's most sustained effort at achieving that "something else," that "acceptable fiction"—the great poem of our time that would stand as a kind of epic of the imagination. Not surprisingly, Stevens's epic is conceived of as a journey, the heroic passage of the ephebe and his ultimate transfiguration by the end of the poem into the fully realized man of imagination, a transfiguration symbolized by his mystical marriage to the "fat girl, terrestrial," his "fluent mundo." As always in such journeys, the *hierogamy* epitomizes a union of opposites: "Soldier, there is a war between the mind / And sky, between thought and day and night.... / It is a war that never ends."[19] With this coda Stevens reiterates the prologue's implication that the shadow side of the imagination is history, and that it is the imagination, properly attuned and employed, that might bring peace.

Though not the apotheosis of the epic's end, the MacCullough is the essential figure of the poem's first movement, that embodiment of imaginative vitality toward which the ephebe first moves. Given Stevens's remarks to Henry Church, the MacCullough is explicitly linked to Ireland not only by being the name of an American secretary of the Treasury when Stevens was at Harvard,[20] but more significantly through the figure's association with what Stevens takes to be an expressly Irish understanding of God. As such, the MacCullough stands between a humanist conception of the world, founded purely in reason, and that "something else"—the imagination, which permits reason to transcend its bounds:

> If MacCullough himself lay lounging by the sea,
>
> Drowned in its washes, reading in the sound,
> About the thinker of the first idea,
> He might take habit, whether from wave or phrase,
>
> Or power of the wave, or deepened speech,
> Or a leaner being, moving in on him,
> Of greater aptitude and apprehension,
>
> As the waves at last were never broken,
> As if the language, suddenly, with ease,
> Said things it had laboriously spoken.[21]

Though surely, as Harold Bloom affirms, the MacCullough is part of a "Nietzschean trope"—the poem's "major-man"—the figure essentially represents human being coming to consciousness of the self as maker, humanity gaining consciousness of its imaginative potential. As Stevens argues in a letter to Hi Simons, "the gist of this poem is that the MacCullough is MacCullough; MacCullough is any name, any man. The trouble with humanism is that man as God remains man, but there is an extension of man, the leaner being, in fiction, a possibly more than human human, a composite human. The act of recognizing him is the act of this leaner being moving in on us."[22]

In quoting this passage, Bloom maintains that Stevens's denial of the Nietzschean influence merely confirms how unconvincing Stevens's denial of influences are in view of his protestations to the contrary.[23] For Bloom, in the MacCullough "we confront Whitman assimilated to Nietzsche, an American Over-Man." To this we may add that Stevens's affirmation of the MacCullough as "any man," a "composite human," merely draws greater attention to the origins of the figure's name within Stevens's preoccupation with Ireland. Therefore, to Bloom's American "grand trope" and "noble synecdoche of Power," we could add an Irish dimension. Why else would Stevens follow his own meditation on the figure of the MacCullough with his consideration of how the Irish envision God? The MacCullough may be an American Everyman, but Stevens casts him in an aura of Irish religious practice. This application of Irishness as a trope in Stevens's personal mythology stands in stark contrast to Eliot's "Apeneck" Sweeney, a figure that within its negative stereotype embodies the degenerate nature of modern humanity.

From the Shannon to the Schuylkill: Tom McGreevy's Double Consciousness

Ireland does not take a direct hold of Stevens's imagination until the late forties, a few years before the poet's death, though his letters show that he had corresponded with Elizabeth Yeats at Cuala Press as early as 1934 in order, among other things, to secure a copy of Italian philosopher Mario Rossi's Irish travelogue, *Pilgrimage in the West*. As Stevens remarked in a letter to Barbara Church in 1947, "Some years ago Mario Rossi, an Italian philosopher, who teaches near Naples, visited Ireland and wrote a little book called *Journey to the West*. It was curious to see what a man whose sight, not to speak of his intelligence, had been developed in the clarity and color of Naples made of the mist and rain of Ireland."[24] What Rossi made of Ireland, among other things, is a romance of "the Irish race" consistent with the Celtic revival. "Ireland itself," so Rossi remarks, "is in reality (to put it roughly) a Celtic country. . . . Irish Celticism is the obstinate permanence of an original spirit athwart all the modern superstructures, athwart mingling of blood, and variations of language and religions."[25]

Rossi's racially infused conception of Ireland and the Irish is even more emphatically in evidence when he remarks that the Irish "Celt celticizes even more evolved races, that is (perhaps) races decayed as to their vital force in consequence of the hybrid quality inherent in civilizations."[26] The undertones of Rossi's view of Ireland are manifestly racist by inference, if not explicitly so, especially considering that Cuala Press published the book in 1933. Then again, traditional Irish nationalism, with its revivalist impulse, has been distrustful of the hybrid, and Rossi's reflections on race no doubt have been deeply shaped by Ireland's particular cultural and historical climate. Not surprisingly, at the end of his journey to the west, Rossi's "celticized" inheritors of the

Irish race—William Butler Yeats and Lady Gregory—come to embody not only the essential Ireland but imagination itself: "This is, I think, the nature of poetry: your soul. Your Irish soul."[27] Here Rossi's conception of "the Irish soul" elides the fact that Yeats and Lady Gregory are both Anglo Irish, a matter that renders problematical his appeal to Ireland's specifically racial identity. Indeed, his notion that the Celt "celticizes more evolved races" subverts from the outset his essentialist conception of the Irish soul, unless one is willing to concede that "Celtic blood" possesses powers of cultural transubstantiation.

Certainly Stevens was not immune to racism, and his prejudice toward African Americans is well documented in his letters and elsewhere. One need only consult the title of his poem "Like Decorations in a Nigger Cemetery," which is now published with the *n* word elided. Yet nowhere is Rossi's talk of vital racial forces and purity of blood reflected in Stevens's interest in Ireland. Whatever Stevens made of Rossi's sojourn, apart from conjoining the journey motif so important to Stevens's work with Ireland and poetry itself, it surely provides evidence of his perception of Ireland as a metaphor for the imagination. "This is the nature of poetry: your soul. Your Irish soul." The soul to whom Rossi refers is Yeats's. Whether by inference or circumstance, here is the Celt as MacCullough, the proto-poet akin to the singer in "The Idea of Order at Key West," an Orpheus *in potentia,* a figure of greater power than modern humanism, which tends to level the axis of transcendence by permitting God to remain human. It is a trope that in the last decade of Stevens's life he came to secure real-life roots in the person of Thomas MacGreevy.

What Peter Brazeau called "the Dublin-Hartford connection"[28] began in the spring of 1948, when Irish poet and critic Thomas MacGreevy wrote Stevens after being informed by Barbara Church that the American poet admired his poetry. And so commenced a profoundly important literary friendship. Friend and collaborator with other giants of modern literature like Joyce and Beckett, MacGreevy is a significant figure within Irish modernism, a poet as well as a cultural figure who among other posts served as director of the National Gallery for many years. In addition to a definitive study of the art of Jack B. Yeats, he wrote one book of poems during his lifetime, which was published in 1934 and which Wallace Stevens admired and commented on in his letters to his Irish friend.[29] By the time of her father's death on August 2, 1955, Holly Stevens tells us that it was with MacGreevy and another friend, Barbara Church, that Stevens felt most himself.[30]

From the outset, in his first letter to MacGreevy, Stevens reveals not only the depth of his connection to the Irish poet's work but something of the place Ireland had assumed in his own imagination. "Ireland is rather often on my mind over here," Stevens writes. "Somehow the image of it is growing fresher and stronger. In any case, the picture one had of it when I was a boy is no longer the present picture. It is something much more modern and vigorous. I don't know whether you feel that change in Dublin. This has nothing to do with propaganda: it is something that seems to take form without one's knowing why."[31] Stevens's confession about his own relationship to Ireland is significant on two fronts. First, it reveals that Stevens had "an image" of Ireland in his mind for the greater portion of his life, though he himself had no Irish ancestry. Second, his inquiry to MacGreevy reveals the interplay of imagination and reality that so possessed his mind and work. We have Stevens's past picture of Ireland, imagined as it is, being tested against the reality of the present. It is almost as if he were himself an émigré, if not from the literal country of his youth than from an Ireland of his imagination. As such, the motif of emigration and diaspora begins to inhere in his work as an explicit theme and to link to Ireland in his imagination. It also becomes explicitly tied to the place through his affiliation with his Irish friend and fellow poet.

Beyond implicating Ireland in Stevens's perennial obsession, this first letter to MacGreevy also raises the issue of Stevens's sense of place. Put bluntly, from the standpoint of the imagination one place might just as well be another for Stevens. As he writes in a letter to Barbara Church, "it interests me immensely to have you speak of so many places that have been merely names for me. Yet really they have always been a good deal more than names."[32] What they were for Stevens, and what they must be for his readers, are fictive embodiments that emerge from the mind's encounter with place. "In what sense do I live in America," Stevens continues, "if I walk to and from the office day after day?" In short, one could live anywhere, unless one's imagination is primed to engage the material of reality.

Yet for Stevens, his sense of place is also determined by his home: "A man living in a twelfth century stronghold in Dublin pluming himself on such a title inevitably makes me think of Tommy Collins, a poor thing at home when I was a boy, who rode around town in gorgeous costumes. The people in the livery stable used to lend him a white horse. He liked the animal and took great care of it and what a cry would go up when children saw him in the distance coming their way and dressed up say like the Admiral of the Schuylkill and its Convivial Streams."[33] What is remarkable in this passage is Stevens's transformation of a distant place—twelfth-century Dublin—into the familiar, and beyond the familiar into an emblem of America worthy of Norman Rockwell.

MacGreevy's idea of America, as Mary Joan Egan observes, "was as stereotyped, and as nearly accurate, as Stevens's idea of Ireland,"[34] though where MacGreevy for all his attachment to Ireland was a cosmopolitan, living for extended periods in London and Paris, Stevens remained in Hartford and "actualized life abroad" through MacGreevy and other correspondents.[35] In any case, what matters to Stevens's sense of place is the *idea* of place by which the imagination might be liberated. He makes the point more directly in a letter to Barbara Church:

> No doubt you are back somewhere in France after your trip to Ireland. I hope that you saw something of the country there because, for all that Dublin may be, it can hardly be more than one expects it to be and that is merely one minor metropolis. But the country could be more than that. I like natives: people in civilized countries whose only civilization is their own land. Not that I have ever met any: it is only an idea. Yet it would be nice to meet an idea like that driving a donkey cart, stopping to talk about the rain.[36]

It would be easy to see Stevens's invocation of the idea of place here as merely a testament to his own American provinciality. Nevertheless, it is not too great a leap from the idea of place to the idea of order. As he remarks to MacGreevy, "the mind with metaphysical affinities has a dash when it deals with reality that the purely realistic mind never has because the purely realistic mind never experiences any passion for reality."[37] Stevens's idea that the metaphysical is part and parcel of the order of reality, and hence is the vehicle of the sense of place regardless of one's home, rescues his remarks to Barbara Church from mere provinciality. He makes his understanding plain to MacGreevy when he asks, "Why should not Mr. Yeats be everything that is said of him and for all the fascination of the details of Ireland why should not his imagination make use of it for his imagination's sake, let alone for the sake of Ireland? The same is true of any land of which any artist is a part."[38] For Stevens, through his encounter with MacGreevy and a lifetime of significant if intermittent reflection, the idea of Ireland had been subsumed into the place of his imagination.

Nowhere in Stevens's work is the assimilation of Ireland and Irishness into the poet's fictive world more apparent than in "Our Stars Come from Ireland," the first section of which found direct inspiration in MacGreevy's own poems "Homage to Hieronymous Bosch" and "Recessional."[39] In the first section of Stevens's poem, as the subtitle tells us, *Tom McGreevy, in America, Thinks of Himself as a Boy*. More than assuming the persona of the stock, nostalgic immigrant remembering Ireland years after his American wake, the poem transforms memory into a self-conscious act of imagination:

> Out of him that I loved,
> Mal Bay I made,
> I made Mal Bay
> And him in that water.[40]

For the "Tom McGreevy" of the poem, Ireland—the place of origin—is created through the act of imagining it into being, as is the original self who is recollected, initially at least, as someone "other" than the imaginer. As Lawrence Kramer points out, there is ambivalence in the poem, especially if one conceives of the speaker as a "transcendental ego" that nevertheless is born of a place.[41] According to Kramer, Tom McGreevy's identity can be affirmed only by the poem's denial of self-separation through the mind's creation of its origin. In such a reading, the transcendental self becomes imagination's fiat by which the passage of time and place—a note of metaphysical as well as historical diaspora—is overcome and likewise the sense of discontinuity within the self.

Undergirding Kramer's view, however, is the tendency to read Stevens exclusively through the ethos of American transcendentalism. Such a view relies almost exclusively on what I have called the vertical axis in Stevens's work. Yet this is not the balanced view Stevens himself suggests in his letter to MacGreevy, where the origin of the poem in the Irish poet's own work becomes evident. In his letter, Stevens offers two views of MacGreevy's lines:

> High above the Bank of Ireland
> Unearthly music sounded,
> Passing westwards.
>
> I thought about these lines of yours. Arranged as they are with the reality in the first line one's attention is focused on the reality. Had the order been reversed and had the lines read:
>
> Unearthly music sounded,
> Passing westwards
> High above the Bank of Ireland
>
> the attention would have been focused on what was unreal.[42]

More than elucidating a minor technical point, Stevens's observations about reality and unreality here capture the essential tension in what would become his adaptation of MacGreevy's lines in "Our Stars Come from Ireland":

> Over the top of the Bank of Ireland
> The wind blows quaintly
> Its thin-stringed music,
> As he heard it in Tarbert.[43]

If anything, Stevens's modification of MacGreevy's poem involves directing the focus of the poem more emphatically toward reality, toward the horizontal axis of his work. As such, a stanza that begins with the speaker's eyes directed upwards ends with an evocation of the ferry at Tarbert, McGreevy's home village in Kerry. The transcendental act of making one's identity, affirmed in the first stanza, is thus qualified by the trope of diaspora that exists as a kind of substructure within the poem. "What would the water have been," Tom McGreevy asks, "Without that *he* makes of it"[44] (my italics). Here, the fictive McGreevy's initial declaration of self-making is transposed to the boy he was and into a kind of transcendental present that has the power to recreate the past. This transformation is signaled by the shift from past tense, the verb tense in which the poem began, to the present tense of the poem's final stanza. Yet it is water, the medium of his passage away from his invented origin, that makes such invention possible. The unearthly music that passes westward in MacGreevy's poem gives way in Stevens's poem to an earthly passage westward that enables the self to become its own muse, an invention that paradoxically invents the self. In this passage, through a surprising figural reversal, the experience of diaspora paradoxically creates an "original" sense of identity by which the self gains its native sense of belonging.

Of course, it might be argued that the voice of "Our Stars Come from Ireland" is actually ambivalent and shifting, and therefore that the McGreevy persona may not be the sole speaker of the poem's first part, thereby disrupting the trope of passage at its outset. From this perspective the "I" that opens the poem is not McGreevy at all but Stevens, who, having assumed the persona of his double, now summarizes his reading of the Irish poet's "Recessional":

> I could hear
> Where listeners still hear
> That far away, dear
> Roar
> The long silver roar
> Of Mal Bay.[45]

While it may be true that the poem evolved out of Stevens's deep emotional response to MacGreevy's lines, to read the speaker of the poem as "shifting" between personas rather than as the speech of a single persona, "Tom McGreevy," is to ignore the subtitle's self-evident direction to the reader: "Tom McGreevy, in America, Thinks of Himself as a Boy." The persona may be a double for Stevens's, but to neglect the poet's clear intention to *fictionalize* the voice is to miss a crucial attribute of the poem's dramatic organization.

In any case, the complex relationship between unreality and reality in the poem, between reality and imagination, inheres in the persona of Tom McGreevy. The Tom McGreevy of the poem is not the Thomas

MacGreevy of the letters, though clearly Stevens intended the fictive McGreevy to echo his real friend. MacGreevy, of course, never emigrated from Ireland despite being well traveled, and so Stevens's persona views his life through the prism of a journey that essentially defines the difference between Stevens's friend and his fictive speaker. From another perspective, the musings of the fictive Tom McGreevy communicate a sense of place nearer to Stevens's own origins:

> These things were made of him
> and out of myself.
> He stayed in Kerry, died there.
> I live in Pennsylvania.[46]

The first section of "Our Stars Come from Ireland" ends:

> The stars are washing up from Ireland
> And through and over the puddles of Swatara
> And Schuylkill. The sound of him
> Comes from a great distance and is heard.[47]

Pennsylvania, the Swatara, and the Schuylkill are place names from Stevens's childhood, as he himself remarks in a letter to his Irish friend.[48] Perhaps, then, it is appropriate to see Tom McGreevy, the "transcendental self" of this poem, as a composite self, a speaker whose voice originates not in Ireland or the United States but in an imagined fusion of both realities—an Irish America of the purely imagined—a conception underscored by any shiftiness in the poem's pronouns. To read the poem in this way is not to deny its transcendentalist affinities, or its compositional origins, but to extend the range of experience that so informs its idea of being American. In the sound of Tom McGreevy's dead self coming from its great distance, and now traced again in the self's long passage west, the unearthly music of MacGreevy's Irish poem gains new embodiment in the imagined reality of Stevens's American idiom.

Nevertheless, to claim that the backward look of "Our Stars Come from Ireland" constitutes an alteration in Stevens's squarely American poetic seems to contradict not only the preponderance of Stevens's most notable critics but the poet himself. In another letter to Mac-Greevy, Stevens observes, "conceding that the generations of people there have not lived in vain, it is still probably true that there are more meanings for Americans in America." More flamboyantly, Stevens underscored the importance of the American locality to his sensibility when he wrote, again to MacGreevy, that "I am, after all, more moved by the first sounds of the birds on my street than by the death of a thousand penguins in Antarctica."[49]

Stevens's seeming lack of environmental conscience notwithstanding, his emphatic embrace of America as the proper arena for his poetry takes on moral import in "Dutch Graves in Bucks County." In "Dutch Graves," what Harold Bloom called Stevens's pugnacious and polemical "stand against the past"[50] underscores both his moral repugnance at the brutal aspect of human history and his hope that America offers the promise of a new beginning. The poet's "semblables" are, among other things, "mossy cronies," "monsters antique and haggard with past thought" whose "crackling voices" bespeak an archaic freedom awful in its power to shape the present. What follows is a view of historical brutality worthy of Heaney's *North* that elaborates its own vision of reciprocal violence, or Derek Mahon's "A Disused Shed in County Wexford," with its evocation of lost peoples and cultures:

> Freedom is like a man who kills himself
> Each night, an incessant butcher, whose knife
> Grows sharp in blood. The armies kill themselves,
> And in their blood an ancient evil dies—
> The action of incorrigible tragedy.[51]

A double vision inheres in Stevens's poem. On the one hand, the past is claimed to be "not part of the present." As such, a genuine freedom—a freedom from the past—appears possible, though only to the poet's dead ancestors. On the other hand, the ancient evil that dies with each historical tragedy lives again in the living, "the violent marchers of the present" who "march toward a generation's centre." Does the double vision of this poem really constitute a purely Emersonian stand against the past, and therefore an affirmation of Whitman's visionary America, the avatar of democratic vistas wholly new? Rather than a pure negation of the past, the poem demonstrates an appropriation of the past with an eye toward transformation. What fuels the poem is Stevens's perennial "rage for order," and not as the poem suggests, "a chaos composed in more than order," the precise arcs of World War II's rumbling armies. What makes that transformational vision possible is the same backward look witnessed in the first section of "Our Stars Come from Ireland." As Stevens affirms in "Dutch Graves," discerning an appropriation of the past is the legacy of "the much too many disinherited" as he called them—the actual, historical throngs of diaspora—who, like the fictive Tom McGreevy, were forced by history to embark on the creation of a new identity out of a convergence of the past and the present.

Stevens's obsession with his personal genealogy during the 1940s and early 1950s surely informed the composition of "Dutch Graves in Bucks County," but beyond the making of any single poem Stevens's fascination with his ancestors deepens his connection with the circumstance of Tom McGreevy in "Our Stars Come from Ireland." "To let a little daylight into the attic of the past . . . to form an acceptable realization of the past," Stevens wrote to Henry Church, is the goal of both the poet and his fictive persona.[52] The parallel between Stevens's obsession with his Dutch ancestry and Tom McGreevy's interest in his Irish origins intensifies in *The Necessary Angel,* in which Stevens recounts a visit to the Zeller house in Tuplehocken, Pennsylvania, which leads him to a meditation on the faith of his forebears. A family of religious refugees, their reality, Stevens observes, "consisted of both the visible and invisible."[53] It therefore anticipates his claim that the joining of imagination and reality in poetry must be in its measure "a compensation for what has been lost,"[54] with the decline of religious faith under the often brutal impress of historical reality. The stars that wash up from Ireland in Stevens's poem suggest the idea of poetry as a "transcendent analogue" achieved through Tom McGreevy's retrospective act of self-creation.

The parallel deepens further in his recollection of a trip with a fellow genealogical enthusiast to Christ Church near Souchsburg. "This stout old Lutheran," Stevens writes, "felt very much about his church as the Irish are said to feel about God. Kate O'Brien says that in Ireland God is a member of the family."[55] Echoing his earlier remarks to Henry

Church about the Irish view of God, the faith of Stevens's fathers—their supreme fiction—again reveals a felt resemblance to the Irish idea of God, at least as Stevens understands it. The point would be incidental were it not for the fact that Stevens repeats the same observation using nearly the same phrasing in letters to Henry Church in 1943 and again to Thomas MacGreevy in 1948.[56]

If what has been called Stevens's "central-perceiving self" was bound exclusively to the mainstream of American transcendentalism, even to the inclusion of his genealogical preoccupations within that critical framework,[57] how was it that in these last years of his life Stevens confessed an affinity with an Irish writer's account of how God is seen in Ireland, and did so not merely in personal letters but in *The Necessary Angel,* his definitive statement of his poetics? The answer is that, in the last great flowering of Stevens's imagination, the Irish experience of historical disinheritance, emigration, diaspora, and need to reconcile that disinheritance with some metaphysical order had become an analogue for the human predicament. Indeed, Stevens's affiliation with Irishness assumes political undertones when he observes to MacGreevy, "It would not surprise me if in time [the United States] came to be much better friends with the Irish in Eire than we have ever been with the English in England."[58] By his own account, this profound resonance between Irish and American reverberates in the common refugee history of Stevens's own family and resounds in both Stevens's poetry and his poetics.

As Stevens observes in his essay "The Relation between Poetry and Painting," "the world about us would be desolate except for the world within us," and goes on to characterize the "interchange between these two worlds" as a "migratory passing."[59] In short, Stevens's implied idea of the poet's work as an effort to chart, as it were, the mind's continuous migration between reality and imagination inheres in the concept of "transport," one of the central recurrent tropes of his work. The primacy of "transport" announces itself explicitly in a poem like "Transport to Summer," though the idea of transport is implied already in an early poem like "The Comedian as the Letter C." On the one hand, "transport" recalls Longinus's use of the term; it describes the soul's migration from this world into the sublime. On the other, it recalls the mass movements within time and history that involved millions forced from their homes by what Stevens called "the pressure of reality." By the pressure of reality Stevens means "the pressure of an external event or events on the consciousness to the exclusion of contemplation."[60] For Stevens, the first meaning of transport as a kind of ascension out of reality into the sublime is meant to redress the second notion of transport and its associations with war, forced migration, and genocide. We could say then that "transport" as a central trope of Stevens's late poetics stands at the point of convergence between the two axial directions of his work.

The moral and imaginative ambition of Stevens's late work is to transform "transport," conceived of as a mere migration commensurate with the historical experience of diaspora, that is, an external event that stifles contemplation, into a figure of possible transcendence in which the pressure of reality is transfigured and not merely released. In addition to its own obvious import for how we view Stevens's work and the place of the Irish poems within his oeuvre, this conception of transport particularly westward bears further reflection in the light of diaspora literatures, including Irish and Irish American. To borrow from Paul Gilroy, the backward look of Tom McGreevy not only reveals a composite self but also encodes a "double-consciousness"[61]—the transported and thereby necessarily "invented self," and the "original self" that it must reinvent. It is this fusion of imagination and reality in the idea of transport, at once essential to Stevens's work and relevant to literary approaches centering on the historical experience of emigration, that saves reality from becoming desolate and the imagination from becoming merely escapist.

In "The Westwardness of Everything," the second section of "Our Stars Come from Ireland," Stevens explicitly takes the reality of Irish migration to America and uses it as one of his most successful tropes of imaginative transport. The stars that wash up from Ireland in the first half of the poem, emblems of an original sublime, are now emblems of a sublime made present in the moment, at once apocalyptic and generative: "the ashes of fiery weather ... luminously wet." The figure of Tom McGreevy disappears, and an anonymous unnamed voice takes over. Yet, now as before, the speaker's reflections do not transport him to a purely transcendent otherworld. Instead, they register the pressure of reality, for he finally likens the green stars to "beautiful and abandoned refugees." It is this migration of imagination into reality that occasions an alteration in the poem's world that can only be called transfigurative:

> The whole habit of the mind is changed by them,
> These Gaeled and fitful-fangled darknesses
> Made suddenly luminous, themselves a change,
> An east in their compelling westwardness,
>
> Themselves an issue as at an end, as if
> There was an end at which in a final change,
> When the whole habit of the mind was changed,
> The ocean breathed out morning in one breath.[62]

In these stunning lines the retrospect of the poem's first section becomes a prospect verging on the edge of time and space in which imagination and reality become joined within the transfiguring presence of "Being." In "Of Mere Being," the coda poem of *The Palm at the End of the Mind,* the tail feathers of Stevens's figural bird of paradise are "fire-fangled" and "dangle down" out of the pure sublime and into the figural world of human language. The poem's "fitful-fangled" stars anticipate that later apotheosis, though they do so by inscribing history, and in particular Irish American history, into Stevens's elaborate figural transfiguration.

Westwardness, of course, is the idea around which this section of the poem revolves, and it is the idea toward which the first section pointed in the very urgency of McGreevy's backward look east. The idea of westwardness had been weighing on Stevens as well around the time of the poem's composition, as his words to Thomas MacGreevy testify:

> What you say in one of your letters about your westwardness as a result of living near the Shannon Estuary interested me. The house in which I was born and lived as a boy faced the west, and wherever I have lived if the house faced the other way I have always been pulling round on an axis to get it straight. But that is the least of this sort of thing. After all, instead of facing the Atlantic, you might have faced London and Paris. The poem I sent you some time ago is one of the two. The other is this very subject: the westwardness of things.[63]

Beyond making specific reference to the two sections of "Our Stars Come from Ireland" and demonstrating again the extent of Mac-Greevy's influence on the poem's composition, Stevens's considerations in this letter reveal him establishing a historical and ultimately imaginative parallel between the circumstance of being Irish and his own American origins. The westwardness of things is the idea that links the two, and it is around this idea that the axis of Stevens's imagination revolves. Of course, "Our Stars Come from Ireland" is not the sole reference to westwardness in Stevens's work. As we have seen, Crispin in "The Comedian as the Letter C" travels west and then east again. In "Tea at the Palaz of Hoon" Stevens's unnamed traveler descends "the western day through what you called / the loneliest air."[64] In contrast, in "Evening Without Angels" Stevens speaks of a "desire for day / Accomplished in the immensely flashing East."[65] The east-west axis is a consistent imaginative orientation in Stevens's poetry, an orientation that follows the perennial path of the sun across the heavens as well as Tom McGreevy and the actual refugees of history across the sea from Ireland and Europe.

Genealogy of the Sublime

At the beginning of "Notes Toward a Supreme Fiction" Stevens claims that the ephebe "must become an ignorant man again / And see the sun with an ignorant eye / And see it clearly in the idea of it."[66] In "The Sense of the Sleight-of-Hand Man," he says again of the sun, "the wheel survives its myths."[67] At such times Stevens emphasizes his desire not to rely on any received mythology, but to force the imagination to find its own source in the thing itself. Of course, as Stevens knows, there can be no perception without imagination, imagination at the origin of things. Hence, again in "Notes Toward a Supreme Fiction," the sun that "must bear no name" is immediately called "gold flourisher." To be in between the thing itself and the naming of things is, for Stevens, to be "in the difficulty of what it is to be." As such, Stevens does not simply abjure old mythologies but reinvents them for his own imaginative needs. Though in "Credences of Summer" he claims that the goal is to "trace the gold sun about the whitened sky / Without evasion by a single metaphor," the sun's rising in the east, passage across the heavens, and eventual descent in the west represent an original migration, the kind of which religions are made and cultures are defined. In such symbolic organizations of space, to turn westward is to look toward death, for it is in the west that the sun completes its journey.[68] Thus the westwardness of everything is a figure for the migration of all things toward death, the final change in a world defined by change, and Stevens clearly intends to let these associations echo in the poem. By comparison, the last third of John Berryman's *The Dream Songs* offers a contrary migration when Henry, his skittery protagonist, journeys back to Ireland from the westward "Country of the Dead."

There are other echoes suggested by the poem as well, since its darknesses are "Gaeled." Tom McGreevy's passage west repeats the western journey found in Irish *immrama,* the visionary passages west of Máel Dúin and Bran and Óisin and Brendan. Moreover, since Stevens's persona is an emigrant from the west of Ireland, his prospects at the end of the poem recall the luminous "New Island" (An tOilean Ur) of the Irish peasant, an America mythologized into a land of gold, a version of the sublime like Tir na nÓg, the Land of the Young in Irish mythology. The American myth of the westwardness of things is yet another version of the sublime. It is Whitman's open road, the place where our destiny as a new people will be made manifest in an ever-expanding American identity. "The sublime comes down / To the spirit itself," Stevens observes in "The American Sublime," "the empty spirit in vacant space."[69] Surely Stevens's "American Sublime" brings us to the limit of Whitman's open road, or perhaps it positions us on the brink of Whitman's imaginative circumnavigation of the globe in "Salut au Monde!"

Luke Gibbons's observation on the myths of the west in Ireland and America is salient here. In *Transformations in Irish Culture* he observes: "For all their similarities as foundational myths—sharing agrarian ideals, an aversion to law and order and to the centralization of the state—it is the differences between them that is most striking. The Wild West is an outpost of individualism, extolling the virtues of self-made man that lie at the heart of the American dream. By contrast, the recourse to the west in Ireland is impelled by a search for community, a desire to escape isolation of the self and immerse oneself in the company of others."[70] Indeed, the Irish and American myths of the west would seem to be irreconcilable. However, in the case of Stevens's persona Tom McGreevy, the sublime is anything but vacant and solitary; it is that which gathers up all the habitations of the mind, as well as its habits, and transforms them. One might say that the Irish influence, clearly evident in the poem, enabled Stevens to reimagine the lineaments of his American sublime. Thus, having followed McGreevy's emigration west, his stars represent the inevitable movement of all life toward its end; moreover, we can discern in that end the enduring human longing to answer death with a new beginning, or as the speaker observes, "an east in their compelling westwardness."[71] As Stevens's poem states, this is an end that entails an issue—the promise of new life transfigured out of death. That transfiguration arrives on a slight horizon to be sure—"as if"—though it is enough for Stevens to envision a final change that reverses westwardness itself, change itself, however demythologized and remythologized. Thus, by poem's end, beginning and end are one: the ocean breathes out morning in one breath. "Naked Alpha," as Stevens says in "An Ordinary Evening in New Haven," has been inscribed imaginatively into "hierophant Omega."[72]

Is this moment of transfiguration merely a "chilly retreat" from Tom McGreevy's initial backward look toward his first place, an abstraction and ultimately an evasion that undoes the very passage that brought both the figural emigrant and the emigrant reader to this prospect?[73] If we read the poem as more than another example of the American sublime, and therefore not merely as an instance of imagination totalizing itself into a pure and solitary transcendence, and instead see in Tom McGreevy's journey west a figural passage grounded in historical reality, then Stevens's stars do not deconstruct his persona's origin—they transport it with them. In Stevens's "fluent mundo," as in the world we sense and know, the journey westward eventually brings us east again. It evinces, in Stevens's words, "an interdependence of imagination and reality as equals."[74] Though that interdependence does not collapse the inherent differences between the Irish and American myths of the west, it does manage to hold them together in a tensive figural unity.

In "Le Monocle de Mon Oncle," Stevens exclaims, "in the high west there burns a furious star." A quarter century later, it is fair to say that in "Our Stars Come from Ireland" Stevens pursued that star to its green apogee. It is also fair to say that in the collection *The Rock* Stevens realized another ideal likewise anticipated in that early poem: "Like a dull scholar, I behold, in love, / An ancient aspect touching a new mind." Near the end of his life, Stevens's "new mind" permitted him to embrace more fiercely and consummately than previously in his work what Ralph Mills called "the possibilities of the created world."[75] The ancient aspect Stevens momentarily beholds in "Le Monocle de Mon Oncle" comprises the major object of his contemplation in *The Rock*, and it marks a major advance in worldview from the nakedly shining star of "Nuances of a Theme by Williams," a reality that "mirrors nothing." By contrast, in the poem "The Rock" sheer physical reality is at once "the starting point of the human and the end," and not merely a lofty otherness seemingly beyond the brink of imagination. It reveals "a desire to be at the end of distances," a desire that like "Our Stars Come from Ireland" affirms the idea of origin through the very distances traversed abroad from the source of self.

Not that Stevens wished to be reduced "to a state of unrelieved realism," a concern he expressed in a letter to Barbara Church. In the same letter, however, he does reflect "that the close approach to reality has always been the supreme difficulty of any art: the communication of actuality . . . has been not only impossible, but has never appeared worthwhile because it loses identity as the event passes. . . . Nevertheless, the desire to combine the two things, poetry and reality, is a constant desire." Remarkably, immediately following these remarks, Stevens recounts the origin of what is one of the finest and most representative poems of *The Rock*, a poem that thereby constitutes one of the most succinct and moving reflections on imagination and reality, and thus the human place within the order of the created world: "Jack Sweeney (the Boston Sweeney) sent me a postcard from County Clare the other day—the worn cliffs towering up over the Atlantic. It was like a gust of freedom, a return to the spacious, solitary world in which we used to exist."[76]

The poem anticipated by Stevens's account is, of course, "The Irish Cliffs of Moher." Perhaps never so much has been made of what Richard Hugo would have called a poem's triggering moment, the arrival of a simple postcard. The poem begins: "Who is my father in this world, in this house, / at the spirit's base? // My father's father, his father's father, his—."[77] More than merely rhetorical, the poem's question establishes a genealogical conceit whereby the poet's imagination travels back to its generative center at "the core of all creation."[78] In that conceit, McGreevy's backward look in "Our Stars Come from Ireland" penetrates beyond the lure of personal origins. In Stevens's vision it travels back "to a parent before thought, before speech, / At the head of the past."[79] In making this visionary journey back through time and space, "The Irish Cliffs of Moher" reverses the passage west traveled in Stevens's other explicitly Irish poem. Just as "Our Stars Come from Ireland" envisioned an east in the world's compelling westwardness, so "The Irish Cliffs of Moher" envisions a west mythologized in the eastwardness of Ireland. Stevens, the American descendant of Dutch emigrants who made the journey west like the emigrant Irish, finds in the cliffs a semblance of eternity. They are not Tir na nÓg, discovered beyond the western edge of the known, though they are of wondrous aspect, rising as they do "out of the mists / Above the real / rising out of the present time and place, above / the wet, green grass."[80] At the crux of east and west, as well as above and below, Stevens's Cliffs of Moher are the embodiment of the earth's own generative imagination, at once prehuman and preconscious and the source of human consciousness:

> This is not landscape, full of somnambulations
> Of poetry
>
> And the sea. This is my father or, maybe,
> It is as he was,
>
> A likeness, one of the race of fathers: earth,
> And sea and air.[81]

To picture the cliffs as simply "a likeness" is to bear witness not merely to an interdependence of reality and imagination but to avow an indwelling of each in the other. To extend that likeness by extending the genealogical trope with which the poem began to its ultimate realization in the human mind's elemental oneness with the world constitutes nothing less than the fulfillment of Stevens's whole poetic quest. It is also now to envision a communal dimension to Stevens's American sublime, one derived explicitly from the west of Ireland. "This end and this beginning are one," Stevens states in "Hermitage at the Center,"[82] and in "Final Soliloquy of the Interior Paramour," "We say God and the imagination are one,"[83] and, finally, in "The Rock,"

It is the rock where tranquil must adduce
Its tranquil self, the main of things, the mind,

The starting point of the human and the end[84]

In Wallace Stevens's "The Irish Cliffs of Moher," we arrive at the center of the poet's life's work, and we have arrived there by charting his fascination with Irishness in poems that are few but of immense importance. That center is a long way from Blanche McCarthy's "unimagined coverts," and yet it appears nascent if not present there as well, amid the symbols going by and the glare of revelations—an idea of self and world glimpsed beyond the dead glass of solipsism, one that we can describe by invoking Whitman's phrase from "Song of Myself": it contains "the similitudes of the past and those of the future."[85]

Near the end of his life Stevens confessed to his friend Thomas MacGreevy, "I have not even begun to touch the spheres within spheres that might have been possible if, instead of devoting the principle amount of my time to making a living, I had devoted it to thought and poetry."[86] The American poet's veiled allusion to Dante in this lament to his Irish friend might seem surprising coming from a poet so wary of old mythologies, at least those unaltered by his own imagination. Yet it is an aspiration with which Yeats would have sympathized, though surely he would have been less sympathetic toward Stevens's American pragmatism, his "paudeen" tendency to place his artistic aspirations within the context of merely economic instead of imaginative reality. Nevertheless, though not essentially Irish or Irish American, Wallace Stevens's poetry—and particularly the poetry of his later years—attempts nothing less than "the figuration of blessedness"[87] and employs figurations of Irishness to secure that achievement even to the end. "The catalogue of early Irish Christian art, from the Sweeneys, came this morning," so he wrote to Barbara Church five months before he died: "The identity of the Irish with their religion is the same thing as the identity of the Irish with their lonely, misty, distant land. . . . I shall study this catalogue with the greatest interest."[88] And so, to judge by the poet's ever more involving conjunction of Ireland with the imagination, he would have.

FOUR

Lines of Leaving, Lines of Returning
John Montague's Double Vision

Only Irish?

In his autobiographical essay, "The Complex Fate of Being Irish-American," John Montague asks why his poem "All Legendary Obstacles" cannot be found in any anthology of American poetry—"Is it because I am supposed to be only Irish?"[1] Montague's question is significant beyond the poet's obvious sense of being slighted by the American poetry establishment. He was, after all, born in Brooklyn in the year of the Great Crash, a child of exile whose "complex fate" had been shaped from the beginning by the same immense historical, political, and cultural forces that have formed the modern world and not just modern Ireland. By birth, at least, he is American, a fact that greatly informs his two master sequences *The Rough Field* and *The Dead Kingdom,* as well as more than a few individual lyrics. As he told Ben Howard in an interview, "I've come to accept that I am at least partly Irish-American, and I have a small number of poems that add up to a description of that world."[2]

By his own account, Montague's "grumpy" demand for admission into the canon of American poetry underscores the insight that his work inhabits a larger literary space than Ireland alone—this despite the accolades and paeans to indispensability brandished across the backs of books. As Robert Garratt observes, "the critical reception of Montague's work . . . depends upon a complex network of critical, literary and political opinion, much of which lies outside the poem itself."[3] Elizabeth Grubgeld extends Garratt's insight when she affirms that "Montague's double birth—as infant in America, and again as a child of four years sent to live with relatives in County Tyrone—precludes an easy entry into his inheritance." Montague's "double birth," so she argues, at once weakens his relationship to Garvaghey—the "rough field" of his ancestors—and "aligns him with a heritage of dispossession."[4] In other words, political and cultural forces that lie outside the work and condition critical opinion also shape the work from inside as a matter of the poet's sensibility and his struggle for imaginative self-possession.

In turn, in one of the few readings of Montague's work that effectively identifies the complex nature of the poet's personal and imaginative preoccupations as well as his achievement, Thomas Dillon Redshaw comments that *The Rough Field* is "uniquely vivid" not only because it "performs an embassy from modern Ireland to the waiting world," but because "it also performs an embassy from the world, and from America in particular, to Ireland."[5] This understanding of Montague's work as the product of a profound reciprocity between the imaginative poles of his dual inheritance is lost on those who perceive him merely as an "invoker of powers," "the poet as oracle," bound by mythic and ancestral ties to his home.[6] By contrast, against those who would limit his poetic "citizenship," Montague reminds us that he has always "kept a double vision,"[7] a vision that incorporates both his Irish and his American births and that characterizes his remarkable achievement as a poet whose work has been prescient of other postcolonial writers and writers of diaspora. In his effort to wrest self-possession from cultural dispossession and personal trauma, Montague's "double vision" ought to be seen as exemplary for our time. Likewise, his "double vision" stands as the manifest extension of Thomas Kinsella's dual tradition from the island of Ireland into Irish America.

When we encounter the term "double vision," either in a poet's description of his own work or within the rubric of critical discourse, it is impossible not to hear an echo of Yeats and his aspiration to yoke together two seemingly disparate modes of being—flesh and spirit, temporal and eternal, immanent and transcendent—within a personal mythology through which he might "hold in a single thought reality and justice."[8] Certainly Yeats's oeuvre, in the individual instances of particular poems and in its cumulative scope, achieves its "unity of being" through the poet's effort to reconcile the oppositions he discerned within his own character. The sum of the poetry may be seen as the imaginative record of the poet's quarrel with himself—his desire "to hammer his thoughts into unity."[9] The effort at self-knowledge thus comes to engage a wide variety of intellectual frameworks in pursuit of an encompassing vision of reality through which the poet might attain, if only in his art, the feeling of being at home in the world—a world perpetually in crisis. Montague shares with Yeats just such a "dialectical approach to knowledge," an approach that makes him "the first Irish poet of consequence to benefit by Yeats's example."[10] Montague's double vision is obviously less obsessed with matters otherworldly and more concerned with those internal conflicts—the quarrel with self—that arise expressly out of the crucible of self and history. Another way of stating this is to say that where Yeats would incorporate the realm of history and politics as well as his own complex life into the Great Wheel of some mythic vision, Montague weaves the vestiges of mythology and the visionary into the *prima materia* of his personal history. That history, by the very fact of his double birth, locates the central conflict of his work in the idea of home itself.

"When Montague asks who he is, he is forced to seek a connection with a history and a heritage; before he affirms a personal identity, he posits a national identity, and his region and his community provide a lifeline to it," so Seamus Heaney argues in "The Sense of Place."[11] Similarly, Gerald Dawe maintains that Montague "sees his work as an artist strictly and reverentially as the sexual, political and cultural communion of his life with his *natural* homeland."[12] Nevertheless, while Montague's connection to his ancestral home and nationalist heritage is incontestable, it is also only part of the story. As Montague himself observed, "there was too much of a backlog of confusion for an early start [in poetry]: Brooklyn born, Tyrone reared, Dublin educated constituted a tangle, a turmoil of contradictory allegiance it would take a lifetime to unravel."[13] Likewise, the limiting tendency of such assessments for our understanding of Montague's work may be witnessed in no uncertain terms in his "Preface" to *The Rough Field,* the "orchestration" of poems that many regard as the epitome of his reverential vision of home:

> Bumping down towards Tyrone a few days later by bus, I had a kind of vision, in the medieval sense, of my home area, the unhappiness of its historical destiny. And of all such remote areas where the presence of the past is compounded with a bleak economic future, whether in Ulster, Brittany or the Highlands of Scotland. I managed to draft the opening and the close, but soon realized I did not have the technique for so varied a task. Although living in Berkeley introduced me to the debate on open-form from *Paterson,* through Olson, to Duncan, I was equally drawn by rooted poets like MacDiarmid.[14]

What ought to be obvious in Montague's reflection on the genesis of his work is how swiftly the contemplation of home and its historical travails dovetails into a meditation on "other remote areas" whose histories resemble that of Tyrone. Rather than fixing him in a highly circumscribed sense of place, Montague's vision of home opens outward to embrace *other* places facing similar turmoil. In a sense, Montague's visionary gaze at his own homeland is, paradoxically, an act of passing through to a still wider sphere of vision. Moreover, what binds these various communities together, what makes them similar, is not a reverence for nationalist affiliation or racial preference but the recognition that their present trouble is in large part the product of economic conditions—conditions whose political import is implied, though without the appeal to nationalism.

In short, Montague's "medieval vision" becomes increasingly modernist and international within the span of his own brief account of its origins and development. In fact, in both its content as an exemplar of "the unhappiness of historical destiny" that transcends its original place, and in its form as a work of art that combines the "rooted" and "the open," Montague's vision of *The Rough Field* embodies the poet's contrary experience of home in a tensive though ultimately reconciling double movement. To paraphrase the poet from "A New Siege," the ancestral lines that bid him to return find the source of their articulation in the very lines that have required him to leave; that is, his goal is to see home not merely as an object of nostalgia and reverence but as an emblem of his own psychic and cultural condition that may, in turn, become available to others through his art.

An Unhealable Rift

Montague's persistent "lines of leaving and lines of returning" constitute what Thomas Dillon Redshaw has called the "bidirectional" nature of his work, a pattern conspicuous in "A New Siege," though nonetheless characteristic of his work as a whole.[15] Shrewdly, even in an early poem like "Emigrants," Montague describes those forced by conditions to leave their homeland as "poor subjects for prose or verse."[16] Nevertheless, Montague's whole body of work may be seen as an extended meditation on the condition of the emigrant, of the exile whose departure from home is a metonym for the poet's own psychic and imaginative passage, the growth (as it were) of the poet's migratory mind.[17]

In another early poem, "Soliloquy on a Southern Strand," the poet's concern with exile as a metaphysical condition and not just a historical reality manifests itself in the ruminations of a vacationing priest. "Is this the proper ending for a man?" asks the aging priest, who once, so he muses, "saw God standing on a local hill."[18] The priest's loss of faith is evident, and though he is merely on holiday in Australia, his very distance from "the local" triggers thoughts that reverberate with the condition of exile. What he feels, though unacknowledged, is the loss of metaphysical assurance attendant on the emigrant's separation from home, a condition that Montague elsewhere judges to leave them "like animals, most piteous."[19] Despite his portrayal of exile in such poems as disconcerting at best and, at worst, portending an almost unhuman existence, Montague nevertheless refuses to envision home as an assuring enclosure worthy of the exile's nostalgia. Indeed, as he observes in "Stele for a Northern Irish Republican," his father "was right to choose a Brooklyn slum / rather than a half-life in this / by-passed and dying place."[20]

Here his ancestral home offers little if anything of what Simone Weil called in "The Need for Roots" the "real, active, and natural participation in the life of a community which preserves in living shape certain peculiar treasures of the past and certain peculiar expectations for the future."[21] Or if it does, the unconscious element that sometimes informs such continuity is rendered suspect when we recognize the implicit association between "rootedness" and "uprootedness" (*racine* and *deracinement*) and the dangers that attend identification by race. In any case, the fundamental "fault" that runs through Montague's poetry emerges from his realization that there will always remain, to borrow Edward Said's phrase, an "unhealable rift" in the very substance of who he is.[22] Yet if the experience of "true exile," as Said defines it, is "a condition of terminal loss," then this sense of loss is redoubled by the fact that, unlike for most exiles, the native place for Montague does not represent his "true home" and therefore eludes nostalgia. In fact, the idea of "nativity" itself becomes problematic in every sense, thereby rendering the poet a native of nowhere.

To be sure, at both the beginning and the end of *The Rough Field*, Montague's "failure to return"—his suspension between worlds—establishes his place as a poet of exile, understood both literally and metaphorically.[23] After all, his is not only a "Dead Kingdom" but a kingdom of the dead in which the vestiges of ancestry, both paternal and maternal, remain a source of agony for the poet. From this perspective Montague's American inheritance assumes the character of a profound psychic and social disruption. As it has for many emigrants, and not only the Irish, the New World offers a duplicitous legacy. Though portrayed as a land whose streets are paved with gold, the "castles of gold" of an America mythologized by the would-be emigrant, the reality of the New World often disappointed.[24] This was surely the case for the Montagues, who emigrated out of political necessity in the mid-1920s and settled with other immigrants, both Irish and otherwise, in a Brooklyn slum.

Montague's own assessment of his origins, "the worst birth in the annals of Brooklyn," speaks to the depth of his awareness of exile as a metaphysical as well as historical condition. A breech birth, Montague literally enters the world through a wound, the love child of a loveless marriage that destines his mother and father for separation. Not only is his biological nativity in doubt, but so is his cultural nativity. As Montague recounts in "The Figure in the Cave," after his mother leaves "the new world" for Ireland—the "muddy cup" she refused to drink—he himself is sent back to Tyrone to live with his paternal aunts, so he is still separated from his mother by seven miles and the anguish of a failed marriage.²⁵ The wound of Montague's birth and subsequent family life reveals the presence of an ever-widening breech, a fault line the poet recounts with remarkable pathos and compassion in *The Dead Kingdom* and particularly in the poem "The Locket":

> Sing a last song
> for the lady who has gone,
> fertile source of guilt and pain.
> *The worst birth in the annals of Brooklyn,*
> that was my cue to come on,
> my first claim to fame.
>
> Naturally she longed for a girl,
> and all my infant curls of brown
> couldn't excuse my double blunder
> coming out, both the wrong sex,
> and the wrong way round.
> Not readily forgiven . . .²⁶

Montague's confession here of having committed a "double blunder" is just one example of how the idea of "doubling" communicates the poet's experience of woundedness. Likewise, in one of Montague's greatest poems, "The Cage," the father's underground life behind the grille of the Clark Street IRT becomes a metaphor for his own life as an emigrant, as an exile who cannot quite make himself at home in his surroundings and hence comes to find a surrogate home in "brute oblivion." The cage itself is thus the emblem of his father's double life, in which he is at once visible and cut off from the world of which he is only marginally a part, as these lines from "A Christmas Card" further underscore:

> Christmas in Brooklyn,
> the old El flashes by.
> A man plods along pulling
> his three sons on a sleigh;
> soon his whole body
> will vanish away.

> My long lost father
> trudging home through
> this strange, cold city,
> its whirling snows,
> unemployed and angry
> living off charity.²⁷

Though solitary and broken, Montague's father is also a double for the son, just as the son is a double for him: "For when / weary Odysseus returns / Telemachus should leave."²⁸ Such duplicitous identifications between father and son recur in Montague's work, as in "The Same Fault," in which the poet observes that both he and his father have "the same scar / in the same place / as if the same fault ran through us both."²⁹ It does. It is the scar of disinheritance so wounding it undermines his very identity:

> How can one make an absence flower,
> lure a desert to a sudden bloom?
> Taut with terror, I rehearse a time
> when I was taken from a sick room:
> as before from your flayed womb.
>
> . . . .
>
> There is an absence, real as presence.
> in the mornings I hear my daughter
> chuckle, with runs of sudden joy.
> Hurt, she rushes to her mother,
> As I never could, a whining boy.
>
> All roads wind backwards to it.
> An unwanted child, a primal hurt.
> I caught fever on the big boat
> that brought us away from America
> —away from my lost parents.³⁰

These lines from "A Flowering Absence," one of the most powerful poems in *The Dead Kingdom,* not only reveal Montague's psychic pain at being an unwanted child but also suggest the father's anguish of losing his family. As husband, he is as "unwanted" as the son, and both irreconcilable losses are explicitly placed within the brooding context of the poet's double disinheritance, from Ireland and America, thereby exposing the grimmer aspect of diaspora. Montague's mother's refusal to live the life of an emigrant wife involves a double rejection. Significantly, then, as he tells us in "The Locket," back in Tyrone Montague courts his mother "like a young man." Once again he becomes the double of his father in an effort to heal a most painful wound that haunts the idea of home itself.

In its obsession with a primal woundedness that renders the world "unhomely," Montague's work resonates with what Homi Bhabha has called, after Freud, the *unheimlich*. For Bhabha, Freud sees the *unheimlich* (the "unhomely" or "the uncanny") as an instance of "psychic ambivalence or intellectual uncertainty" that occurs when repressed expressions of "a cultural unconscious" manifest themselves.[31] Bhabha, in turn, further affiliates "the cultural representation" of such ambivalence with, among other things, "the *unheimlich* terror of the space or the race of the Other" over against "the *heimlich* pleasures of the hearth."[32] From such a vantage, the complex process by which home and unhomely are defined implies that the idea of "the nation" itself is constructed through a narrative. In that narrative, home in part becomes identifiable by what home is not: that is, "the unhomely," the Other in contrast to which a nation comes to derive the image of itself. Nevertheless, as Anindyo Roy observes, "the close identification of home and identity are ruptured [for Homi Bhabha] by the 'un-homely,'" which "stands in the place of the experience of human location and signifies the impossibility of securing a safe continuity for the self."[33] It is for this reason that home comes to be continually reconstructed, at times brutally, at the expense of the Other. Yet it is also the reason why the unhomely continues to exert a subversive power over the idea of home, thereby making the exile something of an "Everyman" for our time.

Just such a portrait is given a distinctly American portrayal in one of Montague's earlier poems, "Bus Stop, Nevada": "This cheapest form of transport gets its trade / From God's worst handiwork, the botched and poorly paid / In a land of honey." By the end of the poem, Montague's biting portrait of an America that has failed to live up to its myths resonates unmistakably with a world defined by the metaphor of passage: "Travelers raise their bored and famished eyes / To where snow and forest limn the weightless skies."[34] In these lines the world of the emigrant is lifted almost explicitly to the status of destitute Everyman, a vision that has informed Montague's work in more subtle ways throughout his career. This does not prevent Montague from portraying the raw edge and disconsolation of the emigrant experience, as he does in "Molly Bawn":

> Emigrating anywhere, suburban
> England, prohibition Brooklyn,
> the embittered diaspora of
> dispossessed Northern Republicans
> scorning their State Pensions;
> a real lost generation.[35]

For someone defined by this condition the key question, as Robert Jerome Smith remarked in reference to Irish mythology, is always "Who am I?"[36] This would be as true for the emigrant as for the conquered native. Harry Marten, by placing Montague's poetry firmly within the scope of Smith's question, essentially effaces the boundary between questions of self-definition and cultural definition. One way in which one might understand Montague's persistent self-mythologizing,[37] then, is to see his work as exemplary of what Freud called "the doubling, dividing and interchanging of the self,"[38] a process that naturally entails questions of individual identity and of national identity. Both inform Montague's uniquely agonistic sense of the "unhomely."

Such "doubling" of the self shapes Montague's portrayal of himself and his father, particularly in poems like "The Cage" and "The Locket." In these poems Montague explodes Edward Said's claim that the enterprise of homecoming, modeled on Odysseus's return, be abandoned in favor of "an unmortgaged modernity."[39] At the same time, Montague implicitly preserves Said's insight that the divided condition of the exile is defining for our time. The poet as Telemachus *is* Odysseus reinvented, the son of exile who can neither return to nor wholly abandon his home, and whose birth fates him to be caught between the desire for a home lost before his birth and the recognition that the consciousness of being homeless may afford him a painful though privileged vantage by which to survey the world and also to live within it. Thus, if Thomas Kinsella diagnosed that "the divided mind" of the modern Irish poet who writes in English stems from the loss of the native Irish tradition, then Montague adds to that diagnosis by articulating the exile's loss of home not only as a matter of linguistic dispossession but also as a matter of physical and metaphysical disruption. To "the grafted tongue" of English Montague adds the exile's experience of displacement.

"Who cut the long wound of poetry into my youth?" Montague asks in "The Figure in the Cave."[40] His answer is never expressly given, though the question comes to be associated with the mother who abandoned him and "the strange figure" of the old woman, the *cailleach*, whom he evokes so movingly in "The Wild Dog Rose." Both, in their own ways, are figures who exist on the margins of their societies: his mother, by being a woman who left her husband and youngest son, and Minnie Kearney, who was mythologized as a witch by the local populace and brutally raped. Both women are wounded—Montague's mother by the choice she had to make and the *cailleach* by her social isolation and physical victimization. Montague's question, by its open-endedness, suggests to him a widening sphere of possible answers: his father and his alcoholism; the authorities who pursued Montague's father and precipitated his exile; sectarian bigots of either stripe who contributed to Northern Ireland's periodic escalations of violence; English imperialists and their plantation policies; the world economic order, whose immoderate practices portended the depressed economic environment into which Montague was born and which certainly contributed to his family's dissolution. To list such figures as mere objects of blame would be absurd. But not to acknowledge the personal, cultural, and social forces they represent would be to lose sight of the contentious yet comprehensive nature of Montague's double vision.

As Robert Edwards observed in "Exile, Self and Society," "the idea of self based on personal identity . . . plays against a self defined by consensus and verified in the roles and repetitions of social life."[41] In Montague's exemplary case, fate has conspired against such verification through a mass migration perhaps unparalleled in human history. We may discern within the multiple textures of Montague's personal "psychomachia"[42] a dialectic in which the self-verifying enclosure that would be home becomes destabilized. As such, the fundamental dialectic of exile that Edwards defined as existing between "inside and outside, center and periphery" becomes something more fraught and insidious than "a release from previous definitions" of self.[43] Witness these lines from "Ó Riada's Farewell":

> With no family
> & no country
>
> a voice rises
> out of the threatened beat
> of the heart & the brain cells
> . . . .
> a voice
> like an animal howling
> to itself on a hillside
> in the empty church of the world[44]

In this cri de coeur we hear one of Montague's starkest articulations of the human being in psychic, cultural, and metaphysical exile. The artist, as exemplar of that condition, becomes a self so bereft he is reduced to a voice crying in the wilderness, a self so bewildered and inconsolable that even the identification of a dialectical limit appears impossible. There is, for him, neither family nor country. Another way of stating this, more pertinent to Montague's own biographical circumstance, is that he is not only at once Irish and American but neither one nor the other. Like the water carrier of his early poem, he exists in between, though the bipolarity of that fact may be figured positively or negatively. In either case the "fictive water" Montague feels arises at least as much from his nearly "animal" impulse to belong in the world as it does from any urgency to define the self anew.

Because Montague's double wound of having no family and no country runs so deep in him, his work is often acutely attuned to the duplicitous nature of any allegiance to either family or country. To examine the fearless clarity with which he confronts both circumspect allegiances we need to return once again to Montague's portrayal of the mother figure. In "Mother Cat" he constructs an allegory of his own condition in which, by association, he becomes a "wan little scut" who "pulls down air / not milk" as the other offspring remain "fierce / at the trough."⁴⁵ What is so striking in the poem, of course, is the mother's indifference. Placed as it is within *The Dead Kingdom,* mother and "scut" stand roughly analogous to Molly Montague and Montague himself. Both "scut" and poet are bereft not only by circumstance but by an active negation of primal love. Yet the figure of the mother in Montague's work is also affiliated with the poet's personal sense of having been abandoned, and so the figure likewise resonates with the Sean Van Vocht (the Sean Bhean Bhocht), the feminine motherland, who must be demythologized by the poet before he can extricate himself from her overpowering control.

In his poem "The Sean Bhean Bhocht" that is exactly what happens. Nevertheless, the figure of the mother in Montague's work never ceases to be associated with the poet's wound of having been divorced from his own mother's primal sympathies, as well as with the more universal wounding of sectarianism and racism. The mother figure, like the father figure, from whom the son inherits "the vomit surge of race hatred,"⁴⁶ is implicated in an idea of home that would violently negate the other entirely. Indeed, perhaps the mother is even more responsible; Montague has his mother confess in "A Muddy Cup" that it was the prospect of inhabiting the same world as

> *cops and robbers,*
> *cigar store Indians & coal black niggers,*
> *bath-tub gin and*
> *Jewish neighbors*⁴⁷

that drove her to return to the verifying enclosure of racial sameness in County Tyrone. For all his family's history of a sectarianism intensified to race hatred, Montague's father remained in the racial and religious mélange of America, a country defined—for all its failures at achieving equality—by plurality. Despite the tragic failure of his life alone amid the multitudes, he remained for most his life a part of that plurality. In contrast, the figure of the mother in Montague finds a double in his "Medusa," in whose womb "the whimper of death is born"⁴⁸ and whose insidiousness resonates ironically in the voice of the folksinger in "The Last Sheaf":

> He keeps us waiting, until he rises,
> Head forced back, eyeballs blind.
> *'An Bunnan Bui'*. As the Gaelic
> Rises and recedes, swirling deep
> To fall back, all are silent,
> Tentacles of race seeking to sound
> That rough sadness....[49]

Every detail of Montague's description is freighted not only with respect for the communal ritual that unites everyone in the hall, but also with his conscious circumspection at the "tentacles of race" that bind this community together. If, as Said reminds us, "nationalism is an assertion of belonging in and to a place, a people, a heritage," and so doing "affirms the home created by a community of language, culture, and customs," then the claim that such essential associations "fend off exile" gives the poet little comfort.[50] Instead, Montague captures here the preconscious attraction of racism by which, once again, identity is achieved through a preemptive elision of the other. Invisible, though present, is the Medusa, the *aisling*'s ugly and violent shadow/double with its alluring sectarian call, an inversion of Ireland symbolized as a beautiful young woman. It is this same power that underlies the ritual recounted in "The Bread God," full participation in which devolves into "a willful surrender of identity and self-hood."[51]

The significance of the mother figure in Montague's poetry, however, clearly ramifies beyond the communal and psychic allures of sectarianism and essentialism the more intractable and potentially violent aspects of home. In poems like "Sheela na Gig," what Terrence Browne referred to as "the feminine principle"[52] in the work assumes the status of a metaphysical fait accompli, at least from the gendered perspective of Montague's male speaker:

> The bloody tent-flap opens. We slide
> into life, slick with slime and blood.
> Cunt, or Cymric *cwm,* Chauercian *quente,*
> the first home from which man is sent
> into banishment, to spend his whole life
> cruising to return....[53]

In these lines Montague's mother, the source of his own abiding sense of loss, his own primal wound, finds her mythological counterpart in the figure of the Celtic earth mother. Both the poet's private familial wound and the cultural exile's experience of banishment become mythologized into an archetypal reality that defines the masculine desire to return to the place of primal union through sexual intercourse. The man can only raise "a puny mast"—his phallus the most intimate emblem of his exile—by which to make the nostalgic journey back to the wellspring of creation.

More specifically, the man's desire to double back, as it were, to the place of origin characterizes once again the parallel quests of father and son, as these lines from "A Muddy Cup" further underscore:

> And warmly under
> a crumbling brownstone
> roof in Brooklyn
> to the clatter of
> garbage cans
>
> like a loving man
> my father leant
> on the joystick
> & they were reconciled
> made another child
>
> a third son who
> beats out this song
> to celebrate the odours
> that bubbled up
> so rank & strong
>
> from that muddy cup
> my mother refused
> to drink. . . .[54]

Here both father and son find their origin in the feminine source, though for both even the most satisfying sexual encounter leading to family also leads inevitably to a heightened awareness of the male's fundamental separation and psychic disjunction—"man's question mark," as "Sheela na Gig" reminds us.

Psychically, then, as well as geographically Montague "fails to return"; his very desire for self-completion through sex becomes, paradoxically, the vehicle of self-obliteration. Understood in this way, Montague's *The Great Cloak* is more than a series of love poems; it recounts the poet's efforts to exorcise the demons of his self-conception. Hence, Montague's plea near the end of the sequence, "Medusa, eyes swollen, snake hair astray, / why will you not allow us some peace,"[55] reverberates with his other duplicitous mother figures. Similarly, in *The Dead Kingdom,* the poet's own journey of return and reconciliation reveals the structure of another process that completes the archetypal mother's labors:

> The structure of process,
> time's gullet devouring
> parents whose children
> are swallowed in turn[56]

From the perspective of "Process," the "moist lips" that Montague invokes in "Sheela na Gig" that "overhang *labia minora* and *clitoris*" (italics in original) may be viewed as merely the generative double of time's gullet, which devours the progeny by which life renews itself. Creation and destruction are mirror images of each other, and as Montague suggests, only the "absorbing disciplines" of love or friendship or art—those "swaying rope ladders / across fuming oblivion"—can afford the person exiled within these conditions a simulacrum of home.

If Montague's mythic and metaphysical sense of exile has its roots in his own historical and deeply personal experience of familial and cultural uprootedness and loss—a loss that always leads to a failure to return—then we may ask whether his "absorbing disciplines" merely offer a diversion from the world's presiding and seemingly indiscriminate process, or whether they might actually offer the possibility of transformation, if not of the world than of the self whose perceptions create, in part, a particular reality within that world. Montague's experience of the world as unhomely, at least at first glance, appears to cancel both home and exile as states of being that are capable of summoning in him the kind of psychic reversal that would ameliorate, if not redress, his almost total sense of estrangement. Nevertheless, just such reversals may be discerned in the work, ultimately revealing the magnitude of Montague's effort to transform exile from a condition of "not-belonging" and woundedness into one of imaginative sensitivity and profound compassion. As he observes in "A Graveyard in Queens," "there is no end / to pain, nor of / love to match it."[57]

It is significant that this reversal, definitive for Montague, comes in a poem that would celebrate his aunt, Eileen Carney, and his uncle, the exiled country fiddler who was his namesake and godfather. Indeed, John Montague the fiddler is another double for John Montague the poet, as his name alone should tell us. "So succession passes, through strangest hands," Montague reflects in "The Country Fiddler" in *The Rough Field*. In "A Graveyard in Queens" the poet sees his "own name / cut on a gravestone" and hears "the creak of a ghostly fiddle / filter through / American earth." To link these two poems, as Montague himself clearly asks us to do, is to displace succession from an idea of racial or cultural inheritance and place it anew within the realm of art. That art, as the poet's identification with his uncle makes evident, is not merely the product of home but the product of exile. And it is an art, filtered as it is through American earth, that can envision home now only through the prism of exile. Hence, as "A Graveyard in Queens" reminds us, the "true Catholic world" is not the world of men enclosed in a Tyrone pub singing nationalist hymns but a graveyard in which "Greek, Puerto-Rican, / Italian, Irish" commune together. What Montague presents here is an alternative to "the rough field" of his home, bound as it is within sharply defined borders. Certainly sectarianism is not absent among these dead—it is a Catholic cemetery. But the graveyard does reveal a world defined more by ethnic diversity than Montague's mother could accept, a world emblematic of emigrant multiplicity and plurality, and therefore of what Montague himself called in another context "the unpartitioned intellect," a cast of mind that would "declare an end to all narrowness" and so remain open to "the many voices, agreeable and disturbing, which haunt our land."[58]

Though Montague's notion of "the unpartitioned intellect" is clearly intended to speak to the question of Ireland's status as a divided nation, it resonates strongly with what Edward Said has called the exile's "plurality of vision," an ability to consider the world "contrapuntally." As Said observes, "the exile is aware of at least two [cultures], and this plurality of vision gives rise to an awareness of simultaneous dimensions."[59] This kind of encompassing vision of the world as at once multiple and simultaneous—or catholic in the larger universal sense—is present in "A Graveyard in Queens" and remains the furthest backdrop for "the rough field" of Montague's home. At its widest aperture Montague's imagination embraces

> the rough field
> of the universe
> growing, changing
> a net of energies
> crossing patterns
> weaving towards
> a new order
> a new anarchy
> always different
> always the same[60]

Here Montague's own "contrapuntal" double vision unites order and chaos, identity and difference, the history of his own province and the metaphysics of the universe, within a single reality that can be expressed only as a *coincidentia oppositorum,* a communion of opposites—a vision of simultaneity on the grandest scale. In order to embrace such a vision the poet must be able to inhabit his own exile, his own experience of the world as unhomely, and transform it into a generative state. As such, in "Border Sick Call," the poet on a medical journey with his brother surveys home like an astronaut "creak- / ing over the cold curve of the moon's surface."[61] The exile's estrangement occasions the poet's moment of transfigured seeing, his ability to conceive of his displaced condition within the "net" of a more encompassing unity. Therefore, as he observes in *The Great Cloak,* "on the edge is best," for it places the poet like the lovers of Montague's poem on a border where, for a moment, "fate relents" and he finds himself able to "fly into risk."[62]

The ability to fly into risk, to transgress and therefore transcend at least partially the given boundaries of one's inherited self-conception, is the common endeavor of both the poet and the exile. It is small wonder, then, why Montague's first volume of poetry is entitled *Forms of Exile*, as though his whole career were an elaboration, both thematically and stylistically, of that most fundamental insight. We find the exile's flight affiliated still more intimately with the poet's desire to risk in language in the birdcall motif that recurs throughout *The Rough Field*, in such poems as "The Northern Gate," and indeed throughout his entire body of work.[63] The poet's persistent affiliation of flight and song in his imagery bears witness to the notion that Montague's "prodigal imagination"[64] is inextricably connected to his consciousness of exile. The bird's flight, like its call, is the exile's condition transformed from the emigrant's alienation into the poet's isolated though nonetheless inclusive vision.

Hence it is the curlew in flight that surveys the United Ireland of Montague's wry prophecy in "The Bread God." In turn, in "Mount Eagle," it is the eagle's aloofness—its austere freedom before the changing world—that so compels the poet before its apotheosis into the confines of myth. Finally, in "Patriotic Suite," the bird's flight and call are revealed, implicitly if not explicitly, to be the poet's. As he meditates on the gloomy images of a provincial Catholicism, a Catholicism quite different from that embraced in "A Graveyard in Queens," he hears again the curlew's "echoing tin whistle" as well as the herring gull's "claims" of air: "Again that note!" he exclaims, "above the self-drive car."[65] Through the juxtaposition of the poem's dropped line, Montague's bird-call motif becomes associated with an image more common to American mythology than to the Irish lore of birds. "The self-drive car" is perhaps the preeminent symbol of American individualism, and its presence at the end of a poem dedicated to the distinctively Irish composer Sean Ó Riada is more than coincidence. Placed as it is, the figure declares the poet's independence from all that is provincial, even as it affirms an artistic allegiance to both the Irish and the American sides of his inheritance. Conjoined here, the bird's flight and the poet's independent drive constitute parallel journeys in which the exile's woundedness becomes the occasion for the artist's ecstasy—his own free flight into the risk of poetry.

In the Irish and American Grains

That Montague's double vision should be evident in but one singular though exemplary instance of his work ought not surprise us. Doubly born of Ireland and America as well as doubly exiled from both, for nearly fifty years Montague has shaped a body of work that amounts to an extraordinary experiment in stylistic hybridity. One can open his *Collected Poems* to nearly any page and discern subtle technical effects in which the poetry achieves a heightened clarity of expression through the poet's internalization of his American poetic inheritance. Here is the first stanza of "What a View": "What a view he has / of our town, riding / inland, the seagull!"[66] Both in its subject matter and syntax the stanza recalls the poetry of the early Irish hermits, nature poets whose work displayed the simplicity and clarity of haiku. At the same time, the taut pattern of short lines and sharp enjambments that keep the syllable count to five and, simultaneously, drive the poem down the page rings of Robert Creeley's work and, less insistently though no less significantly, of Montague's mentor William Carlos Williams. Certainly Montague has acknowledged his indebtedness to those Americans who constituted in his view "the best generation of poets since the great Romantics"—Pound, Eliot, Stevens, Williams, Moore, and Crane.[67]

More specifically, as Harry Marten observed, after having experienced the new developments in American verse in his sojourns at Yale, Iowa, and San Francisco in the 1950s, in his workshops with Lowell and Berryman and his friendships with Duncan and Roethke, Montague brought back to Ireland "the possibilities of verse composed in the contemporary idiom, using local cadences and images that present moments of physical sensation and interrelate ideas and things."[68] As evidenced in just the few lines quoted above, beyond any individual instance of American influence Montague brought back a sensibility that joins American objectivism with its love of the plainspoken and particular to a mythopoeic urgency that underlies a substantial part of the tradition of Irish verse from *The Tain* to Yeats, Kinsella, and Heaney.

Such a communion of stylistic opposites is, in part at least, what Montague has in mind when he remarks, "I had glimpsed a panorama of what the Americans were going to do, and was able to keep an interested eye on them, a sympathetic eye . . . while using what I had learned for my own purposes."⁶⁹ Hence his long sequences of poems may be read as verse collages in which the objectivist lyric gains in gravity through its elaboration into orchestrations of epic proportions. Conversely, the epic mode, always in danger of losing touch with the *prima materia* of the ordinary, gains in immediacy and personal urgency through the lyric focus on individual emotional experience. In works like *The Rough Field, The Great Cloak,* and *The Dead Kingdom,* lyric intensity finds its completion in epic extension, and vice versa.⁷⁰

Deeper still, we may discern in Montague's efforts to bind together lyric and epic modes a stylistic equivalent to the sensibility of exile. In his discussion of Oliver Goldsmith's "The Deserted Village" in his essay "Exile and Prophecy," Montague takes from the eighteenth-century Irish expatriate poet a model for poetic montage whose most salient characteristic is movement:

> The term *painting,* in poetry, perhaps implies more than the mere assemblage of [such] pictures as affect the sight; sounds, tastes, feelings, all conspire to complete a poetical picture: hence, this art takes the imagination by every inlet, and *while it paints the picture, can give it motion and succession too.* What wonder, then, it should strike us so powerfully! Therefore, not from the confusion or obscurity of the description, but *from being able to place the object to be described in a greater variety of views,* is poetry superior to all other descriptive arts.⁷¹

What do Montague's own master sequences do if not attempt to maximize what Goldsmith saw as the essence of poetry's superiority as an art? Each would form, by its own union of movement and stasis, by its own use of montage as a means to describe its subject, a complex order that is composed of a variety of views. Perhaps so pervasive a reliance on movement as the ordering principle of such sequences is sufficient evidence for the centrality of exile to Montague's own modern imagination. Thus, with Montague we hear in Goldsmith's reflection on poetry inklings of the modernist experiments of Pound and Eliot, whose application of movement, of montage, needs no further elaboration here. Clearly, in Goldsmith, Montague recognizes a kindred soul whose sensibility marks his own with the stigma of exile, a marking to which his own modern historical experience adds an American imprint.

Moreover, a similar unification of contraries appears to lie behind Montague's efforts as an anthologist. In his introduction to *The Book of Irish Verse* he reflects: "An Irish poet seems to me to be in a richly ambiguous position, with the pressure of an incompletely discovered past behind him and the whole modern world around."[72] Montague's insight that the ancient and incomplete needs to be connected through the poet's work to the modern and enveloping quietly reiterates his obsession with his dual heritage of Ireland and America, for in it Ireland's tragic past is yoked to America's modern sprawl. As he further observes in "American Pegasus," "in a world dominated by American-type modernity, expatriation is the problem of the European artist; influence the prerogative of the American."[73] Tellingly, in this regard, he entitles the aforementioned introduction "In the Irish Grain." In addition to being a small homage to his mentor and an admission of American influence, his unmistakable echo of Williams's manifesto *In the American Grain* underscores his tendency to perceive not only his own work but the entire tradition of Irish verse in part through the dual lenses of Ireland and America—as if through the eyes of the expatriated, the history of the *patria* might be surveyed anew.

Nevertheless, despite the force of America in Montague's work through the motif of exile, it would be wrong to limit our reading of his work to his dual inheritance. After all, as he observed himself, Montague has "three umbilical cords": Ireland, America, and France. In the poet's own mind, France binds him to a tradition of Irish writers like Beckett, Joyce, and (to a lesser extent) Denis Devlin, who sought a path into their Irish identities through a Continental exile. Montague's internationalism, and its antithesis, may be discerned again in his claim that a poet needs to balance "the desire to ransack a great many literatures" with the need to "come from some place."[74] Neither the literary dilettantism of a Pound nor the geographical stolidity of a Frost is sufficient unto itself. And as Eamonn Wall observes, "Patrick Kavanagh spoke of the parochial and provincial: perhaps an appropriate binary notion for the future will be the parochial and transnational."[75] In light of such views John Montague's effort to reconcile the aesthetic and temperamental extremes in his work offers a model that anticipates the poetry of the New Irish in America and elsewhere. He therefore reveals himself to be a poet not only of his time but in crucial ways before his time.

"Standing stones and streams are not part of Brooklyn, nor are *cailleachs*." So Montague muses in "The Figure in the Cave,"[76] though to this observation we may add the poet's claim that the ideal method for poetry "is, on the one hand, continually to dig deeper in your own garden patch, in whatever garden patches you have been given or you have claimed, and on the other hand, to try to discover anything across the world which can become accessible to you."[77] Montague's idea of a poetry that is at once regional and global—the final collaboration of his double vision—emerges out of his own unflagging confrontation with the harrowing circumstances of familial abandonment, cultural exile, personal alienation, as well as racial and sectarian division—all the demons of his poetry. His globalized regionalism also bears witness to his work's achievement and its consistent ability to transcend the very conflicts that have spurred its creation through the poet's refusal to succumb to what Wallace Stevens called "the pressure of reality."[78] Against such pressure Montague has exerted and continues to exert the movement of his mind in the act of making poems that are, among other things, talismans against speechlessness and promises of the same harmony he would discern, despite the amplitude of confusion around us, within the ongoing process of life itself. From this vantage, John Montague's double vision—his wisdom for balancing loss and gain, flight and return, woundedness and healing—has the look of absolute clarity.

FIVE

Starting from Wexford, Ending in the Sublime
The Poetry of James Liddy

Out of the Golden Cave, onto the Open Road

Does the writer have any purpose? In an interview given in 1983 to *Adrift,* James Liddy answered this question with these words: "I have never been very good on purposes; I don't see the poet as an analytic thinker except in a very compressed way. I don't see my purpose; I can see the general usefulness of literature in the education of society towards an increase of mental and imaginative vigor."[1] It is apt James Liddy affirmed this cunning disavowal of the writer's purpose in an American literary journal devoted to Irish and Irish American writing, particularly since the imaginative vigor of the poet's own work draws pervasively from bardic poetry on both sides of the Atlantic. Yet where in the bardic tradition in Ireland the poet assumes an official social role, in Liddy's version of the contemporary bard it is the poet's own self-delight that spurs a collective increase in imagination. In Liddy's conception, then, the overtly public role assumed by the likes of John Boyle O'Reilly in the nineteenth century pursues its avenues of inspiration with a more subtly democratic appeal to individual consciousness instead of to the masses.

Still more significantly, when Liddy declares the usefulness of literature to rest in its ability to increase the mental and imaginative vigor of society, he assigns a purpose to poetry deeply resonant with that proposed by the most bardic of American poets, Walt Whitman. Setting forth his own purpose in the preface to the 1855 edition of *Leaves of Grass,* Whitman binds his work to the development of "a corresponding largeness and generosity of the spirit of the citizen," an idea he echoes near the end of his life when he speaks of a poetry "with cosmic and dynamic features of magnitude and limitlessness suitable to the human soul."[2] In light of such statements, both by circumstance and by virtue of his own mental and imaginative vigor, James Liddy is a poet whose work ought to be read in significant measure as an extension of the American tradition that begins with Whitman and may be traced through Lawrence, Williams, Crane, O'Hara, Kerouac, Ginsberg, Spicer, and Snyder, and not only as an exemplar of Irish avant-garde writing during the last third of the twentieth century.

Of course, Liddy's own *"salut au monde"* (recalling Whitman in *Leaves of Grass*) began in County Wexford and in the rocky western stretches near Kilkee, County Clare, before he emerged as a central figure of Dublin's bohemian set in and around McDaid's Pub on Henry Street in Dublin in the early 1960s. There, in his own words, he "stood his rounds" with Patrick Kavanagh, who was the presiding literary spirit of an emergent group of artists and literati, among them Anthony Kerrigan, Anthony Cronin, Paul Funge, Liam O'Connor, and Michael Hartnett, as well as Liddy himself.[3] By Liddy's own lights, the "golden cave"[4] of McDaid's was a raucous, competitive, and wildly vitalizing arena for a young poet, particularly one like Liddy, whose sexuality in the otherwise repressed fabric of Ireland at the time would certainly have brought disapproval from those who were less liberal in their social and religious views.

Out of the circumscribed but vivid otherworld of McDaid's before Kavanagh's death in 1967, Liddy, along with O'Connor and Hartnett, started *Arena,* the magazine that succeeded *Kavanagh's Weekly* in providing a forum for many Irish poets and writers who eventually gained major recognition, among them Derek Mahon, Macdara Woods, and John Montague.[5] In the 1970s and 1980s, *The Gorey Detail* succeeded *Arena* and remained an influential if lesser-known literary publication. Published in affiliation with the Gorey Arts Festival in Wexford, the *Gorey Detail* brought together poets from both sides of the Atlantic, largely because Liddy himself had departed for America in 1967, just in time to arrive in San Francisco and the "breezy cauldron" of Haight-Ashbury, for the Summer of Love.[6] What undoubtedly prompted Liddy to move from Ireland was not merely the collapse of McDaid's charmed bohemian circle but something Eamonn Wall understands as endemic to Liddy's fundamental sensibility as a poet—his commitment to "disorder, fluidity, a sense of always wanting to move on" that exists in direct contrast to formal order.[7] In short, something of Whitman's "open road" inherently informs Liddy's vision for the art of poetry.

Perhaps it is not surprising that in his memoir, *The Doctor's House*, Liddy calls San Francisco a "second Dublin." It is undoubtedly true, as well, that after several peripatetic stints around America and a year of living in New Orleans, Liddy settled on the east side of Milwaukee for the final twenty-five years of his life; the poet's arrival in Milwaukee meant that he had, in fact, found his third incarnation of Dublin in the Midwest of the United States, and his last before his death in 2008. The importance of his American home for his work is incontestable, despite his annual trips home to Wexford, along with his occasional visits to a Dublin that had become increasingly altered since the Kavanagh years, when it informed his early life as a poet. In America, Liddy's sympathy for the Beat generation came to the fore, as his response to Mike Wallace's interview with Jack Kerouac suggests: "Mike Wallace asked Jack Kerouac, 'This Beat Generation is a seeking generation . . . What are you looking for?' The response, 'God, I want God to show me his face,' strikes me as similar to Kavanagh's desire to find the same face in a cut-away bog."[8]

Liddy's embrace of the American Beat generation involves nothing less than a bold act of translation—literally a carrying over—of Kavanagh's aesthetic of the parish to the American vista. And if one's view of God determines the whole imaginative cast of a poet's mind, then Liddy's God is clearly Janus-faced, looking back to Ireland while looking ahead into America. Liddy's embrace of the Whitman tradition and his move away from the strictures of a more insular society enabled him to risk a more expansive and transgressive poetry while at the same time retaining the informing intimacy that comes ideally with the communal network of parish life.

The essence, then, of Liddy's embrace of an expansive American tradition with its capacious, visionary yoking together of personal experience and the quotidian with primal and ultimately sacral energies may be discerned in these marvelously suggestive lines from the poem "Cantico":

> Walt Whitman
> existed either yes or no
> in love/the body what is practical
> what anyone can bear[9]

"Walt Whitman," that is, the individual person who is "turbulent, fleshy, sensual, eating, drinking and breeding" and in his very particularity is "a kosmos," is invoked here by Liddy as a kind of kindred spirit presiding over his work's rich catalogue of quotidian details as well as its ever-present sense of spiritual energy and stylistic play. Nevertheless, the line "existed either yes or no" immediately calls into question that assured sense of self and of self-presence in a manner that rehearses Whitman's own confrontation with "the terrible doubt of appearances," with the seeming irreconcilability of life and death. This most profound of confrontations finds its redress in the very next line, "in love/the body what is practical." For Liddy, as for Whitman, it is the realization of the fundamental ritual union of love and the body—of spirit in and through the flesh and vice versa—that occasions the transfiguration of death itself from mere dissolution to what Whitman in "Starting from Paumanok" called "death's outlet song of life." It is because of this union that the ordinary is recognized to be extraordinary. And so the poems of materials, "what is practical"—the clank of shod horses on Whitman's granite floor, the case of Blatz in Liddy's refrigerator—are also the most spiritual. In turn, it is by recognizing our common ground in them, and in "nature without check with original energy" (to use Whitman's phrase from *Leaves of Grass*), that we realize the path of the individual is the path of all. That is, the poet exemplifies for all "what anyone can bear." In the body he bears witness to the story of the common human soul, or as Brian Arkins observed, "since energy is of the body cum spirit the poet must turn it into the special, but not the transcendent."[10] These lines from "Cantico," then, do more than gloss Whitman's achievement; they open a window to some of the most distinctive observances of Liddy's own work.

Doubtlessly one of the chief observances about Liddy's poetry is the role of his personal life, starting from Wexford and Clare, the counties in Ireland where he was brought up, and embracing the United States, to which he emigrated. It is certainly a noteworthy coincidence that Liddy's parents emigrated back to Ireland from America, for his work is perhaps the most prodigious hybrid of Irish and American literary sensibilities. His mother, Clare, was born in America to Irish parents, and his father was a town doctor in Coolgreany, County Wexford. Liddy's artistic cast was imprinted early on by both worlds. In his poetry, then, we can discern the marriage of Kavanagh's parochial affections and Whitman's democratic vision. This uniquely realized union of Ireland and America is prescient even in Liddy's early work and can be felt in the poem "Personal Odyssey."

Dedicated to his father and mother, "Personal Odyssey" is a declaration of the poet's vocation that calls up images reminiscent of Whitman himself:

> Yes, I promise I will spread my sails to leave you
> because when I was young I took an oath
>
> to make myself an individual however peculiar
> I might look or however far I might have to travel[11]

This linking of the outward quest and the centrality of the individual to the vocation of the poet is one of the legacies of Whitman. Beyond this vision of the poet's portrayal of himself, Liddy's poem quickly and distinctively ushers the reader toward "the million falling leaves of experience," which enable him to declare, like Whitman, that he "found his future waiting in the nearest field." There, through a visionary encounter tellingly spurred by the grass, Liddy uncovers a theme that will be essential to his work:

> the flames I held against my body implored: *love*
> *should be given to others in our brief stay,*
>
> *friends are our connectors with Divinity*
> *as the spirit requires in its journey and return home.*[12]

In these lines, the body becomes the mediator for the soul, and vice versa; in turn both body and soul together converge on an apotheosis of our common humanity, our divinity. "Behold, the body includes and is the meaning, the main concern, and includes and is the soul," declares Whitman in his poem of vocation, "Starting from Paumanok," an insight that is the seed and telos of his work. Similarly, as "Personal Odyssey" suggests, Liddy's own poetic journey begins with a vision of the spiritual integration and codetermination of body and soul. Like Whitman, he will travel outward, singing the materials, celebrating nature and our common humanity, celebrating sex, candidly expressing his own personality. He, too, will become a poet of comrades.

For Liddy, as for Whitman, the odyssey of the poetic vocation and the consequent journey outward to travel among, embrace, and catalogue experience begins with an acute awareness of origins, in particular of the mother. Near the end of "Personal Odyssey," Liddy envisions "the creature he seeks" entering his belly, as if he will himself give birth to the poet he will become. This fusion of the generative imagination with the feminine power to give birth resounds throughout Liddy's poetry. "My mother's body is a legacy / the pages woven from her ordinances," he confesses in "Poem for My Sister Nora, at the Reading," the epigraph to his *Collected Poems*. Similarly, in "Starting from Paumanok," the poem that defines the poetic odyssey of *Leaves of Grass*, Whitman sees his journey beginning "from fish-shaped Paumanok, where I was born, / Well-begotten, and raised by a perfect mother."[13] It is no coincidence that Liddy and Whitman confess their indebtedness to their mothers in poems clearly intended to articulate their sense of themselves as poets. For both poets the incorporation of the feminine, generative power of the mother is essential to the procreative powers of their own imaginations. With Whitman, of course, it is the vast primal mother of the ocean that pervades the imagery of so many poems, as well as the fluid rhythms and lines of virtually all of his work. Similarly, many of Liddy's poems seem to locate their creative propensities in watery media: oceans, pools, rivers, the liquid release associated with alcohol and sex.

Perhaps nowhere is this more evident than in Liddy's "Epithalamion," a poem that is meant to commemorate his parents' wedding but in fact commemorates his own initiation into the sexual life. Reading the lush descriptive fluency of the poem's first section, one finds it hard not to recall section 11 of "Song of Myself," with its twenty-eight young men bathing by the shore and the woman whose unseen hand passes over their bodies. It is one of Whitman's most famous paeans to sensuality, and Liddy's poem, with its dark-eyed fisher boys and the feminine fury of the Inch River, echoes the American poet's fervor. By the end of the first section Liddy has given us an image of "the body in genuine human experience." The lines "I swim, I laugh, I look about, / I watch your freckles curve, I lavish and place my lips / and march down your back"[14] could easily have been spoken by Whitman himself, had he removed his woman's mask and joined his twenty-eight bathers. And indeed, the poem's second section invokes

> The dream bard out of the hedge
> [who] stands on the edge
> and dissolves into poetry . . .
> splashes a young nubile figure
> in the parting stream.[15]

These lines picture the making of poetry as a kind of fecund dissolution, a flow that seems to find its source in the feminine river itself. To be sure, Liddy asks earlier, "What is the Inch River?" "It is the racking songs of sense love," he answers. Poetry, like sex, ought to be a fluid communion of energies, or as "Epithalamion" itself tells us, "the initiation is to transfer sexual / purpose—everything that is energy—into the creative not the sublime."[16]

By Whitman's own estimation *Leaves of Grass* was "avowedly the song of Sex and Amitativeness,"[17] and the vision of sex as an emblem of primal creative energy that also fuels poetry is perhaps the most significant insight Liddy has in common with him. It is perhaps for this reason that Liddy at first glance at least eschews "the sublime" and its intimations of otherworldly transcendence for "the creative" and its affiliation with the immanent life of the body and of nature. From this perspective, even Liddy's landscapes are suffused with fleshly life and seem emanations of a presiding creative sexual energy. For example, in "My Neighbor's Two Brothers," placing himself and his friend in a landscape surrounding Croghan Kinsella near his family home in Wexford, the poet asks, "Does our aura of sex ride up or down / from Croghan / through the natural hallway of its slopes?"[18] And in the early poem "Coolgreany" Liddy's catalogue of observations ends with the doctor's son kissing someone. Sex, what Whitman called "the procreant urge of the world," is at the root of Liddy's imaginative perception, as Arkins once again reminds us when he writes that "for Liddy, as for Whitman, sex is clearly the central part of the ordinary experience: just as Whitman affirms that 'Sex contains all,' Liddy equates sexual purpose with 'everything that is energy.'"[19]

In *Corca Bascinn* that perception extends into his apprehension of the land itself. To borrow a phrase from Liddy's "Katherine Young," *Corca Bascinn* may be said to comprise "a voluptuous landscape of ancient mothering."[20] "I went down to give the / Flesh. Wonder / Land of," Liddy writes in the opening sequence "Shore," which also discerns allegories of creation in the "male cells attracted to the female / by some chemical substance given out by the female."[21] The sequence develops its reading of the landscape through these fluid, often imagistic allegories of sexual combination and creation. Finally, the insights derived from Liddy's observations of Corca Bascinn and his imaginative excursions into it pertain as rightly to poetry as to the natural phenomena and legends alive within the land: "Sensuality so ordered it seems / Like brothel anarchy but isn't" is both an apt description of Corca Bascinn the place and *Corca Bascinn* the book. Just watching a seagull prompts the poet to exult, "By God's wounds / Give me Mick Jagger's fag / Dancing."[22] By the end of the book there is a double movement. On the one hand, Liddy arrives at a Roethkean and even Franciscan embrace of the sacral dimension of nature: "Say never ending Masses, fishes. / Put a cowl on me, Brother storm. Sing low with me, Sister waves."[23] On the other, he shrewdly advocates a Blakean assent to heterodoxy: "The road of sex leads to the brothel of wisdom," he writes in "Proverbs of Corca Bascinn."[24] Both movements in fact derive from the insight that the "original energies" of sensuality and sexuality are what bind human beings to the universal creation and are therefore, as in Whitman's eyes, sacred.

Liddy's proverb, of course, is a playful riff on Blake's "the road of excess leads to the palace of wisdom." The implicit association of sex and excess in Liddy's alteration of one of Blake's "Proverbs of Hell" points to the depth and pervasiveness of his faith in the life of the body, and specifically in the body's sexual nature, both as an end in itself and as a way of attaining moments of transfigurative union. For Liddy, as with both Blake and Whitman, excess and the transgression of social taboos may indeed engender a visionary merger of the soul and the body with an all-embracing procreant flow of life energies. "I'll be reckless," declares Liddy at the end of one of his early poems, "To the Memory of Sylvia Plath: A Personal Note,"[25] and in "Dear Anima, Show These Words," he writes, "I have the observance of the sexual life."[26] These declarations, as well as Liddy's Whitmanesque embrace of "amitativeness," become fully realized in *Baudelaire's Bar Flowers*. Baudelaire, of course, is another poet of excess. By using the French poet's *Les Fleurs du Mal* as an engendering text, Liddy explores the transgressive, liberating, and imaginatively generative power of his own homosexuality:

> Island of sweet festivals of the body
> The incredible ghost of Venus
> Pours over your seas like perfume
> And fills us men with decadent love.[27]

Worthy of the spirit of Cavafy as well as that of Baudelaire, these lines from "Voyage to Cythera" exemplify the balance in *Baudelaire's Bar Flowers* between Liddy's technical control and the Dionysian luxuriance of his vision. We hear this same delicate balance in "Prayer of a Pagan" where Liddy exults:

> Voluptuousness torturer of bodies
> Do not lessen your flames.
> . . . .
> Voluptuousness
> Be my queen
> Take the mask of a Siren
> Made of flesh and velvet
>
> Pour over me rich sleep
> In formless mystic wine
> Voluptuousness resilient ghost.[28]

"Smile O voluptuous and cool-breathed earth," Whitman writes in "Song of Myself," and "I am not the poet of goodness only, I do not decline to be the poet of wickedness also."[29] *Baudelaire's Bar Flowers* is Liddy's assent to both these elements of Whitman's expansive vision. "Voluptuousness" is in fact the most important single word in *Baudelaire's Bar Flowers,* resounding as it does throughout the sequence and incorporating as it does the mirror realities of sexual self-transcendence and personal obliteration. Having likewise been "scorched by Beauty," Icarus also celebrates his anonymity, the myth in Liddy's hands having become an allegory for cruising bars as well as for the mystical union of bodies. Here, in his own way, Liddy sings "the phallus," sings "the muscular urge and the blending," sings "the mystic deliria, the madness amorous, the utter abandonment," sings "the bedfellows song," and finally sings "the act divine."[30] What Lawrence wrote about Whitman is thus similarly illuminating for Liddy: "He seeks his consummation through one continual ecstasy of his own reaping and merging with another, with others; the sword-cut of sensual death."[31]

"Sex contains all," Whitman proclaimed, and nowhere is this more resonant in Liddy's poetry than in its exploration of the relationship between eros and thanatos. As the mystic knows, the consummation of sexual love and the consummation of death resemble each other. Merger, whether of the soul with God or of the bodies of lovers, involves the mystery of the descent into formlessness and death: self-transcendence mirrors self-obliteration. Liddy confronts this notion head on in "Delphine and Hippolyta," when Hippolyta cries out, "Pull the curtains Delphine / Let fucking bring us peace / I wish to be destroyed in your body / And find in your breast freshness of the grave."

This same paradox lies at the heart of Whitman's work ("copulation is no more rank to me than death is," he wrote in "Song of Myself") and forms the visionary crux of such poems as "Out of the Cradle Endlessly Rocking" and "When Lilacs Last in the Dooryard Bloomed." In both these poems, it is the "dark Mother," Death, as conveyed through the images and rhythms of the sea, that is at once the source of identity and poetry as well as the mysterious "outlet song of life." "Death, death, death, death, death," the sea whispers in "Out of the Cradle." It is hard not to hear Whitman's chant resound in "Afterword," the final poem of *Baudelaire's Bar Flowers*:

> Our votive offering is
> To die fainting on our bodies like golden fish.
>
> . . . .
>
> Trembling we have made it
> The gilded ocean in Hell city
> Down down through the mermen waters
> Drowning drowning drowning drowned drowned.[32]

For both Whitman and Liddy, death must show itself to be the purposeful—that is, the generative—continuity of existence.[33] More pointedly, death must be envisioned from the standpoint of the greater reality of love. "Is it love not gender that is / trapped in our bodies?" Liddy asks in "Cantico." To answer in the affirmative is to place the ultimate scope of Liddy's poems outside the powers of accident and within the purview of an unabashed "Yes" to existence. The moral element in Liddy's work is thus strikingly similar to what we find in Whitman: "there is nothing human that he cannot touch with reverence and love."[34] In fact, it must be said that the figure of the beloved in Liddy's poetry is not simply a sexual object but a true subject that fosters the soul's ecstasy as well as the body's ecstasy. As Liddy remarks in the poem that opens his first volume, "In a Blue Smoke," "we are blinded by love and that is the way forward."[35]

This celebration of sexual ecstasy, not only in *Baudelaire's Bar Flowers* but throughout Liddy's poetry, finally brings us to the ecstatic, sacramental embrace of existence, of being itself at its most immediate and incarnational, rather than as philosophical abstraction. Bodily voluptuousness is merely a dimension of the soul's rapture. As such, in Liddy's words, "there can be no going no death / the Northern lights are that pure / so seeing they are god's eyes god's eyes."[36] Opening up his own "scuttle at night," Whitman saw "the far sprinkled systems" and observed "wider and wider they spread, expanding always expanding, / outward and outward and forever outward."[37] This ecstatic, aboriginal, visionary awareness of immanent divinity, common to both poets, comprises the binding sensibility that enables them to hold even the most diverse experiences together in poetic unity when each is "afoot with his vision." But while Whitman looks to Vedic sources to inspire his version of the sacred, Liddy finds corroboration in his own heterodox Christian faith:

> Christ is not the sun
> Christ is not the rose
> Christ is not the window
> Christ is the glass.[38]

This epigram from "Art Is Not for Grown-Ups" suggests a vision of Christ as Dionysus, as the glass that inspires both the communal joining together of persons and the poet's encompassing embrace of life through language. Christ is not the theologian's intellectualized "sun," "rose," or "window." This Dionysian Christ, though not the singular important figure in Liddy's work ("Our lyre-mouths extend all the way / to the four first things: Bacchus, Love, / the Muses, Apollo," he writes in "Kerouac's Ronsard Dance"),[39] is nevertheless crucial, for in Christ Dionysus the voluptuousness of the bodily life and the soul's rapture are joined in perfect communion through the double entendre of "glass" as at once visual medium and vessel. Liddy's heterodoxy, remarkably enough, becomes more resonantly orthodox than the implied or explicit dualisms of theologians in his provocatively literal celebration of the incarnation:

> There are those who spoke and listened
> who said mercy, forgiveness
> so they became temples—not temples
> of the Holy Ghost, that sick joke told
> by Christians who want to have nothing
> to do with Christ's body, His body holy
> only to those who know what bodies are.[40]

In his later poems, Liddy's sacramental embrace of the unity of body and soul becomes still more deeply interfused with his celebration of the divine body of the universe as revealed in the most ordinary occasions. As such, in the poem "Last Light in Clare's Mind," at peace in the beauty of the landscape and enjoying the company of friends, Liddy hears Jesus contradict a priest's denial of the miraculous. "I shall officiate right here," Jesus says, in words that recall not only Whitman but Teilhard de Chardin, who likewise believed that for the communion of the one and the many to be incarnated in the world, "all we may need is to imagine our power of loving developing until it embraces the total of [humanity] and of the earth."[41] Liddy, like Whitman before him, is a poet of just such imaginative development.

"Literature is about kissing," Liddy notes in "Art Is Not for Grown-Ups," a remark that echoes an observation made by Denis Donoghue about Whitman's work: "A life of continuous intimacy, a life of contact, is [his] ideal human image."[42] The same certainly ought to be said about Liddy. We may add to that one of Whitman's own observations: "The known universe has one complete lover and that is the greatest poet."[43] It is this ideal that has inspired poets as various as Lawrence, Williams, Crane, the Beats, and others to locate their imaginative matrix in the work of the American bard. From the first Liddy's poetry has aspired to just such a comprehensively loving vision, or as he said himself, "in the cinema of my life the flashing epic."[44] It is a very different epic vision from that, say, of John Montague, who like Liddy drew from the instructive well of American poetry a decade earlier, but whose handling of the line is tighter—one might dare say fraught—with his imagination's deep-seated sense of disinheritance. Not so James Liddy's poetic line, which is a more fluid and less vertically driven affair, as if it committed itself entirely to the process of generation for the sake of generation, almost as though to embody the feminine that causes Montague such anxiety in his unending quest for home. Liddy, in contrast, makes his home anywhere—Ireland, California, New Orleans, Milwaukee—the democratic vista and the parish wedded together. Starting from Wexford, and bridging the floodtide of late-twentieth-century America, Liddy is a poet who would be part of an American company as well as an Irish company of, in Whitman's term, "camerados."

Figures in the Set: An Art of Transport

A lone man in a sweeping longcoat, his right hand confidently gripping a walking stick that props him with an almost incongruous formality at the edge of a vast prospect, surveys at his feet a firmament of clouds stretching onward seemingly to infinity. He is solitary and pleased to be so, his back turned even to the viewer, for whom Caspar David Friedrich's painting has become a window to the sublime, that immeasurable arena of feeling and imagination in which a person may come to "transcend the human."[45]

Scene shift. The alpine precipice has become the winding Healey Pass across the Beara Peninsula, and Friedrich's aristocratic contemplative of eternity a German tourist in spandex, his bicycle propped against a hulking mass of rock, a stepping-stone for goats and sheep. Or maybe it's an American, his Maury's Europcar wedged uncomfortably into the side of the road.

Let's shift the scene again, to Clare and the wild limestone landscape of the Burren, or better yet to Corca Bascinn, with its tidal pools, sea cliffs, and cormorants—"as in poetry, as in the beginning," so James Liddy memorializes the place in an early sequence of poems. No, we're in the pub—"whiskey fire in the night / Kilkee's pre-discos." Now Vincy is "playing accordion at bar closing time / which goes on forever in a village."[46] He is likewise "Bacchus of the lounge as his fingers stroll / the aisles of Vergil, Livy, and Horace," and here, as in Axel's Bar in Milwaukee, the whole universe begins to flutter in the poet's "taverned" mind. In the bar's closed, smoky space, among the laughing friends, loudmouths, and cruisers of the milling crowd, we appear as far from the Romantic's solitary ecstasy as we can be. This is what Friedrich's "Walker above the Mists" sought to leave far behind—like the German film director Leni Riefenstahl's exultant paeans to the purity of the rock face or the Reich, a cinema of transport. Though it is here, well below the mists, amid the bar smoke and rabble, that James Liddy's own cinematic eye embraces his alternative sublime.

It seems an insurmountable contradiction, the idea that the sublime might exist among rather than above the circumstances of everyday life. As Schiller observed, "the beautiful is valuable only with reference to human being, but the sublime with reference to the *pure daemon* . . . the statutes of pure spirit."[47] Or as Thomas Weiskel concisely summarized, "the humanistic sublime is an oxymoron."[48] This notion that the sublime must by definition be bound to the utterly transcendent, to something beyond the limits of complete representation though nonetheless a presence that calls for revelation, we first find in the Roman Longinus's *peri hypsous*—"transport" or "ecstasy"—the Greek word *hypsous* embodying in its root meaning, "height," the very image Friedrich gives us of the sublime eighteen hundred years later.[49] We find this same image embedded in poem after poem of Wordsworth, in Shelley's "Alastor," notoriously in Byron's "Manfred," evoked, mistrusted, and critiqued in Mary Shelley's *Frankenstein*. And of course there is Wallace Stevens's "American Sublime":

How does one stand
To behold the sublime,
To confront the mockers,
The mickey mockers,
And plaited pairs?[50]

As Stevens continues, "The sublime comes down / To the spirit itself, // The spirit and space, / The empty spirit / In vacant space."[51] The confrontation with a disturbing vacancy lies at the heart of Sylvia Plath's psychically intense and ultimately destructive version of the sublime, and the like is true of Robert Lowell's "monotonous sublime"[52]— the metaphysical emptiness of time as it reveals itself to be devoid of transcendence, the sublime imploded into memory's desire to reiterate "what happened." Each of these, to borrow Keats's famous phrase, is an example of the "egotistical sublime" in which a psychic solitude becomes the prime mover of the poet's imagination, a solitude that reverberates back to the origins of the imagination in the primordial solitude of Coleridge's "the eternal I AM."[53] The Romantic poet's urgency, in turn, is to discern something more deeply interfused, an immanence through which the transcendent might paradoxically disclose its presence and secure the poet's identity, though that interfusion at best only obliquely places the poet in relationship to the human plane of friendship and social life.

The sublime in James Liddy's poetry has a different vector, one that shifts the postmodern model from Lowell's confessional "what happened" to something closer to Finn McCool's "music of what happens." Even when they focus on the past, James Liddy's poems tend to elicit the illusion of a continuous present:

The sun piling on forgetful grass—
village doors opening—
the door of Rafferty's pub open—

Old neighbors drink in Sunday best—moths
they drown in airy warm waves—
a Japanese cherry and a copper beech back from the street—

> The Dispensary House—
> Virginia creeper—the doctor's beautiful wife drinking
> inside—the doctor's son kissing someone—[54]

These lines from the early poem "Coolgreany" inscribe the past as a suspended present—a fullness of time rather than the transmutation of time and memory into some cold eternity. That suspension of time is underscored, of course, by the poet's use of dashes, and so one senses that this mellifluous list could extend backward and forward into infinity. Yet this sublime present hardly leaves the reader with a feeling that life is a monotonous succession of meaningless juxtapositions. Rather, each particular is a cause for wonder, and that wonder includes not only the natural landscape but, even more emphatically, the social realm of pubs and kissing. Liddy in Coolgreany is no Boy of Winander hooting with his mimic music to the owls. Already he is sexually transgressive, and indeed sex will become for him one of the essential vehicles of sublime transport.

Likewise, contrary to Schiller's divorce of the beautiful and the sublime, in Liddy's poetry the beautiful and the sublime "interfuse." There is no conflict in Liddy's poetry between humanity and sublimity. In "The Sound of a Moment at Scariff" he declares, "It's the opposite of boorishness / I say, it's what we should be / when we disappear. A sweetness / a rich current."[55] Contrary to the realm observed in Stevens's "The American Sublime," a harbinger of death, this sublime is anything but vacant. Even disappearance brings sweetness and a richer current "ever more about to be," to interject a phrase of Wordsworth's. In fact, the sublime as encountered in these early poems of James Liddy is not entirely different from the sublime we encounter in Wordsworth, though Liddy humanizes the transport and in so doing repositions the sublime away from nature and toward the human:

> A view of the universe
> of brighter stars (us) as
> it would appear to
> an observer transported
> into space outside or beyond
> our universe of stars (our ways).
> They all "were" now.[56]

The universe in these lines, again from "The Sound of a Moment at Scariff," seems literally fueled in the extreme by an anthropic cosmological principle. The traditional realm of the sublime, the stars, transubstantiate us. Up has become down, as the end of the poem further directs us, now back in the shared community of the bar:

> The bottle is poured again in
> the glasses. Tongues are dipped
> into it, small smiles raised.
> Peace, peaceful direction.[57]

The sublimity of this peaceful direction, which is the human direction of outgoing embrace from the "sole self" to the other in community, is given still more emphatic credence in the poem "A White Thought in a White Shade," a title that does nothing if not evoke the sublime in its most removed incarnation:

> there can be no going no death
> the Northern Lights are that pure
> so seeing they are god's eyes god's eyes
> destinies perfect-shaped white
> and we come to the transfiguration[58]

Here, again, the compass of Liddy's imagination directs us first into the sublime of traditional Romanticism, the liminal sublime of passage out of this life, though just as quickly the poem evokes "Marilyn Monroe high in her moon," another kind of star and a human embodiment of transport sexually charged. The poem looks up again and sees a friend who has climbed into a tree during a drunken night out. By the poem's end we are transported not to the North Pole of so many sublime passages, but "the lighting-up apartment" transfigured in place by the dawn sun and the intimate transport of shared friendship. We find the trope reiterated in Liddy's late work, as in the poem "Our Party Art on Earth" in *Gold Set Dancing,* in which, after reflecting on the deserted West Clare of his youth ("Open roads / no holy places") he further reflects:

> And yet in dreams and otherwise—
> the curtain of the real morning
> rises in slow motion,
> space is filled with shrine
> flowers and even garden flowers
> trees and after a distance people.⁵⁹

Once again, up and down have become oddly inverted through the poet's figurative transport, and as such the distance of the sublime brings us back to people rather than into an awesome empty space that surpasses the human. In this way Liddy's sublime also confounds Edmund Burke's claim that the social nature of beauty is precisely what distinguishes it from the sublime.⁶⁰ Where Burke, like Schiller, splits the sublime and the beautiful into opposing forces, Liddy conflates the two so that the beauty of the ordinary attains a majesty normally consonant with the sublime. Likewise, to use Burke's term, there is a "negligence" to Liddy's poetry, a profusion of utterance by which the poet's voice conveys nothing less than a sublime sense of creation. The energy is sexual and suffused with Blakean excess:

> The initiation is to transfer sexual
> purpose—everything that is energy—
> into the creative not the sublime.⁶¹

In these lines from "Epithalamion" Liddy eschews the sublime understood within the traditional model of a titanic desire for power that in turn becomes projected into solitary nature. At its apex, then, the sublime denies the very nature it aggrandizes into an image of the transcendent because it denies the unifying creativity within nature, and so within the human. For Liddy such a version of the sublime is masturbatory rather than an optimal splurge, as it were, of the primal sexual energy.

Generally speaking, then, what we find in James Liddy's work is a version of the sublime that might be characterized as *relational* rather than egotistical. This tendency to encounter the sublime in human relationships rather than in solitude, "the thing that stands alone" as Keats called it, and even to affirm the anthropic cosmological principal in nature as the immanent image of the transcendent, proclaims itself throughout James Liddy's work. Of course, as a practitioner of Beat poetics James Liddy is no stranger to the poetics of transport, a poetics that wants to give the impression and feel of spontaneous composition. In the work of Ginsberg and Kerouac, poetry is a vehicle to both celebrate and practice the experience of ecstasy, as well as to celebrate what Whitman called "the need of comrades." Liddy's work locates itself within this tradition, though the particular way it foregrounds what I am calling the relational sublime represents a marriage between European and American Romanticism within a cross-cultural Irish American context.

James Liddy's collection *Gold Set Dancing* could be seen as his most conspicuous treatment of the sublime as it manifests itself within human instead of beyond human circumstance. Divided into three sections, the first comprising poems set in Ireland, the second a prose memoir of his grandparents, and the third set in his adopted home of Milwaukee, *Gold Set Dancing* coheres as an essential collection within Liddy's body of work largely as a result of the poet's thematic organization of the book across these separate sections. This is especially true of the poems in the first and third sections, which, while focusing on the poet's relationship to Ireland and America respectively, nonetheless resonate mutually with the poet's abiding desire to discern the sublime in the midst of the human community rather than at the fringe—a relational sublime that manifests itself near to us rather than far from us. In "Sitting on a Waterbed at Knute's and Edna's," for example, it is the company of friends and fellow poets and writers that takes precedence over the austere sublimity of the nearby Cliffs of Moher, famously evoked by Wallace Stevens: "Who is my father in this world . . . at the spirit's base?"[62] Liddy's question has a quite different focus: "Why must I sing the fermented ways / of maiden men and women?" As always in Liddy's work, "the fermented ways" of shared drink suggest a movement outward from the self toward the other, and often with erotic implications. It is here with friends and fellow artists, and not in some remote hinterland, that the poet in search of the sublime pursues his quest: "The radical soul climbs up the wall. / Laudamas Te."

In keeping with the book's desire to locate the sublime in human relationships, *Gold Set Dancing* also celebrates poetry and poets as vehicles for sublime encounters. In the first section, poems like "Tribal City," "The Apparitions," "Mac Liammoir's Moonlight Is Mine," and "Omos do Seán Ó Ríordáin" envision poets and the life of poetry as sublime manifestations of how to live in mutually sustaining community rather than as lone figures brooding away at their solitary art. And in true sublime fashion the community of poets travels beyond death through the sublime medium of moonlight. At the same time, in a figure linked less to the traditional sublime and more to the pub world of friendship, palaver, and fermented eroticism, the sublime becomes manifest in "whiskies that are surpassing kisses."[63] This ideal of "surpassing" oneself through eros and the ecstasy-engendering powers of alcohol links the beautiful to the sublime in ways unforeseen or ignored by Schiller's conception, since this kind of eroticism is wedded for Liddy in the conjugal act of making poetry itself—"literature is all about kissing," he writes in "Art Is Not for Grown-Ups."[64] The last poem of *Gold Set Dancing*, "Casey's Light"—yet another poem written in homage to a friend—reiterates the poet's guiding vision, now through the medium of light:

Light made

Made it moves
light is a star attraction
among a number of field trips

light doesn't masturbate
just throws itself into eyes
gazing at everything[65]

As these lines suggest, the primordial act of making—light—is itself movement, a transport of nature that is to become deeply interfused with everything. Rather than directing the human world away from its messy parish, Liddy's light levels the hierarchy and links the gazer to everything, not only what stands above the human: "Light is trash that stays trash / the kind the muses descend on"[66] to make poetry—news that stays news. Typically, by the end of the poem, the poet redirects us once again and places us within the purview of the human:

> or light is a guy who buys a car
> on his student loan or in
> another era would buy a small farm
>
> being driven through the city
> walking the fields
> you feel surpassed.⁶⁷

Light in "Casey's Light" is a mode of transport, and by the end of the poem the ordinary car becomes a vehicle for just such metaphorical transport on the human plane—it enables one to become surpassed and so to surpass oneself in a wonder of the ordinary. Similarly, in the poem "The Sea Is Great," love is the manifestation of the divine present in the world, but most especially within human relationship. Far from any Gnostic otherworldly light, this light is incarnational, a commingling, a communion, like love itself, the supreme transport of the relational sublime:

> Love is the Buddha fetus that knows its roadside noises
> Love is an orphan driving an unlicensed car
> Love is a car with the wrong plates.⁶⁸

"Eros fires the mind," Liddy writes in "For Jeff, 1978," and "honor is to love the friends that last." In poem after poem of *Gold Set Dancing*, friendship and eros—and often both commingling—manifest an intimation of the sublime and ultimately an intimation of immortality: "Roses petals are souls of the dead. / I reset you with neck and mouth / kisses like no tomorrow,"⁶⁹ so the poet declaims to his beloved friend. Such evocations of the relational sublime find stylistic manifestation in Liddy's tendency to accelerate the movement of lines in poems through quick scene cuts and associations, as in "Wearer": "Mother dies father dies trees and bushes / hearses plumed hearses run by motors / reading cards in the Officers' Mess / rose of Castleconnell or is it Annacoty / they carry the same wept flower petals."⁷⁰ The sublime is also found in the incantatory use of anaphora, as in "Venice Poem for Nora's and Tom's Return" and "A Keening," which like many of these poems is also infused with the poet's wit and humor.

Laughter, too, is a kind of transport. As the book's title poem suggests, dancing brings the surpassing ensemble together:

> It's the figures in the set, what they do,
> how they execute their wins and weave
> they come a little closer than you imagine,
> how they start being great friends
> thanking/being thanked for attentions.
> The walls belong to them and me.[71]

From here the poem recounts the entirety of James Liddy's life as lover and poet, binding once again his "poetry mouth" to the evocation of the sublime manifested in great friendships as well as in the erotic—"mouths, limbs, kiss-talking"—so that the apparently confining walls of the venue transform themselves into the scene of a sublime belonging that anticipates eternity. In this anticipation, the longing for love itself becomes part of a dance in which even the unattainable desire—Liddy's love for a friend who has just been married—finds release in a brightening glance that sees "gold," the unalterable, as an essential presence underlying the dance's own elaborating, transporting, and surpassing movement. Likewise, poetry need not be a sedentary trade, Liddy would have us believe, nor a walk above the mists in the borderlands away from town. Solitary reapers. Leech gatherers. Poets ought to be dancers, figuratively if not literally, and preferably among the throng, turning toward you in a shaggy Irish sweater, with a welcoming pint, and always pushing the pub doors open.

SIX

Two for the Road

The New Irish Routes of Eamonn Wall and Greg Delanty

Wandering Towards

About a week after the 2008 presidential election, a college friend of mine of Irish American descent, with an ardent consciousness of that history and strong ties to Galway, forwarded me a web link to the One Eyed Parrot Dance Club and its YouTube performance of Hardy Drew's "No One as Irish as Barack OBama." Timely, witty, hilarious, celebratory, and brilliantly opportunistic in the best Irish way, the band's performance and Drew's lyrics capture the political and social exhilaration of a remarkable historical moment with a frivolity that is as irrepressible as it is seriously illuminating about Ireland's relation to America and the world. Here is how the song opens:

> O'Leary, O'Reilly, O'Hare and O'Hara
> There's no one as Irish as Barack O'Bama.
>
> You don't believe me, I hear you say
> But Barack's as Irish, as was JFK
> His granddaddy's daddy came from Moneygall
> A small Irish village, well known to you all

Toor a loo, toor a loo, toor a loo, toor a lama
There's no one as Irish as Barack O'Bama.¹

With a playfully shrewd immediacy Drew's lyrics winningly put the lie to a version of Irishness commensurate with the island of Ireland, as well as any version of "ourselves alone," and instead pitch the full compliment of Irish identity outward to a diaspora community that has long been sequestered into the margins. For one familiar with Irish history, it is difficult not to hear reference in the song's opening gambit to John O'Leary, the nineteenth-century poet, political, and cultural advocate for Ireland immortalized in Yeats's "September 1919": "Romantic Ireland's dead and gone. It's with O'Leary in the grave." It is difficult, also, not to note John Boyle O'Reilly among the eponymous O'Reillys, O'Hares, and O'Haras that bridge us to the one and only Barack Obama, the supreme embodiment of Irishness according to the song, the equal even of the iconic JFK. Moreover, one cannot help being won over by the song's rhetoric as it incorporates the objection of the naysayer, "You don't believe me," before it proceeds to elaborate the genealogical proof of the African American president's Irishness in its witty lyrics—lyrics that slyly shift the terms from Ireland to a transnational conception of identity of which Irishness is only a part:

He's as Irish as bacon and cabbage and stew
He's Hawaiian he's Kenyan American too.
He's in the white house, He took his chance
Now let's see Barack do Riverdance.²

As the lyrics continue, they invoke the cheers of the Irish in Kenya and in Yokohama, and while clearly Drew intends the whole orchestration to be tongue-in-cheek, the song is unrelentingly subversive of revivalist insularity and also of its opposite: the contemporary exportation of Irishness as a entertainment/tourist commodity of which Riverdance is the most self-parodying manifestation. With its mention of Riverdance the video flashes an image of Barack Obama dancing spontaneously on stage during a campaign stop, a moment to which my colleague the novelist Kim McLarin (stifling her laughter at the whole production) responded by observing, "If he keeps dancing like that, we'll have to throw him out of the race!" "No One as Irish as Barack OBama," for all of its brash levity, exemplifies an acutely forthright awareness of the complexities inherent in determining and articulating Irish identity and Irish American identity—or any ethnic identity for that matter—in a world defined as much by routes as by roots.

Near the end of Hardy Drew's song, he calls Barack Obama "our famous president," as though Ireland possessed him as much as the United States, or as though the new American president had been imaginatively repatriated to the country of his great-grandfather and bound once again to the parish of "old Moneygall." In a sense, in addition to exemplifying the complexities of identity, "No One as Irish as Barack OBama" invests a newly elected president of multiple ethnic ancestry with a new Irishness, or the newest kind of Irishness, the kind that welcomes back those long departed in diaspora regardless of their family's genealogical intricacy. Such would be a New Irish of a different kind than the appellation given to the Irish who emigrated from Ireland in the decade before the Celtic Tiger, an emigration experience that already began to place the question of Irish identity in a global context.

New Irish poet Eamonn Wall reflects on this shift in sensibility and self-understanding in *From the Sin-é Café to the Black Hills* when he writes, "Perhaps an appropriate binary for the future will be the parochial and the international."[3] What Wall signals here is a paradigm shift from Kavanagh's binary between the "provincial" and the "parochial" to a decidedly more encompassing and far less insular pair of parameters. The insight anticipates the response in Ireland to an exemplary figure like Obama—Irish ownership of the long departed made "other" by the passage—as much as it bears witness to the circumstances of those emigrant Irish who in the 1970s and 1980s, as in times before, were forced by economic conditions to leave home.

Written ten years before Obama's candidacy, Wall's remark is prescient indeed and exemplifies the kind of insight born of his sensitivity to deeply prevailing social as well as literary trends. Born in 1955 in Enniscorthy, County Wexford, Eamonn Wall is, with Greg Delanty, one of the two most accomplished poets of the New Irish diaspora in America. As Wall recounts, the unofficial center for the expatriate artists of the New Irish emigration was the Sin-é Café, located on the Lower East Side of Manhattan.[4] The café had more in common, as Wall notes, with "the Nuyorican Café than it did with the up-town American Irish Historical Society," and indeed the Nuyorican Café still exists in "Loisada" just a few blocks from where the Sin-é Café opened its doors. Wall himself lived for years with his young family in the Inwood section of Manhattan while pursuing his doctorate in literature at the City University of New York.

The poems of Wall's first book, *Dyckman 200th Street,* reflect his years living in that richly multicultural neighborhood filled with immigrants from all over, but especially Latin America and Ireland. He moved there after having studied poetry with James Liddy at the University of Wisconsin–Milwaukee, and indeed the older emigrant poet out of Wexford as well as Kavanagh's Dublin was instrumental in influencing Wall's decision to come to America to advance himself in the art rather than remain at home. Founded by painter Paul Funge, another Wexford artist, the Gorey Arts Centre also played a role in Wall's formation, particularly through the Barnum-like energies of Liddy, who became the chairman of the arts center and "the boss of the literary side," and who brought to Wexford not only Irish poets and writers but American luminaries such as William Dickey and John Ashbery.[5] Undoubtedly Wall's early exposure to such American poets, as well as to the poetically and culturally cross-fertilized work of James Liddy, conveyed the younger poet some considerable way personally toward his general observation that "to the Irish man or woman, this progress from Ireland to the United States is a natural right-of-way which has long been forged by history and practice."[6]

Degrees of artistic progress and poetic practice, of course, can mark differences in sensibility after the journey to the United States has been made individually. For Eamonn Wall the right-of-way to become an Irish poet in America meant a radical engagement with the work of American poets, work that in substantial ways differs from the kind of practice adhered to by exemplars of the art in Ireland. He makes the case explicitly when he writes "to be able to write convincingly about America, the contemporary Irish poet must be able to unlearn what he or she has picked up in Ireland and produce newer hybrid forms which are part-Irish and part-American."[7]

The absorption of "American influences and styles," Wall continues, has been crucial to the success of New Irish artists such as Larry

Kirwan, the principal writer and performer for the rock band Black 47, whose work evinces the quality of a "dynamic hybrid" between Irish and American sensibilities. For poets specifically, Wall envisions a perfection that "lies somewhere between Derek Mahon and Anne Waldman," since from his perspective "the perfectly formed artistic work combines the precise closed forms employed by many Irish poets with the open forms of American poets." In Wall's view, this hybrid kind of poetry, in which "the old themes of exile and loss" find their expression in open forms, "represents an important development in Irish writing."[8] At the same time, one can also say the development of such an American-influenced Irish poetry deepens and extends influences already advanced by Liddy, as well as by Boland and Montague and (to a lesser extent) Kinsella and even Heaney. Each of these Irish poets spent significant time in America, and that engagement at crucial periods in their development has undoubtedly influenced the degree to which each poet has employed and adapted what is perceived to be more of an American management of the line, though it should be said that none have found the American grain quite so enabling as Wall himself.

Wall signals the pervasive influence of the American grain in his poetry with the epigraphs to his first four books of poems. The epigraph in *Dyckman 200th Street* draws from the poems of James Schuyler, *Iron Mountain Road* from Frank O'Hara, *The Crosses* from Lucille Clifton, and *Refuge at DeSoto Bend* from William Stafford. Both Schuyler and O'Hara are Irish American poets who made a significant impact on the canon of American poetry, and their affiliation with the New York School, along with Ashbery, underscores their centrality to postmodern American poetry. Lucille Clifton is an African American poet who likewise has assumed a significant presence in the American poetry scene over the course of the last two decades of the twentieth century and into the twenty-first. Stafford is one of the most prominent American poets to come to the fore in the 1960s and carries in his work a strong sense of the American West. It is an implied but important directive on Wall's part that he implicitly repositions his work aesthetically relative to Ireland by using the work of four American poets as portals to his first four books of poems. One has to come to *A Tour of Your Country* before finding an epigraph to a book by a poet who is not American—in this case Emily Bronte.

The pitch and approach of Wall's earlier poems exemplifies the conversational and deceptively one-off style of Schuyler and the O'Hara of the *Lunch Hour Poems*. In a similar vein, Wall's work seeks to capture the immediacy and verve of the speaking voice in the moment of perception. Here, for example, are the opening lines of "The Grassy Garbage of Inwood," which mark the entry point to *Dyckman 200th Street* and hence to Wall's whole body of work:

> If anyone walks through here from out of town
> he /she /it will hardly be pleased by grinding
> boomboxes, the leaves of twenty autumns and
> every brand of beer can, bottle, and cigarette
> known to the bodega owners of this great city.
> And I agree that Inwood Park is an unholy mess
> and would be hard pressed indeed to write the
> Fall/Spring/Summer/Winter poem the *New Yorker* demands
> for each pristine season because I don't think
> that he/she/it in the dentist's waiting room in
> Cincinnati would like to read a nature poem
> with a beer can in it. No Way . . .[9]

The most striking fact about these lines and the opening sentence that weaves through them is their energy and momentum—their swiftness. What Wall has absorbed, and what he has mastered at this early stage of his poetry, is the kind of supple and propulsive, uniquely American brand of vers libre practiced by O'Hara in a poem like "The Day Lady Died," in which the lines move with kinetic intensity through the poet's lunch-hour observations only to halt, devastatingly, at the realization of Billie Holiday's death. That poem is one of the great elegies of the past fifty years, and its technique of acceleration and accumulation—the line breaks intensifying the poem's pacing relative to the poem's syntax—serves to orchestrate the feel of a rapid passage through quick takes and scenes. Wall employs this same technique in "The Grassy Garbage of Inwood," which is at once a kind of antipastoral pastoral and an *ars poetica* that rejects the poetry of more reserved tastes for a more expansive vision of beauty. By the poem's end, the "unholy mess" becomes "the belly hair of paradise" and "a brilliant world of grass and radios." In short, the unholy mess has become holy, worthy, and indeed necessary, and it is the orchestration of line and syntax that propels the poem so convincingly toward its epiphany, the arrival of which is nothing less than cinematic in the way it unfolds.

As I have suggested, the *kine* (Greek for "movement") of "The Grassy Garbage of Inwood" works so successfully in the poem primarily because of Wall's ability to modulate sentence and line so ruefully and evocatively. The poem's first sentence advances through five lines; the "and" at the end of the third line, with its strong enjambment, pushes the sentence even more emphatically forward. The "and" in the sixth line beginning the second sentence, followed by the "and" at the beginning of the seventh line, underscores the pattern of acceleration and accumulation in such a way that the two sentences may just as well be one long sentence moving the length of nearly twelve lines before the reader hits the abrupt stop, "No Way." Wall's use of slash marks to compress pronouns and the names of seasons further emboldens the lines' rapid movement. By the time we reach "No Way," the poem has already come a very long way and will continue to move forward with similar deft modulations of syntax, line, and tone until what might have been overlooked is gathered together in the poet's vision of immanent holiness—a holiness of the unholy, of the neglected.

Wall's aesthetic of embracing the overlooked and his use of accelerated pacing find equally strong examples in "Junk Food" from *Iron Mountain Road*, "Election Day" in *The Crosses*, and "Homeland Security" in *Refuge at DeSoto Bend*. Each of these poems underscores Wall's sense of comic and ironic timing without allowing these attributes to devolve into glibness or wordplay. Indeed, Wall's employment of accelerated pacing manifests itself throughout his work, from *Dyckman 200th Street* through *Iron Mountain Road, The Crosses, Refuge at DeSoto Bend,* and *A Tour of Your Country*. Thematically, it is appropriate that the titles of his books—including *From the Sin-é Café to the Black Hills*—emphasize routes taken, of passages made and journeys ongoing.

We find technique, theme, and Wall's self-consciousness as an Irish poet in America coming together brilliantly in "Four Stern Faces/South Dakota" in *Iron Mountain Road*:

> I was living in a bedsit in Donnybrook
> when John Lennon was shot outside the

> Dakota apartment building in New York City
> and that's what I'm thinking this morning
> piloting my family through the hollow
> darkness on Iron Mountain Road, trespassing
> on the holy ground of the Lakota nation.[10]

In these lines the technique of accelerated movement through strong enjambments (in lines two and five in particular) serve now to capture an entire passage through time and space, from a parallelism of the personal and historical in Donnybrook and New York City to the further distances across the American continent into the West. The figural as well as literal locale that ties together the entire poem is the Dakota—at once the famous apartment building in New York where John Lennon was murdered and the traditional home of the Lakota nation in the Black Hills. The most important verb in these opening lines is "piloting," aptly placed at the beginning of the fifth line as this initial strophe moves toward its landing pad in the moment: the poet with his family "trespassing" on a contested ground that is holy for those whose history has been effaced by "the four stern faces" of Mount Rushmore.

As the poem progresses, Wall manages to weave his children's interests and his own concerns and ambivalences about obtaining American citizenship together with what he knows best—postmodern American poetry. What he doesn't know, comically, is everything required by the citizenship test. The poem is ruefully self-mocking, though in it deeper parallels are developed between the Sandhills of Wall's native Wexford and the Black Hills of South Dakota and Wyoming.

Even more emphatically than "The Grassy Garbage of Inwood," "Four Stern Faces" creates a fictional present in which the poet's seemingly personal reflections venture into historical, cultural, and even cosmic territory. The Irish emigrant-to-be transmutes into the American-to-be with a family, and their trip together transposes into a meditation on the nature of holiness and loss:

> Being woken one ordinary workday to Lennon
> being dead, 'Imagine' on the radio, remembering
> the grown-ups weeping in late November '63,
> one morning in Dublin when it finally struck
> that heroes are flowers constantly dying on

> these black and holy hills we spend the years
> wandering towards till light reveals a universe
> beyond stony victorious faces bolted to a rock.[11]

The end of "Four Stern Faces/South Dakota" very nearly catapults the poet, and hence the reader, to the brink of hyperspace. Irish American history and Native American history—those dual roads—open to an awareness of the migrant nature of life that enjoins the metaphysical, or at least the ontological. The repetition of the word "being" in the beginning of this final strophe at the front end of its first two lines parallels the two words at the front end of the final two lines—"wandering" and "beyond" (there is also the phrase "wandering towards" in the penultimate line of the poem)—which only serves to underscore that, despite Wall's emphasis on dynamic movement through propulsive syntax across lines, the formal architecture of his poems display a solidity that renders their rapid cinematography and scene shifts effectively secure. In the case of "Four Stern Faces" the formal orchestration of the poem also matches the poet's presiding content to the richest possible degree. "Being...wandering...beyond" is, at its broadest aperture, the fundamental theme of Wall's work over and above its important occasion in Irish American experience. That theme is charted in a journey in which minute-to-minute details and incidental experiences find their place in an evolving and essentially migrant pattern of manifesting itself poem to poem, book to book, en route.

At the same time, throughout his body of work, Wall never loses touch with the specific historical and cultural circumstances that led to his own emigration from Ireland as one of the New Irish at a particular moment in Irish American history. Several poems from *Dyckman 200th Street* speak movingly to the fate of those Irish immigrants to America who left uncertain prospects at home to face uncertain prospects in their new country. In a poem like "A Christmas Card from Ireland" the view is retrospective. The poet reflects on the sea near his Wexford home and muses about Homer. In doing so he implicates his own future odyssey in the meditation. Wall treats the emigration theme explicitly in such poems as "A Radio Foretold: Green Card," "Outside the Tall Building: Federal Plaza," and "Two Stops on the River," all of which recount the poet's trepidation as he maneuvers through the bureaucratic complexities of securing the right to stay in America at a time of restrictive immigration laws. These poems compose something of a sequence throughout the book, adding to the book's dramatic arc.

One of the most significant of these poems is "Hart Crane's Bridge," in which Wall envisions rows of immigrants facing west, as though standing at the gateway to an entire continent. Indeed, they are standing at the edge of an entire imaginative continent as well, for Hart Crane's long poem constructs nothing less than a myth of America, and not just America: "Vaulting the sea, the prairie's dreaming sod, / Unto us lowliest sometime sweep, descend / And of the curveship lend a myth to God."[12] Wall's intentions are scaled more to the human level, but nevertheless the immigrants of Wall's poem resonate with Crane's lowliest as they face the prairies and the west—the journey Wall himself would take as if in pursuit of "the westwardness of everything," to borrow Wallace Stevens's phrase. Wall allows Crane's mythic context to simmer below the poem's surface as he narrows its scope to the personal detail: "Where in the forest grows / the green card? / Is it what surrounds the primrose / on the Wexford Road?"[13] With these lines the poem's tone shifts from something akin to the documentary detail to something verging on the fairy tale, which is what America is for many immigrants if not, in some instances, a full blown myth.

In what is one of the defining poems of Wall's early work, "Song at Lake Michigan" evokes the ambivalence of the New Irish experience most vividly and places the reader in the no-man's-land between longing, nostalgia, present loneliness, and the prospect of a future liberated from old definitions of self and history:

> I walked to Lake Michigan
> with thoughts of a sea nearer home
> where we swam under clouds of departure
> Maria, my father, and me.
>
> I walked towards Wisconsin's waters
> to take wind of some boats and rocks
> a child of the green on the waterfront
> faces of the past in my eyes.

> This country is drinking itself
> working by day for the right not to sleep
> galloping along without comment or thought
> content that some time is at hand.
>
> But here I can sing to myself
> unbound by traditions of death
> I'm not working for brothers or nuns
> I'm drinking slowly at the wild neon bar.[14]

In contrast to poems in which Wall accelerates the relation between syntax and line through strong enjambments and other means, "Song at Lake Michigan" takes its time, moving with greater solemnity through lines that perfectly interleave meaning and syntax progressively through four end-stopped quatrains. The only departure from standard usage is his elision of traditional punctuation inside each stanza, which has the effect of creating a measure of speed through scenes. The parallel openings of the first and second stanzas underscore the progressive action between them, while the third stanza breaks the pattern and advances the immigrant's perceptual and judgmental engagement with his new home, which is not quite home. It is this turn in Wall's poem that enables him to render so convincingly the double vision of the last stanza. There, the poem reveals brilliantly the immigrant's simultaneous experience of feeling freed from the traditions that formed his old self and yet utterly alone in a world that has become "wild," existing as it now does outside the confines of those earlier definitions. In "Hart Crane's Bridge" Wall asks, "What does Whitman mean?" In "Song at Lake Michigan" he gets his answer: the American experience of singing a song of one's self on an open road leading to an open-ended future.

In his essay "The Black Hills, the Gorey Road and Object Lessons" Eamonn Wall reinforces the insight we gain in "Song at Lake Michigan" of the emigrant's experience of liberation when he says, "one factor that excited me most about leaving Ireland for America was that my new home offered the possibility of escape from history."[15] Wall's essay goes on to refer to Ireland's history of "old battlefields" scattered around the island, like Vinegar Hill just above Wall's hometown of Enniscorthy, to which he returns often in his poetry. Though he affirms he grew up knowing "that my home area was important to both Irish and European history," entry into the American context brings him a deepening awareness of another, wider history that nonetheless enjoins the Irish context through Wall's examination of the emigrant motif. That extended history begins with his connection to other immigrant populations in New York and grows until he probes the full reach of the continent. In his own idiom and with his own Irish American history and family in tow, Wall embarks on the open road of Whitman as well as the archetypal journey into the West of the setting sun, significant to all peoples, whether Native or European.

For Wall, the journey westward is not a solitary passage, a song of the self only; it is a communal journey. Many of Wall's most characteristic poems include his family and imply that the family is the nexus of community that at once enlarges the poet's imaginative engagement with his new country and reminds him of his origins in Ireland. "What's solitude[?]" he asks himself in "Winter Thoughts from Nebraska" in *The Crosses*. His answer is "What I fear the most, I reckon."[16] In *A Tour of Your Country,* poems such as "Homework with Her Cat" and "Mother and Daughter Aubade" offer wryly poignant depictions of domestic life, and this inclination remains consistent and central to Wall's work from the outset. He is one of the most domestically grounded of poets, and in his work the errancy of the journey finds security—he carries his roots along his routes. Wall's embrace of domestic life within the context of the journey suggests that such family travels exemplify a communal passage in microcosm. They enable him not only "to imagine journeys my own children would make when they were grown" but also to affirm that through those journeys he gains critical perspective and ultimately a vantage through which he can examine America's own complex and often violent history "of Native extermination and slavery."[17] His vantage is given greater credence in his wife's own ancestry, which includes Native American predecessors. Above and beyond the personal circumstances, the domestic world in Wall's poetry stands as a recognition of a still wider human community. Solitariness, if not solitude, is a potentially dangerous illusion, and to be "islanded" is not a satisfactory condition. That is the emigrant's important lesson for us.

With each book of poems Wall travels more deeply and pervasively into the wide American expanse of geography and history, and as such his engagement with both geography and history becomes ever more attentive and expansive. At the same time, his work refuses to lose sight of its sources in Irish experience. In "The Westward Journey," even as he begins "the busy work of forgetting / Mr. Pedro's large hands" and realizes that he has "stored away" his children's cries of being born," he nevertheless owns that his life would be "unimaginable without the Slaney humming / 'Son, you breathe.'"[18] As an Irish emigrant to America Wall sees himself "doubled in every way." Nevertheless, his poetry imaginatively enacts continuities across boundaries—between Ireland and America and also between the expansive distances and indigenous locales of America itself.

The journey westward requires, as he says, "someone to write this down."[19] It is the poet's job. Wall's travels in poetry as in life include more than touring the American West and trips back to Enniscorthy and the west of Ireland; they also include journeys to Mexico in the early work and, most recently in *A Tour of Your Country*, trips to European locales other than Ireland. Such poems, especially those from his most recent book, exemplify Wall's ambition to push the migrant motif of his work beyond the binary of Ireland and America into a global context. The aesthetic of a poem like "A Rose in Coyoacan" from *Dyckman 200th Street*—"I watched your face / thorned by many winters / become a rose"[20]—or a poem like "Helsinki Sequence" from *A Tour of Your Country*—"Kansallismuseo / sled-runner from Lapinlahti: / six men work to ferry children out across the frozen land"[21]—demonstrate Wall's receptivity to other tonalities in the poetry beyond the aesthetic of the New York School. The result is his poetry's respect for the sights and sounds of places other than the landscapes of Ireland and America.

Likewise, in Wall's poetry the journey west settles in strongly as a pervasive motif. It suggests the idea that the very otherness of places can awaken one to the otherness, the spiritual estrangement, of simply being in the world. As such Wall's poems once again venture into metaphysical as well as physical territory. In his moving poem "The Crosses," for example, Wall memorializes the death of a friend, Don Martinez, who is an exemplar of the migrant life, a man who moved from one job to another across America's southwest. Wall's remembrance of Martinez's life of migration prompts the poet's realization of the relative insignificance of the human place. Thus his friend becomes the human medium for Wall's encounter with the sublime:

You underlined for me the desolation
of these highways: the mockery of
place names among great continuities:
rising to dryland, descending onto grass.[22]

At the same time, the place names, in this case Las Cruces, New Mexico, can also mark the human place at the crossroads of the human and the sublime:

We were driving back to Denver from
Don Martinez's funeral on an April day
under the clearest of skies,
the brightest of light. Under the crosses
he has joined the dry ground.[23]

Wall's experience in the American West is an estranging encounter that places the human journey in relief of what forever surpasses the human. Martinez's life and death bring Wall to the brink of death's own clarifying otherness. Conversely, in "Puye, New Mexico," a climb up the walls of an ancient Native archeological site underscores a profoundly ritualistic connection to the source of an abiding sense of place, regardless of locale or manifestation: "Mesas, arroyos, evergreens call you back / to the cool centre of the backed lands, mother / Of roots, mother of the dew. All share one way home."[24] And in "Finding a Way Home," Wall asks, "Don't you know your place?" and concludes, "my home is where I am."[25] Home, in short, is not so much a locale but a condition of being, the inner parish of the encountering self.

The idea of knowing one's place is yet another important motif in Wall's poetry, though he does not use it as an injunction to curtail one's sense of self or one's place in the world. Rather, the phrase resonates with his poems' pervasive call to the openness of relation. Such is, again, the lesson of the migrant mind, or the migrant-minded soul: "And / everything you / silently / had seen / remembered you," Wall writes in "Know Your Place," from *Refuge at DeSoto Bend*.[26] The poem suggests that the horizontal journey across space and time is something more than a mere passage: it constitutes the gradual and indelible compilation of relationships in which the epistemology of "knowing" conjoins with the pervasive ontology of all things encountered in their uniqueness. In such poems, the historically founded experience of one New Irish poet pushes beyond the situational confines of history and personal background into a wider awareness and scale of relevance. "There must be someone to write this down," Wall affirmed in "The Westward Journey," because writing is a way of remembering, a way of affirming relation, which is why in "How You Leave," the first poem in *Refuge at DeSoto Bend,* the call is, once again, to record: "On the road dodging landmarks of migrating geese / a big rig motors southward to Kansas city & such / are sundry details that must be added to record, with / notice, of how you leave Nebraska."[27] Though "How You Leave" pays homage to the poet's departure with his family from Omaha, Nebraska, to a new life in St. Louis, all of Wall's work is, broadly speaking, a record of departures—from Wexford to Milwaukee, Milwaukee to New York, New York to Omaha, Omaha to St. Louis, as well as the many briefly visited locales across the American West and in Ireland, in Mexico and in Continental Europe. Yet it is precisely through the inevitability of departure that Wall affirms his vision of continuities made across the boundaries of time and place: "Now face East where hills are full of our late season: / the highway on a cold night will remember your hands."[28] Likewise, in *A Tour of Your Country* the poem "The Art of Forgetting" ranges still more broadly over cultural inheritances from Anglo-Saxon lore to Greenland, Norway, Newfoundland, Celt, Viking, Norse folk, and even, as the poem tells us, "birds and fish crisscrossing cloud and sound" in order to ask, "Who are we, did we recall?"[29] The answer, implied by a fiddler's struck communal note, is that we are nothing less than "all of us remembering all."

From book to book Wall's poetry has advanced continually along the paths of geographical migration spurred by his own experience of emigration only to partake of an equally compelling imaginative migration that urges him to embrace something akin to a humanly communal vision. One of the poet's most important callings is to remind us of those hidden connections across our more insulating boundaries. At the same time he has always embraced his connection to Wexford, his original home, even while the idea of self becomes understood ontologically—that is, where one *is* rather than where one is from. His fourth book of poems, *Refuge at DeSoto Bend,* concentrates with greater intensity on the Irish sources of his work. One of the finest poems of the book, "Revelation," speaks eloquently to his engagement with home in the more limited sense of where one originates. At the same time, the world of Enniscorthy, like that of Las Cruces or South Dakota, comes to open outward to a more encompassing vision of place:

> We are bedded down in ring
> Layers of time, split by rivers, united by
> Bridges. We recall old spirits struggling
> Still to climb our great hills, their songs
> Frozen in December's air, these names
> Unwritten in the great book of history.[30]

As he travels in his semi-commuter life back and forth from America to Ireland, and journeys within his adopted country, Eamonn Wall recognizes that the poet's fundamental charge is to gather up the incidentals of time and place through memory in order to record them in a book of history, a book that bears witness to their importance in an order that lies outside the records of history.

Wall's stature as one of the foremost Irish poets of his generation has been well established through the steady evolution of work that stands as a centrally important depiction of the New Irish experience of immigration to America, culminating in *A Tour of Your Country*. His work also stands as an exemplary witness to the migrant nature of human existence as ontological as well as historical errancy. At the same time, Wall's ambition to create a technically hybrid poetry that draws from the aesthetic resources of both the Irish and the American traditions of verse making likewise finds greater and greater impress in the work, as well as greater and greater variety.

"A Route to Dunbrody," the first poem in *A Tour of Your Country*, showcases Wall's deft management of strongly enjambed couplets, the employment of the form creating a kind of modulation that slows the pace of the poem even as the poem progresses, accumulating details and interweaving the poet's ruminations on history and the landscape of South Wexford. "All the Worshippers," another poem in couplets set in Missouri, exemplifies a similarly deft use of the form:

> All of our ministers are busy. Their churches full
> from Bompart to Lockwood. I am walking through

our leafy city, dodging worshippers' parked cars.
To walk is a form of worship as to sit and listen

is a form of walking. . . .[31]

The short sentences that move across these couplets are differently paced from those employed in "A Route to Dunbrody," though the approach here only underscores Wall's ability to inhabit the form to varying effect. The poem offers a teasingly ironic inversion of what it means to worship. Taking a walk is no different from worshipping in church. The tone is breezy, though it turns quietly ominous when the poet acknowledges that his refusal to comply with the Sunday rites means that he remains "a part of the broken world which only at your / peril can you forget."[32] At the same time, what Wall cannot forget as well are the old monks in the Ireland of his youth chanting a song to the sun in a kind of ecumenical hybrid of paganism and Christianity, and if that memory is a marker of his difference from the Missouri where he now lives, it also stands as the source of his present embrace of a secular form of the sacramental: "To cook is a form of worship, / to laugh a hymn of exuberant annunciation." Wall's accomplishment here matches the wider accomplishment of the entire volume, which is his arrival at an impressive level of artistic maturity.

If Wall's attentions turned more prevailingly east in *Refuge at DeSoto Bend,* what we find at the outset of *A Tour of Your Country* is an interleaving of poems about place—Enniscorthy and the Wexford "sloblands," the American West, Helsinki. Such interleaving has characterized the shape of his books of poems, though the effect is particularly emphatic in the most recent collection. If the arc of *Refuge at DeSoto Bend* moves from Nebraska east to Wexford, then the arc of *A Tour of Your Country* moves from Wexford to the far west of Boise, Idaho. It is as though Wall were encoding in the very arrangements of the two books a pattern of crosscurrent and dialogue between Ireland and America, now with stops inside the wider landscape of Europe as well. The poem "Ballagh" is juxtaposed with "Dawn in Pennsylvania," which in turn is juxtaposed to "Midsummer's Eve," a short brilliantly cutting poem about the widely protested destruction of the area around the Hill of Tara, the traditional political seat of ancient Ireland, to build a highway—the worst possible manifestation of the American attitude of expendable culture. One of the most vital of these juxtapositions comes when the poem "Of Multitude" sits beside "Lewis and Clarke: Omaha, Nebraska." Akin to "The Alphabet Calendar of Amergin," "Of Multitude" is a list poem that conjures the natural world in all its collectivities—clumps, schools, nests, rookeries. Yet the poet's invocation of these communities resolves in a single petition in the poem's last line, "Remember me." It is a stunning lyric performance in which the poet's voice manages to enjoin the tonal purity of an Irish hermit wandering afield from his beehive hut.

By contrast, in "Lewis and Clarke: Omaha, Nebraska," Wall employs a tightly modulated vers libre, approaching the cadence of blank verse, to record, as he does so expertly in his poetry, a single moment in time. That moment finds the poet sitting outside the Con Agra corporate complex, where, the poet tells us, "chefs created the TV dinner."[33] At first, as in one of O'Hara's lunch-hour poems, Wall appears to be interested only in the surface details of experience, the thoughts of a man musing beside the Missouri River in a smallish modern America city. Very quickly, however, the poet's portrayal of the scene deepens, and he begins to conjure depths of history just below the surface:

> Above,
> cast by the bridge, a rocking gray shadow
> folds old light into a shiny new envelope.
> When great bridges are sunk in place,
> history, our great brown God, is hurled
> over gaslights onto the curb, then clothed
> in shelter belts—all the way to Kansas City.[34]

The old light that folds onto the "new envelope" of his city was shaped, as all cities are nowadays, by technology and comes from a place that lies, the poem implies, outside human history—just as the "great brown God" of the Missouri (with due homage to T. S. Eliot's "Four Quartets") suggests a power ultimately uncontainable by human means. The poem ends by projecting the reader back into time, with Sacajawea washing her hair beside the river and Meriwether Lewis "naming this world" in his hubris as though it had never been named before or it needed his naming to enter into viable existence. Here, then, as in "Of Multitude," we find effusion reduced to singularity, though the juxtaposition of the poem also enacts a counterpoint. The individual who calls out for remembrance in "Of Multitude" is a man of the twenty-first century who seeks a connection with nature that predates the unfolding of technological history. He appears to be passing away, rather than the natural world. The figures of Sacajawea and Lewis, juxtaposed at the end of "Lewis and Clarke: Omaha, Nebraska," place us at the pivot moment of loss accomplished through an act of naming that does not take account of nature, as it should, in the spirit of right regard. The poem leaves us with an image of dangerous solitariness devoid of respectful relation, the image of a man willing to encounter the world only on his own terms.

If *A Tour of Your Country* begins en route, it likewise ends, appropriately, en route with "Leaving Boise." It is the kind of broad-ranging historical poem that so characterizes Eamonn Wall's work and that he has perfected so masterfully over the course of his career. "Leaving Boise" begins with a second person address that stands as an invitation to the reader to place himself or herself in the role of the speaker, whose attentions move from the Sawtooth Mountains to Thoreau in Concord to a backward look in which the speaker has become so intertwined with a continent and a country it is now nearly commensurate with his life:

>   For you, now, these twenty years
> America indivisible from children's names called out
>   across a backyard at dinner time,
> indivisible from a night in deep December above
>   a throbbing street when, finally,
> transfigured home, you wept in joy the final hour
>   of your wedding day,
> finally poised, you knew, for fondness, responsibility,
>   and due regard from this America
> on whose sheets you stretched, the plough a steady
>   sentinel atop the city lights.[35]

These lines move sinuously in their syntactical felicity and control through the poet's retrospective, not unlike so many of the rivers that appear in his work. The backward look continues as the speaker recounts seeing a liner depart for the "shuttered waters of the sea," then shifts to the present trip west in a rental car, in which conversation remains at once "bright with pushing forward / then backward into history."[36] That double passage is, in essence, what the poem performs though the speaker's own transfigurations, his imagined passages into moments of local history and, finally, his evocation of the lives of Irish immigrant miners who left their mark on Boise with its own Ha'penny Bridge, as if to make a Dublin away from Dublin.

Beyond these transfigurations and evocations of Irish and Irish American history, Wall is interested in depicting this kind of migrant experience as the defining experience of human life. Every arrival presages a leave taking. As a poet sensitive to all brands of migrant experience, Wall's life as a New Irish immigrant has given him the vantage of embracing a vision of "all of us across time" with our particular histories intersecting; the "many destinies we had managed to escape"[37] shadow our lives like alternate universes. Time, of course, as the poet notes, is the very life of the train that ends "Leaving Boise" as well as *A Tour of Your Country,* "continuing, always, to pick up speed." It is Eamonn Wall's exceptional achievement as a poet to have extended the sources and vision of his work on the open road of America while remaining vividly in step with whatever he encounters anywhere, and to have done so without losing sight of the horizon of the past likewise expanding intricately behind.

Errancy and Transfiguration

The growth of a poet's mind, to borrow Wordsworth's well-trodden phrase, can be followed in part by the distance covered from the first place to the wider arenas of experience beyond a poet's original world. That journey may be solely a matter of the quality of consciousness, like Emily Dickinson or R. S. Thomas, or it may be literally as well as consciously enacted—here one thinks of Wordsworth himself, and Bishop and Walcott. Either way the poet's work has to evolve artistically, has to carry those first inklings of poetry from what was initially seen and felt to what was unforeseen and unexpected, and it must do so by continually drawing the line between them and further out again. Like Eamonn Wall, Greg Delanty is the second kind of poet, a poet for whom the *errancy* of the journey is a spur to the artist's vital perspective not only on where he comes from but on where he proposes to go.

Few poets of Greg Delanty's age—he had just turned forty-eight when Carcanet published his *Collected Poems*—have the benefit of a retrospective volume covering the breadth of their career still unfolding, though in the case of Delanty's poetry the publisher's decision to bring out such a volume affords readers the opportunity to survey under a single cover his substantial body of work. Paul Muldoon is another, though a collected volume for a poet so young is virtually unheard of in the United States, suggesting perhaps a substantial difference between the reception and publication of poetry on the American side of the Atlantic relative to Ireland and Britain. As a New Irish poet Delanty inhabits both worlds. His body of work, like Eamonn Wall's, is shaped extensively by the poet's emigration in the 1980s from his home in Cork, Ireland, to America and eventually to Vermont, where he now resides and teaches.

Born in 1958, three years after Wall, Greg Delanty writes a poetry that speaks to the long history of Irish emigration as well as the experience of being a contemporary Irish immigrant in America. Like Wall's work, it also arises out of the poet's desire to make his individual journey emblematic for his time, and its fundamental tensions cross the domestic with the wayward, the retrospective with the prospective. The result, likewise, is a body of work that has grown steadily from book to book in depth, invention, and ambition. At the same time, Delanty's poetry inhabits and embodies the emigrant experience and its resultant tensions differently from that of his slightly older New Irish contemporary, and that difference manifests itself in the work's overall sensibility and form.

The generative tension between Delanty's domestic inclinations and the spur of departure manifests itself throughout the poems of his first two books, *Cast in the Fire* and *Southward,* which are combined in his *Collected Poems.* The felt attentions of these early poems turn to family, young love, home, and place, and they gradually open onto travel and the emigrant's life abroad in America; naturally what follows are the considerations his move to America forces on his relationship to home. Appropriately, Delanty's first book was published in Ireland with Dolmen Press and his second in the United States with Louisiana State University Press. Like Wall he is a poet of at least those two worlds from early on, though unlike Wall his publishing history better reflects the dual inheritance of Ireland and America. (Wall's work is available only through Salmon, his Irish press, which also publishes a number of American poets.)

Where Eamonn Wall's trajectory of work begins decidedly in America and in the American grain, Delanty's first poems situate themselves in the poet's home city of Cork and are grounded more emphatically in the formal practices of poetry in Ireland. There are strong echoes of Patrick Kavanagh in Delanty's early work, as in the last line of "Leavetaking," in which the departing emigrant and his father wave "eternally to each other," recalling Kavanagh's own "In Memory of My Mother." Formally speaking as well, in these first books Delanty is prevailingly a poet of the parish, whose emigration positions him in a retrospective relationship to his home:

> After you board the train, you sit & wait
> To begin your first real journey alone.
> You read to avoid the window's awkwardness,
> Knowing he's anxious to catch your eye,
> Loitering out in never-ending rain,
> To wave, a bit shy, another final goodbye;
> You are afraid of having to wave too soon.[38]

Delanty's formal orientation to the line in "Leavetaking" reveals none of Wall's early embrace of the propulsive syntax of New School poetics, the strong enjambments, the intended inculcation of a hybrid American/Irish orientation to the art. What we do find in "Leavetaking," by contrast, is a patient and elegant coincidence of syntax and line combined with the poet's nuanced metrical sensitivity and his finely tuned ear for rhyme, internal rhyme, and off-rhyme. The cumulative effect is to create a feeling of slow motion commensurate with the complex emotional resistance of the father and the son in the experience of separation, rather than a swift acceleration through the scene.

Delanty creates a similar effect in "The Emigrant's Apology," a deftly turned sonnet that features a scene in which the poet as a child attends church with his mother and a contrasting scene in which the mother prays alone after her grown son's departure. Both structurally and sonically, Delanty's sonnet closes in on itself. The long *u* sound from the poem's second and fourth lines returns in the final couplet, along with the ending phrase, "a front pew." In short, rather than employing more open modes to underscore emotion and scene, Delanty here and elsewhere seeks strong formal closure. The sonnet literally clicks shut with its final word, its sound a formal registering of the mother's solitude and separation from her now distant son.

At the same time, in these early poems Delanty tests his more traditionally formal inclinations by taking in the influence of American free verse, as he does in "Epistle from a Room in Winston-Salem, North Carolina," "The Fable of Swans," "The Loudest Sound," and other poems. For example, in "Observation by a Pond at Dusk in Gainesville, Florida," he writes, "A squirrel gallivants up / a telegraph pole, / skedaddles across a tightrope / of a humming power line."[39] Delanty's management of free verse in these lines is far less kinetic in approach than the free verse methods of Wall's early poetry. What gives the lines their energy, by contrast, is Delanty's employment of diction—his use of the verbs "gallivants" and "skedaddles," which have a decidedly Irish ring. Such verbal displays suggest that the hybrid influence in Delanty's poetry emerges most strongly through the work's conjunction of Irish and America dictions, rather than through the movement of line and form.

Thematically, despite his emigration, the draw and celebration of the home life is strong in these early poems and remains consistently so throughout Delanty's work. Strong also, however, is an emergent "wayward" current surfacing from under, as in "Nightmare," one of the very best of Delanty's early pieces:

> Though it has never happened, you know
> How it feels to fall overboard at night;
> To discover your cries go unheard by the crew,
> Drowned out by the wind, sea and boat.[40]

Delanty's formal management of this sonnet with its off-rhymes showcases again his ability to work conversationally inside a demanding form, a facility owed in part to Heaney as well as to Kavanagh. Beyond its formal achievement, however, the poem succeeds in transforming the nightmare description into metaphor: "It is not water you tread, but darkness. / The dreaded creatures baiting you are in you." As in other strong poems like "The Master Printer" and "Home from Home" from these first books, "Nightmare" is quietly suggestive of the trajectory of Delanty's subsequent work—an outward journey that mirrors the inward journey of the poet negotiating personal, political, artistic, and spiritual allegiances. Or as he reflects in "Home from Home," "perhaps now I understand the meaning of home / for I'm in a place but it's not in me."[41]

If Delanty's first two books introduce a young poet who practices his craft with laudable facility and distinction according to the prevailing practices of his home, then the books that follow showcase a poet deepening into maturity and coming into his own with a distinctive voice that takes account of other practices without losing original orientation. *American Wake* includes many fine poems that explore the life of the poet as both emigrant and immigrant and yet somehow never wholly one or the other. Here is the beginning of "The Fifth Province":

> Meeting in a café, we shun the cliché of a pub.
>   Your sometime Jackeen accent is decaffed
> like our coffee, insisting you're still a Dub.
>   You kid about being half & halfed.[42]

The insecurity of being, proverbially, neither one thing nor the other is admirably evoked by Delanty's precise depiction of the American scene, which is counterpointed by his use of Irish diction—"Jackeen" and "Dub"—and further heightened by the witty repartee about being "half & halfed." Such wordplay and his commingling of Irish and American idioms characterize Delanty's way of registering his own hybrid practice in the art, which is less formally manifested than Eamonn Wall's. As the stanza continues, the confusion of identity turns inward— "the people populating your dreams now are / American," the poet observes, though they are back home in Ireland.

In the stanzas that follow, the poem pursues its exploration of the emigrant's ambiguous sense of identity by moving us from dreamscape to legend—Brendan's voyage and Hy-Brasil—to history without leaving the café, and it does so believably, without forcing its conceit, because of the confidence and ease of Delanty's voice. It is no small achievement to be able to carry off a poem of seeming immediacy without disrupting what John Gardner in another context called "the continuous fictional dream," the sense of inhabiting the world created by the writer. So much of contemporary poetry wants to dazzle and dazzle loudly on the page, as if the poet really had very little confidence in what was being written—*written* and not *said*. The result is often cacophony or melodrama. Delanty's poems invariably *speak* to the reader; they invite the reader into the scene, and upon rereading the poems reveal the nuances of their artistry.

"The Heritage Center, Cobh 1993," "America," "On the Renovation of Ellis Island," and many other poems in *American Wake* evince this quality, a quality of Delanty's conversational voice on the page that can manage folding together serious emotional content, intellectual ideas, politics, historical and literary allusions, and dramatic scene, often with a comedic riff. One senses that, for Delanty, comedy is how he keeps the darkness that surfaces in the early poem "Nightmare" at bay, but it never devolves into slapstick or vacuous irony, as it does in many a lesser poet. In "The Heritage Center, Cobh, 1993," for example, the poem's retrospective movement takes effect with a train ride to this seaside town in County Cork from which so many thousands departed in the worst conditions imaginable. The train "might be a time machine" shuttling back through a modern Ireland "shrouded in smog" to the simulated coffin ship inside the center itself. While remaining attuned to the inevitable tongue-in-cheek nature of such dioramas with their "canned clamour"—how could they begin to evoke the trauma of such forsaken departures?—Delanty nonetheless manages to convey the depth of the loss by hedging "the doomsaying theatrics." He implicitly likens the poet's passage into the wreck of history to a diver who enters the "fathomless eternity" of the wrecked *Titanic*. It is Delanty's management of tone that carries the poem.

"On the Renovation of Ellis Island" offers an apt vantage from the other side of the emigrant voyage: "What is even worse than if the walls wept / like a mythical character trapped in wood / or stone is that the walls give off nothing."[43] Delanty's evocation of those "chalk-branded for a limp," and the others whose silence echoes throughout the American heritage center, is starker than the previous poem, though both evince the poet's urgency to contend with history.

In *American Wake* the Cobh Heritage Center and Ellis Island stand as opposing gateways of the journey from emigrant to immigrant, and together they mark the Janus-faced nature of the experience—the one looking forward, the other back, and both doors opening toward the unknown. Unlike Eamonn Wall, Delanty does not so much move through such spaces gathering momentum and historical gravity as he stands before them in a kind of trenchant stillness in order to penetrate the scene. The poem's orientation to movement, therefore, is what characterizes the difference between a memorial poem like "Four Stern Faces/South Dakota" and "The Heritage Center, Cobh 1993" and "On the Renovation of Ellis Island." In "Four Stern Faces" the poet's witness gains amplitude through a dynamic, active movement through the scene and in memory; in Delanty's two poems history and memory largely rise up to the poet who stands before the scene as receiver. Those differing orientations speak to differences in poetic sensibility, which in turn mark differences in each poet's management of pacing, line, and form. Both are exemplary poets of the New Irish in America who, together, share the emigrant experience of their time, though, poetically speaking, they arrive at their achievements by different aesthetic routes.

From the outset, generally speaking, Wall inhabits the doubled condition of the emigrant writer with a prospective view toward both his life as an immigrant and his life in the art. Delanty, by contrast, particularly early on, assumes a largely retrospective vantage toward that same condition. When in "The Yank" the poet returns "a retuned Yank himself" and is mocked by letting slip the words "restroom" and "gas station," the slippage of idioms becomes a marker of his otherness, not only to his friend but to himself. They constitute a kind of inverse shibboleth that separates the Irish Americans from the "Irish Irish," to whom the poem is ruefully dedicated. Importantly, it is as if such Irish American usage had simply accrued on Delanty's tongue, whereas Wall indulges in the idiom of his New World with unapologetic abandon: "I don't cook so good" he declares at the end of "Junk Food." Where Wall drinks by himself, gladly one feels, in the wild neon bar in "Song at Lake Michigan," Delanty portrays himself in "In the Land of the

Eagle" pub-crawling through the Irish bars of the Bronx among the other "legals / and illegals longing to go back" and cursing American Guinness.

In "Tracks of the Ancestors," in turn, Delanty vividly dramatizes this awareness of a gulf between Ireland and America that likewise signifies a complex sense of connection:

> Along a boreen of bumblebees
>   blackahs & fuchsia,
> somewhere around Dunquin,
>   you joked that Pangea
>
> split there first and America
>   drifted away from Kerry
> and anyone standing on the crack
>   got torn in two slowly.[44]

Addressed to the Irish language poet Louis de Paor, Delanty's poem at once offers a vivid metaphor for the separation of Ireland and America and the fate of those caught between them, and it also suggests that the two poets are nonetheless held together by "songlines" across the differences of prairie and bog, like "walkabout aborigine." At the same time, though often retrospective, the poems of *American Wake* chart Delanty's acceptance of the otherness forced on him through emigration, or as he says in "The Shrinking World," "I sing now like the North American brown thrasher / who at one point in its song orchestrates / four different notes: one grieves, another / frets, a third prays, but a fourth celebrates."[45]

Tracing the arc of how the poems are arranged in *American Wake*, one sees that they are carefully placed to move from poems of the emigrant's life in America, infused as it is in the poet's mind by history and legend as well as the gradual acceptance of his place apart from Ireland, to his poem "The Splinters," which experiments with multiple perspectives and is something of a tour de force suite for voices. "The Splinters" takes the form of an Irish dream vision in which figures from Irish literary history from Amergin to Louis MacNeice step up, as it were, to the camera to tell their tales. The poem constitutes an extended meditation on the idea of tradition in Ireland, though notably it does not include any poets who made the journey away from the island. The book ends with "The Children of Lir," again an evocation from Irish legend but still an analogy for "all the exiles."

If *American Wake* explores in detail the complex experience of the emigrant's life and his backward look homeward while seeking a new conception of home abroad, Delanty's next book, *The Hellbox*, takes a slightly different tack. The book moves from poems about his father's life at the Eagle Printing Shop in Cork to the son's life as an emigrant in America, the land of the eagle. It is this movement that signifies the book's complex orchestration of continuity and difference between Ireland and America. Many of the poems in this volume are not only moving elegies for a dead father but performances on the page that use the lingo of the printer's art both to evoke the lost world of the father's trade and to examine the nature of invention in the son's trade of poetry, which has become a trade practiced by the emigrant away from home. The book, to a poem, is rife with invention, turning sonnets to new effect, and in one case—"The Printer's Devil"—turning the print around entirely so one must read it upside down and backward in a mirror. In effect what Delanty does in this poem, and also in "The Broken Type," is make the physical poem on the page part of the performance actively as well as aurally. Beyond this daring formal effect, "The Broken Type" offers a conceit for the emigrant poet when it asks the reader through its blurred and fractured settings to "consider now the broken type and worn types / thrown without a word into the hellbox of America." The hellbox, where the printer casts defective type, stands as a wrenching conceit for the immigrant's sense of being cast off—no longer "the type," as it were, to be wholly identified with home.

Delanty's thematic emphasis on the emigrant's backward look in his early work begins to shift, however, in several poems in *The Hellbox*. His embrace of the American influence can be felt strongly in the poem "We Will Not Play the Harp Backward Now, No," which answers Marianne Moore's "Spenser's Ireland" by using the syllabic line adopted by that poem:

> We, a bunch of greencard Irish,
>   vamp it under the cathedral arches
>   of Brooklyn bridge that's strung like a harp.

> But we'll not play
> the harp backward now, harping on
> > about those Micks who fashioned
> this American wind-lyre
> and about the scores
> > who landed on Ellis Island
> or, like us, at Kennedy and dispersed
> through this open sesame land
>
> in different directions like the rays
> of Liberty's crown. . . .⁴⁶

Thematically Delanty's poem dovetails neatly with Wall's "Hart Crane's Bridge." Both poems take account of the New Irish immigrants within the context of other immigrant populations, and like Wall's poem Delanty's acknowledges the dispersal of the newcomers across America. If Wall's poem finds its shape through a tightly managed American free-verse line, Delanty's conversational tone finds conducive form in Moore's syllabic line. Yet even while Delanty situates the poem both thematically and formally in the American grain, the poem's metaphors—the bridge span as harp, the figure of Earl Gerald from Irish legend that Moore herself drew on for her poem—recall their Irish sources. This is no fault of the poem and no fault of the poet's orientation to America or his art. Rather, for Delanty, the trick (as the poem says) of "turning ourselves into ourselves" personally as well as artistically requires in his case a strong dose of Irish tradition even within the relatively "anonymous," anything goes context of America.

That said, in a poem like "Ligature," in which Delanty addresses Walt Whitman at the site of the *Eagle* newspaper in Brooklyn, where the poet of the American open road first set *Leaves of Grass* to type, the perspective turns toward "the composing room of America," where, again, "it is time to set our own lives down . . . with our own measure."⁴⁷ As such, in addition to being exemplary of the New Irish experience in America, the poems of *The Hellbox* are also about their own artistry—about the poet's emergence from the cultural, personal, and artistic sources of home into a new "type" of person and poet, one who is more radically self-composed.

If Seamus Heaney is correct when he suggests that the line and the life are intimately related, then the poems of *The Hellbox* and Delanty's subsequent collections register the change from his early work. For example, the longer line employed in a poem like "Striped Ink," or the shorter free-verse lines of "^" and "Bad Impression" reveal a poet willing to translate something of the American grain into the compositional space of Ireland as well. The more expansive lines of "The Lost Way" examine profoundly Delanty's self-conscious equivocations about his doubled identity as Irish and American:

> In our rent-a-car Chevrolet Troubador
> I seanchaí-ed how I ate the lotus of emigration,
> never in a decade of Sundays imagining I'd be here
> to stay, wincing at the word *emigrant*
> that, once uttered, seems to filch me of myself
> the way they say a camera steals a soul.
> And there is the stranger word *immigrant*
> that I've become and that my tongue that night
> stuck on, the stammer itself
> intimating the meaning.[48]

At once alluding to Odysseus, the paradigmatic exile, and echoing Montague's "A Grafted Tongue," these lines trace the translation, as it were, from "emigrant" to "immigrant" through the trope of changing from one word into the next. At the same time, Delanty's ideal appears to be to seek a more contentious and combustible formal mixture of Irish and American than that which we find in Eamonn Wall's poetry.

This combustible admixture of Irish and American modes is present, in particular, in the title poem of *The Hellbox,* in which Irish diction and Cork slang mixes with an expansive American cadence running down the page. That vocal admixture comes more and more to characterize Delanty's poems, and it speaks to the inclusive art he seeks to achieve. "The Hellbox," as an autobiographical poem about Delanty's arrival in America and the personal circumstances leading him to stay put here rather than return, adopts not only an expansive cadence but an expansive arc of inclusion as well. At times he appears to dismiss the past and Irish tradition, especially the Irish emigrant tradition of the

"American wake," as when he states, "But to hell with all that American waking, that bull, / that myth-making crap." Other times he appears likewise resistant to his transformed American self, as when he observes, self-consciously, "Look, even my own poems are getting blasted bigger."[49] The result is a vision of the emigrant/immigrant as a kind of monstrosity:

> I'm cross-fertilizing my regular, leprechaun-small strain
> with the crazy American variant, as if the Irish to-mat-o
> was crossed with the whale of the Yankee to-mate-o
> that itself looks like one of those radioactive mutants
> of Chernobyl. . . .[50]

As such, as a poem "The Hellbox" must be understood as an *ars poetica* in which the poet declares the inherent theatricality of the transformation from Irish to Irish American:

> All I want is not simply to parrot American voices,
>   reminding me of how the immigrants learned
> a new tongue, mimicking gramophone records
>   or following theatre stars from show to show,
> pronouncing actors' lines, always a fraction behind,
>   till they knew every word. . . .[51]

Instead of parroting, Delanty spurs himself through multiple vocal exercises, from those as performative as the actors he invokes above, through a bit of self-conscious, self-mocking mimicry, to "the cocky young cleric at St. Brendan's door, / refusing to leave till I've played the music of the world." To be sure, we find "cockiness" in Delanty's poems, or more rightly an engaging confidence in the "mutant" if not hybrid voice, though that voice is anything but standoffish. It is inviting. The binding motif and ambition of Delanty's work from *The Hellbox* onward reveals a desire to play the music of the world, both intimately in poems of domestic observance and more encompassingly in poems of searching migration.

In his two most recent collections, *The Blind Stitch* and *The Ship of Birth,* Delanty's ambition, like Wall's, is to hold within a single thought the domestic and the errant. Also like in Wall's poetry, the geographical preoccupations of the work advance significantly beyond the dual imaginative poles of Ireland and America. Nevertheless, poems in *The Blind Stitch,* like "The Speakeasy Oath," "The Memory Quilt," and "Tagging the Stealer," explore what by now is Delanty's inhabited territory of emigrant life between his two homes, though these poems refuse to settle into complacent patterns. Each is an address—to an Irish poet-friend, to an American poet-friend, and to an American seamstress-friend—in which the poet with characteristic verve and wit manages to portray human affection without affectation or sentimentality while at the same time articulating his art's ideals. "Give us each just once / a poem equal to that unknown man's talking hand," the poet muses, watching the sign language of the catcher to the pitcher during a baseball game. It is a kind of shibboleth for reading America as well as bringing its language into his art.

Here, again, we find Delanty's interest in language as a signifier of culture, just as in *The Hellbox* we saw typeface itself as a sign highlighting the luminal, shifting sense of identity, the transitional signification of self from immigrant to emigrant. "Tagging the Stealer," however, addresses itself to Canadian American poet David Cavanagh, and as such the poem-as-address offers the experience of a shared language between friends. In addressing his poet-friend, Delanty compounds one Americanism after another in his description of the ballgame:

> How often have we waited for the magic
> in the hands of some flipper throwing a slider,
> sinker, jug-handle, submarine, knuckle or screwball?
> If we're lucky, the slugger hits a daisy-cutter
> with a choke-up or connects with a Baltimore chop
> and a ball hawk catches a can of corn. . .[52]

By incorporating the ball game's American lingo the poem offers itself as a kind of play space of communication and friendly communion across difference. Delanty's poem is thus not so much a portrait of a day at the baseball game with a friend as it is a playful inquiry into shared connection across linguistic and cultural difference.

We find the poet probing the deep significance of "the lingo" in "The Speakeasy Oath" as well, written to Irish-language poet and fellow Corkman Liam Ó Muirthile. Composed largely in a lively marshalling of Cork slang, Irish, and English, the poem offers itself as an ideal of linguistic hybridity in which "speakeasy" is a double entendre for an American watering hole and a mythical polyglot in which the localities of usage become an enduring conjunction between friends across distances in "the dark eternity of America." We sense that conjunction of friends again in "The Memory Quilt," an elegy he calls a "crochet of words" in the image of a dead friend's gift to the poet.[53]

The conceit that weaves the poems of *The Blind Stitch* together, however, begins with the thread that appears in the first poem, "To My Mother, Eileen," and finishes with the final poem, "The Blind Stitch," a love poem for his wife. The book unfolds between two movingly depicted domestic scenes, though Delanty's poems about India are what distinguish this collection. These add a still more worldly scope to the work and extend the poet's imaginative engagement beyond the dual poles of Ireland and America. As Delanty's American poems suggest, *The Blind Stitch* is a book of correspondences. "Like so many, I grew up in a town with a beloved river the color of slime / I took for the natural color of all waterways," Delanty muses humorously in "Homage to the God of Pollution in Brooklyn."[54]

In the poems of the collection that wander further afield than Ireland and America we find still more wide-ranging correspondences. Delanty finds in India and Sri Lanka a kind of Asian objective correlative to Cork (there is even an "Emerald Isle"), though poems like "Behold the Brahmany Kite" engage that still more distant world on its own terms, which is something one expects of a Delanty poem—the world embraced as it is given but nonetheless reflected through the prism of the poet's idiosyncratic sight:

> And, in my way, I too believe in the kasti—the sacred
>   thread—of the elements
> stitching us all together, and would rather the kite pluck
>   the flesh from my bones
> than I be laid in the dolled-up box of the West.[55]

In these deftly modulated lines of free verse Delanty steps outside of the polarity between Ireland and America that so animates his work, like Wall's, and in so doing he enlarges the scope of his poetry by casting his art even further afield than the binary terms "immigrant" and "emigrant." The errancy of his passage out has come to embrace the wider world.

Nevertheless, what I have been calling Delanty's waywardness and errancy is not really the antithesis of his poetry's "homelier" impulses, but it is, as it were, the flipside of the domestic coin, the yang to its yin. (Masculine and feminine poles also interplay in Delanty's work—his father is the presiding spirit of *The Hellbox,* his mother and his wife the presiding spirits of *The Blind Stitch.*) The title of *The Ship of Birth* embodies the idea of the errant, the wayward, the journey, but that journey arrives perforce in the domestic world, which is ultimately the world we all share in spite of the separate realms of our private lives. In this world, where journeys and arrivals are at once miracles in themselves and harbingers of wider realities, the birth of the poet's son in the poem "The Alien" bespeaks the emigrant nature of every life:

> I'm back again scrutinising the Milky Way
>   of your ultrasound, scanning the dark
>   matter, the nothingness, that now the heads say
>   is chockablock with quarks and squarks,
> gravitons and gravatini, photons & photinis.[56]

If "The Alien" joins together beautifully the seemingly contrasting impulses of Delanty's work, then it also exemplifies one of the most appealing facets of this poet's voice—its welcoming quality that at the same time doesn't leave him at a loss for wit and imaginative play.

The grand organizing structure of *The Ship of Birth* is, in fact, the impending birth of the poet's son, and the poems as a sequence follow the process of his emergence closely. As "The Alien" establishes at the outset, the book's guiding conceit is the ship of birth as a kind of spaceship. The child arrives at this earth gradually in the capsule of the mother's womb. Of course, the conceit of the ship's passage is not lost on Delanty, and consequently the alien voyage here resonates with other emigrant voyages. His son will be an immigrant not only to America, like his father, but to this world. As such *The Ship of Birth* presses the emigrant motif into the service of the poet's ontological concern as well as his historical and cultural concerns. We saw a similar evolution in Eamonn Wall's work, though the aesthetic temperament of the two poets remains quite different. We sense the difference in these lines from the book's title poem:

> Listen, the horns, the horns are blowing,
> trumpeting you, our dear humacorn,
> beckoning you onto the ark
>   out of your first watery dark.[57]

Here, Delanty playfully evokes the son's embarkation in a figural double vision that enjoins wordplay, the fabulous, the biblical, and the evolutionary in equal measure. His deployment of line here keeps the restrained cadence of more traditional modes and even uses a perfectly rhymed couplet to underscore closure at this moment in the poem, an impulse different from Wall's propulsive energy down the page.

Delanty's enrichment of the formal sense emerges through his tonal adjustments at once conversational and filled with imaginative play. Several sonnets in the book, among them "According to the Nepalese," "The God of Drymouths," "The Arrival," and "The Coronation," demonstrate that Delanty's expertise in this tight rhetorical form has advanced in large measure through his ability to adapt the flexibility of the American line to the strict requirements of the traditional sonnet structure. Often this means adjusting the rhyme scheme according to improvisational need. For example, in "According to the Nepalese" the rhyme scheme proceeds as follows: *abccbaddefefgg*—not a strictly traditional sonnet. The poem opens with a strong enjambment underscoring the sentence's conversational syntax:

> The kith and kin souls of those who've gone hover
>   above the couple making love, elbow into
> the woman's underworld, drinking the man's buttermilk
>   in their ghostly death-drought to recast our ilk.[58]

The sway of these lines follows suit through the remainder of the poem, long lines offset by shorter lines, so the poem moves its invocations of the dead, including "all the Danny Boys" of the poet's paternal ancestors, who will shape the invisible code of the child's features as well as his temperament—his *duchas,* the physiological cast of his natural inclinations emerging from the past, a heritage in the most intimate sense. For the Nepalese, so for the Irish.

Delanty's feel for the weave of lines, long and short, and his increasing use of the page's space to register shifts in tone and music in these most recent poems suggest the poet has internalized some of the practices of American open-form poetics, what Charles Olson dubbed "projective verse." In projective verse the whole page is used as a way of registering a poem's complex music, and not just variations within the metrical line. Delanty has not embraced the program wholeheartedly, but the line adjustments relative to the page in the poems of *The Ship of Birth* reveal a subtle influence. Nevertheless, Delanty has not abandoned his connection to more traditional practice—he can still complete the requirements of a sonnet for strong and haunting closure: "We toast you now, our ancient child risen from the tomb, / kidnapped by a band of ghosts, bound in your dark room."[59]

As "For the Nepalese" exemplifies, *The Ship of Birth* is a book about miraculous arrivals. At the same time it is a book of departures. The ship of birth is also, inevitably, a coffin ship. Interlaced with the poems celebrating the birth of his son, therefore, are moving elegies for Delanty's mother, whose slow passage out of this world from cancer coincided with the child's passage into it. These elegies are continued in the section of new work, titled "Aceldama," in which also appear a number of political poems about our disastrous treatment of the environment, among other brutal realities of our time. In fact, a number of overtly political poems are scattered through Delanty's work, like those in the pamphlet *Children of Chernobyl.* Again, Delanty's progress as a poet has been to extend the range of his concern, so it is not surprising that his early political poetry has expanded to more vocal and pointed engagements with contemporary issues. Still, he remains a poet of more intimate affiliations as well. The poems written for his mother's death are deeply moving in that regard, though clearly Delanty intends these poems to be resonant beyond his own singular loss. This is especially true of the poem "Aceldama."

"Aceldama" refers to "the field of blood" purchased by the priests and elders with Judas's thirty pieces of silver thrown down in the temple after he betrayed Christ (Matthew 27:5–8), and the poem of that title powerfully changes the context and resonance of the work that comes before:

> We drove down what seemed the curve
> of the earth, sandwiched in our Ford Anglia.
> We were happy as the colors of our beachball,
> a careless car full of mirth and singalong songs,
> songs that were mostly as sappy
> as the soppy tomato sandwiches sprinkled with sand,
> which is why they're called sandwiches our father said,
> sandwiched himself now in the ground between his mother
> and ours. What's the meaning of dead?[60]

The poem's first sentence places us at once in the domestic car and on the curve of the wider world and then moves us seamlessly line by line through the evocatively digressive thoughts of the poet recalling the scene. The syntactical movement through the lines is deceptively simple and brilliantly deft. We come at once to be in the poet's mind and in the child's, both arriving at the ultimate irrevocable question. From there the poem moves us more intimately inside the domestic bubble of the Delantys' Ford Anglia: the mother serves as a kind of guide to the children and the now recollecting poet as they survey a local "hill field" where the dead have been buried without recognition or headstone. The mother is an ordinary woman transformed quietly by the poet into the family's Virgil, explaining the nature of this remote field, which has become an image of the lost world, despite all its beautiful cities. And what she awakens in the children, the poet, and the reader is not only the sense of human loneliness that "shrouds" the family's "bright time" and joins everyone together on the journey through birth and life into death, but the transfiguring presence of compassion. Delanty's music in this poem—the last in his *Collected*—has become the measure of this transfiguration.

Both Eamonn Wall and Greg Delanty would have us encounter in their poetry a world that transcends the social, historical, and cultural occasion of New Irish writing. Though each began his journey in the art as a New Irish poet who sought to reconcile his experience as an emigrant from Ireland and an immigrant to America, both had to negotiate a dual literary inheritance in order for the work to grow in mastery and significance. While Wall and Delanty negotiate the dual inheritance of Ireland and America differently, their journeys have brought them both to a more encompassing vantage of history, as well as a deeper appreciation of what is at stake in the art within and beyond the occasions of circumstance. For each the experience of "exile" broadly conceived rises in significance to an ontological condition and not merely a sociological one. In a world increasingly defined as much by passage as by place their work stands as exemplary beyond the confines of Ireland and America.

SEVEN

The Parish and Lost America
The Witness of Michael Coady's *All Souls*

First Worlds

In the Brooklyn neighborhood where I grew up, one locale that most impressed its oddly indigenous vitality into my sense of place and self was Bay Ridge Post 157 of the American Legion. My father bartended weekends at the post, where he was elected commander in 1955, the year before my older brother was born and ten years after he had been discharged from the navy. He had enlisted at the age of seventeen in 1942 and fought in North Africa as well as in the Pacific theaters, most dangerously in the Battle of Leyte Gulf. I would come to learn how tough the fighting was in the Philippines in documentary footage and in college history courses, but as preteens my brother and I were fascinated sufficiently by the medals commemorating the battles he had been in, medals that he'd framed and placed on the hallway wall outside our bedroom. We were fascinated, too, by the box of photographs in the family hope chest—men at a distance moving deliberately under palms, Bob Hope spoofing at the USO recognizable even in the closely cropped black and white of the snapshot, and most starkly the Japanese soldier staring up at me from the sprawl of his death some fifteen years before I was born.

Every weekend, while my father bartended and chatted with his fellow veterans, my brother and I would play around the post, exploring the upstairs function hall or running around the block's tightly parked cars playing tag or army with the other "Sons of the Legion," sometimes in our own snappy gray caps and uniforms if it were Memorial Day or Veteran's Day. I can still rattle off the names of many of my father's cronies—Eddie Beale, George Lewis, Charlie Kerr, Frank Dillon, Sylvester Devlin, Eddie Caravone—and their faces lift to attention in my memory. Sylvester Devlin, bald, heavyset, with a pencil-thin black moustache, was an amateur illustrator. Every holiday he'd adorn the mirror behind the bar with elaborate scenes drawn and painted in washable ink—sleighs and snowscapes at Christmas, Irish hills and cottages on St. Patrick's Day—a range of low to high-grade kitsch brought off brilliantly that would disappear from the broad glass like Tibetan sand paintings once the day had passed. Each one of these men, with their wives and children—everyone talking for hours at the bar or bellying up to the piano for the Saturday night sing-alongs—embodied a unique and unrepeatable intersection with history, whether directly or, like my brother and me, generationally. Here, with all of its ingrown welter and indigenous verve, was the parish life—not at first self-evidently worthy of a poet's fledgling effort at commemoration: some would-be Patrick Kavanagh of the American parochial capturing a speck of the universal in the particular, its familiar faces washed from the bar mirror along with the holiday dazzle.

Of course, the crucial importance of Patrick Kavanagh for the generation of Irish poets succeeding those who practiced their art in Ireland in the immediacy of Yeats's shadow is by now a commonplace. Kavanagh's temperamental and aesthetic decision to privilege the parochial over the provincial opened an imaginative laneway for poets like Kinsella, Montague, and Heaney, whose reputations would come to range beyond parish, province, and nation to enter the region of global recognition. It was always Kavanagh's assumption that the local housed the universal and that what Heaney (echoing Eliot's "Burnt Norton") would later call the "first world" was actually the whole world in microcosm. Though more the classically oriented poet, Michael Longley's evocations of Carrigskeewaun follow Kavanagh's precept, as does Eavan Boland's labor to make the suburbs a viable locus for her poetry, itself a combination of the parish and an Irish adaptation of American feminist poetics. Derek Mahon's "Glengormley," by contrast, evokes the poet's refusal of the local as a repository of the universal, so fraught is home with conflict and deadly sectarian conflict. Mahon's "The Hudson Letter," in turn, reveals that poet's assent to the condition of homelessness in the multicultural diaspora of contemporary America. In a different vein, Paul Muldoon's eclectic and at times esoteric *immrama* chart an elaborate subversion of Kavanagh's idea of the parish. Rather than centering itself in the local, Muldoon's work finds its dominant trope in eccentricity, in the irrepressible subversion of the parish in favor of a global quotidian.

This tension between center and the passage away from the center—passage that leads potentially to the erasure of the center as a sustainable ground—defines the general drift of the postmodern milieu. Yet while apologists for this reified notion of postmodernity would efface the fundamental tension between center and passage in favor of a world defined by errancy alone, it is the conscious exploration of the tension between center and passage that makes a poet's work definitive for our time.

Kavanagh himself felt the depth of the conflict in the evolution of his own work from *A Soul for Sale* to his last poems. When in the introduction to his *Collected Poems* Kavanagh observes that he lost his "messianic ambition" and that now his "purpose in life is to have no purpose," he is doing more than merely announcing a widely acknowledged shift in sensibility between his early and late work. More than just exemplifying a change of temperament brought on by his survival of lung cancer, Kavanagh here articulates the shift from the almost premodern appeal to place as the locus of meaning to the postmodern condition of displacement. The barely hidden "transit" within his "passionate transitory" underscores the shift from the rootedness of parish life. It is a condition to which he willingly assents in the late work and which he ultimately celebrates. The path of Kavanagh's life from Monaghan to the Grand Canal (to allude to Heaney's important essay) traces that passage. As Kavanagh declaims in his poem "The Hospital," "Naming these things is the love-act and its pledge; / For we must record love's mystery without claptrap, / Snatch out of time the passionate transitory."[1] With these words Kavanagh's parish gains transport out of its central space in its immediate environs to become primarily a function of time—a visionary clearing in which the transitory and not the local reveals its subtext in some universal "mystery" to which the ephemeral bears witness.

From the standpoint of postmodernity's distrust of universals, however, it could be argued that Patrick Kavanagh's late-life "shift" merely reiterates the poet's premodern connection to the stable parish in another guise. Nevertheless, the older poet's "purposeless poetic" readies the ground for the wilder excursions of Muldoon and Paul Durcan, not to mention a plurality of voices that collectively extend the attentions and possibilities of Irish poetry beyond the fixation with place. But are the parish and the passionate transitory really at odds fundamentally? As a body of work rooted almost exclusively in parish life, Michael Coady's work disputes the claim. Coady's first book, *Two for a Woman, Three for a Man,* appropriately won the Patrick Kavanagh Award. His second, *Oven Lane,* appeared in 1987, followed by *All Souls* in 1997 (with a revised and expanded edition in 2001). *Full Tide: A Miscellany* appeared in 1999 with *One Another* following in 2003. He has lived all his life in Carrick-on-Suir in County Tipperary. Yet, especially in *All Souls,* Michael Coady's long sojourn in the parish has been the occasion for his passage beyond the particular center of his inherited world. More specifically, in Michael Coady's work the undeniable though usually hidden correlation between the parochial center and the eccentric passage beyond its boundaries finds one of its most incisive examinations in all of Irish and American poetry.

In *All Souls* Michael Coady chooses for his epigraph the same lines quoted above from Patrick Kavanagh's "The Hospital," and the master's intention to "snatch out of time the passionate transitory" profoundly informs the disciple's work in *All Souls* and elsewhere. The hybrid nature of Coady's three most substantial books, *All Souls, Full Tide,* and *One Another,* speaks to his desire to use poetry, short prose pieces, and photographs to illuminate the dynamic nature of the moment, the "transitory's" transit from the depths of the past and not merely an evocation of the ephemeral. The first two sections of *All Souls,* "Voices" and "Visitations," underscore Coady's bricolage structure of orchestration, the organization of his books around bits and pieces—voices and voice-overs—that, juxtaposed, manifest the unique textures of a world. It is the exemplary model for all of Coady's subsequent work, though the rootedness of Coady's approach in Kavanagh's "passionate transitory" also tellingly calls to mind the routedness of America, as Coady himself suggests in "A Local Habitation": "It's true that the sense of place has, at least up to now, always been a strong element of our culture, right back to the *dinnseanchas* of the ancient literature. If two Americas bump into each other at a bar or in an airport the initial inquiry is likely to be 'What do you do?', whereas the Irish question is surely 'Where are you from?'—meaning county, town, village, townland or even street, depending on context."[2] Coady's contrast between Irish and American ways of self-identification has some basis in fact and says something honest about how one derives one's sense of self in an island culture like Ireland's as opposed to the United States, where even regionalism, much less the parish, begins to succumb to a deadening homogeneity, to the urgency of work and accomplishment rather than place as the central source of identity. The equation has shifted in Coady's estimate from being to doing, and that he suggests is still the difference between Ireland and America.

Though my father and his fellow veterans at Bay Ridge Post 157 might yet see themselves as members primarily of a community and a self-identifying locale, Coady's point is well-taken. There can be a prevailing effacement of depth in American culture. Coady, in turn, further characterizes the encounter experienced by his American travelers as exemplifying "the horizontal dimension of place," or as he says, "what you see: the people currently walking around, the state of the tide at this moment in the river, who is being buried or born today."[3] The horizontal, of course, is as present in parish life as in the milling anonymity of airport bars. But in addition, what the parish possesses for Coady is "a vertical dimension of place." As he observes:

> Unlike most writers I still live where I was born. I've remained on site and that enables me an intimate focus. The vertical dimension is the absent presence, what lies underneath and invisibly all around; the deep, deep accumulation of lives and living on the site: what has gone before for a thousand years in terms of people and lives and destinies and seasons and days and nights, in the exact place with its streets and lanes, straddling the same river, with the cosmic dimension of its twice-daily cycle of tides and its fifteenth century bridge.[4]

Here the parish life of Coady's Carrick-on-Suir constitutes something of an axis mundi, where the horizontal and the vertical dimensions of place meet, a dynamic communion of orientations that is harder and harder to find in a world where the local looks and feels like the local everywhere. Moreover, as a poet Coady is less interested in dazzling surface effects than in letting his imagination enter the vertical spaces, the way a scientist lifts a core sample of mud or ice to register the climate centuries ago. The orchestration of his books as miscellanies intends to manifest an ideal axial unity of his horizontal and vertical dimensions.

This method is underscored by the female speaker of "The Blind Arch" in *All Souls,* whose nostalgic reverie announces Coady's concern with recording both the passionate transitory and the mystery of being toward which it points:

> Here on this slope your man is fishing for names and dates
> that are told on stone. Maybe he'll learn it's not about
> things fixed on stone at all, but about a river of moments
> where everything filters down to the bed and nothing at all
> is lost.[5]

As the woman's remark implies, the River Suir is a parochial emblem that at once puts the reader in mind of Heraclitus's well-worn adage—you can't step in the same river twice—and announces the stability of some metaphysical ground, the bed, beneath the flow of each moment. One suspects that this view underlies Coady's aesthetic as well, since the poems that follow in these first two sections—one the voice of a Carrick cot-fisherman, one in lines that commemorate a servant girl, another evoking an evening of thrilling music "where every gathered / soul again became / an infant at the breast"—all suggest a deep faithfulness in the art's ability to preserve what is essential and universal in the particular; that is, what is most vitally human. To use Wordsworth's phrase, each is intended to be a "spot of time," and yet these spots are not intended solely to reflect on the singular identity of the poet. Rather, the poet intends these short pieces to be evocations of the communal life of his town, relics of a transpersonal history.

Both the narrator of "The Blind Arch" and the titles of Coady's opening sections, as well as the title *All Souls,* announce the collection's fundamental preoccupation with religious matters. Yet, though the title derives from the holy day on the church calendar when the dead are reverently brought to mind, Coady is not interested primarily in representing the role of religion in the life of the parish, or as merely an exploration of his own practice within the Catholic faith. Instead, his concern with religion resonates with Paul Tillich's idea of faith as "ultimate concern."[6] It is existential urgency that finally directs the reader to consider the fate of everyone who has ever lived and who will ever live—"all the living and the dead," as Joyce evokes in Gabriel Conroy's epiphany. Coady's parish, like Joyce's holiday party in "The Dead," is as much a metaphysical space as it is a physical place. "All Souls," the long poem from which the collection gains its title, begins with an epigraph taken from Elizabeth Bishop's poem "Filling Station"—"somebody loves us all." The epigraph is appropriate both for its rootedness in Bishop's fascination with ordinary details and commonplace subjects and for the fundamental humility of its assertion of faith. Like the epigraph from Kavanagh's "The Hospital," the quotation from Bishop's poem suits Coady's aesthetic perfectly. At the same time Coady's poem also intends to be more encompassing than Bishop's short lyric. It names locals, alludes to town and county history as well as national history, and exults in its Whitmanesque litany of familiar sites, personalities, and lore.

Coady's guiding trope in "All Souls" is the journey, in this case the passage within that familiar, parochial world. Nonetheless, in its humble way, the poet's journey is consonant with the grander archetypal pattern of the errant soul descending to the underworld only to return with greater insight into the human condition as well as a renewed spirit:

> Then I'm on my own and heading toward
> the town clock salmon swimming above
> the West Gate that's seen every soul who ever
> set foot in this place for a thousand years[7]

Without being ham-fisted, the West Gate is the gate that eventually opens into the Land of the Dead. Such is "the westwardness of everything," as Wallace Stevens called it in "Our Stars Come from Ireland." Unlike Stevens, who in his poem considers the broad canvas of emigration, Coady's passage takes place entirely within the fixed compass of the parish over the course of a single night, as the speaker walks home from a pub. The salmon referred to in the lines above alludes to the salmon of wisdom in Irish lore. Coady does not need to leave the parish to embark on his *immram,* since time itself is his medium, a living element like the flowing river that at once sweeps through the life of the parish and preserves all its souls.

That preservation includes the Irish language and by extension the civilization that existed before English became the dominant tongue. As such, nearly midway through, Coady's poem transforms into a dual language text:

> **A Mháthair Dé coimeád cúntas réidh**
> O Mother of God keep ready account
> > **ar an slua scáil ina n-aiséirí**
> > of this host of resurrected shades
> **gach fear is bean a mhair cois abhann**
> all souls who saw the river flow
> > **is a shiúil thar droichead le linn a saoil.**
> > and crossed the old bridge in their day.[8]

If for Thomas Kinsella all of Irish literature is haunted by the gulf at the core of its dual tradition since the "grafted tongue" of English (to enjoin Montague's phrase) brought the Irish language to near extinction, then for Michael Coady's "All Souls" the double nature of Ireland's literary inheritance speaks more openly to a vision of cultural enlargement and not merely to loss. "All Souls" then is an effort at comprehensive redress, a welcoming to Irish within the pervasively English language text rather than a farewell to English in the manner, in turn, of Michael Hartnett. Part archetypal journey, part catalogue of names and events, part parish record, part dual language text, "All Souls" is a poem that finally reveals the parochial to be anything but uniform.

With its shifts in perspective as well as its reliance on a variety of formal choices from anaphora to catalogue to prayer, Coady's "All Souls" constitutes a passage inside the center in which the enduring presence of community takes precedence over the transformations of the poet's individual identity—his transit, as it were, through transitory states. There is no psychomachia at work in the speaker's consciousness as we find in Montague's work, and consequently the self's sense of continuity is never at risk. There is stability under the flow, within the flow, a metaphysical "bed" below the transitory.

From this perspective, "All Souls," is also the antithesis of a poem like Kinsella's "Nightwalker" that, while brilliant, nonetheless "cogitates" in a manner reminiscent of one of Beckett's talking heads. It also differs from Montague's "The Rough Field" and Heaney's "Station Island" to the extent that those poems locate transformation within the self's rite of passage toward renewal, in spite of the poet's sense of displacement. In the case of Montague's sequence, community is finally lost to history's upheavals. It is "going, going, gone . . ." as the end of "The Rough Field" tells us. In contrast, Coady's "All Souls" ends with its "hero" snugly home in bed and his wife wryly asking, "Were there many below in the town?" For Coady, all souls are there, and nothing is finally lost. While this affirming vision may be seen by some to face inadequately the magnitude of historical and metaphysical loss, it does appear to fulfill Kavanagh's later precept that tragedy is merely incomplete comedy. At the same time, Coady refuses the self-reflexive and intertextual journey narratives of a Paul Muldoon. Instead, with a wry, unsentimental sincerity rather than subversive wit, "All Souls" adds a new dimension to the journey poem in contemporary Irish poetry. Thus there is an inherent humility in the witness of Michael Coady's work, though that humility does not undermine its ambition to portray the irreducibly communal nature of our lives, caught as we are in the crosshairs of the vertical/horizontal axis of which Coady speaks. The parish life exemplifies this condition in microcosm.

Bridge and Memory

One sees Coady's vision at work again in the title poem of his book *One Another,* in which the human need for comfort in the face of loss bridges onto the subject of memory:

> *And afterwards, in the*
> *accustomed way, there will be*

*a shared remembering
that could include you*

*some things that you yourself
may already have forgotten,
or never realised,
or would prefer unspoken.*

*Then, within a month,
that communal recall
must make way for
the beginning of forgetting*

*for it is remembrance
that allows us
little by little
to forget.*

*Bleak shelter, this, for
all our nakedness,
but out of it quite suddenly
a surge of unexpected joy*

*at how you're blessed
amongst those men and women,
one but individual
in their natures at the bar.*[9]

The same interfusion of private and public finds equally moving expression in the prose piece "Nightdress," in which the sense memory evoked by the object brings back the immediacy of grief at the loss of a child. This individual grief—"I have looked into the depths," Coady writes—opens compassionately outward into the recognition that others have felt and experienced the same, as all will: "How many times did this happen before in the town? And everywhere. Beginning with a man and woman making love, and having a child. And losing the child. I never thought of them before. All the demented parents. People we never heard of. The names and stories lost and forgotten. But going through the same things as ourselves in their time."[10]

Michael Coady's affirmation of community and continuity with place and tradition—of the parish in every sense—perhaps finds its most fitting emblem in the town's Old Bridge, which recurs as a figure throughout *All Souls*, as well as in *One Another*. As he reflected in *Full Tide*, "one of the great, simple free pleasures of life for me is taking a cot out on the tide and drifting under the arches of our 1447 bridge." As these words reflect, though Michael Coady has no intention of advancing anything so grand as Hart Crane's epic vision, Carrick's bridge is suspended across the river of history as well as the literal river running through town. Beyond history, as he observes again in *Full Tide*, "if its old stone arches could talk we would have tales enough to see us through all the dark nights of a lifetime of winters. God only knows how many human beings of all kinds and conditions have crossed over it."[11]

In the poem "Checkpoint," the Old Bridge moves beyond these descriptions to convey an ontological import that still deepens its resonance:

> Out of the deep galaxies
> of detail and the blind ways
> that we go and the light
> or dark that shines on us
>
> there is the measure of
> the nitty-gritty impact
> that I've made so far
> upon the earth:
>
> an unreckonable fraction
> of a millimeter in
> wear-down of polished
> kerbstone, the first
>
> on the bridge,
> southwestern side,
> after I step half-past
> midnight out of

Maggie Dunne's
in Carrick Beg
to cross again
(no record of how many

times in all, of which
no two the same
in one direction
or the other),

cross again that old bridge
built before Columbus,
on my way to sleep
in Carrick Mor

where the weir plays
when the tide's away
and sometimes
between quays

I'm pulled up
and asked where
I've come from
and where I'm going

by stars
that stand
on night-watch
in the river.[12]

"Checkpoint" exemplifies brilliantly Coady's penchant for discerning the universal in the simple diurnal rituals and common landmarks of the parochial, the call of the infinite in the fraction of time and space inhabited by the attentive life. The Old Bridge is a liminal space that has endured for centuries on the margins of world-making historical events. It also poises the poet, and the reader, at the edge of a sublime cosmic immensity that, in effect, calls the poet's attentions—and the reader's—to fuller consciousness, and so calls us with the poet to step outside the habitual.

Coady underscores the cosmic significance of the bridge again in "Recycling the Universe," a poem that first appeared in *Full Tide* and that he reprinted in *One Another*. Here, after portraying the "ancient bridge" as "only / five centuries made after all," he quickly expands the time frame from that of the parish and the stonemasons who built it to that of geologic and finally cosmic time:

> the river itself
> did not flow until
> the great meltdown
>
> some twelve or so
> thousand springs ago,
> and even the fabled mountain
>
> of Fionn and the women
> had a distant day when it did
> not yet stand over the valley.
>
> If you would hold in your hand
> some inviolable
> nugget of permanence
>
> you could reach down
> for any unremarkable
> pebble—but then you stand
>
> by a breaking wave and know
> that sand between your bare
> toes was rock of ages,
>
> just as truly as certain stars
> defining the firmament
> may already be aeons dark.[13]

The subtle infiltration of religious diction in these lines—"rock of ages," "firmament"—places Coady's warp-speed reversal of planetary and cosmic evolution within an implicitly religious context. Likewise,

Coady brackets this movement back through ages, which takes place in the space of a moment, between a portrayal of the stonemasons who built the bridge, and who lived pretty much as the current inhabitants of Carrick-on-Suir, and a portrayal of the town council "dustmen" of more recent times, who sweep the streets. Coady's implication is clear—we are all dustmen, albeit composed of cosmic dust. Here again, the faint religious echo insinuates itself, now from the Ash Wednesday ritual: "Remember man that you are dust; from dust to dust you shall return." In a manner that recalls Montague's relationship to his home ground (though far less fraught), the Old Bridge in "Recycling the Universe" as in "Checkpoint" reveals itself to be the luminal span between the parish as centering space, *heimlich* space, and the parish as defamiliarized space, *unheimlich* space—a sublime cosmic amplitude that Coady calls in "The Friction of Feet in Time" the "gravity of darkness."[14]

That same gravity as it bears down on the individual is given a strongly personal turn in the poem "Extra-Corporeal Circulation," where the poet evokes the circumstances of his open heart surgery and questions the very nature and endurance of consciousness.[15] Thus for all of their ease with the parochial, Coady's poems prod us quietly toward the recognition that human consciousness is inherently—and at best fruitfully—at odds with itself, suspended as it is between being at home and being en route.

The experience of being en route as well as stretched between Coady's horizontal and vertical axis of existence likewise finds expression in both *All Souls* and *One Another*. The past of the parish includes the past of the Irish language and its continued presence in the parish as an important nexus of continuity in the parish's peregrination through time. Two short prose sections from *All Souls*, "The Things They Say," with its proverbial snatches of conversation, and "Five Airs from an Older Music," consisting of translations from the Irish, assume an enduring identification with place over time despite traumatic events like the Great Famine, acknowledged by the poet in his translation of "Na Pratai Dubha," a traditional song/poem from the Ring *gaeltacht* (Irish-speaking region) in County Waterford. Coady's intent is to affirm an enduring community through the hard-won persistence of the Irish language, and he extends this important awareness of continuity to other languages resident on the island and beyond in *One Another*. There Coady prints an old story from the Ring *gaeltacht*, "The Gift of Tongues," in English, Irish, Ulster-Scots, Scots Gaelic, and Welsh. The gesture is subversive of purist and essentialist versions of Ireland's linguistic history, and one can only assume that Coady intends to affirm his communal vision across even traditional linguistic boundaries.

This profoundly faithful affirmation of continuity in the face of time passing more emphatically animates the short prose memoir "Three Men Standing at the Met" in *All Souls,* though it likewise initiates that book's thematic counterflow, its expansion beyond parish life both horizontally and vertically, as it were, in its obsession with the emigrant experience. "Three Men Standing at the Met" begins with the poet listening to Verdi's *La Forza del Destino,* the satellite transmission "overleaping the ocean" in a reversal of the passage made by his father and two uncles in 1927. The guiding trope underlying Coady's evocation of his father's flirtation with a life in America is synchronicity. For the poet, his father's evening at the Metropolitan Opera some seventy years ago is really happening again, as if the microsecond transmission had somehow transubstantiated the past into the present. "There are conspiring shades about me, standing again, listening to *La Forza del Destino* as they did on that November evening at the 'Old Met' in 1927," Coady writes. Jimmy, the eldest brother, will stay in America and never see Ireland again, though his daughter will return to tell stories of her father's life apart from Ireland and the parish. George, the poet's father, and the poet's Uncle Peter return to Carrick after the start of the Great Depression.

What Coady's brief memoir offers the reader is a glimpse of individual lives within the context of momentous historical events. From these experiences the poet will glean a poem, "Assembling the Parts," about his father's job in the Underwood typewriter factory in Hartford, Connecticut. Similarly, in *One Another,* the poem "On the Record" recounts the preservation of an old Irish song by a Connemara woman, who learned the piece "When she was young / from a boat-builder's sister / who left for Chicago and never / was heard of after." Here again the parish discloses a hidden transport to a lost America.

Underlying the poet's act of making in both of these instances is Coady's faith that "all things connect in time"—a vision of how things are that contrasts starkly with, for example, Montague's understanding of time as a great wound. Once again, the potentially tragic vision of a world defined by separation finds its appeasement in the poet's faith in time's wider economy, its ability over time to reconcile discontinuity and loss. Nevertheless, Coady's generally affirming vision does not ignore the more intractable magnitudes of loss, as "On the Record" acknowledges when the poet observes that the "sound of salvation" preserved by the folklore commission, its "blind-eyed innocence," was caught in "the year of the Warsaw ghetto, / packed trains pulling into Treblinka."[16] In Coady's work the parish is not impermeable to the massive losses and brutalities that exist seemingly outside its limited domain, so the Jewish genocide—a central manifestation of what Kavanagh called in his poem "Epic" (culpably in my view) "the Munich bother"—places the world of the parish in relief of the wider march of history. The poet's biting irony here cannot be missed—the word "salvation" freighted with Christian meaning stands in stark counterpoint to his evocation of the death camps. In essence, Coady would bring the parish's experience of continuity to bear on historical loss as an act of imaginative healing, though he would do so with full knowledge of what cannot be healed.

Nevertheless, nowhere is Coady's intention to bear a healing witness more richly and eloquently realized than in his long reflective memoir/essay "The Use of Memory" in *All Souls*. Inspired by lines from T. S. Eliot's "Burnt Norton," "The Use of Memory" recounts the long-secreted circumstances of a family wound: the abandonment of Coady's grandfather and namesake in Carrick by his great-grandfather, James, who decided to emigrate to America out of economic desperation and grief over his wife's death and never returned. What we have in this family story is the kind of personal and historical trauma worthy of Montague's essentially tragic sensibility, and a story of seemingly irretrievable loss. "The Use of Memory" is not Coady's first effort at recovery. In "At Home Abroad," in *Full Tide,* he acknowledges that growing up in Carrick he knew nothing of a Newfoundland connection to the town through the emigration of families during the time of the Great Famine. The essay goes some way toward recovering those connections in detail. Still, the reason for the work of remembrance, he underscores, has to do with a pervasive loss of memory brought on by cultural trauma incurred at the local level: "Community tradition had long-since forgotten all this in my town: human migration, of its nature, leaves little Trace in the original homeland. Moreover, the local folk memory must have been blocked out by the trauma of the Great Famine and the subsequent mass exodus, not to Newfoundland, but to the United States."[17]

In his essay "The Sea-Divided Silence," however, Coady emphatically shifts the circumstance from passive forgetting to something more culpable: "Consider the uncreated conscience of the diaspora. Whatever about cunning, there has certainly been silence and exile. A quite astonishing degree of silence, in fact, whether willed or otherwise. Apart from the ballad tradition, the experience of emigration—perhaps the most definitive historical reality for millions of Irish people over the last two centuries—has never articulated itself in anything like a commensurate literature of substance and dimension, either at home or abroad."[18]

Coady goes on in the essay to suggest the absence of the emigration experience from Irish literature may well constitute a "hiding-hole of denial and evasive amnesia in the national psyche," which may be viewed as tantamount to "an Irish solution of surgical simplicity and finality, ensuring complacency and security of the establishment at home," so much so that the light shining in the window of Aras an Uachtarain, symbolic of the diaspora Irish, reveals for him "a truer instinct for both our unexamined story and our buried guilt with its self-serving amnesia."[19] Coady's words are strong indeed on the subject of the potential culpability of memory and tradition—the willed forgetting that has led to remarkably "scant expression" of the diaspora experience of the Irish. Perhaps now, however, the scarcity of expression is beginning to give way to something closer to a refusal of recognition. In any case, "The Use of Memory" is Coady's moving and brilliant effort at redressing a massive cultural denial.

In "The Use of Memory," Coady recounts the fact of his great-grandfather's departure for America, like the Famine emigrants of Carrick never to return. When years later a mysterious letter arrives addressed to Michael Coady, the poet's grandfather, and it turns out to be from his long-absconded father now near death in Philadelphia, the still-wounded and unforgiving son destroys it in front of the poet's father. It is a scene Coady also recounts in his radio talk "A Local Habitation" and elsewhere, and so the centrality of the event for the poet's work is incontestable. Coady's poem "The Letter" from *Oven Lane* (reprinted in *All Souls*) was written, in part, as an answer to that angry and definitive refusal, as well as an attempt at healing the wound by avowing the lost connection between father and son across generations:

> Out of the maze of circumstances,
> the ravelled tangle of effect and cause,
> something impelled you,
> brought you finally
> to bend above
> the unmarked page—
>
> an old man
> in some room in Philadelphia
> reaching for words to bridge
> the ocean of his silence
> pleading forgiveness of the child
> of Oven Lane.[20]

As these lines suggest, Coady's poem is the imaginative act that completes the failed intention to heal the rift brought on by circumstance and flawed human choice. It is therefore "the bridge" by which his great-grandfather's future reaches back into the past to liberate memory. The poem is also a definitive act of refusal to maintain "the sea-divided silence" of a culture and not only a personal rift. Coady coins a term to describe this action, essentially a reversal of "the ravelled tangle of effect and cause" that is history. He calls it "presequence"—a mode of imagination that constitutes "a knowing return to a seminal moment in the past from its own future." For Coady this is nothing less then the imagination's work of embodying time's essential continuity, and hence the continuity of the self with the whole of the past. "Here I discover myself already nested in the possible," the poet further explains.[21] In "The Use of Memory" it is the recognition of the self's presequence in the past that leads the poet to further bring to light his family story, and as such to further make manifest the intimate and pervasive connections of time with transitory life. The poet accomplishes this through the unlikely marriage of genealogy and imagination.

In Coady's hands genealogy becomes a compelling tool of the imagination and not merely a dry schema of births and deaths and generic social circumstances far removed from the drama of the present. Rather, in Coady's poem genealogy offers a path into the vertical dimension of his axis, which places each life both in a historical context and in the context of "all souls." "The Use of Memory" begins in the parish registry with the poet poring over entries two hundred years gone. Importantly, and with great compassion, Coady reminds us that "the individual transience of two centuries of lives densely manuscripted here dismays the heart, yet each entry also embodies a quality of immediacy still on the page." The dead continue to have potency, which stimulates the imagination of the living. Still more trenchantly, Coady reveals the real purpose of genealogy, which, he says, "should not be the neat assembly of pedigree culminating smugly in self, but its exact opposite: the extension of the personal beyond the self to encounter the intimate unknown of others in our blood." Inheritance, for Coady, is a "darkly woven-basket," a web of connections that genealogy helps to reveal but that only imagination can reanimate. Together, despite loss, displacement, and willful rejection of the past, they illuminate time's irreducible continuity: "Every future will become a past for other futures."[22]

Were Michael Coady's "The Use of Memory" just a deeply moving memoir, that would be a fine enough achievement. The sad failure of his great-grandfather's life in Philadelphia—the death of his second family, the evocation of his loneliness in the lodging house at 321 Kimball Street during the last ten years of his life—conjures a strange coterminous affiliation between parishes, the one in Ireland that he left and the one in the America to which he emigrated, boatman of the Suir and of the Delaware. "This is the story of two rivers and two places an ocean apart," so Coady reflects. Still, the story's double life manifests the synchronicity of time in its retelling: "I fly eastward through the dawn to Ireland while on the ocean more than five miles below James Coady passes me in another dimension and direction, sailing westward to America in 1885. He looks up at the sky, wondering what lies ahead of him."[23]

This passing of destinies a hundred or more years apart is nonetheless an act of repossession in which the lost America of Coady's great-grandfather finds an unforeseeable reconciliation in the poet's perception of the fullness of time. Still more importantly, "The Use of Memory" is also an essential work that vividly portrays the enduring human drama of the Irish diaspora. As the poet himself reflects, "the story's tangle of individual human destinies was also a tiny fragment of the great epic drama of migration from Ireland to America."[24] Michael

Coady is right in calling the Irish diaspora "a vast human and spatial landscape"[25] and right also in saying it is an epic that has been "little articulated" in Ireland or America, though the history of Irish American poetry demonstrates that wide and varied imaginative responses have emerged gradually out of the Irish experience of diaspora. Still, Michael Coady's "The Use of Memory," like his poem "The Letter," stands as a major, culturally urgent response to the self-imposed amnesia he articulates so bravely in "The Sea-Divided Silence"; likewise, his periodic trips to Philadelphia over the years find their place within his efforts of national and transnational as well as personal recovery.

Few writers have taken on the subject of the Irish diaspora as directly and vividly as Michael Coady does in "The Use of Memory" and elsewhere in his work. That gap in attention largely inheres in Irish poetry as well, with exceptions to be found in the New Irish poetry of Eamonn Wall and Greg Delanty, as well as James Liddy and Eavan Boland, whose poem "The Emigrant Irish" speaks to an almost willful sin of forgetting: "Like oil lamps, we put them out back / of our houses, of our minds."[26] Colm Tóibín's novel *Brooklyn* stands as a more recent and equally brilliant effort at redress. Michael Coady's work begins in the parish where he was born and raised and where he has lived his life, and he rightly praises it, as he does in "Munster Aisling" at the end of *One Another*:

> Here is my *cuan*,
> where I began, and where I live,
> this settlement of souls at the tide-head of the river,
> all its living or lost hearts in place and time
> under the abiding breast of Slievenamon.[27]

It is a recognition that would have gone over well among the denizens of Bay Ridge Post 157, though their tides were those washing up against the wall of Shore Road's concrete bicycle path and their Slievenamon the winter sledding hill at Owl's Head overlooking the old Sixty-Ninth Street Pier, where the Staten Island Ferry used to dock before the Verrazano rose above the Narrows. The rooted experience of the parish always has routes, however hidden, stretching out to other lives elsewhere if only in recognition and resonance. Unlike the vast majority of Irish writers, Coady's significance depends in fact on his resolute commitment to the undeniable reality that the parish for all of its local presence is not insular, however profoundly trauma might have led to the historical erasure of those forced to leave in diaspora. In a review of Coady's *All Souls,* Ciaran Carson observed that he "would like to think that such a book could only have come out of Ireland," and yet Carson's wishful thinking here reiterates the historical and cultural amnesia that refuses to see across the categories "Irish" and "Irish American." The fact is Coady's work is the product of both Kavanagh's parish and the lost America of the Irish diaspora, and his witness is directed generously and unflaggingly to both worlds. Until the indisputable connection between these imaginative landscapes is still more fully acknowledged and explored by the literature of Ireland and America, and recognized as an essential part of tradition by critics, scholars, and writers, the double life of Irish and Irish American inheritance will remain largely lost to us.

EIGHT

Back Through Distance

Currents of Tradition in the Poetry of Louise Bogan and Thomas McGrath

Heritage and Disinheritance

Some twenty-five years ago I enrolled in a class on modern drama with the aim of broadening the course of study for my doctorate. Though my abiding interest was poetry, as an undergraduate I'd taken an introductory course in continental European drama that included Goethe, Racine, Molière, Ibsen, Strindberg, Chekhov, and Beckett, and I had read some of Yeats's plays on my own, particularly the later, strange one-acts like "Purgatory," seeing them as extensions of the poetry rather than works of drama in their own right. I had not read much if any twentieth-century drama other than in the Irish grain—Synge, Yeats, Lady Gregory, O'Casey, Beckett. In particular I had not read much American drama, which is what attracted me to the present class, in addition to the felt need to gain a greater sense of what had been written for the theater in the middle to late twentieth century. On the first day, when our distinguished but affable professor handed out the syllabus with its reading list that included, among others, Shaw, Brecht, Pinter, Stoppard, Miller, Albee, and Williams, Eugene O'Neill's absence felt like a palpable slight against a figure who, I thought, should have been included. How do you leave out a Nobel laureate from a course in modern drama? That unspoken sense of insult deepened when our professor underscored his selection by drawing attention to the reason for his intentional omission: "You'll notice there is no O'Neill in the reading. That is because he's overrated—a caricaturist of the human condition, a sentimentalist." My Cambridge-educated professor had asserted his judgment, forthrightly ex cathedra, to a seminar of would-be professors.

Still, I could not help sensing that what remained unspoken in the room was my professor's rejection of what he saw to be O'Neill's ethnic illegitimacy: his Irish Americanness. And one can hear something of O'Neill's own artistic insecurity in the poems he wrote before turning to writing plays, like these lines from "The Lay of the Singer's Fall":

> A singer was born in a land of gold,
> In the time of the long ago
> And the good fairies gathered from heath and wold
> With gracious gifts to bestow.[1]

It is impossible not to hear the young Irish American seeking, rather desperately, a model both for his art and his lost Irishness in these lines, which sound as though they had been written by one of the imitators Yeats called his "fleas." It is impossible not to hear also, however, O'Neill's willed artistic self-assertion in these lines from his poem "Submarine," written five years later, in 1917, when he was twenty-nine:

> My soul is a submarine.
> My aspirations are torpedoes.
> I will hide unseen
> Beneath the surface of life.[2]

O'Neill's assertiveness echoes Stephen Daedalus with the same need to advance artistically by stealth and cunning. Likewise, I would venture, one feels the submerged fury of the artist's self-disdain, the product of his inbred insecurity, in the desperate, often outsized characters of his plays. It is good that O'Neill turned away from poetry, good that he took up confronting the fierce human wreckage of his plays, since theater appears to have been his native imaginative means to wrestle with the haunted inheritance of his family life, its theatrics rooted as much in a lost Irishness as in the routing of that identity into the errancy of diaspora in America.

Nevertheless, there is something in O'Neill's albeit fraught Irish American inheritance and in his artistic treatment of that inheritance that resonates distinctly and deeply with the Irish notion of heritage in all of its knotted complexity. Beyond residing as a signifier on the website for the Irish Heritage Service, *dúchas,* the Irish word for "heritage," carries within it meanings beyond its English equivalent. Embedded in the Irish word *dúchas* are conceptions of birthright, heredity, and one's innate capacities and qualities as derived from ancestral sources, as well as one's affinity with one's native place. The word, as such, implies something more intimate than culture and history broadly conceived. The intimacy of the term was brought home to me some years ago in conversation with an Irish-language poet who spoke of a neighbor's fraught secretive behavior, nonetheless known to the locals, as an example of "the *dúchas,*" meaning an inheritance that can determine how one lives in the world and that may well be deleterious—something akin, almost, to karma. It would appear, then, to draw out the implication native in the word, that the experience of disinheritance, of being misbegotten socially and culturally, can be as much a part of the *dúchas* as any affirming standard of belonging to a tradition. Such an experience of disinheritance is common not only to Eugene O'Neill but to two of the most important though insufficiently celebrated Irish American poets of the twentieth century, Louise Bogan and Thomas McGrath. Taken together, their achievements exemplify the shaping influence of what might be called the Irish American *dúchas* on the poet's work as well as the Irish American poet's effort to employ Irish and American literary traditions as a dual foundation for artistic redress.

Born in 1897 in Livermore Falls, Maine, to parents of Irish ancestry, Louise Bogan died in 1970. As such her life and work span the transformation from late Victorian and Georgian poetry through the rise of modernism, the renewal of formalist poetry in the 1950s alongside confessionalism, the Beats, projectivism, the advent of postmodernism, and, most important for her legacy, the impact of feminism on poetic practice in the United States. Born of the nineteenth-century Irish diaspora to America, Bogan likewise lived and wrote during a period of tremendous historical upheaval and cultural transformation in which the United States rose to political and cultural world dominance over the course of two World Wars, the Great Depression, the expansion of America's military industrial complex, and the Civil Rights Movement—in short, very nearly the entire unfolding of the so-called American century.

For all of the great historical, cultural, and literary transformations indicative of the time, very little of that grand opera overtly enters Louise Bogan's poetry. The one exception is her delicately beautiful and moving elegy for her brother, Charles, who was killed in action shortly before the end of World War I. Rather, hers is poetry of intense, thoughtful, and emotionally probing lyric compression—"compactness compacted" as Marianne Moore described it[3]—that nonetheless aims at an immediacy and vibrancy of expression Yeats regarded as personal utterance. As Elizabeth Frank observes, "like Emily Dickinson, Bogan searched for the axiomatic and the general in experience rather than the particular."[4] Nevertheless, along with their intricate rhythms, her lyrics are dramatic in their approach to syntax as well as in their expressiveness. Dickinson and Yeats are, in fact, her two most prominent aesthetic lights, and a great many of her poems read as if written by the impossible but inspired offspring of these two starkly contrary poets, the one reclusive, the other theatrical.

Louise Bogan's real-life parents were likewise stark opposites, though their lives together were as painful in their way as those encountered in an O'Neill play. In her magisterial literary biography, Elizabeth Frank recounts the traumatic circumstances of Bogan's early life growing up in the "incredibly ugly" New England mill towns where her father, Daniel Joseph Bogan, whose family came from Derry, Northern Ireland, found work as a foreman and where her mother, May O'Neill Murphy Bogan, followed with her two children.[5] As Frank succinctly reflects, "From very early on [Louise] was present at scenes of violence between her parents,"[6] and it is certain that the "spirited" May had many affairs, sometimes leaving for stretches of time, at other times bringing her daughter on the elicit trips away from her family life. May was herself the child of lost parents—her mother, who disappeared, was originally from Dublin, and her father was killed in the Civil War. She was brought up by another Irish American family named Shields.[7] The emotional trauma of Bogan's early family life had a long-lasting impact on her own relationship with her first husband, whom she married in order to escape life with her parents. It likewise had an effect on her choice to separate from him. Subsequently, she also chose to leave her daughter with her parents in New England while she pursued the life of a poet in New York. The traumatic experience of Bogan's childhood had an impact on the failure of her second marriage and on her lifelong battle with depression and alcohol.

From early on, then, Bogan regarded her childhood as tragic and poetry as the way to escape the lower-middle-class *dúchas* of her familial inheritance. Poetry was also her way of engaging her fraught birthright imaginatively. She makes the psychic link of her childhood unhappiness to the potentially assuaging power of poetry in her prose portrait of her mother:

> I do not see my mother. I see her clearly much later than I smell and feel her—long after I see the solid fractions of the house and fields. . . . I must have experienced violence from birth. But I remember it at first as only bound up with flight. I was bundled up and carried away. In the town of Milton violence first came through. . . . I began to write verse from about fourteen on. The life saving process then began. By the age of eighteen I had a thick pile of manuscripts, in a drawer in the dining room—and had learned every essential of my trade.[8]

Despite the fraught nature of her relationship to her mother in later life, she nonetheless regarded May Bogan as an admirable person, and indeed the source of her facility with words—the "Celtic" source of her gift for poetry.[9] She likewise contrasted that side of her family inheritance with the other side, what she called after Yeats the "Paudeen" side of her birthright.[10] From early on Bogan retained a sense of her Irish identity, even before she traveled to Ireland in 1937 as an extension of a Guggenheim year abroad.

Typically, her awareness of her Irish identity was spurred by the experience of exclusion and prejudice while she was enrolled in Girls Latin School in Boston before entering Boston University (and eventually turning down a scholarship to Radcliffe to elope with her first husband, an army officer, to Panama near the end of the First World War).

The headmaster, one Ernest Hapgood, made a point of calling her into his office to explain to her that "no Irish girl could be editor of the school magazine." As Frank observes, "it was this incident in particular that Bogan perhaps had in mind when she later wrote, 'It was borne in upon me, all during my adolescence, that I was a Mick, no matter what my other faults or virtues might be.'"[11] What we find from the beginning in the life of Louise Bogan is her consciousness of endemic family distress linked to contrary perspectives on her Irish ancestry, the one highly problematic but the bearer of the gift of poetry, the other narrow and hidebound in the world of having to make do— like so many emigrants who sought to raise themselves into positions of meager prominence in mills or factories that were themselves part of the legacy of emigration. Onto this impose a consciousness of the legacy of exclusion ("No Irish Need Apply"), and what you find manifested is the *dúchas* experienced as a heritage of violence born of failed aspirations, limited attainment, loss of community, and the enduring experience of disinheritance. It is no wonder she sought to escape first into a hasty marriage and finally into the bustling literary milieu of New York in the 1920s.

When she did escape to join a burgeoning scene of writers, artists, and publishers, she mingled with other important Irish American contributors to American culture, among them Lola Ridge, Marianne Moore, and Kay Boyle, as well as the emigrant Irish poet Padraic Colum, who with fellow *New Republic* reviewer Maxwell Anderson founded *The Measure*,[12] an important literary journal of the time. Bogan's mature poems first appeared in its pages. Clearly Bogan was acutely conscious of her Irish roots, and while she sought to make her way in the American literary milieu, it must have resonated with her to have such positive and evident Irish American role models among the vital literati of New York. The complex *dúchas* of her Irishness remained with her throughout her life, and her equally complex engagement with her heritage becomes evident in the mixed feelings she articulates on her visit to Ireland, a journey she made if not to trace her roots, then to encounter the maternal and paternal soil from which she grew, if only at one remove. In a letter from Ireland to her friend and publisher, Edmund Wilson, she wrote, "[Dublin] is perfectly beautiful. But it's cruel and shut up and full of conspirators, believe me. . . . You don't know what's up. The most moveless faces in the world confront you on all sides. I saw one woman, at a matinee, at the Gate Theatre, who had looked as though she had never moved her face, from birth. How she managed to eat or speak I can't imagine. Now I know where Yeats got his idea, his obsession, with the mask."[13]

Bogan's description of Dublin is a perfect mirror of her attitude toward her family and her upbringing—an early life filled with her mother's conspiracies and simmering, secretive pressures that could erupt into violence. In such circumstances exposure of the self is far too risky. There was for her, pervasively, a sense of being frozen in place. For the young Louise Bogan, poetry was the necessary vehicle to foster movement out of the "moveless" life into which she was born, though the poet's progress likewise required a way of confronting a psychic wound—an obsession—that could not be confronted head on.

Here is the opening of Bogan's early great poem "Medusa," from her first book *Body of This Death*:

> I had come to the house, in a cave of trees,
> Facing a sheer sky.
> Everything moved,—a bell hung ready to strike,
> Sun and reflection wheeled by.
>
> When the bare eyes were before me
> And the hissing hair,
> Held up at a window, seen through a door.
> The stiff bald eyes, the serpents on the forehead
> Formed in the air.[14]

The poem's first two stanzas evoke a scene in which movement and stillness stand at equipoise. Everything is moving, but the bell is ready to strike. The bald eyes of the Medusa are stiff while the serpents form in air. As the poem unfolds, Bogan declares, "this is a dead scene forever now. / Nothing will ever stir," as if she were portraying an eternal condition, the psyche's hypostasis into myth and vice versa: "The water will always fall, and will not fall, / and the tipped bell make no sound." In addition to Yeats's idea of the mask as a catalyst for self-making, Bogan was also greatly influenced by Freudian psychoanalysis and especially Jung's conception of the collective unconscious. "Medusa" draws inspiration from all of those wells. In the myth of the Medusa the female figure turns the beholder to stone—what could be more "moveless"? The poet, like Theseus, must make a reflection through a fiat of artistry in order to survive, though by so doing the figure of female monstrosity and its maternal embodiment of the wish to die are at once preserved and controlled inside the poem. The poem itself is the mirror that frames the horror, allows it to be seen, and transforms its harmful power into the power of art. As Deborah Pope observes, "after this apparition, the speaker is frozen in a landscape that categorically evades the death-wish of the youth . . . yet through agency of the Medusa any threatening process is also evaded. In this fantastic realm, the speaker has it both ways, much like the figures adorning Keats' Grecian urn."[15] All this happens while the speaker "stands like a shadow / under the great balanced day."

Knowing the severity of her early home life and its effect on her, and placing that life in the context of her early poem "Medusa" as well as her ruminations on the "moveless" faces of Dublin, one can see Bogan's art as an effort at transfiguration, an attempt, as Louis Untermeyer wrote, to plumb "the secret behind appearance."[16] Her poetry is a confrontation with the shaping forces of her life managed without recourse to the confessional mode and an effort to transcend those forces—the proverbial momentary stay against confusion. We find the presiding symbolic figure of the Medusa again in a less troubling though no less moving encounter in Bogan's later poem "The Sleeping Fury," from her third book of the same title:

> You are here now,
> Who were so loud and feared, in a symbol before me,
> Alone and asleep, and I at last look long upon you.
>
> Your hair fallen on your cheek, no longer in the semblance of
>   serpents,
> Lifted in the gale; your mouth, that shrieked so, silent.
> You, my scourge, my sister, lie asleep, like a child
> Who, after rage, for an hour quiet, sleeps out its tears.[17]

There is a profound emotional reversal in these lines from the stony terror of "Medusa." The Medusa has transformed from a motherly embodiment of *thanatos* to a sisterly child, as if Bogan were encountering now her own youthful doppelganger. The address "You, my scourge, my sister" echoes purposefully Baudelaire's "You hypocrite lecteur, mon semblable, mon frère." "You lie in sleep and forget me / Alone and strong in my peace, I look upon you in yours"—so the poem ends. The lines underscore the speaker's sense of acceptance, of reconciliation with the fraught inheritance of the past.

At the same time, Bogan's poetry refuses to gloss its bitterness. It is a bitterness that extends beyond the circumstances of her individual cultural past into the lot of women some thirty or more years before Plath, Sexton, and especially Adrienne Rich pushed the feminist perspective to the forefront of American poetry. As her other Yeatsian mask, "Cassandra," declares: "I am the chosen no hand saves: / The shrieking heaven lifted over men, / Not the dumb earth, wherein they set their graves."[18] The sound of shrieking in these lines, the call of Bogan's Medusa however becalmed, asserts something more universal than the muted anger of an individual woman born into a troubled home. It is a gendered outburst raised to the highest pitch that at once displaces the male heaven and negates a speechless, maternal earth. Cassandra's shriek, as wild and potent in its way as Munch's, only exacerbates the irony of Bogan's early poem "Women," in which she writes, "Women have no wilderness in them, / They are provident instead, / Content in the tight hot cell of their hearts / To eat dusty bread."[19] In Bogan's poem, Cassandra's shriek is the wild cry from women's suppressed and unregarded wilderness.

Though emerging out of her troubled childhood and the *dúchas* of Irish American disinheritance, Bogan's poetry from this standpoint is exemplary not only for its intense lyricism as well as emotional and intellectual perspicacity but also for its profound importance for the emergence of poetry by women in the twentieth century. Nonetheless, her work is resolutely anticonfessional. Any direct representation of documentary, autobiographical circumstance remains almost exclusively outside her aesthetic sphere of interest. Perhaps even more emphatically than in Yeats's work, in Bogan's poetry there is always the mask. Nevertheless, as her one-time student and lover Theodore Roethke trenchantly observed, "her best lyrics, unlike so much American work, have the sense of civilization behind them. . . . Invariably these effects are produced with great economy, with the exact sense of diction that is one of the special marks of her style." And he continues with equivalent insight: "The ground beat of the great tradition can be heard, with the necessary subtle variations. . . . Bogan is one of the true inheritors."[20] Her poetry's embodiment of tradition should be understood as an expression of the poet's effort to push back against what Wallace Stevens called "the pressure of reality," which in her case most prevalently is her familial past—the *dúchas* of her origins.[21] Her work aims to assert in Stevens's phrase "a violence from within against the violence without," and as Roethke similarly recognized, "Bogan is a contender, and opponent, and adversary, whether it be the devouring or overpowering mother, or time itself."[22] The poet pushes back against the pressure of reality by naming the adversary and holding a mirror up to it, thereby diffusing the Medusa's power. The counterforce of such empowerment in the art is obtained by hard labor to secure a place in tradition's unfolding inheritance.

Yeats for Bogan is more than any other poet the principal exemplar of tradition's power to counter disorder through the poem's transfiguration of reality into art. As such, Roethke's insight that her work is unlike much of the poetry bred in America is not surprising, for through the presiding figure of Yeats it is her Irish inheritance—the residuum of the *seanchas,* that other Irish term for "heritage"—that asserts itself most emphatically in her work. As Elizabeth Frank notes, Yeats was Bogan's "first and most important literary influence," the poet to whom she had paid the closest attention since she first encountered his work in 1916.[23] In the late 1930s until shortly after his death Bogan wrote several short reviews and one brief essay on Yeats's work. The title of her essay, "The Greatest Poet Writing in English Today," written two years before the great Irish poet's death, underscores how profoundly she regarded his work and his example. In it she praises Yeats's imaginative vitality into old age, his dedication from early adolescence to "training of the personality" as well as in the art, and most significantly "the naturalness, sincerity, and vigor" of his late style.[24] Significantly, she does not see these stylistic virtues as "approaching the secret" of his work. Rather, she observes, "what impresses us most strongly in Yeats' late work is that here a whole personality is involved. . . . A complex temperament (capable of anger and harshness as well as tenderness) and a powerful intellect come through; and every part of the nature is released, developed, and rounded."[25]

In a brief portrait written three years earlier, Bogan further summarizes the ideal when she affirms that "Yeats grew from a singer of a few snatches of pure song into a master of technical subtlety and intellectual power.... His native gifts—the extraordinary ear underlying his technical brilliance, his heritage of blood in which run wit, bitter intelligence, and a fund of beautiful common speech—always stood him in good stead."[26] Such aesthetic ideals were Bogan's own, and her love of Yeats's work and his steadfastness in the art enabled her to pursue her vision in spite of her experience of adversity.

It is significant, however, that Bogan invokes heritage in the midst of her list of Yeats's virtues, since it is such heritage, the *dúchas* positively construed, that she perceived herself mostly to lack except for her mother's "Celtic" speech. In a sense, the compacted emotional and intellectual urgency of Bogan's poetry is born, as Harold Bloom notes, in "a conflict of contraries" he deems akin to Blake's and Yeats's.[27] The inherent contrariness of her poetry comes to the fore in "Summer Wish," which Bogan wrote as a kind of dialogue of self and soul in which two voices contend with what to make of natural process and, ultimately, the fate of consciousness. Throughout her work, as in "Summer Wish," she seeks the kind of technical and musical virtuosity she admires in Yeats's lyricism as a means to embody and express often explosive emotional content. For example, in her early poem "Stanza" Bogan appears to be in direct conversation, and disputation, with Yeats on the matter of women's experience:

> The eyes that opened to white day
> Watch clouds that men may look upon:
> Leda forgets the wings of the swan;
> Danae has swept the gold away.[28]

In Bogan's revision of the myth of Leda and Danae, rape is neither mythologized nor secured within an overarching historical narrative; rather, both female figures obtain a ruthless psychic self-assertion through courageous acts of erasure against the very forces that have violated them. The brutality of the male gods and their violent sway are simply brushed aside. The poem's final gesture is remarkable, for with it the incessant conflict between male and female in Bogan's poetry, rooted as it is in her early life, reaches a kind of momentary stay through an answering psychic dismissal granted to the women. For the moment of the poem the *seanchas,* the tradition of art and poetry, has trumped familial *dúchas,* that heritage defined by power, violence, and disinheritance. As "Stanza" further suggests, while Bogan holds Yeats in the highest esteem as a poet, she nonetheless is willing, and able, to contend with him.

Bogan's achievement in such poems is more than a necessary variation on tradition. Rather, her achievement constitutes the beginning of a revision of that tradition from the inside. We see this operation of intensive revision through mastery of the *seanchas*—her art rejects outright dismissal of the tradition in favor of a mastery that is as subversive at times as it is secure. In her great poem "Hypocrite Swift," for example, Bogan incorporates significant selections from Swift's own journals, though she hammers those portions together with her own fierce portrayal of the man, his social and political milieu, and his relationship with Stella into a sequence of taut, shapely, variant Sapphic quatrains:

> Hypocrite Swift now takes an eldest daughter.
> He lifts Vanessa's hand. Cudsho, my dove!
> Drink down Wexford ale and quaff down Wexford water
> But never love.[29]

Beyond its technical achievement, "Hypocrite Swift" marks Bogan's engagement with specifically Irish subject matter, and she employs that subject matter to her own imaginative ends. In the poem Yeats's estimation that Swift "served human liberty"[30] is turned inside out with respect to his young wife, to whom the bodily liberation of erotic love will be denied: "Stir / the bedclothes; hearten up the perishing fire. / Hypocrite Swift sent Stella a green apron / And dead desire."[31] Unlike Zeus, whose power finds expression in the rape of mortal women, Swift's power exerts itself through social standing and the subjugation of the beloved despite his advocacy for the poor and his fierce critique of human social, moral, and spiritual degeneracy. This is his hypocrisy for Bogan—a betrayal of intimacy, eros, the supremely personal.

Nevertheless, despite her willingness to subtly dispute with the master in her poems, Bogan agreed with Yeats about formal poetry— that ancient salt is the best packing. Or as she herself states in "The Pleasures of Formal Poetry," "formal art—art in which the great tradition is still alive and by which it still functions—is as modern as this moment, and as ancient as the farthest antiquity."[32] Beyond her formal affiliation with Yeats as well as Auden and Rilke, Bogan's admiration for the Irish Nobel laureate stems from his example of rectitude and dedication in the face of failure. As she wrote to her publisher Morton Dauwen Zabel, after the loss of Maud Gonne, Yeats was "shot to pieces." "And then what happened," she reflects, "in a few years he is back on his feet again. . . . He began learning how to write all over again. . . . He began to face reality even more." It is her understanding of Yeats as a "fighter" that most pervades her estimation of him and his importance for her, despite any disagreements latent in the poetry. For her the later poems come out of "a break, a tragic break, which he lived through and got over and mended from."[33] Come build in the empty house of the stare. Leda forgets the wings of the swan.

While Yeats is surely the most significant artistic connection to Ireland's poetic heritage for Bogan, it is important to recognize that she also read widely in the work of Louise Imogen Guiney, another Irish American poet whose work anticipates the explosion of women's poetry in the twentieth century. She did not, however, think highly of Lola Ridge's poems (and one can see why, given Ridge's very different relationship to form) and felt that Marianne Moore treated her kindly, "but rather like some assistant more or less invisible to her."[34] Both Moore and Bogan worked in the New York Public Library at the time, and both were poets, though Moore was a decade her senior.

Beyond Bogan's deep dedication to the great tradition of English language poetry and her serious engagement with the poets of her day, in at least one poem she plumbs the source of the Irish *seanchas* directly and brings the inspiration forward into the modern, and American, sensibility:

> Back through clouds
> Back through clearing
> Back through distance
> Back through silence
>
> Back through groves
> Back through garlands
> Back by rivers
> Back below mountains[35]

Written under the influence of onomatopoeic chants, "Train Tune" sounds as though it might have been written by Amergin himself. The return passage through groves, garlands, by rivers, below mountains—back through distance—is simultaneously an invocation, a calling forward, of the dual heritage of cultural birthright and artistic tradition. It is surprising, then, that so exemplary a poet as Eavan Boland makes no mention of Louise Bogan in her literary memoir *Object Lessons,* though she invokes the examples of Elizabeth Bishop, Sylvia Plath, and Adrienne Rich. The lack of any mention is ironic, since in 1952, while Bogan was poetry reviewer at the *New Yorker* under William Shawn, she recommended the poetry of one Adrienne Cecile Rich for publication.[36] Also ironic is Boland's encounter as a child in New York with Padraic Colum, with whom Louise Bogan would have worked and socialized in the literary salons of mid-twentieth-century New York.

In an interview Boland reflects, "I'm a feminist. I'm not a feminist poet. I've said somewhere else that I think feminism has real power and authority as an ethic, but none at all as an aesthetic."[37] In *Object Lessons* Boland also speaks candidly of the role of women's poetry relative to tradition: "if the woman poet makes a new custom and a different sign, she is not by that process alone, free of her engagement with the old signs. She must renegotiate a position with the poetic past which is appropriate to her project and faithful to her imaginative freedom. But which is also generous to that past and delicate in the manner of a tradition which sustained her."[38] Both of these reflections offer judgments to which Louise Bogan would have assented wholeheartedly, though Ruth Limmer speculates whether Bogan's "deep admirations" for male poets like Yeats and Rilke might have impeded the reception of her work by women poets of the generation maturing in the 1960s and, in particular, by feminist critics and academics.[39] If so, they miss the profound importance of Bogan for the development of women's poetry in the twentieth century, an importance evidenced in the poems themselves, if not in her proclivity to praise men poets more than she praised women poets.

One also has to wonder whether Bogan's embrace of the great tradition of Irish poetry, particularly through Yeats, might render her less significant an influence on an Irish poet like Eavan Boland, for whom America's "tradition of experiment"[40] is something she admires and is attracted to. After all, Boland was born culturally and artistically into the more conservative Irish tradition and sought to free herself from its masculine dominance by embracing such American poets as Plath and Rich. Bogan's significance for women's poetry, in turn, might well be hidden from the likes of Irish women poets precisely because she embraced the largely male-dominated tradition from which they seek greater purchase on their own terms, if not liberation. Nevertheless, it is Adrienne Rich who proclaimed on the jacket of *The Blue Estuaries* that Bogan's work "is a graph of the struggle to commit a female sensibility, in all its aspects, to language" and further affirms that "we who inherit that struggle have much to learn from her." One can only hope that in time Louise Bogan's achievement will be recognized rightly, in Ireland as well as America, as an outgrowth of the contraries of a double heritage that should itself be acknowledged, interrogated, and affirmed in all its generative complexity.

Radical Routes and the Poetry of Community

The problem of obtaining this kind of extended recognition is, as is so often the case, a matter of audience—not only securing an audience but defining it. Throughout her life Bogan was granted the peculiar moniker "a poet's poet," which means apparently that her technical resources were such that those who admired her work most were themselves practitioners of the art. This does not say much for the audience for poetry, nor by implication for the "trade" of many practicing poets. Auden and Roethke were among Bogan's admirers, and with the publication of her *Poems and New Poems* in 1941 she was widely expected to win the Pulitzer Prize.[41] She did not. The fickle and often arbitrary nature of awards is, proverbially, what it is, though the fact that her final poetic testament, *The Blue Estuaries, Poems 1923–1968,* received almost no notice when it was published at a time when poetry written by women had climbed to the forefront of American literature suggests a more endemic problem.

She lived at a time when a poet could make a living reviewing poetry, and consequently she was not herself an academic. She lived also during the time when the locus of recognition for poetry shifted decisively to academia, with the attendant emphasis on theory over practice, though as her essays demonstrate, she was a brilliant practical theoretician in the art as well as an acute and articulate critic. As the American poet Michael Ryan ruefully acknowledges, "the poet's idea of his audience (which may or may not be accurate) is fused to his idea of his cultural role (which may or may not be realistic) and thereby influences and even generates his poetry."[42] Bogan's idea of her audience is irrevocably linked to the great tradition, even as her work embeds other, less visible aspects of her familial, social, and cultural heritage. She had no conception of the poet's great cultural role—she certainly did not see herself in the role of the *file*—though it also might be said that her conception of the audience for her work eventually revealed an incompleteness with regard to the place of women's poetry in America. That is ironic, considering her importance for women's poetry. Her own production certainly dwindled as she aged, though she always wrote slowly and deliberately. Likewise, the broader recognition that might have given her wider appeal before the reclamation of Frank's biography and a growing number of critical works also failed to take hold. Thanks initially to the dedication of her former student, Ruth Limmer, the work of Louise Bogan is posthumously winning a wider audience in some parts of the academy, in addition to the continued attention of fellow discerning practitioners of the art.

In stark contrast temperamentally and formally to the work of Louise Bogan, though likewise less widely appreciated than it should be, the poetry of Thomas McGrath embodies the spirit of a leftist counterculture that affirmed an alternative national narrative over the course of the American century. Where Bogan remained deeply circumspect toward politics of whatever persuasion (at times chastising leftist friends such as Rolfe Humphries to avoid ideological idealism), McGrath from his early adolescence threw in his political and imaginative lot with Marxism. Born in North Dakota in 1916, the grandson of Irish Catholic emigrants, McGrath is an inheritor of the Irish American emigrant experience of exile prompted by idealized tales of freedom and prosperity for those homesteading on the northern plains of the American West. Such ideals met with the hard realities of living and working in a rural nineteenth-century community of farmers whose investment of land and lives was to come to nothing in the Great Depression and in the Dustbowl of the 1930s.[43]

The consciousness of that emigrant heritage, the encounter with America, and the betrayal of the labors of generations of family by powerful political and corporate interests deeply marked him. When asked by Reginald Gibbons about the sources of his radicalism, he responded, "Well, I guess what happened is I got a basic kind of radicalization out of my father and out of the people around him, and people who passed through when I was a kid, working. Somewhere in high school I read a little Marx, and that seemed to pick up these things that my father had talked about, in a different kind of way. My father says, 'Can't trust any of those sons-of-bitches,' and Marx talks about the ruling bourgeoisie. And eventually I guess I made some kind of connection."[44] What becomes clear very quickly in this reflection is that McGrath's political and eventually his imaginative cast of mind emerges directly from the heritage of dissent communicated to him by his father. Any theory merely builds on that foundation.

Beyond this, McGrath's awareness of his family's history is imbued with an indelible awareness of his Irishness, and like Bogan the *dúchas* of a heritage of dispossession. When he recounts the story of his mother's father settling in North Dakota near Maple River outside of Fargo, and his father's father "with his savage anti-English recollections of the Irish Potato Famine,"[45] his musings exemplify the kind of oral tradition common to emigrant family narratives:

> And that's where he started out. He sent back to Ireland and he got a wife who was about three times his size from over the Shannon, where the English said they would drive the Irish to hell or Connacht. And so he got one of those beauties from over there (and probably she *was*). She was a Gaelic speaker, whereas his Gaelic was very, very little. . . . My father's father [also] came from Ireland to Canada, and from Canada came down and eventually wound up at a little place called Fort Ransom, homesteaded, got killed by a runaway team, the farm went under, and everybody went every which way.[46]

Such knowledge of family history can be quite common, needless to say, and McGrath's relation of his family stories of emigration sound as if they could have been recorded for an oral history project. The difference, however, is that McGrath is considered by a substantial community of contemporary poets and critics to be "as close to Whitman as anyone since Whitman himself."[47] Echoing such poet-critics as Reginald Gibbons and the late Terrence Des Pres, E. P. Thompson proclaims with equal enthusiasm that McGrath "will be remembered in one hundred years when more fashionable voices have been forgotten."[48] The cornerstone of McGrath's achievement as a poet rests on his exploration of heritage, culturally as well as politically and artistically. As Terrence Des Pres trenchantly observes, "every aspect of [McGrath's] heritage—the place, the hard times, the religious and political culture—informs his art in a multitude of ways."[49] That heritage includes his Irish Catholic upbringing as well as his sense of lived Irish and Irish American history.

One can see his Irish heritage influencing his poetry in the late poem "Offering," an elegy for his father, in which the archetypal emigrant journey informs the poem's conceit as the poet bears witness to his father's endurance over a lifetime:

> Father, you must have been,
> Like now—
> On a tiny raft while the big ship went down.
>
> You had taken our mother aboard
> While the decks were still awash.
> Then for a little time, it must have seemed almost like heaven—[50]

Like many other Irish Americans, McGrath worked for a time as a longshoreman. He also worked on boats while a soldier in the Aleutians during the Second World War, though he won a Rhodes Scholarship to study at Oxford—eventually giving it up to travel in Spain when he could not bring himself to conform to the requirements. Still, the emigrant journey exerts its power from below in "Offering," in which, like the subtext of a palimpsest, it underwrites the surface meaning. At times, however, McGrath's sense of connection to his Irish *dúchas,* as well as the *seanchas* of his Irish heritage, manifests itself directly rather than metaphorically in a vivid convergence.

In the final movement of his twentieth-century epic, *Letter to an Imaginary Friend,* McGrath incorporates—of all things—Ogham into an unfolding quest guided largely by Native American kachina traditions and the vestiges of his sacramental Catholicism, the strands of multiple traditions woven into an autobiographical Irish American family narrative presided over by his Marxist vision of history. We can see how emphatic and committed McGrath is to that vision in these lines from his early poem "The Topography of History," lines in which one can also hear the sweeping drive of his Whitman-like cadences so unlike the taut formal lyricism of Louise Bogan:

> Beyond the corrosive ironies of prairies,
> Midnight savannahs, open vowels of the flat country,
> The moonstruck waters of the Kansas bays
> Where the Dakotas bell and nuzzle at the north coast,
> The nay-saying desolation where the mind is lost
> In the mean acres and the wind comes down for a thousand miles
> Smelling of the stars' high pastures, and speaking a strange
>   language—
> There is the direct action of mountains, a revolution,
> A revelation in stone, the solid decrees of past history,
> A soviet of language not yet cooled or understood clearly:
> The voices from underground, the granite vocables.
> There shall that voice crying for justice to be heard,
> But the local colorist, broken on cliffs of laughter,
> At the late dew point of pity collect only the irony of serene stars.[51]

Had Robinson Jeffers been inclined politically to the left these are the lines he might have written, in which the natural world becomes infused with a sublime materialism that chastens the human presumption of control. The natural world in "The Topography of History" exerts something of an incipient Marxism, a kind of preconscious materialism that sets matter itself in a relation that should ideally be made manifest in the human drive toward community and justice. The poet therefore postulates a "soviet of language" that has not yet found its place in the American grain. The land was not ours before we were the land, as Frost believed. It is not ours even now, for McGrath.

The poet's attack on the failure of capitalist America to live up to its ideal of social justice recurs in many poems, though perhaps nowhere more movingly than in his antiwar poems, as in "Blues for Jimmy," written for his brother killed in the Second World War, when soldiers moved "among the murders to the sound of broken treaties."[52] What distinguishes McGrath's poetry and rescues it from mere propaganda is the emotional urgency of it, an urgency born of a real and vital relationship to his subject as well as to the cadence of the line and a specificity of image whereby language is rescued from mere ideology and becomes freighted with a genuine, transcendent human concern:

> The bee that spins his metal from the sun,
> The shy mole drifting like a minor ghost
> Through midnight earth—all happy creatures run
> As strict as trains on rails the circuits of
> Blind instinct. Happy in your summer follies,
> You mined a culture that was mined for war:
> The state to mold you, church to bless, and always
> The elders to confirm you in your ignorance.
> . . . .
>   But, in another year,
> We will mourn you, whose fossil courage fills
> The limestone histories: brave: ignorant: amazed:
> Dead in the rice paddies, dead on the nameless hills.[53]

These lines from "Ode for the American Dead in Asia" resonate well with those moments in Yeats's "Meditations in Time of Civil War" when public speech and personal feeling conjoin to effect a mutual empowerment. At such times what fuels McGrath's poetry is something that cannot be identified as merely his political animus toward a cultural and social power structure to which he cannot give credence or assent. What we have in McGrath is a profoundly essential American poet who is fundamentally at odds with the vast majority of his fellow Americans, though whose work affirms the quarrel with self in and through the quarrel with others. His is a radically communal vision. It is not surprising that his poetry has been ignored by what Reginald Gibbons calls "the highly sanitized canon of American poetry."[54] McGrath's is an inverse vision of Whitman's open road, a counter version of a possible America grounded securely in the values of community and labor rather than in the profit-driven manifest destinies of corporations. In his own words the poet's goal is "to create a past in order to rescue a future that has been stolen from us."[55]

From this standpoint McGrath's whole imaginative and political enterprise as a poet—the two are intimately and inextricably commingled—stands as a stark countercurrent to the poet's relationship to the idea of an audience as practiced in America or, for that matter, in much of the English-speaking world. Notwithstanding the advent of a plethora of writers' organizations at least in the United States, the poet's trade has become ever more solitary, particularly since poets have become predominantly if not exclusively their own audience. Michael Ryan ties this development to the growth of industrial capitalism and more recently to the growth of writing programs, as well as to the relative "material worthlessness" of poetry as a product except for the usefulness in securing for the poet a teaching appointment[56]—the latter ever more desperately. For Ryan, that relative worthlessness along with the relatively humble patronage of the academy brings a kind of freedom to the work of making poems. Likewise, one "result of the poet's freedom," Ryan reflects, "is a dizzying proliferation of styles and almost no commonality of taste, which unhappily makes critical judgment seem arbitrary, reputations disproportionate, and awards meaningless."[57] Certainly the reception and reputation of McGrath's poetry has suffered because of his political beliefs, which led in 1952 to him being called before the House Un-American Activities Committee. He refused adamantly and eloquently to cooperate, and as a result he lost his teaching position. He sought work outside the academy in a variety of jobs, among them as a documentary film editor—a job he also lost as a result of his refusal to regard the members of HUAC as anything more than "usurpers of illegal powers."[58]

Central to McGrath's refusal, and central to his art, is the idea that the poet's freedom must be exerted against the forces that collectively disengage us economically and culturally from community. McGrath is, above all, a poet of community, a poet whose work intends to speak to the broader collective and only out of the poet's individual consciousness, the locus of a privatized inner world. As Dale Jacobson explains in his introduction to McGrath's posthumous collection, *Death Song*, "deliverance of the individual from the stasis of isolation" is the leitmotif that runs through his poetry. "Not only do his poems show us the need to be nourished by the emotional exchange of community, but they also reveal the depth of that need," Jacobson underscores, for "community is a necessity that goes to the core of our own sense of value.... Our identity can be properly experienced only through and with others."[59] This core of McGrath's essentially ethical and relational vision for the art and for society can be heard resonantly in his poem "The End of the World":

> The end of the world: it was given to me to see it.
> . . . .
>   the awful traditional fire
> Hearing mute thunder, the long collapse of sky.
> It falls forever. But no one noticed. The end of the world provoked
> Out of the dark a single and melancholy sigh
>
> From my neighbor who sat on his porch drinking beer in the dark.
> No: I was not God's prophet. Armageddon was never
> And always: this night on a poor street where a careless irreverent laughter
> Postpones the end of the world: in which we live forever.[60]

In McGrath's materially realized eschatology it is work, neighborliness, and a presiding irreverence toward the rulers of the world—including the religious rulers—that keeps the world in some measure of well-being and avoids catastrophe.

With its radical commitment to leftist politics, McGrath's vision resembles that of his predecessor, Lola Ridge. The difference between the two poetries is McGrath's refusal to grant the sacramental a reality and transcendence beyond this world. For McGrath, Christ is "a holy man" and nothing more, and he is holy because he was one who would raise human consciousness.[61] Not surprisingly, while steeped in the craft of poetry going back through "the great tradition" of English as well as American verse, McGrath additionally seeks to enlarge his artistic inheritance to include non–English-speaking poets like Pablo Neruda and Ruben Dario, whose left-leaning dedication to social justice he praises along with their artistry. "With the fury of cinders, with the despair of dusty / Great meat-eating birds stuffed under glass . . . They are hunting for you, Neruda,"[62] he writes in "A Warrant for Pablo Neruda," with intonations that echo his Chilean mentor—intonations we hear again in "Lament for Pablo Neruda": "I want to believe you, Neruda, old Commissar of roses!"[63] The commerce between McGrath and the poetry of Latin American communism gains greater purchase in his poem for Ruben Dario, "A Visit to the House of the Poet":

> To carry this grand opera of the morning south: down:
> The horny and plumed back of the vast flinty cordillera:
> Green backbone of the continent under which Quetzalcoatl sleeps.[64]

To carry Whitman's "native grand opera of America" south along the spine of the continent is an imaginative journey as well as a gift that greatly extends the heritage of poetry as it is practiced in the United States. Such major gestures on McGrath's part speak, again, to his idea of an audience and hence to the elaborated cultural and artistic heritage in which he practices his craft.

Multiple heritages manifest themselves in McGrath's work—English, American, Spanish, Latino, Native American, and, significantly in *Letter to an Imaginary Friend,* Irish. As in any traditional epic, even an autobiographical one, the "hero" makes a descent to the underworld, however metaphorical. In "The Prelude," Wordsworth confronts the traumatic violence of the French Revolution. In McGrath's poem, appropriately in the middle of the journey, "the descent" occurs on the docks where he welded battleships during the war:

> They are sending me down to the ways where I don't want to go.
>   But I go
> Under the ghost-walking gantries . . .
> . . . .
>   But I am umbilical: tied to a war
> By electric cable, by a blower to breathe out the poisonous fumes
> From the iron I weld.[65]

In the midst of this descent he encounters Packy O'Sullivan "down from the wilds of the Irish Bronx." Packy is the personification of worker discontent, irreverence, and subversion—"After / The war we'll shake the bosses' tree till the money rains / Like crab apples. Faith, we'll put them under the ground."[66] Or as he toasts at "Paddy-the-Pig's," "*Slan leat!* . . . Down all bosses! After the war we'll get them!"[67] Through figures like Packy O'Sullivan and through his own family history, McGrath's sense of Irishness and his Marxism are linked together imaginatively, supplanting his family's Irish Catholicism, if not the consciousness-raising potential of a sacramental view of reality. In McGrath, the sacramental is linked to the affirming relations of communal work and not to a vision of transcendence: "History is the labyrinth, Art is the curved arrow, but Labor / Is the gunstraight line to our common heaven."[68] McGrath's "gunstraight" line likewise finds embodiment in the line of poetry through which just social relations may be made ideally, imaginatively, and genuinely possible for the community. For all of his allusiveness and learning, McGrath is preeminently a populist poet.

Embedded in McGrath's populism is his embrace of what Michael Ryan identifies as one of the essential roles of the *file* in early Irish society: "the identity of the individual poet was nothing in light of the social function of his poetry."[69] The connection emerges strongly in *Letter to an Imaginary Friend,* and not merely with his incorporation of Ogham into the text of the poem. From the first, McGrath's ideal for poetry is intimately bound to the poet's traditional social function. While his poetry intends to preserve the prevailing and defining narratives of his family that narrative is conceived of as socially and historically exemplary. It embodies the life of our times and the nation as well as the blueprint for the ideal of a better society. Though differently tuned in every respect from Louise Bogan, like her he is not a conventionally confessional poet. At the end of *Letter to an Imaginary Friend* his evocation of his Irish roots has everything to do with unearthing the routes of community imaginatively and little, if anything, to do with genealogy.

However comically and hyperbolically, McGrath locates the social ideal expressly in the *seanchas* in the world of the *file,* though he does so by unfolding a progressively more outrageous hagiography:

> From my place, adoze at the edge of the light, the half-heard talk
> Fills in a children's map of a magical place I've heard

Named "Ireland"...
    "Irelan"...
        "Eire"...
            "that damned country"...
                and "the Ould
Sod."
    And I've heard of Tuatha, the ancient hierarchic stronghold
Of the McGrath kings: that rests at the exact center of the world.
It was here my family ruled for a full fifteen minutes
Before the creation of Adam.
. . . .
At the same time Tuatha is tiniest of all the villages of the earth.
Some ancient curse (laid on them by Fomorians no doubt!)
Has reduced the enormous lands of the McGrath kings to a mere...
—In fact we lost the whole shootin' match: all kit and caboodle—
Including the vast horse herds (through which we're related
To the Oglala Sioux) . . .[70]

Surely these lines exemplify what Terrence Des Pres calls McGrath's "carnivalesque" approach to poetry. The poet's joking and hyperbole at once constitutes the integration of his Irish heritage into the body of his definitive magnum opus and the subversion of that heritage as an exclusive narrative by which history may be encoded to the detriment of others and the aggrandizement of oneself and one's tribe. The linkage to Native America is likewise at once affirming and subversive. Indeed, Irish and Native America become con/fused at the end of the poem, and all are rendered outlandishly exaggerated. The Sheas of his mother's side make their appearance as well, from "ten thousand miles south of Tuatha, in County Kerry." McGrath's progressively more outrageous account of origins as his epic nears its end constitutes nothing less than a fantastical creation narrative, a narrative of origins reminiscent of non-Western native cultures.

    In the poet's account, an American tall tale to be sure, the original McGrath arrives in the image of Wallace Stevens's major man, the McCullough, from "Notes Toward a Supreme Fiction." *Letter* is McGrath's supreme fiction in which the original ancestor takes "Creation in hand," except, in a stark reversal of gender roles the Major Man of origins becomes a Major Woman:

> And then THE MCGRATH (*She*)
>> created the MAGH RUATH
>> from whom all subsequent
>> McGraths derive certain divinatory
>> powers in regard to the Social
>> Revolution. And an almost fatal
>> skill at catching snipe in a plain
>> brown wrapper.[71]

The poet's role is founded on this origin, which is simultaneously outrageous, carnivalesque, a lampoon of myth and genealogy, and deadly serious in its communal and social significance:

> And this work is to be completed by
>> the least of the McGraths among
>> us, or by his son, *MILLE*
>> *FAILTE* AND UP THE
>> REVOLUTION![72]

Here, McGrath emphatically binds his sense of Irishness to his revolutionary vision. Shortly after the Blue Star Kachina doll appears at the end of *Letter to an Imaginary Friend,* the poet completes his wildly unfolding narrative with nothing less than an ode to labor and the laborer: "Bless! Grant him gift and gear, / Against the night and riding of his need, / To seed the turning furrow of his light."[73] Importantly, McGrath's ambitious epic ends not only with an image of work but with field work, a gesture that harkens back to labors deeply resonant with his Irish heritage, with his *dúchas,* as well as the *seachcas,* the plough turning back again in its earthy verse.

For all of its playfulness and wild literary cunning, *Letter to an Imaginary Friend* is a work of the highest poetic ambition. At the same time, like all of McGrath's poetry, it remains undeniably populist in tone and scope while nonetheless manifesting its artistic intricacy and allusiveness. In its carnivalesque aspects its recalls the transgressive aspect of James Liddy's work, though Liddy eschews reductive materialism in his own sacramental and relational vision of the poet's art. Similarly, by lampooning the *file* in *Letter,* McGrath inadvertently draws near to fulfilling the bardic aspirations of John Boyle O'Reilly, though with a decidedly different sense of American history and with an air of postmodern irony that nonetheless grounds itself in a desire for real-world justice, whether or not one agrees with his politics. Moreover, in its playfulness and allusiveness McGrath's poetry also reminds one of Paul Muldoon's, though the two poets could not be further apart in their conception of their audience or in their temperaments.

Brilliantly intricate, formally masterful, playful, subversively comic, hyperbolic in every way, Muldoon's work positions itself for an audience that is solidly academic, critically based, and assured by theorists to last in creative writing departments and departments of English and Irish Studies for the foreseeable future. McGrath's work has no such prevailing academic caché—his banishment from the academy as well as his resolutely socialist vision has assured his absence from the canon, at least in the near term. Though, as Tim Kendall has observed, the mock epic "Madoc" "reveals the strong moral drive which underlies so many of Muldoon's parables and evasions,"[74] McGrath's *Letter to an Imaginary Friend* even at its most allusive eschews artistic evasion for the prevailing ethos of its populism. The vision of the poems is primarily and insistently communal and social and refuses the figure of the poet as solitary inventor, even if the invention itself exhibits the most dynamic vitality for being inhabited by language and tradition. This is perhaps to say that where Muldoon is intensively playful, burrowing down allusively and associatively through tradition, sharing McGrath's penchant for the carnivalesque, McGrath is extensively so. His iterations finally constellate in a vision outside the poet's self-generating inventiveness. That vision abjures the often self-enwound signposts of allusion in favor of paths to enjoin communal involvement in changing the world, however unpopular McGrath's politics might be.

In his poem "The Impossible Marriage," Donald Hall shrewdly and wittily fantasizes about America's two defining poets, Dickinson and Whitman, and what their imaginative conjugation might mean for the art of poetry in America. Likewise, the vastly different poetries of Louise Bogan and Thomas McGrath, like that of Dickinson and Whitman, reveal stark contraries of sensibility and practice. At the same time we find in their achievements alternative ways to make useful the imaginative resources of their shared Irish and American heritage—something

Eugene O'Neill, as the one of the most preeminent Irish American writers, was unable to accomplish in his poetry. His great plays, of course, are another matter, like *A Long Day's Journey into Night,* in which the brutal karma of his family heritage finds its most devastating artistic embodiment. Where in contrast to his drama O'Neill's poems exemplify the failure of the Irish American poet to own tradition efficaciously and inventively, Bogan and McGrath demonstrate how various the influences of heritage can be in the hands of Irish American poets who make themselves masters of the art. Taken together, Bogan and McGrath constitute a masterful odd couple of Irish American poetry, as odd a couple as Dickinson and Whitman in the tradition of American poetry at large. We find in their work currents of tradition shaping the poetry in conscious and unconscious ways, ways that hail another seemingly impossible marriage—that of Irish and American poetry. In the dual accomplishments of Bogan and McGrath, and the variously achieved poetries of many others, it is a union that has already been consummated.

CROSSINGS

What would the water have been
without these indelible stains—
slaves heaving dead slaves overboard
while the ship cleaves its cargo to port;

and north of that middle course
this other, likewise riding west:
refugees, brutalized, abandoned,
bones gnawed by the dogs of famine?

Each changes the habit of mind
out of its distance, unheard,
until what's made returns to emend
what it is, and its origins.

The sea from its luminous east
churns in the length of its chains.
This ocean bears more than stars
on the cold aesthetics of the waves.

III

Crossings

NINE

The Need for Routes
Genealogy in Irish American Poetry

Roots and Routes

One of my first memories to become more than a hazy backward prospect into the beginnings of my conscious life, the kind of memory that by force of ritual shapes itself into one of the primary channels of identity, is my lying awake nights in my room in our walk-up apartment listening to foghorns sounding on the Narrows. Our four-room flat was five blocks from Shore Road and the white-capped harbor with its newly risen bridge, named for the Italian explorer Verrazano, the first European to pilot his boat up the strait. It was before Third Avenue in Bay Ridge, Brooklyn, had become the acoustic for car alarms and late-night club goers, and the likely streetwalkers at that hour were men like my father—or my father himself on a Friday night after poker and drinks with his cronies—making their way home to their wives and families, maybe a little wavery in the glow of whiskey and cigars, two if not three sheets to the wind.

Already my old neighborhood, a paved-over grid of apartment buildings, rowhouses, and privileged homes near the shore, had changed from the Norwegian, Italian, and Irish enclave it was when my parents moved there after the War. Bakeries and other shop fronts with Greek and Middle Eastern names, some in Arabic script, now lined the avenue. Sally's Luncheonette around the corner smelled of hamburgers, brisket, falafel, and tabouleh. In St. Anselm's schoolyard at recess we asked each other our nationalities—"What are you?" "Irish." "Greek." "Lebanese." Nationalities flashed between us like team names on baseball cards. We'd play basketball on the courts beside the Belt Parkway and, later, would drink smuggled beers behind the park house. And always the ship traffic crowded the harbor—freighters, tankers, the big liners steaming back to Europe. My best friends, Bobby and Tony, were Syrian and Lebanese, and my parents—whose idea of exotic food was spaghetti with clam sauce or Beef Lo-Mein—sampled spinach pies and baba ganoush one Sunday afternoon at Bobby's parents' house. My first world was hyphenated, the noun "American" always qualified by other histories. The sons and daughters of emigrants, we breathed the atmospheres of our inherited histories like air.

What we did not consciously perceive was ourselves as part of a vast ongoing movement of people, part of a great passage composed of innumerable routes across geography and history. Still, throughout the neighborhood, the names of buildings inscribed traces of the new arrivals that mingled with first settlers: Anastasia Court, named after a Mafia don shot getting a haircut; the Barkaloo, a Dutch family that built the first farm below New Utrecht on this ridge above the bay. From every corner, every block, history whispered to us. Perhaps that's what I heard those nights awake in bed, the murmuring confluence of history and our own small lives in the shifting currents of the Narrows, which, like history, defined our common ground. Tonight, as memory has it this time, my brother and I in the shared bedroom in Pearl Court, my parents asleep across the hall, I listen to the intermittent tones of ships churning in the harbor where the Hudson empties into Gravesend. Each sounds like the haunting call of an animal in the middle distance or a summons made out of hollowed wood or shell to convene the tribe.

Often, when one invokes the metaphor of a tribal call, it brings to mind what Seamus Heaney called circumspectly "the shared calling of blood."[1] Despite his vaunted genius for evoking the sense of place and the poet's almost numinous connection to his home ground, Heaney's circumspection about the source of his own imaginative powers reflects a deeper current of skepticism that wisely rejects the claims of tribal identity—whether spawned by sectarian or racist estates. Though Yeats's greatness and example for the art of poetry is indisputable, we hear a muted though powerful version of the shared calling of blood in "Pardon, Old Fathers," the prefatory poem to *Responsibilities*. There, among the guiding figures of Yeats's ancestry are "merchant and scholar who have left me blood / That has not passed through any huckster's loin." For Yeats, character is blood, is pedigree, and poetry, as the end of "Pardon, Old Fathers" makes clear, is a redress or at least a sublimation of that exclusive calling—"I have nothing but a book, / Nothing but that to prove your blood and mine."[2] At this moment, implicitly if not explicitly, poetry has merged with genealogy. Poetry has become the analogical proof of the poet's genealogical connection to a rarified past and so inscribes, as it were, the family seal of both his identity and his imagination. In Yeats's work particularly, and as exemplar of the modernist cultural enterprise generally, this collusion of poetry with a culturally, socially, and racially conceived use of genealogy can make for powerful poems, though often it makes for dubious and dangerous politics. It goes without saying that too ardent a celebration of roots can lead to the worst kind of xenophobia, the most volatile kind of racial identification.

No wonder so many contemporary American poets write as though they had taken as axiomatic the injunction U.S. poet laureate Billy Collins makes in his poem "Some Final Words"—"The past is nothing. . . . Leave it behind."[3] Given the history of the twentieth century, and our short foray into the twenty-first, we have every reason to be circumspect if not incredulous about history's claims and genealogy's allures. Genealogy is nothing but history understood as the cipher of identity encoded in the cellular text of the body, and as such it may be seen as a trace, as a representative strand of a larger historical narrative. At the same time, in contrast, a call to an artistic practice that rejects history and so, broadly speaking, the self's quest for understanding of its place in the human lineage assumes implicitly that language comprises a hermetically sealed *spielraum,* an innocent play space, the poet's untroubled linguistic sandbox. Hence, another poem about "my" sad childhood, or "my" husband or wife or child, or "my" backyard—what C. K. Williams called the poetry of "domestic obsessiveness."[4] Conversely, there are poems—and these seem to be proliferating—in which irony thrives supreme and, like kudzu, chokes out all other growth, other tones, and other possible epistemological obsessions a poem might engage. In such poems, I would argue, irony can become a shield against innerness, a pose of risk. The first kind of poem can be hampered by its own earnestness, while the second may never rise above its own self-absorbing wit.

Of course, there is all manner of postmodern poem, and many fine poets writing in all manner of styles, and so finally the issue is not so much a conflict of schools and sensibilities but a question of how poetry can speak to the desire for continuity that so shaped the obsession of Yeats's "Pardon, Old Fathers," that human need for a shared calling, though without recourse to thankfully bankrupt notions of cultural, national, and racial purity. In a world defined by hybridity rather than purity, by diaspora rather than place, what purpose does poetry have that takes genealogy as its subject, that uses genealogy as a plumb line into history and identity instead of as a proof to assuage the insecure self with an illusory pedigree?

Addressing herself to the question of the soul's fundamental needs while living near the nadir of the last century's descent into apocalyptic horror, Simone Weil in *The Need for Roots* observes "that because of its continuity a collectivity is already moving into the future" but at the same time "a collectivity has its roots in the past."[5] For Weil, the presence of continuity is essential for the soul's well-being, and the violent transgression of roots by which both physical and metaphysical security are undermined eradicates not only our confidence in identity but also the foundations of humanity. Of course, equally obvious is the recognition that the perpetrators of such world-shattering violence obtain ethical justification for their actions, however perversely, through equally unyielding claims to continuity. What is National Socialism, or any brand of racism, but a fiction of continuity enforced in the most extreme condition to obliterate the continuity of the other both culturally and genetically? From this perspective the need for roots may be seen as a suspect desire, a human wish that can in its worst manifestations create systems of unparalleled cruelty. Better to forget the past, or if not the past then forget—or better, uproot—the wishful need in which such brutal delusions find their origin. At the very least avoid making poems that would indulge in "the shared calling of blood," and surely not poems that would make genealogy the impetus for their own generation.

On the other hand, does removing the need for roots from the purview of poetry do anything more than uproot poetry from the complex, fraught, and ultimately emblematic continuity of our particular history as well as the wider human collective? As we have seen earlier, alert to such concerns in both literary and popular American culture, Paul Gilroy in *The Black Atlantic* seeks to negotiate the focus on "roots" with a concomitant emphasis on its homonym, routes. Focusing specifically on black political culture, Gilroy seeks to explore the relationship between seeing identity as rooted and seeing identity as "a process of movement and mediation."[6] It is this need to be mindful of *routes* and not only of *roots* that I find most urgent for a poetry that would locate its subject in the inquisitive processes of genealogy. The roots of American poetry, like its culture, spring from the diverse and, in some cases, traumatic *routes* by which Americans arrived on this continent, even those, so we are now coming to realize through archaeological evidence, whose claims predate the European arrival to these lands. Nevertheless, scientific initiatives like the Human Genome Project have done nothing if not awaken us to the fact that our individual genealogies are precisely what bind us together through an immense and increasingly traceable web of origins. A Native American woman living in Oklahoma may be related literally by her mitochondrial DNA to a Japanese man in Tokyo; likewise the Mayo publican to the businessman in New Delhi. Though we hardly knew it in my Brooklyn schoolyard, our roots are woven through our routes. Far from being an enterprise founded on exclusion, genealogy should waken us to our physical, familial connection to each other. In our time, poetry that would find the spur if not the means of its generation in genealogy likewise needs to be mindful of both the routes and the roots that have brought this preoccupation to the forefront of a poet's concern.

Despite the unsavory nuances, certainly in Yeats's poetry the preoccupation with genealogy spurs a process of imagining that shapes the poet's whole sensibility. At such times, genealogy becomes poetic generation, or at least a shaping code in the body of the poem. Yet, in the canon of American poetry, one has to look arduously to find genealogy as an explicit concern. Strangely, as we saw previously, genealogy manifests itself marginally but notably in the poetry of Wallace Stevens. It is the subject, albeit at one remove, of his late poem "Our Stars Come from Ireland." Though not Irish himself, Stevens imagines the emigration to America of his friend and correspondent, the Irish poet Thomas MacGreevy. More rightly, Stevens invents a doppelganger for his friend who did not himself emigrate. In the poem, the fictional Tom McGreevy becomes a figure for "the westwardness of everything," or the mind's inevitable route away from the "luminous east" of origins, from roots. In an earlier poem, "Dutch Graves in Bucks County," Stevens turns directly to his own forebears, his "semblables" in their "sooty residence" underground, where "the old flag of Holland / Flutters in tiny darkness." Yet "Dutch Graves in Bucks County" is, in a sense, a genealogical poem against genealogy, for by its end Stevens has chastened his semblables by declaring they should "know that the past is not part of the present . . . / that your children / Are not your children, not yourselves."[7] No doubt the Stevens of "Dutch Graves" would look approvingly on Billy Collins's injunction to "forget history." At the same time, the poet's urge to confront history through genealogy undermines that claim. In essence, Stevens reproves Yeats's indulgence in the blood of his ancestors by facing the subject head on instead of by ignoring it. He refuses to take his own advice, and so he is, imaginatively, the *father* of his ancestors—after all, they are *his* semblables.

Anyone who has engaged in genealogical research knows that, in fact, it is impossible to recapture the past, to reconstitute entirely the roots of one's history. Gaps always inhere in the process, yet these absences in the recorded history comprise the impetus for the whole endeavor. Genealogy itself is an imaginative enterprise, as much an act of making as a process of discovery, and therefore it is potentially at least a kind of incipient poetry. In contrast to Stevens, Robert Lowell's work and, more importantly, his work's obsession with history, both personal and national as well as cultural, originates in the knowledge of an imaginative inheritance. The fact of his birth into one of the founding families of the United States, as well as his artistic legacy by virtue of his genetic relationship to poets Amy Lowell and James Russell Lowell, profoundly shapes Lowell's conception of himself as both a poet and a cultural figure. He is part of a poetic lineage. Indeed, he is the full flowering of that lineage, the imaginative heir to American history as well as America's place in Western culture. In essence, he is American poetry's embodiment of the ideal that defines such groups as the Daughters of the American Revolution. As C. K. Williams observes, Lowell saw himself at least in part as "the heir of a living body of events which were in his blood, as much as by concept."[8] Of course, the idea that events were in his blood *is* a concept, one shaped by his sense of genealogy. For all the turbulence and self-recrimination in his work, that genealogical and social bequest allowed Lowell to "prove," in Yeats's sense, the value of his book without any sense of cultural or historical insecurity.

Despite the psychological strain that might be levied on a poet born into so self-evident a coupling of art and history, Lowell's circumstance is nonetheless enviable, since it immediately gives his work access to a largeness and legitimacy of concern. When Lowell writes about his parents, their position renders them emblematic of an important social and historical sphere in American life. His genealogy, even if he did not have the poetic talent, gave him an open door to the mainstream of the American imaginative inheritance in a way that the daughters and sons of later immigrants must earn, often by dislodging themselves from a far less privileged past. Americans are often chided for their limited sense and connection to history. The idea of America as the New World, untainted, a forward-looking "open road" as Whitman pictured it, is central to our myth of national identity. The injunction to forget history, however painful, lies deep in our cultural consciousness and informs, consciously or unconsciously, much of American poetry in the same way that, eventually, so many of the various nationalities in my neighborhood schoolyard blended, at least in part, into the singular identification "American," as my friends grew up to become policemen, firemen, stockbrokers, and the like. Though not entirely forgotten, our different routes to becoming American were surpassed by our common experience of being American. For most of us, bringing those various cultural histories to mind meant the partially conscious rituals of family gatherings or perhaps the occasional political discussion.

It should be one of the poet's jobs, however, to explore the intersection between self and history and, in so doing, to give form to the profound questions inhering in that unavoidable and indelible relation. In his essay "The Poet and History," C. K. Williams raises the issue of how difficult it is in poems to take oneself as the case historically; that is, to write poetry that takes as its subject the intersection of one's personal history and history at large. Indeed, he observes that it seems hardest of all for Americans to do just that. "How am I to reconcile my sense of limitation, even of inadequacy, in terms of my own actual position in history," Williams observes, "with the apparently heroic self which these sorts of meditations seem to call for?"[9] For Lowell, access to such heroic self-portrayal is resident in his blood. At the same time, need the "heroic self" as Williams understands it, with all of its potential grandiloquence, be linked so rigorously to a history narrowly defined by social privilege?

In contrast to Lowell's Brahmin sense of imaginative belonging, the poetry of African America breathes the painfully brutal history of the antithetical American inheritance of slavery and social injustice. Such poetry is, by contrast, an affirmation of human and historical adequacy affirmed against the starkest and most malignant kind of limitation. In poems like Robert Hayden's "Beginnings," for example, the preoccupation with the self's place in history—a theme profound in Hayden's work—announces itself in specifically genealogical terms, and in so doing the heroism of the poet taking himself as the case sheds any pose of grandeur and acknowledges its vulnerability to historical circumstance. Though it leaves the poet with no access by blood or social standing to figures like Cotton Mather, Jonathan Edwards, or Nathaniel Hawthorne, it goes without saying that the history of racism in America is nonetheless inescapable for our identity. In both sequences, Hayden's treatment of genealogy is lyric and anecdotal—Grandma Easter, a Virginia freedman Indian's bride, "at ninety could still chop and tote firewood," though the brevity of the telling and the limitation of what is told quickly become representative of the absence at the center of the quest. The routes to the roots can bring us only so far.

In turn, Rita Dove's Pulitzer Prize–winning sequence about her grandparents, *Thomas and Beulah,* can be understood as a still more sustained effort to dramatize the family story into presence against the backdrop of twentieth-century American history. The genealogical aspect of the work is curtailed—Dove only goes back one generation. She also dramatizes her grandparents' lives from an omniscient perspective, thus effectively eliding the voice of the questing self from the work. Nevertheless, the impulse of using genealogy as spur to imagination and even a method of writing poetry remains at the heart of Dove's book, and with Robert Hayden and others her work illuminates alternative bloodlines in American poetry.

Just as significantly, taken together, the absence of a complete family story in Robert Hayden's "Beginnings" and the cumulative narrative arc of the lyric vignettes by which Rita Dove portrays her grandparents' lives in *Thomas and Beulah* illustrate two contrary approaches to the problem of writing poems based on genealogy. Hayden's approach is to write a poem that embodies the confrontation with incompleteness, and as anyone knows who has done genealogical research, that confrontation is inevitable and makes all the more significant those moments when a line of inquiry sheds genuine light on the family lineage. Dove's approach, on the other hand, is to create the illusion imaginatively of her grandparents' presence through the accumulation of dramatically realized moments. This is, of course, a fiction, like Dante's descent into the underworld. We are meant to believe they are before us through the medium of the page. Neither approach can be adopted purely, however, since Hayden has to shape the fragments of his genealogy imaginatively, and Dove's lyric moments likewise outline the contours of absence around which her grandparents' lives come into relief.

Eavan Boland confronts the same dialectic in an Irish context when she imaginatively recounts in *Object Lessons* her grandmother's hospitalization and eventual death in the National Maternity Hospital in Dublin in the fall of 1909. Discussing Boland's reconstruction of her grandmother's past, James Rogers aptly calls her efforts a process of "genealogical filling-in." Indeed, Boland's evocation of her grandmother's tragic last days, like a genealogical search, begins with the most fragmentary materials. "I know nothing about her childhood," Boland writes. "There are no photographs. No letters. Nobody ever recalled her to me as living memory. It is another erasure." Here, as elsewhere in her work, Boland confronts the eradication of the past by recorded history. What does survive, by the frailest margin, is a story that Boland calls "so odd and strange that it has the power to upstage all those icons and arrangements that survive the recorded childhoods of official family histories."[10] That, of course, is the story she "fills in" in *Object Lessons*. It is the imaginative endeavor to fill in the gaps of history that binds Boland's endeavor to the efforts of African American poets like Hayden and Dove whose work, whether genealogically based or otherwise, seeks to shed light on the neglected stories outside the official historical record.

More broadly, in the American context, the imaginative importance of filling in the record has influenced poets as diverse as Ellen Bryant

Voigt and Edward Hirsch. Voigt's poem "Short Story" explores variation in the genealogical record through the family story of how her grandfather killed a mule, or maybe it was a horse—the poem explores that narrative incongruity. In "Ancient Signs" and "Fever," Edward Hirsch evokes the lost world of his grandparents, both Jewish refugees from Poland on the eve of the Nazi devastation. Still more elaborately, Allen Grossman's poetry takes on the imaginative burden of locating itself within the cultural and familial lineage of Jewish thought and history—"Everyone must write a book of mother, and / Father," so he affirms in his poem "Of the Great House."[11] There are many other examples scattered across the landscape of American poetry. Undoubtedly the horrendous and indelible erasures of slavery and other subsequent injustices have profoundly shaped the imaginations of African American poets. "Slavery itself and the memory of it," as Paul Gilroy observes, have prompted specific kinds of countercultural invention in spirituality, music, politics, and literature.[12] Likewise, the impact of the Holocaust on Jewish American poets hardly needs to be elaborated, while Voigt's poem "Short Story" demonstrates that genealogical themes can arise in poets whose personal histories are distinguished by neither great privilege nor great social evil.

At the same time, given the brutal historical and political circumstances that forced Irish emigration to America, particularly in the nineteenth century, one has to wonder whether with regard to genealogy Irish American poetry has been in a prolonged state of amnesia. The brutal and wholesale obliteration of bloodlines through the slave system was a horror Irish emigrants did not have to endure. Nevertheless, the atrocious conditions in Ireland during the famine years; the vast loss of life both at home and en route on coffin ships, and later in America's crowded urban ghettos; the unhappy ritual of the American wake performed by families well into the twentieth century—all provide ample and more than sufficient cause for the kind of imaginative response Boland articulates when she writes in her poem "The Emigrant Irish," "what they survived we could not even live"—and many did not survive. Prior to the traumas of the nineteenth century, Irish peasants in the eighteenth century were "the most miserable representatives of their class in Western Europe," so Lawrence McCaffrey observes, with a standard of living "probably lower than that of black slaves in North

America."[13] In addition, it should be remembered, Irish slaves worked alongside African slaves in the Caribbean and were vilified as "white niggers," particularly during the Famine years in the urban centers of New York, Boston, and Chicago, while blacks were deemed "smoked Irish."

As Toni Morrison observed, "in matters of race, silence and evasion have historically ruled literary discourse,"[14] and the like is true emphatically of how this complex and often fraught social relationship between Irish Americans and African Americans has been represented in literature. Studies like Noel Ignatiev's controversial *How the Irish Became White* bring the issue to the fore historically, and far more needs to be done in the arena of race and literary discourse. My point at this juncture is only to emphasize that a common experience of diaspora shapes the historical identity of these two groups, as well as others, and that saying so ought not to obscure our awareness of both the qualitative and the quantitative differences in that experience as initiated and maintained by racial injustice. While the Irish entry into modernity was not shaped by the incomparably brutal experience of systematic slavery or wholesale genocide, it nonetheless shares with other immigrant groups—to paraphrase Robert Hayden—a traumatic legacy of passage to life on these shores.

Bridge and Breach

Remarkably, despite the urgency of these large historical matters and contemporary Irish America's seemingly insatiable interest in tracing roots back to Ireland, this tragic legacy has been mostly absent from Irish American poetry. If there has been a need for roots, the exploration of the routes by which that need arose has been neglected until recently by the vast majority of Irish American poets. Though a profound sense of Irishness informs the poems, as well as an engagement with Irish and American history, in the nineteenth century there was little in the way of genealogy shaping the imagination of Irish American poets. One exception is Sarah Whitman's "Don Isle," which is spurred by the poet's effort to imagine back to the place of origin and its castle "wrecked in the wild Cromwellian wars."

> Lonely beneath the silent stars
> > It stands, a gray and moldering pile,
> Wrecked in the wild Cromwellian wars,
> > The sea-girt castle of Don Isle.
> The wild waves beat the castle wall,
> > And bathe the rocks with ceaseless showers;
> Dark heaving billows plunge and fall
> > In whitening foam beneath the towers.[15]

Whitman's evocation of place in her poem is vivid but willed. The original connection to place has been broken by history. James McHenry's "The Haunts of Larne" expresses a more immediate paean to place—"Ah! lovely Larne! must I ne'er see, ne'er see thee more?"[16]; despite its obvious emotion the poem's nostalgic tone is unmistakable.

In any case, what one feels in each of these poems is a different sense of generational connection from what Seamus Heaney articulates in his personal essay "Mossbawn," in which he meditates on the pump behind the family farm:

> That pump marked an original descent into earth, sand, gravel, water. It centred and staked the imagination, made its foundation the foundation of the *omphalos* itself. So I find it altogether appropriate that an old superstition ratifies this hankering for the underground side of things. It is a superstition associated with the Heaney name. In Gaelic times, the family were involved with ecclesiastical affairs in the diocese of Derry, and had some kind of rights to the stewardship of a monastic site at Banagher in the north of the country. There is a St Muredach O'Heney associated with the old church at Banagher; and there is also a belief that sand lifted from the ground at Banagher has beneficent, even magical, properties, if it is lifted from the site by one of the Heaney family name. Throw sand that a Heaney has lifted after a man going into court, and he will win his case. Throw it after your team as they go out on the pitch, and they will win the game.[17]

Here genealogy is not only proximate to the place of origins and the sacred center of the *omphalos* but a magical conduit or passage to the source of identity by virtue of the family name. Genealogy and its literal embodiment in place are the foundation of the poet's imagination. In contrast to Heaney's fortunate circumstance with regard to his sense of place, Sarah Whitman's "Don Isle" is significant for Irish American poetry because its willed effort to imagine back to the foundation of identity records a breach rather than an identification. The like is true of James McHenry's poem. In each case, the source of identity and imagination has been broken, and as such the poet's identity and imagination find their origin in the gap of longing rather than in the security of connection. The center has not held. Both Sarah Whitman's and James McHenry's genealogical affiliations with place find their true imaginative spur in diaspora.

In contrast to Heaney, John Montague's genealogical sense of place is more fraught at the primal level of self-identity by historical trauma. Though his connection with the "rough field" of his home is strong, Montague, as we saw in chapter 4, is the product of diaspora. Born in Brooklyn, Montague has deep psychic wounds, and in a profound sense his parents' separation—the mother who returned to Garvaghey, the father who stayed in America—embodies the conditions of diaspora that have shaped the modern world. At the same time, in Montague's work one finds genealogy forming an imaginative bridge to bind together the poet's breached sense of identity.

In his poem "A Graveyard in Queens," the link to the past is realized by the recognition of his own name on the stone of his uncle and namesake:

> I submit again
> to stare soberly
>
> at my own name
> cut on a gravestone
>
> & hear the creak
> of a ghostly fiddle
>
> filter through
> American earth.[18]

The name he sees—his own—is both bridge and breach, at once the conveyor of identity and the emblem of irretrievable loss. In addition to his awareness of "the unhomely," what Montague's example underscores is the recognition of genealogy as at once the identifying code in the body of the poem and the trace that inscribes an unhealable absence—the sound he says in "A Flowering Absence" that a wound makes.

Beyond the parameters of Montague's work, the idea of genealogy as both poetic bridge and poetic breach suggests that what I would call the genealogical imagination may be understood as a method of inquiry not into identity alone but into an anxious awareness of historical and metaphysical absence that precipitates the poet's effort of identity construction as well as the generation of poems. To put this another way, genealogy as a shaping influence on poetry traces the poet's effort to establish a home in time apart from the assurance of place, though as anyone who has done genealogical research knows, the journey is always partial, filled with gaps and dead ends. Ideally, the genealogical imagination prompts an effort on the part of the poet to plumb that more encompassing idea of home beyond the point where the idea of home can be easily affirmed, if at all.

Both Heaney's meditation on his family roots in the soil of Ulster and Montague's obsessive contemplation of family routes in the diaspora of twentieth-century America provide vivid examples of how memory, and in particular genealogical memory, can foster the poetic imagination. The like ought to be said of Sarah Whitman's "Don Isle," which, while more reverie than meditation, nonetheless reveals an early Irish American poet's effort to extend memory back beyond the limits of personal recollection into the ancestral past. In contrast, Billy Collins, both an Irish American and the former poet laureate of the United States, looks with considerable circumspection on the kind of poetry that is, as he says, "driven by the engines of memory rather than the engines of imagination." Though Collins hedges somewhat by stating that his "complete lack of experience with grandparents probably accounts" for his "minimal participation in producing such poems," he clearly finds poems preoccupied with "personal experience" an indulgence.[19] What could be more of an indulgence than a poem driven by the preoccupation with ancestral memory, as though the poet's extended life story were so important as to trace his or her arrival on the planet back generations? Hence the irony of Collins's essay "My Grandfather's Tackle Box": the box doesn't exist.

Billy Collins's wry misgivings about memory-driven poems, like his urgings to forget history, are symptomatic of a growing distrust of the personal in contemporary American poetry, the sometimes wary and sometimes condescending rejection of any poem that even hints of confessionalism. Collins is right, in part at least, when he identifies the limit of such poetry. "The key risk in writing the memory-driven poem," Collins observes, "is a failure to take advantage of the imaginative liberty that poetry affords.... A poem suffering from such a disadvantage wanders around in the past and may amount to little more than a record, an entry in the log of the self's journey, a fond reminiscence, a photo in a family album, or worse, a carousel of color slides." In contrast, the poem of imagination adds to experience what Collins calls "the light that never was," which is a light that transcends the self's "reiterated fictions" and therefore allows poetry to become something "more than reminiscence."[20]

For all of Billy Collins's well-taken observations about the limits of memory-driven poetry, one has to wonder whether the binary that exists in his discussion between memory and imagination doesn't privilege the latter at the expense of the former. A memory poem that fails to transcend reminiscence, that fails to compel the reader with its own artistic achievement and not just by begging the indulgence of its subject, is a bad poem. There are many bad poems written directly out of personal experience, but then again many bad poems are positively Gnostic in their efforts to escape both the world and the poet's personal experience, poems that, to paraphrase Brendan Galvin, have no sense "of life lived beyond the margins" of the poem itself.[21] Such poems reject out of hand taking oneself as the case, much less taking oneself as the case historically, as do poems rooted in the genealogical imagination. Yet the kind of poem I am speaking about inhabits genealogy in order to step beyond the narcissistic journey of the self into the expansive imaginative boundaries of history and what lies outside history.

Perhaps the most exemplary Irish American effort at such a poem is Robinson Jeffers's "Patronymic":

> What ancestor of mine in wet Wales or wild Scotland
> Was named Godfrey?—from which by the Anglo-French erosion
> Geoffrey, Jeffry's son, Jeffries, Jeffers in Ireland—
> A totally undistinguished man; the whirlwinds of history
> Passed him and passed him by. They marked him no doubt,
> Hurt him or helped him, they rolled over his head
> And he I suppose fought back, but entirely unnoticed;
> Nothing of him remains.[22]

The question with which Jeffers begins his poem is the fundamental genealogical question, the question that would penetrate to the center of origins. Unlike Heaney's direct access to his Ulster roots through the Heaney name, Jeffers's name is both the means of self-identification and a cipher. Joseph Jeffers, the poet's paternal grandfather, emigrated from Monaghan in the early 1800s and settled in Ohio with his family to become a frontier schoolteacher.[23] Despite the accessibility of the poet's immediate ancestry, the linguistic migrations of the Jeffers name in the poem give testimony to diaspora and suggest that in fact the poet's identity lies more in the idea of diaspora than in the idea of origin. Jeffers likewise eschews Yeats's response to the predicament of modernity—the embrace, or invention, of a privileged family history. Jeffers's name is an "erosion," but the ancestral origin is nonetheless "totally undistinguished." The whirlwinds of history passed him by, though as Jeffers observes they may have "marked" him. How they did so is impossible for the poet to say, and so instead of easy reminiscence, the genealogical impetus of Jeffers's poem urges his imagination toward an inevitable confrontation with the absence that lies at the heart of recorded history: What remains? Literally, nothing.

What is the poet's response to this predicament, which is the predicament of the genealogist as well as the poet? Jeffers's response to the impasse is not just to fill in the gap confronted by the imagination but to illuminate the process by which the poet at once confronts that absence and seeks to transcend it imaginatively. "I should like to meet him," the next stanza begins, "And sit beside him, drinking his muddy beer." Jeffers's act of identification is neither affirmed absolutely nor elided. Rather, Jeffers acknowledges the provisional nature of the imagination in tracing the path back—"I *should* like to meet him" (my italics).

In a subtle but stunning sleight, Jeffers's tense shift transports the poet back through time into the past. The limits of the quest implied in the poem's initial question are again brought to bear on the poet when he further observes, "I *think* his tales of woe / Would be as queer as ours" (my italics). At the same time, however, this confrontation of limits permits an identification between poet and ancestor, as well as affirms a correspondence of lives beyond the self and the long-negated past. "His tales of woe / Would be as queer as *ours*" (my italics), and "his mind was as quick as ours, / But perhaps even more credulous," Jeffers claims, and so he deftly shifts the personal identification of the poem to a collective one, but a collective that includes all humanity and not merely a privileged race or lineage, as if to say we are bound to each other by suffering and the knowledge of suffering. Jeffers's imaginative path traces the action of thought and evokes the mind itself as the common bond across the obliterating centuries. Beyond its genealogical premise, the true subject of Jeffers's poem is consciousness.

As expansive as the poem's imaginative movement is, at the same time Jeffers continually raises the issue of limits, as in the third stanza, when the poet declares, "I am not dreaming back into prehistory." Still, though his paternal ancestor was "a Christian / No doubt," that indubitable historical fact prompts yet another expansive shift in the poem into metaphysics. "Godfrey" means "the peace of God," but ironically Jeffers speculates his ancestor never found it in his life, though in death "it found him" in the "forgotten British graveyard, nettles and rain-slime," where he continues to "moulder" after "six or eight centuries." Lifting off from the genealogical and historical quest, the poem finally arrives in the realm of metaphysics, though without ever leaving the groundwork of the name, or of language itself:

> Nettlebed: I remember a place near Oxfordshire,
> That prickly name. I have twisted and turned on a bed of nettles
> All my life long: an apt name for life: nettlebed.
> Deep under it swim the dead, down the dark tides and bloodshot
>   eras of time, bathed in God's peace.[24]

In the poem's final rhetorical crescendo Jeffers brings the genealogical imagination to a place resonant with Gabriel Conroy's epiphany at the end of Joyce's "The Dead," a visionary glimpse beyond the self at once rooted in language and routed through the nettlebed of life, understood as a community or collectivity of the dead and the dead-in-waiting. Though, as Billy Collins points out, there are limits to the memory-driven poem, Jeffers's "Patronymic" at once faces those limits and transcends them by venturing into the common ground of our own inevitable disappearance among the dead, while at the same time remarkably leaving those limits in place.

In his essay "Autobiography and Archetype" Stanley Plumly muses that "our identities depend so much on that with which we identify and that which identifies with us," and further that "seeing, or remembering, is a way to get the meaning, the idea as well as the image, just as experience itself repeats and returns, becomes general, common."[25] Plumly's observation about the relationship between individual experience and archetypes, those primordial images or ideas—Mother, Father, anima, animus, and the like that tie self to wider collective life—assumes that a poet's work needs to transcend the limits of the individual life. Though it may well be an overstatement to see genealogy as a means to venture into the archetypal—archetypes assume access to a supra-historical reality, and not merely a historical connection—poems that take genealogy as their subject nevertheless likewise seek to locate the general life in the individual. What could be more original to self-identity than one's family history, and what could be more general than the fact that this is true for each of us, regardless of our personal lineage?

If Robinson Jeffers's "Patronymic" explores this question by affirming his distant, gap-filled connection to family origins, Thomas Lynch's narrative poem "The Moveen Notebook" examines the same melding of the individual and common life by recounting his journey to his family's ancestral home in Moveen, County Clare. Unlike Jeffers's poem, Lynch's elaborates his genealogical connection through family stories that prod the poet's imaginative resources. Patrick Lynch, his grandfather's grandfather, "was given this cottage as a wedding gift," the poet observes, "when he first brought Honora Curry here / from somewhere eastern of Kilrush." In Lynch's poem, narrative is the conveyor of the poet's seamless connection to the past and to place, as well as the formal embodiment of an assurance that Patrick Lynch is "our common man."[26]

There is nothing disjunctive in Lynch's approach to his family past, and in a manner that approaches the security of Heaney's relationship to place, the poet gains access through his genealogical knowledge to a confidence in the continuity of time itself, which is nothing other than the poem's effort of "trying to set these lives and times into / Life and Time in the much larger sense." As such, as though to embody the antithesis of Montague's fraught ancestral identification through the inheritance of a common name, the poem affirms that it is a Thomas Lynch who departed Ireland and a Thomas Lynch—the great-grandson and poet—who would return. As such, genealogy, like poetry, involves the repetition of subtle patterns over time, patterns that confound "the ineluctable modalities":

> how we repeat ourselves like stars in the dark night,
> and after Darwin, Freud and popes and worlds at war,
> we are still our father's sons and daughters
> still our mother's darling girls and boys,
> aging first, then aged, then ageless.
> We bury our dead and then become them.[27]

Here, as in Jeffers's poem, the genealogical quest ends in the ageless "archetypal" reality of death, which is now strangely assuaging, the end that marks our continuity into a future that is essentially the same as the past and therefore able to overcome history itself. Autobiography in Lynch's poem would indeed fuse with archetype.

Like Thomas Lynch's "The Moveen Notebook," Leo Connellan's book-length poem, *The Clear Blue Lobster-Water Country,* uses an at once headlong and recursive narrative to examine in this case the fictionalized speaker's connection to a dominant male ancestor. In Connellan's poem, however, the pattern of repetition that is also the speaker's social and cultural inheritance reveals itself to be inextricable from the "ineluctable modalities" of history, in particular immigrant history:

> Oh many an Irish immigrant youth
> cursed by Saint Patrick myth and
> stupidity, foolish pride bragging how

> they were able to succeed enough to spare
> their children what they had to do, and in
> doing this, making many Irish American youth
>
> as crippled as he is back home in
> rough green Irish Sea country. [28]

In contrast to Lynch's affectionate embrace of the genealogical place of origin, Connellan sees Catholic Ireland governed by guilt and repression, a pattern that is repeated in the New World. The "rough green Irish Sea country" is ruthlessly demythologized in the poem and becomes instead the source of grief in Irish emigrant Maine. The "Clear Blue Lobster-Water Country" is the antithesis of the Land of Youth in Irish lore. Rather than fostering his imaginative growth, the ghosts of historical failure trail the fabled grandfather to the New World:

> so ended American promise
>
> in Michael The O'Dock . . . so ended the chance taking, the
> beautiful riskers that are the greatness of a country,
> ended the functioning that must come from
>
> inside us in each and everyone of us, promise
> gone as much to the bottle here in America
> as any Irish farmer with Ireland,
>
> green Ireland, violent Ireland grape in its yearning
> Ireland always green in his eyes but alcohol
> his early death with all the old boys crying
>
> for The O'Dock who sailed away, his hand clutched
> in his mother's forever from Ireland, Eire
> of my soul my flesh wanders the earth.[29]

As these lines bear witness, *The Clear Blue Lobster-Water Country* is Connellan's version of Kavanagh's "The Great Hunger," an epic recounting of social and moral and finally imaginative degradation. Michael The O'Dock, the inverse of Wallace Stevens's The MacCullough, the American poet's archetype for imaginative humanity, breeds impotence in Michael's son Big Billy and so in his grandson, Young Billy. Unlike the two Thomas Lynches in "The Moveen Notebook," the inheritance of the name signifies the pathos of an apparently inescapable failure. Nor is there much hope for the music of empathy, as in John Montague's identification with his namesake uncle.

The continuity the poem envisions is destructive of both personal and collective energy, and as such, in a tone reminiscent of Berryman's Henry in *Dream Songs* (that other Irish American epic of the psyche), Connellan's fictive voice declares:

> We are a damned breed, the Irish. Young Billy gave
> his whole identity to Big Billy just to try
> to have his love
>
> . . . . . .
>
> destruction of ourselves by ourselves
> until we are all forgotten
> dead among the dead.[30]

In Connellan's poem we are back with Jeffers and Lynch gazing into the great absence that is death, only now the poet's genealogical obsessions lead him to the brink of an absolute forgetting, rather than "God's peace" or an assuaging congruence of generations. In Connellan's somber vision the Irish become an archetype for our shared human futility—"we are all forgotten / dead among the dead."

Line and Lineage

Leo Connellan's *The Clear Blue Lobster-Water Country,* Thomas Lynch's "The Moveen Notebook," Robinson Jeffers's "Patronymic," and John Montague's "A Graveyard in Queens" together constitute an assortment of patrilineal meditations. Though each poem is distinctively expressive of its poet's individual stylistic signature, taken as a whole they demonstrate the Irish American male's obsession with the father's extended genetic inheritance. Identity is bestowed through the name, the "patronym" of Jeffers's poem, and the patronym in turn becomes the vehicle for self-transcendence beyond the limited historical moment. The identification is redoubled in Montague's poem, as well as in Connellan's and Lynch's, since in each a namesake and not just the patrilineal surname reinforces that connection to the past, however fraught the connection might be. Though it is particularly emphatic in these male poets, obsession with the name and especially the ancestral namesake can be found in recent Irish American women poets as well.

In "The House of My Birth," for example, Susan Donnelly envisions a retinue of female ancestors imaginatively coinhabiting the domestic space of her home, an "alto-soprano of daughters / doing the Sunday dishes" who seamlessly transform into the mermaids she hears singing. Unlike Prufrock's sirens, they do sing to the benefit of the protagonist's questing consciousness. "One trails / her long green hair / like moss from a window," Donnelly observes. The third visitor from this feminine generational sea is her namesake, who "climbs to the tower of bone." "What is darkness? / What is light?" she sings. And above her / the family motto: / Amor et silentium."[31] Donnelly's handling of the genealogical motif in this poem comprises a figure of ascent, which is "figural" in the most emphatic sense: the questions she asks are positively Dantean in their metaphysical import. That her namesake speaks these questions under the banner of the family motto only reinforces the poem's implicit understanding of genealogy as a vehicle for identity and self-transcendence in the largest possible sense.

In addition to Susan Donnelly, Mary Swander and Kathryn Stripling Byer are contemporary poets of Irish American ancestry for whom genealogy is a shaping and sustaining influence. Unlike those male poets for whom the patronym is the bearer of the lineage, or Susan Donnelly's matrilineal namesake, both Swander and Byers locate tropes for imaginative succession in objects of folk art and physical attributes. In Swander's "Succession," for example, the poet's connection with her female ancestors manifests itself through an almost ritualized participation in the art of knitting sweaters:

> It doesn't matter if the light falls.
> Tonight, my fingers move automatically
> Along rows, each stitch
> As familiar as a bead of the rosary.

> I simply follow the family pattern
> My Irish grandmothers knit into sweaters
> For their sons, the fine threads
> Spun off the skulls of Nordic sailors.³²

As Swander's poem implies, the ancestral art of knitting sweaters is itself a generational pattern by which the lineage—both female and male—finds continuity down through the generations. Here again, however, through the poem's imagery, Swander's deft use of implication and metaphor, the genealogical motif verges on the metaphysical. The stitches are familiar as "rosary beads" and suggest this generational work is indeed a kind of ritual action. Moreover, it is this action that keeps one sustained in spite of the dark. As in Donnelly's poem, "Succession" at first orients the reader inward toward the domestic world of women knitting then conveys the reader outward into the depths of a generational ocean:

> Let down the nets, the great walls
> Of the house, and float out,
>
> The tides, the full moon, a tangle
> Of yarn, pulling me in, cell by cell,
> My flesh unraveling. . . .³³

Where in Donnelly's "The House of My Birth" the sea becomes a metaphor for the watery source of individual family identity, in Swander's poem the walls of the house fall away as in a kind of meditative trance until through the contemplative action of knitting the flesh of self diffuses into the wider body of the world—no scars, no fingerprints, no face. Here, paradoxically, rather than unfolding toward a figural crescendo, the genealogical imagination breeds an almost Buddhist awareness of the self's fluid realization in all that is not self.

In yet another contrast, Kathryn Stripling Byer's genealogical interests manifest themselves in poems that inhabit the voices of Appalachian women who share her own Ulster ancestry. Some of these poems affirm continuity with the past and the quest for identity in genetically transmitted physical characteristics. Here is the opening of "Lineage":

> This red hair
> I braid while she
> sits by the cookstove
> amazes her. Where
> did she get hair the color
> of wildfire, she wants to know,
> pulling at the strands of it
> tangled in boar-bristles.
> I say from Sister, God knows
> where she is, and before
> her my grandmother you
> can't remember because
> she was dead by the time
> you were born, though you hear
> her whenever I sing.[34]

Byer's poem goes some way in making hair color a fetish of identity. That in itself may not be surprising, but the poem goes further by associating the child's inherited red hair with the speaker's ability to sing. According to the poem's female speaker, song, like the red hair, does nothing less than make the past present, a near transubstantiation of the ancestor into the moment. The dead are not "dead among the dead" for Kathryn Stripling Byer. The dead are among the living, embodied in the living, and "Lineage" affirms this identification through its effort to make the song of the speaker's voice ring in its own tumbling lines.

Both Swander's "Succession" and Byer's "Lineage" use images of knitting and braiding to quietly suggest the nature of inheritance as a kind of weave, which indeed it is quite literally in the woven strands that make up the double helix of DNA. Again, in his short memoir "The Use of Memory" Irish poet Michael Coady reaffirms this same insight when he remarks, "we are each given a darkly woven basket of inheritance, but it comes open-ended into our hands."[35] Prompted by the process of writing his poem "The Letter," Coady's memoir is an extended reflection on the ill-fated journey of his great-grandfather who emigrated to Philadelphia in the late nineteenth century, having abandoned his son back home in Carrick-on-Suir in County Tipperary. It is also one of the few specifically Irish works that treats the Irish diaspora to

America directly in any substantive way. In addition to being a moving account of family loss and tragedy and the poet's attempt at healing, Coady's work brilliantly theorizes about the nature of genealogy and its purpose for the imagination. As Coady observes, "the purpose of genealogy should not be the neat assembly of pedigree culminating smugly in self, but its exact opposite: the extension of the personal beyond the self to encounter the intimate unknown of others in our blood."[36]

Coady's standpoint could not be further from Yeats's in "Pardon, Old Fathers." Furthermore, Coady intends his reflection to be more than merely a meditation on the imaginative uses of genealogy; rather, he perceives in the genealogical quest, with its gaps and discoveries and the urgency of its need to connect past to future in an imaginative act of self-extension, a "paradigm for the mystery of the written word." Coady's faith in transcending the personal through the self's genealogical quest likewise could not be further from Billy Collins's suspicion of memory and the personal in "My Grandfather's Tackle Box." For Coady, each line of personal history is indelibly enwound with the histories of others—those of our immediate "blood" and, by extension, all humanity. As he observes, his own family's "story of individual human destinies was also a tiny fragment of the great epic drama of migration from Ireland to America—that vast human enterprise of millions which, remarkably, has been so little articulated in a literature on either side of the Atlantic."[37] Nevertheless, this little-articulated epic theme binds the Irish American experience of diaspora to others within the still wider context of modernity's world-transforming Great Migration. This interwoven web of routes is what comprised the backdrop of my schoolyard interchanges so long ago, incomplete as they were.

Even Walt Whitman's epic myth of America does not quite do justice to the vastness of the experience, since for Whitman the emigrant had already been imaginatively adopted into the citizenship of the open road without full comprehension of the loss of the world that came before, or of the brutality for many of the arrival. Nevertheless, more and more, genealogy's role in the poetry of Irish America is to give us some measure of insight into the magnitude of that epic journey of migration through the individual stories, the fragmentary lines that have been woven into our extended inheritance.

Maura Stanton's "Elegy for Snow" from her Yale Younger Poets Award–winning first book, *Snow on Snow*, goes further than the poems I've surveyed thus far in exploring specifically the imaginative inheritance of genealogical knowledge. The poem begins with a family story, or more expressly with the story of a recurrent dream Stanton's grandmother experienced in Ireland before she emigrated. It is a dream of metamorphosis in which horses transform into swans. The imagery of horses becoming swans, like creatures penned in the mind's illuminated manuscript, prefigures the grandmother's own emigration: "It meant travel, snow," the poem tells us.[38] Both horses and swans have prominent places in Irish mythology—Cuchulain's wild horses of the water, the Children of Lir—and so the grandmother's dream is likewise an open door into the collective unconscious of her ancestors and her granddaughter's.

In contrast, the poet's dreams "are blind, without prophecy." A child of the American Midwest rather than the west of Ireland, Stanton sees herself cut off from the magical world inhabited by her grandmother, a world experienced through the prism of dream and shaman-like transfigurations. At most, she sees her grandmother "float across" her own dreams or imagines herself a snowmaiden as she rides the Rock Island line through Illinois in winter, when snow becomes the ghostly medium that poises the child's imagination for its encounter with the dead. In turn, the grown-up poet only has ritual to bridge the loss with the past:

> Sometimes I light candles
> for the old Irish who fiercely
> outlive their bodies, insisting
> on a resurrection in the hot
> mouths of their children's children.
> All I want is her dream, though—
> those red horses signaling
> movement over a continent, home
> through the Illinois snow
> to an imprisoned memory, not her,
> but myself, myself, myself.[39]

Stanton's longing by the end of the poem is for a larger, more comprehensive identity, one that would unite the ancestral past with the present, and as such one that would unite the island with the American continent, as if the red horses of her grandmother's dream had emigrated with her and transformed themselves once again, not into swans this time, but into the wild horses of the plains. Imprisoned by historical fate, memory charges the backward look toward home. Yet, in a line that bespeaks both great economy and panoramic vision—"movement over a continent, home"—Stanton's elegy accelerates the emigrant imagination's journey back into the inaccessible past, her route back into her imaginative roots. The poet's desired self-completion in the lost collective memory is never wholly achieved, of course, though the self is transformed by an act of longing, an imaginative act that is nothing less than the poet's assent to the fierce insistence of the dead for resurrection in the mouths of the living.

If the tone of Maura Stanton's "Elegy for Snow" establishes the poet's imaginative sense of loss and the concomitant effort to ground her identity in her genealogical roots as a matter of serious consideration, Brendan Galvin's "The Gang from Ballyloskey" considers the same matter from a typically wry perspective. Of all the Irish American poets rising to the fore over the last generation, Brendan Galvin is perhaps the most sustained and wide-ranging in his engagement with his Irish American identity and with the specifically genealogical aspect of his relationship to the past. Galvin's large body of work is replete with poems about Ireland and its history, and even in his American poems the sense of place reverberates with a peculiarly Irish affection for "the parish." At the same time, Galvin's imagination continually embarks on its return to the place of his ancestors—even when he did not know the exact location of that place in Ireland.

Confronted with the absence of a genealogical record (or rather the withholding of that record by a cousin), Galvin invents the place of origin in his poem "Inventing Ballygalvin." As the title implies, the poem is more about imagination than it is about recollecting a lost ancestral memory. Nevertheless, the poem brings us to the same recognition of the dead enmeshed in the lives of the living, now envisioned as a reversal:

> Turns out that the faces in Ireland
> are the faces in Boston,
> somebody's rotating
> the living and dead.[40]

Unlike Stanton, Galvin's tone is wryly comic, and by the end of the poem he worries about meeting himself rounding a corner as a red-haired woman "who I promised once I'd murder Cromwell for her." There is more than a rotation of living and dead in this comic confrontation with self once removed. The poem speaks to the question of the poet's identity by envisioning identity itself as a self-enwound conundrum of historical repetitions and recognitions.

"The Gang from Ballyloskey" is even more emphatic in this regard. Written after Galvin discovered the real place of origin in Donegal, Ireland, the poem imagines the encounter with ancestors—a "human compost" that pushed him "out into this vale of duffers and fumblers"—as a raucous haunting of faces that offer commentary and side bets on the poet's habits until the poet sees eternity "as spectator sport." The first face he sees, a farmer's, confronts him in the mirror while he shaves—it is a "face like a woodknot with blue eyes." This initial encounter quickly opens to a crowd of dead ancestors:

> Sometimes in wind I can almost
> hear them rooting for me, all the dead
> from Ballyloskey, point of origin.[41]

The verb "rooting" here inscribes a brilliant pun that joins together the two conceits of the poem: sport and organic process. Galvin reiterates the yoking together of these opposing metaphors near the end of the poem, when he pictures his ancestors as a "lineup / of root vegetables, nobody too far off the ground." Galvin's playful interpolation of sport and organicism in the poem suggests a commingling of imaginative construction—the complex orchestrations and designations of play—with the natural process of generation, the dead as "human compost" for the living. Here, again, the routes of imagination bring the poet to the roots of identity, and the roots of identity fare forward, traversing the routes by which the poet incorporates genealogical obsessions into his art.

"Discovering the provenance of the name, / he marvels again at what fidelity / the genes exact,"[42] so Brendan Galvin writes in "Against Genealogy," and yet that discovery bears witness to the poet's obsession with genealogical matters rather than his rejection of them. To the provenance of the name we may add the provenance of the face, the hair, the weave, and the dream—all traces of the past that recur and give testimony to the human diaspora across reaches of time of which the living are at once the remnant and the genomic embodiment. Genealogy, conceived rightly as a way of transcending the personal through the personal in order to encounter the other inside ourselves, the other who we are, branching outward forward and back and through us, should be a crucial element in the process of defining our humanity and not just our individual lineage.

In his essay "The Mystery of the Family," Gabriel Marcel sums up this ever-widening scope of human interconnection revealed through lineage:

> My family, or rather my lineage, is the succession of historical processes by which the human species has become individualised into the singular creature that I am. All that is possible for me to recognize in this growing and impressive interdetermination is that all these unknown beings, who stretch between me and my unimaginable origins whatever they may be, are not simply the causes of which I am the effect or the product. . . . Between my ancestors and myself a far more obscure and intimate relationship exists. I share with them as they do with me—invisibly; they are consubstantial with me and I with them.[43]

This lineage, as Marcel further states, is finally "co-extensive with the human race itself." Ideally, from this perspective, genealogical poems serve to make the relationship to ancestors less obscure, and they serve also to speak to our mutual inherence in the web of human generations over time. Such poems implicitly, if not explicitly, seek to embody the process of defining what it means to be human, and as C. K. Williams observes, "the process of defining our humanity is always a dialectic between our vision of what we see before us—the evidence—and of what we can conceive ideally for the human."[44] The primary evidence is always first "the singular creature that I am." The secondary evidence, given by genealogy, is that I am not singular. A poetry that takes genealogy as its subject, that sees genealogy as an extension of the quest for self-definition, does well to keep in mind that the human ideal is at once singular and plural and almost never reveals itself except in the teeming neighborhood of our common interdeterminacy: "What are you?" "What are you?" "I am . . ."

TEN

From Crispus Attucks to Mr. Bones
Race in Irish American Poetry

Race and Invisible Irishness

It is amazing how the invisible shapes our perception. In the "dry" Zen garden at Ryoan-ji outside Kyoto, a rectangular expanse of white, raked gravel composes an ocean in which five islands of stones arranged in a precise, though seemingly random, pattern affects the eye so pleasingly that its power has been the subject of speculation for centuries. Most of the garden is empty, an expression of the Zen aesthetic of *wabi*—understatement, simplicity—though fifteen stones cluster in the five remote islands and, it is said, visitors can see only fourteen of the rocks at any one time. In deep meditation, *satori* (enlightenment) is achieved at the moment one sees the fifteenth. Most recently, using a technique called "medial axis transformation," which computes complex lines of symmetry in a spatial layout, scientists have discerned a hidden tree-like pattern in the arrangement, and it is the subliminal recognition of this pattern that, they say, "contributes to the enigmatic appeal of the garden."[1] Whether to please the eye or jolt the mind out of its habitual perception, in Ryoan-ji the invisible exerts a powerful influence over the perceiver. It also prompts me to reflect on how invisible patterns in the more tangled and buffeted thicket of culture and history shape our understanding of others and ourselves.

In *Playing in the Dark* Toni Morrison identifies the construction of "literary blackness" and "literary whiteness" through "embedded assumptions of racial language" as an inescapable, hidden pattern that has shaped American literature.[2] We ignore that pattern at our risk and impoverish both our literary and our social understanding by neglecting to see its shaping significance underneath the island landmarks of the canon, as well as noncanonical works that speak to the migrant nature of American history. America's is an inherently traveling culture, and such cultures are epitomized by the circumstance of "black America" according to Paul Gilroy in his essential work, *The Black Atlantic*.[3] The phrase "traveling culture" also appropriately describes the emigration experience more broadly considered. This is certainly true of Irish America, though the shaping imprint of traveling culture has remained largely invisible until recently in Irish American poetry of any literary value. Likewise invisible has been any critical consideration of how in certain important instances Irish American poetry employs representations of race to articulate identity. In such instances, poetry written by Irish Americans reveals something of the complex mechanisms of racial construction that pervade the wider culture, as well as the perception of shared patterns of self-definition that have remained largely invisible.

The concern with racial configurations in Irish American poetry is certainly part of what Toni Morrison sees as a "large and compelling subject" that in her view has attracted a relative "paucity" of critical energy, and one that amounts to an "evasion . . . in our literary discourse." In particular, for Morrison, the uniquely American manifestations of the romance tradition in Melville, Emerson, and others amount to a construction of blackness that permits the writer to explore "terror," the disruptive and potentially devastating shadow path to freedom's open road, an expression of fear directed toward the very freedom that has been codified by the national consciousness as most desirable. African Americanness thus becomes a convenient literary vehicle for white America to express, often unconsciously, an evolving national identity distinct from its European origins by constructing what Morrison calls that "fabricated brew of darkness, otherness, alarm, and desire that is uniquely American."[4] Likewise, the brutal historical fact of slavery comes to highlight the ideal of freedom at the same time as it subverts that ideal to the core.

If we place Morrison's meditation on the construction of literary whiteness and blackness alongside Matthew Frye Jacobson's exploration of racial construction in emigrant America in such books as *Whiteness of a Different Color* and *Special Sorrows,* the relationship between African American and Irish American comes still more strikingly into view. For Jacobson, race has no essential reality. Race defines public fictions that appear and disappear in history, a "palimpsest of race maps," like the Celts, Teutons, and Anglo-Saxons of the nineteenth century,[5] though obviously race as a felt affiliation—justified by varieties of cultural representations including the literary—exerts a powerful cultural influence. As Jacobson recounts, for the emigrant Irish, like all European emigrants, becoming American involved a process of shifting one's identification from subnational, almost tribal social affiliations first to national affiliations and finally to a more encompassing formulation of white racial identity by gradual assimilation, though it must be said that Jacobson cautions against the notion that the process has been one-directional and complete.

It is neither class competition nor economic competition alone that serves as catalyst for the transformation of the Irish in America from racially suspect to racially acceptable, but in Jacobson's view, it is affiliations of "national subjectivity and national belonging as they both inflect and are inflected by racial conceptions of peoplehood, self-possession, fitness for self-government, and collective destiny."[6] In short, Jacobson is ultimately more concerned with the history of racial relationships evidenced in cultural expressions than with advancing a master narrative of how the Irish "became white," or any monolithic cause for their assimilation (or any other European ethnicity) to the exclusion of African American people.[7] From this perspective, shared patterns in the often harrowing experience of becoming American can be as enlightening as any historical antipathy—and perhaps more so, since it may provide a glimpse of the deeper structure of imagination that shapes the pursuit of identity and not merely the dubious embrace of racial identification.

The common lot behind the fraught relations of Irish Americans and African Americans resides in the experience of historical trauma. The fact that class, economic, transnational, and racial power structures—not to mention the seemingly genetic human proclivity to band into tribal affiliations—forced these two peoples to compete, often in the most intimate and ruthless way, for a foothold in an America that had already betrayed the promise of its egalitarian vision in the obscenity of slavery does not eradicate the root connection between them. If what defines us establishes the conditions for our separateness, our contrary narratives of identity, it is also what binds us together at a still deeper level. This fact does not mean that complicity with oppression on the part of Irish Americans should be glossed over, nor does it minimize the brutal betrayal of humanity inherent in the more savage expressions of this historical confraternity from the off-handed slur to large-scale social disfigurements like the Draft Riots of 1863 and the South Boston bussing riots of the 1970s. Moreover, as Lawrence McCaffrey reflects, "Boston's Irish response to school integration through bussing revealed frustrations of people with the same psychological afflictions as African-Americans. They had little self-esteem and were left behind in Irish-America's march to middle class status, their psyches victims of economic and social prejudices." As such, according to McCaffrey, Irish Americans "should understand that their ancestors not only pioneered the urban ghetto in the United States but also were the 'blacks' of the United Kingdom, victims of imperialism, racism, and manorialism."[8]

My own family history is a microcosm of such tangled historical destinies, transgressions, and connections, and it is therefore at once unremarkable and exemplary. James Tobin, my father's great-grandfather, arrived in St. John, New Brunswick, from Cork sometime in 1850 or 1851, having survived the worst years of the Famine, with its million or more dead of starvation and disease and its further millions torn from their world and the world of their ancestors. With hundreds of others escaping a devastated culture, James Tobin boarded an emigrant ship at Cobh that had been emptied of its cargo of Acadian lumber only to be filled for its return voyage with human ballast. He endured the terrors of the hold recounted in coffin ship journals, the deaths of fellow exiles at sea, disease, and seasickness, before he came ashore on Partridge Island in the Bay of Fundy. After surviving the fever sheds and quarantine station, he found work in St. John on the lowest rung of the economic ladder, in and around the teeming docks, while he lived nearby in one of the poor Catholic wards.

It is unclear from the record whether he married during the passage, but he and his wife, Catherine ni Donovan, raised their family in

St. John until his death in 1880. He is buried with other Irish immigrants in an unmarked mass grave in St. Mary's Cemetery in the shadow of an oil refinery. His eldest son, Edward—who had yet to raise himself above his father's station—moved with his own young family and his mother to Brooklyn, New York, in 1882. James Tobin and his family endured the Irish diaspora like millions of others, in desperation and uncertainty that continued long after the initial scorching trauma of death, departure, and deepening absence, the ever-receding horizon of a first world that had once defined the boundaries of home.

In seeking to reposition the idea of diaspora from a narrative of immigration founded on "arrival and settlement" to a narrative of emigration founded on "departure and absence,"[9] Matthew Frye Jacobson brings the experience of diaspora during the time of the Irish Potato Famine imaginatively closer to the monstrous brutalities of the African Middle Passage without committing the conceptual misrepresentation of affirming an equivalence. Irish culture, as Luke Gibbons observes, experienced "modernity before its time,"[10] and the epitome of the modern is the experience of radical displacement. Paul Gilroy sees the Middle Passage as a "catastrophic rupture," "pre-modern tradition's most comprehensive erasure."[11] Nevertheless, to affirm the Irish diaspora spurred by the horrors and displacements of the Great Hunger draws on comparable patterns and motifs of cultural catastrophe, trauma, and erasure is not to expropriate the nearly unendurable history of injustice inflicted on African Americans. Moreover, it in no way affirms what Luke Gibbons and others have called a "simplistic equation" between Irish American and African American experience, an equation that James Byrne has argued "dominated the history of Irish American assimilation" in order to "either undo or secure the Irish right to American whiteness."[12]

At the same time, Byrne further argues that Irish American identity had already been shaped by a legacy of otherness endemic to living under English rule in their lost homeland—living as it were "beyond the pale," spatially, constitutionally, psychologically, and racially. What I venture here should be regarded as an effort to locate both experiences—African American and Irish American—within a range of historically significant suffering that, while acknowledging the defining difference in magnitude between them, should create opportunities to explore how what Jacobson calls the diasporic imagination shapes poetic expression, particularly when the poetry includes direct representations of African American experience by Irish American poets.

On the one hand, like other displaced European peoples, the emigration experience naturally encouraged the immigrant Irish to assume a backward look that gradually helped them to form stronger national identifications with the lost homeland. On the other hand, as Jacobson observes, "Euro-American racialism provided an alternative logic" by which their destiny "could be accepted, and even applauded."[13] If, as McCaffrey further reflects, "many aspects of western civilization were imposed on the Irish from the outside by their conquerors,"[14] then perhaps the gravest imposition was the assumption of race as a category of essential identity. It only makes sense that representations of race in Irish American poetry can at times manifest the emigrant's profoundly ambivalent circumstance. Add to that the economic, political, and social pressures of life in the mélange of the nineteenth-century urban ghetto, as well as the Irish emigrants' questionable racial affiliation according to the tenets of the day, and we can discern the outlines of a common encounter with the underside of the American ideal.

To this end, one need only briefly compare the simian-featured Celt of Thomas Nast's cartoons with the ape-like visage of African Americans in similar editorials.[15] Even Ralph Waldo Emerson condemned both the "African race" and the Irish to the lower echelons of the human family.[16] And if one looks further back, as Luke Gibbons does, to Edmund Spenser's advice to Queen Elizabeth "that until Ireland can be famished it cannot be subdued,"[17] the long legacy of mass human suffering haunts the histories of African Americans and Irish Americans alike. As Gibbons further notes, the Irish were transported to the New World as part of slavery, an institution that involved whites as well as blacks,[18] and the British colonization of Ireland "provided the template," according to Matthew Frye Jacobson, for colonizing "the North American savages."[19]

None other than Frederick Douglass grieves over the conditions of the Irish poor on the eve of the Great Famine in a letter to William Lloyd Garrison, the editor of the abolitionist newspaper *The Liberator,* when he writes, "During my stay in Dublin, I took occasion to visit the huts of the poor in its vicinity—and of all places to witness human misery, ignorance, degradation, filth and wretchedness, an Irish hut is the pre-eminent." Douglass's compassion for the wretched of Ireland finds its source in his recognition of the common bonds of all humanity. Thus in the same letter he writes, "Though I am more closely connected and identified with one class of the outraged, oppressed and enslaved people, I cannot allow myself to be insensible to the wrongs and sufferings of any part of the great family of man. I am not only an American slave, but a man, and as such, am bound to use my powers for the welfare of the whole human brotherhood."[20] Still, and rightly so, Douglass underscores the supreme injustice of chattel slavery in a speech he gave in 1850, in which he reflects, "The Irishman is poor, but he is not a slave. He may be in rags, but he is not a slave. He is still the master of his own body."[21]

The stunning difference in the literary history of both groups is that for Irish Americans very little, if any, of that traumatic past has found anything like adequate expression in the poetry. More often than not, Irish history and the Irish American diaspora exist between the lines of a poem like Marianne Moore's "Spenser's Ireland," in which Jacobson's "diasporic imagination" remains hidden in the complex arrangement of details or perhaps asserts itself obliquely like a face that suddenly manifests in the dazzling composition of an elaborately painted still life. And so it comes to be revealed as a subliminal pattern: the forgotten historical ghost in the poetic machine.

An exception to this predominant theme is Eamonn Wall's "The Class of 1845," a poem of the late-twentieth-century New Irish experience of emigration that places the Irish diaspora and its history in the forefront of the poet's imaginative concern:

Those who were broken
crawled by brown ditches
into coffin ships

In the new world
they were known as
filth, disease, and silence

In their motherland wise men sang:
"brothers and sisters in New York

> send us your loot."
> In hell's kitchen
> on the lower east side
> turf-bedevilled irish
> fought against black and jew
> worked their skins away
> sent their money home.[22]

Wall's poem is bluntly ironic, an evocative gloss on the conditions of the emigrant Irish at the onset of the Great Famine. The poem's raw articulation of historical circumstance calls to the surface the invisible pattern of history latent in Moore's more allusive version of Irish American identity. As a leader of the New Irish poets who emigrated to America in the 1980s during a time of economic deprivation before the advent of the Celtic Tiger, Wall's engagement with history is immediate and uncensored. Moreover, as a poet born in Ireland and schooled in Irish history, he has available to him a poetic tradition in which the history of Ireland is engaged and inscribed.

Born in America, Marianne Moore has a different relationship to Irish history, as evidenced in "Spenser's Ireland," one that is undoubtedly filtered by a romance with Irish identity. She does not have the historian's awareness of Ireland's bitter history, including the history of emigration; or as one emigrant wrote of his own work, "competing with Free Negroes" in America: "nothing but driven like horses . . . a slave for the Americans as the generality of the Irish are out here."[23] Central to Wall's poem, in contrast, is the competition between the Irish and other ethnicities in diaspora—"black and jew"—with racism and anti-Semitism perpetuated by the struggle to succeed in the New World. More surprising still is the confrontation with the betrayal of the emigrant by the world left behind. The relationship with the lost hearth is likewise disrupted by American capitalism, counterfeiting bonds of identity and, in some instances, breaking them over the course of generations. As a powerful expression of the diasporic imagination, "The Class of 1845" directly enjoins the Irish emigrant experience of historical trauma with those of other ethnicities, including African Americans, and thereby raises to the forefront the delicate issue of what might be shared imaginatively in the experience of diaspora among different groups.

Typology and Type Across the Racial Divide

My fundamental question—"what representations manifest themselves across the racial divide in Irish American poetry?"—may be understood as a more specified inquiry emerging from a series of questions posed by Toni Morrison in *Playing in the Dark:* "How does literary utterance arrange itself when it tries to imagine an Africanist other? What are the signs, the codes, the literary strategies designed to accommodate this encounter? What does the inclusion of Africans or African-Americans do to and for the work?"[24] The central judgment behind Morrison's searching interrogation is that the encounter with the African American other may be discovered in "signs" and "codes" hidden in representations of race that have been, in part at least, invisible to the critical attention of American literary tradition and perhaps even to the writer. The "disembodied voice" at the end of Ralph Ellison's *Invisible Man* pervades American literature—like the infusion of black his unnamed speaker from the African American underground must use to obtain the whitest paint.

In the social context perhaps my own family history can once again serve as an example through the figure of my lost Aunt Edna—"lost" because she had been written out of the family history for, among other unforgivable transgressions, running off with her African American lover sometime in the early 1940s. Her black children have disappeared into the wide ocean of American ethnic identity. They are like the last stone in Ryoan-ji, invisible in the simple and yet intensely complex arrangement of relationships.

Likewise, the treatment of race as a subject is largely absent from Irish American poetry, though with some notable exceptions. John Boyle O'Reilly confronts the theme of race and the representation of African Americans head-on in his work. A monumental figure in his time, O'Reilly embodied in both his life and his literary efforts the wrenching conflict between the Irish emigrant's path to acceptance in America and his recognition that race relations between Irish Americans and African Americans at their worst constituted a betrayal of a possible solidarity through which the egalitarian promise of America could be realized.

Here is the end of "At Fredericksburg," a poem commemorating the confrontation of the Irish American soldiers from the Georgia Brigade and the Fighting Sixty-Ninth in one of the crucial battles of the Civil War:

> Bright honor be theirs who for honor were fearless,
> Who charged for their flag to the grim cannon's mouth;
> But honor to them who were true, though not tearless,
> Who bravely that day kept the cause of the South.
> The quarrel is done—God avert such another;
> The lesson is brought we should evermore heed:
> Who loveth the Flag is a man and a brother,
> No matter what birth or what race or what creed.[25]

The tragic irony of the Battle of Fredericksburg in which Irish fought against Irish on opposite sides of a war that would decide America's fate as a nation as well as its self-definition on matters of race was not lost on O'Reilly. O'Reilly's solution, not entirely satisfactory, is to uphold the conflict to the standard of a higher "glory," a synthesis, a new, greater union rising out of the binaries "North" and "South" into which Irish Americans had been divided. O'Reilly's gendered evocation of manliness and brotherhood is understandable for the time. Remarkable in the poem is O'Reilly's inclusion by universal affirmation of African Americans in that filial union. In the face of draft riot and race riot, of decades of competition and a warping myth of racial division and white supremacy that conditioned Western perceptions for centuries, O'Reilly represents African Americans as united with Irish Americans—all Americans—in a vision of human equality that, it must be said, equals the standard of the most liberal minds of his day.

The extraordinary passion, courage, and achievement of John Boyle O'Reilly as public man have their equivalent in the conviction and broad-mindedness of the inner man, particularly regarding matters of race. From his position as editor of the *Pilot* he advanced the causes of African Americans and Native Americans, as well as Irish Americans. Still more significantly, as Thomas Keneally recounts in *The Great Shame*, O'Reilly even embraced the idea "that the destiny of the coloured American, not the liberation of Ireland, was the chief agenda for the

United States."²⁶ This certainly would have placed O'Reilly in conflict with many of his fellow Irish Americans, as would perhaps his comparison of the land movement in Ireland during Parnell's rise with antislavery agitation, giving the latter as much prominence in his thought as the former.²⁷ Furthermore, in his editorial about the writer and politician Wendell Phillips, a former slave, O'Reilly wrote, "the day is fast coming when this man's claim cannot be answered by a jest or a sneer. . . . This man's children and grandchildren are coming, and they are receiving the same education in the same schools as the white man's children. In all things material before God and man, they will feel they are the white man's equal. They are growing above the prejudice, even before the prejudice dies."²⁸ Without question both O'Reilly's personal history as an Irish emigrant who experienced the full force of oppression palpably in his own life and his convictions as an American intellectual with uncommon foresight on matters of race make him an essential figure, though sadly forgotten—one for whom the sorrows of diaspora offered a possible common background for a shared sense of history and possibility.

Nowhere is this hope more manifested in the poetry than in his ode "Crispus Attucks." Where in "At Fredericksburg" O'Reilly articulates his affirmation of a human fraternity that transcends the perception of racial division in general outline, in "Crispus Attucks" he confronts the problem head-on and in no uncertain terms:

> Shall we take for sign this Negro-slave with unfamiliar name
> With his poor companions, nameless too, till their lives leapt forth
>   in flame?
> Yea, surely, the verdict is not for us, to render or deny;
> We can only interpret the symbol; God chose these men to die
> As teachers and types that to humble lives may chief award be made;
> That from lowly ones, and rejected stones, the temple's base is laid!²⁹

As the first casualty of the American Revolution, Crispus Attucks is a central figure in the American promise of freedom, but ironically so, since as a freed slave whose burgeoning nation had not yet divested itself of the moral burden of slavery he stands at the juncture between the flawed actuality of history and history's ideal. Toni Morrison rightly encourages us to read for signs and codes of how African Americans have been featured in the mainstream of American literary imagination, but in "Crispus Attucks" the problem of racial signification and codification is placed front and center. In doing so, O'Reilly inverts the paradigm: Crispus Attucks, "Negro-slave with unfamiliar name," *is* the sign not merely of his own Africanist presence but of America's unrealized but incipient egalitarian ideal. In him sign becomes symbol, a shift from a condition of merely pointing toward a reality while standing apart from that reality to the condition of an embodiment.

The shift here, to use a distinction Morrison makes, is from the "metaphorical" to the "metaphysical" uses of race.[30] Attucks is no mere metaphor, no mere sign of an invisible likeness among all peoples; he is the embodiment of that communion both in his "Negro-ness" and in his underlying oneness with the rest of humanity under God. As such, he is, like all the "lowly" and thus like the figure of Christ, yet another historical manifestation of the last made first. The temple, or *templum*, O'Reilly evokes at the end of this first stanza is at once the sacred and secular dwelling place of a new kind of nation in which neither race nor any other kind of division supervenes the undergirding unity that Attucks, by his very otherness, his unfamiliar name, makes manifest.

Though O'Reilly can only "interpret" the symbol, the gravity of Crispus Attucks as symbol only deepens. As the poem unfolds, Attucks clarifies America's destiny as a nation and the hidden destiny of the entire human family over time. "Oh, blood of the people! changeless tide, through century, creed, and race!" O'Reilly declares. In this momentous line the poet at once subverts and revolutionizes the logic of racial division, by which blood typifies ethnic and tribal identities and, in particular, white supremacy. He does so by making "blood" the guiding metonymy for our genetic history not as a fictive proof of genealogical purity, but as the actual common bond of human genomic identity. We are all, as O'Reilly envisions, "one as the sweet salt sea is one." It is the sea's sounding, then, that "unifies all"—"Negro, Saxon and Celt, Teuton and Latin and Gaul. . . . / One love, one hope, one duty theirs! No matter the time or ken / There never was separate heart-beat in all the races of men!" In celebratory terms, O'Reilly assumes typological nineteenth-century racial signifiers only to subvert their power to mark racial stratification.

Moreover, as if to link his subversive trope to the motif of diaspora, O'Reilly employs the figure of the sea as the vehicle for his simile to communicate humanity's underlying unity—the same sea that bore coffin ships and Ireland's exiles to America and conveyed the unimaginable horrors of the Middle Passage. The sea as the poem's unifying trope reveals the diasporic imagination pushing back, as Wallace Stevens would have it, against the pressure of reality. Here is an instance of an Irish American poet whose personal experience of oppression and loss enables rather than cripples his ability to feel the plight of others in diaspora, especially African Americans. In contrast, through yet another reversal, the "Tory" and "Patrician" who employs racial division to secure his own aggrandizement both financially and culturally becomes in O'Reilly's eyes history's own self-proliferating traitor—"whatever his age or his name"—and ultimately the true slave "who wields the lash." By the poem's end, O'Reilly's appeal to historical justice finally trumps even the metaphysics of his communion encompassing all races. Forgiveness comes only after "wrong has been turned to right."

While it might be incautious and inaccurate to imply that John Boyle O'Reilly confronted the issue of race in "Crispus Attucks" without some appeal to what Morrison called in another context "a fabricated, mythological Africanism,"[31] it is certain that O'Reilly's effort in the poem is to demythologize spurious and destructive racial codes in favor of a more encompassing "supreme fiction," and one that may just be true: our common, genetic embodiment in and through each other across the human family as the necessary, felt recognition that heralds a truly just body politic, both nationally and globally.

Significantly, Paul Laurence Dunbar's elegy for O'Reilly recognizes the capacious nature of the Irish American poet's embrace of racial unity, and it does so in a way that constitutes a kind of call and response across the American racial divide:

> Of noble minds and noble hearts
>   Old Ireland has goodly store;
> But thou wert still the noblest son
>   That e're the Isle of Erin bore.
> A generous race, and strong to dare,
>   With hearts as true as purest gold,

> With hands to soothe as well as strike,
>   As generous as they are bold,—
> This is the race thou lovedst so;
>   And knowing them, I can but know
> The glory thy whole being felt
>   To think, to act, to be, the Celt!
> Not Celt alone, America,
>   Her arms about thee hath entwined;
> The noblest traits of each grand race
>   In thee were happily combined.[32]

Dunbar's elegy, like O'Reilly's declamatory odes, suffers from the bathos endemic to those poetries driven more by message than by artistic concerns. He also invokes the power of racial identification, though as a celebratory affirmation of difference that may spark nobility. At the same time, Dunbar's appeal to racial stereotypes brings him to the vision of O'Reilly as a figure of race-transfiguring miscegenation. He is for Dunbar a transracial *Übermensch,* the most perfect distillation of the most desirable traits for humanity embodied by all races. As such, while Dunbar asserts the same kind of racial demarcation typical of his time, like O'Reilly he uses the fiction of race in a way that seeks to undermine its power to divide and oppress. "The cause of all oppressed was thine," Dunbar opines near the poem's end. As in O'Reilly's "Crispus Attucks," the metaphorical and metaphysical uses of race shift toward evocations of historical justice, and thereby seek to alter the racially inflected consciousness from inside by awakening us to a shared admission that as human beings emergent in time on this planet we are all the children of diaspora.

Bigotries and Empathies

Like Daniel O'Connell, who in his efforts to seek justice for Ireland through the repeal of the Penal Laws encouraged Irish Americans to empathize with African Americans as "another group that had suffered cruelty and enslavement, to join the abolitionist crusade, and to demand full civil rights for blacks when they were free,"[33] John Boyle O'Reilly understood that the sufferings of oppression and diaspora could bind disparate groups together in a deeper unity. Clearly Paul Laurence Dunbar saw this same virtue in the example of O'Reilly's life and work. More broadly, by "pioneering the American urban ghetto,"[34] the emigrant Irish not only blazed the trail for other European emigrant groups but also shared with African Americans the underside of modern capitalism as America grew in power and world dominance. They did so in a manner that foreshadowed American ghetto life throughout the twentieth century even as many middle-class Irish Americans left the cities.

O'Reilly's celebration of Crispus Attucks grows out of an empathy born of his own exemplary trials as a man who knew prejudice and injustice intimately. Unfortunately, as Lawrence McCaffrey further reflects, unlike O'Reilly the vast majority of "the Irish did not convert their experiences with bigotry into empathy for its other victims. Instead, they responded to prejudice with prejudice," and so, "compensating for the psychological wounds inflicted by nativism and for their unskilled working class status, the Irish took out their frustrations and low self-esteem on African-Americans," refusing "to equate the miserable conditions of African-American slaves with their own unfortunate historical experience."[35]

We witness that refusal in Charles G. Halpine's poem "Sambo's Right to Be Kilt." Written in the persona of Private Miles O'Reilly, the poem exemplifies the kind of raw bigotry that spurred the New York Draft Riots in 1863, when mobs of Irish rampaged through the city in protest of being conscripted to fight for the union on behalf, they felt, of the very African Americans who were their competition for the lowest unskilled jobs:

> Some tell us tis a burnin shame
> > To make the naygers fight
> And that the thrade of being kilt
> > Belongs but to the white:
> But as for me, upon my sowl!
> > So liberal are we here,
> I'll let Sambo be murthered instead of myself
> > On every day of the year.[36]

The Irish-inflected voice of Halpine's bigoted Union army private is likewise racially inflected in the most unabashed way, regardless of the poem's blazing irony.

In contrast, James Jeffrey Roche, who succeeded John Boyle O'Reilly as editor of the *Boston Pilot,* employs an irony equally as scorching against the idea of white supremacy in his poem "The White Wolf's Cry":

> We are the Chosen People—look at the hue of our skins!
> Others are black or yellow—that is because of their sins!
>
> We are the heirs of ages, masters of every race,
> Proving our right and title by the bullet's saving grace;
>
> Slaying the naked red man; making the black our slave;
> Flaunting our color in triumph over a world-wide grave.[37]

Roche's denunciation of whiteness as a tool and expression of racial dominance, socioeconomic power, and empire building is nothing short of scathing. In "The White Wolf's Cry" the logic of racism as supported by Christian theological hypocrisy finds its most searing criticism in the vehicle of its own racially inflected voice. If, as Toni Morrison observes, "American means white,"[38] then in Roche's poem we find an American, white Irish subverting the terms of whiteness at the source of our most ethically devastating confusion.

In less caustic terms, the lost abolitionist poem *Avenia,* published in 1805 by Thomas Branagan, earnestly condemns slavery as an inhuman practice, denounces the Christian slave traders as bloodthirsty religious hypocrites, and seeks to ennoble Africans and their way of life by modeling their warriors on Homeric heroes. The poem, not surprisingly, suffers greatly under the weight of its epic models, particularly Homer and Milton. If the warriors Angola, Mondingo, and Louverture are Homeric in their bravery defending the African homeland and Avenia, their queen, then the white slavers Hawkins and Lambert find their exemplars in Milton's fallen angels, straight from the city of Pandemonium. Branagan sees the slave trade as a war against Africa, a titanic battle fated to be lost by the righteous "Heathens" through the superior technology of the whites. The African warriors die nobly. Avenia, like thousands of her subjects, is carried off to a plantation in the West Indies; she commits suicide after being ravished by her master.

The poem, for all of its derivative imagery, tonal bombast, and formal hubris, succeeds in evoking something of the horror of slavery however conventionally rendered. Here is Branagan's rendering of the slaves' arrival in the New World after the Middle Passage:

> To separate the hapless, weeping throng,
> The cowskin hero wields the knotted thong,
> And as he wields, applies the dreadful blow,
> While streams of blood in purple torrents flow.
> Smit with the sign, which all their fears explain,
> The children still embrace, their knees sustain
> Their feeble weight no more; their arms alone
> Support them, round their bleeding parents thrown.[39]

As poetry, Branagan's epic is not up to the task of communicating the horrors of the slave system, though he himself sailed from Liverpool on a slave ship and witnessed firsthand the savagery endured by African slaves.[40] The very form of the poem as epic, written in pentameter couplets, feels nostalgic. Received through the mainstream of European literary history from antiquity, Branagan's generic employment of the epic mode cannot sustain or express its subject. The savage realities of slavery witnessed by Branagan are part of a new, malevolent modernity in which the humanity understood as the raw material of the state will be employed in ways almost beyond imagination. It will take works like Morrison's *Beloved* and, in poetry, Robert Hayden's "Middle Passage" to render the horror of the African diaspora.

Born in Dublin in 1774 and dying in Philadelphia in 1843, Thomas Branagan lived one Irish version of diaspora. According to Noel Ignatiev, Branagan's empathy for the African American experience was likewise limited by later concerns with miscegenation.[41] Nevertheless, Branagan's depiction of the slave trade in *Avenia* begins a sporadic but complex engagement with African Americans on the part of Irish American poets.

The poems of O'Reilly, Roche, and Branagan are notable for their representations of African Americans as well as their vigorous repudiation of racism at a time when a great many Irish Americans denied a logical empathy with the suffering of African Americans and gradually accepted "whiteness" as a condition that helped to define them as fully invested citizens in an America divided by race. As such their work runs counter to the prevailing tide of race relations between Irish Americans and African Americans in the nineteenth century. Their work should gain greater currency for that reason alone, though it would be impossible to argue that any of them stand out as forgotten masters. With the advent of the twentieth century, Irish American poets do find their way into the canon of American poetry in figures like Louise Imogen Guiney, Edward Arlington Robinson, Marianne Moore, and Robinson Jeffers.

Very little Irish American identity manifests itself in Robinson's poetry (though one could argue Mr. Flood of "Mr. Flood's Party" manifests Irish American type in addition to his surname), and Marianne Moore, as we have already seen, demonstrates a circumscribed awareness of her Irish American inheritance. Jeffers, in contrast, is the first fully historically conscious Irish American poet whose work achieves artistic prominence in the canon of American poetry. None of these poets tackle the issue of race or even broach the subject. It is as if the whole history of racial interaction between Irish Americans and African Americans—addressed so ardently by these key figures in the earlier generations—has been utterly forgotten or rendered unacceptable as subject matter for poetry.

There are exceptions. Though direct treatment of the subject of race almost never occurs, as we move into the twentieth century, a few Irish American poets reveal a fascination with African American music, particularly jazz and gospel. While it is not unusual for white poets to write out of or in sympathy with the jazz tradition, it is significant that a self-consciously Irish American poet like Leo Connellan pictures jazz as inspiration in a way that resonates with an artistically neglected social history. Here are the opening lines of his poem "Jazz":

> Real horn men risk, when everyone's
> playing loud, fast, covering, Miles Davis

blowing slow found us where
we were lost and brings us back.⁴²

The music of Miles Davis, like Coltrane's earlier in the poem, gives the listener access to a hidden sensitivity, a "soul moan," that Connellan ascribes not only to himself but to a community of listeners—the "us" of the poem. There is, in Connellan's phrasing, a salvific power to the music. Davis finds us where we were lost and "brings us back." Is there anything specifically Irish American about this "us"? Not really, but if one reads Connellan's figural association of the supreme jazzman as a type of good shepherd in conjunction with Susan Donnelly's "The Gospel Singer Testifies," a sense of recognition and affiliation begins to emerge that has the force of an awakening:

> When she spoke, I looked down
> the way I would if she'd begun undressing
> before everyone, not to entertain
> but to show things about ourselves
> we knew to cover. So aware that beside me
> a Jewish friend listened—or didn't—
> to her praise of Jesus.
> I wanted to signal, "We're not all like that."
> But my friend is, we are, like that:
> having something we'd get naked for
> before a whole group of people.
> That is, if we're lucky.⁴³

Where Connellan's poem effaces the notion of the poet's racial difference in favor of a shared emergent soulfulness, Donnelly's brings consciousness of race and ethnic difference to the fore as the true but "covered" subject of the poem. In Connellan's "Jazz" covering carries a different literal meaning, that of covering a tune, and Davis's genius in turn is to uncover a commonality of soul that finds the listeners where they have been covered over by the scales (pun intended) of everyday perception—perception that includes, implicitly, how racial definitions shape identity. Donnelly's gospel singer, like Miles Davis, strips away what covers the listener to arrive at a core experience of humanity. Her listener, however, arrives at a formerly invisible "nakedness" of identity through the manifest acknowledgment of racial collusion with her Jewish friend. At the same time, the women's relationship likewise manifests their ethnic difference. What binds them together is their whiteness relative to the blackness of the gospel singer.

More emphatically than Connellan, Donnelly makes race a subject of the poem. By the end of "The Gospel Singer Testifies," however, Donnelly, like Connellan, likens the African American music she hears to spiritual activity:

> So my body heard
> before I did, with tears at the corners of my eyes,
> as the words that had begun in song *Thank you, Jesus!*
> dissolved back into song, or a finer
> distillation, and the singer closed her eyes,
> *Thank you!* bent like a bowstring
> shot forth her nakedness to save me.[44]

In both poems, the song of an African American artist constitutes a saving action for the hearer. Are these poems instances of stereotyping "blackness" or "black song" as a kind of mystical power that can transform the white audience? On the contrary: both poems employ the metaphor of salvation to describe the musicians' effect on the white listener as the uncovering of some lost duende from a time before the Irish had been identified with whiteness, and both also reveal legitimate admiration for the artistry witnessed, which has such a transforming effect. There is a consciousness on the part of both poets, particularly Donnelly, with respect to the subject that exemplifies an honest encounter across the historically and socially maintained racial divide.

James McManus in "Two Songs for Hendrix" brings the Irish American poet's fascination with African American musical figures into the rock-and-roll generation. In McManus's poem, Hendrix is a figure of towering musical genius as well as a man who, because of that genius, is able to uncover hidden reserves of significance.

> Whenever we hear the national anthem
> because a war is about to get started, fought

> by soldiers in camouflage or surrogate warriors
> in eyecatching uniforms, we have to think of Jimi.[45]

At the end of the first song, "Star-Spangled Banner," Hendrix's version of the national anthem raises issues of "surrogate warriors" and "camouflage." As in the earlier two poems, the racially charged matter of "covering" in every sense emerges; only now the action is more subversive than salvific. It asks us to "think" rather than feel, to uncover a habit of mind "antiphonal" to received notions of patriotism and the nature of being American.

In each of these poems, the African American figure serves in some way as a force of illumination for the Irish American poet. If not quite a force of illumination, the maid Patsy Houlihan in Gwendolyn Brooks's "Bronzeville Woman in a Red Hat" shows how an Irish American figure can appear in a poem by an African American poet as a possible model of endurance for the "black" maid who succeeds her:

> But the Irishwoman had left!
> A message had come.
> Something about a murder at home.
> A daughter's husband—"berserk," that was the phrase:
> The dear man had "gone berserk"
> And short work—
> With a hammer—had been made
> Of this daughter and her nights and days.
> The Irishwoman (underpaid,
> Mrs. Miles remembered with smiles)
> Who was a perfect jewel, a red-faced trump,
> A good old sort, a baker
> Of rum cake, a maker
> Of mustard, would never return.
> Mrs. Miles had begged the bewitched woman
> To finish, at least, the biscuit blending
> To tarry till the curry was done,
> To show some concern
> For the burning soup, to attend to the tending

Of the tossed salad. "Inhuman,"
Patsy Houlihan had called Mrs. Miles.
"Inhuman." And "a fool."
And "a cool
One."[46]

Brooks's omniscient narrator characterizes Mrs. Miles as an insensitive bigot who only waxes sadly over the departure of her former maid now that an African American replacement has been sent by the agency—"a dusky duffer," "a lion," "a puma," "a black bear" poised at the door. Dehumanized, an "it," the new maid makes Patsy Houlihan appear infinitely more appealing—a "perfect jewel," a "good old sort" who is defined almost entirely by her job in the eyes of Mrs. Miles. Yet from the narrative context we find that the Irishwoman's economic and class background is haunted by the same violence as possibly any poor ghetto life. Nevertheless, she correctly sizes up Mrs. Miles as "inhuman" when her employer chastens her for mistakes made in the thick of grief. Though she will never see Patsy Houlihan, Brooks's African American maid will have to face the same kind of insensitive treatment—and worse—and like Patsy Houlihan she will have to tread the difficult, racially charged line of at once behaving humanly in the Miles household and seeing Mrs. Miles for the racist she is. They share a common path.

Would Patsy Houlihan have embraced her successor in Mrs. Miles's house? The outward manifestation of their shared endurance is doubtful, perhaps, but in any case unnecessary. Rather, in her poem's superimposition of parallel lives Brooks has illuminated the invisible history of Irish America and African America crisscrossing along the racial divide. In doing so, she recaptures something of the responsive spirit by which poets and writers of the Harlem Renaissance, and in particular Claude McKay, found inspiration and a model for cultural action in the Irish literary revival.[47] It is this same spirit that nearly a half century later empowered Catholic marchers protesting for civil rights in the North to find strength and a model for action in the American Civil Rights Movement, led by Martin Luther King Jr. Across the racial divide such instances of mutual empowerment and cultural reciprocity point toward a deeper set of complex correspondences.

Black Irish, Black Voice

Despite powerful divisions of race, in each of the aforementioned poems some guiding perception or insight on the part of the poet uncovers a common experience, whether artistic, religious, or social, that abbreviates the separation and challenges narrow conceptions of identity. Still, one feels the distance, particularly in Donnelly's and Brooks's poems, of worlds that have been substantially cordoned off from each other by history. Music goes some way toward collapsing the gap, though even in Connellan's "Jazz" and McManus's "Two Songs for Hendrix" a certain translation has to occur. Some of the phrasing of Connellan's poem, for example, affects jazz idiom ("The horn has a thing with tin / if tin has a thing with a horn"), but "Jazz" is not a jazz poem the way Yusef Komunyakaa's are jazz poems. The like is true of William Matthews's poems for Charles Mingus. The point, of course, is not for the white poet to "sound black" (or black poets like Robert Hayden and Marilyn Nelson to "sound white" by writing with an ear attuned to the intonations of the mainstream Western poetic tradition) but for the poet to achieve something of his or her own unique idiom. Nevertheless, confluences of tones and influences run like undercurrents through poems, and they trace at times the complex, racially inflected patterns of identity.

Perhaps nowhere in Irish American poetry is this more honestly encountered than in two poems written by Ernest Walsh, "Irish" and "Poem for a Negro Voice." Born in 1895, Walsh was a member of the Lost Generation of American writers who along with Hemingway, Pound, Stein, and others found themselves in Paris after the First World War. He died prematurely in 1926, a promising poet coming into his prime tragically lost and now almost entirely forgotten. The raw, obsessive subject of Ernest Walsh's poetry is his Irish American identity. Remarkably, in his encounter with his own Irishness he does what no other Irish American poet has done: he questions and confronts the fallacy of his presumed whiteness. Here is the opening of "Irish":

> Must I being born Irish
> and with black eyes

and black hair
and the white skin of the hot-blooded

Be always a mad boy
fighting the wind
coaxing the sun to play
thundering at thunder
spitting at lightning
hitting out with my knuckles
at the rough bark of trees.[48]

In these lines, Walsh's sense of identity is a violent conjoining of black and white experienced and known proprioceptively, that is, in the self's apprehension of its bodily existence. As the poem continues, it becomes obvious that Walsh does not experience himself as purely white or even principally white. "Why should I," he writes, "being black-browed Irish / Appear like a black moon in the gray dawn / and drive all the white-faced boys into a corner."[49] Walsh's sense of identity is a throwback to a period when the whiteness of the Irish was seriously in question. Indeed, he is "black-browed" and fights "the white-faced boys." To be Irish is to be in some sense black, not white, and it is the internal conflict between these poles of identity that is externalized and thus manifested through violence. That violent response is predicated on an inversion: white is "hot-blooded," not black.

In its second and third sections the poem's concern with shaping influence of "blackness" and "whiteness" on the poet's identity shifts into sexual territory:

I played on the grass with Mary
And loosened her dress at the throat
And I kissed her young breasts

And with her face whiter than they
She said *I'm a pure girl.* . . .[50]

Clearly, the whiteness of Mary's face is intended by the poet to be seen in contrast to his own black brow. At first glance, then, Walsh's self-figuration is analogous to the hypermale stereotype of the African American pursuing white women. The contrast between the implied speaker and the white women becomes more intense, and further sexualized, in the poem's final section:

> Ah how they called me the white white girls
> In Venice they were mist floating close
> Suddenly to vanish in a pocket of sunlight
> Or they were lights that laughed at me out of the darkness
> And left me dreaming in the dark.[51]

By the end of the poem, Walsh's women transform into a "white white parade." Yet as whiteness becomes more prominent and defining for their appearance, Walsh's blackness paradoxically disappears. The white women "laugh him out of the darkness." Among these white women are those "that ran all over the hills of Ireland." The poem thus finally comes to challenge its own initial binary assumptions about Irishness itself. The difference between Walsh and the Irish women is not that they are Irish and white and he is Irish and black but that he is Irish American and black and it is they who help make him white since white skin, as the poem initially tells us, is "hot-blooded." Walsh's poem postulates whiteness as an attribute that gains power over the speaker, paradoxically, by distancing himself from America. Against the backdrop of European "whiteness," Walsh's "blackness" loses its palpability. It becomes a dream. By having sex with white European women the black Irishman from America becomes white, or at least less black. By the end of the poem, Walsh is the women's "dark rider" who has dreamt in the dark an alternative to conflicting masks of identity, though that rider remains "unseen by his horse," suggesting in the figure that the conflicting terms of identity set forth at the beginning of the poem remain always partially hidden and never fully resolved.

One way to read Walsh's poem "Irish" is to see it as an example of poetic "blackface" performance. As Eric Lott reflects in *Love and Theft: Blackface Minstrelsy and the American Working Class*, "the blackface performer is in effect a perfect metaphor for one culture's ventriloquial self-expression through the art forms of someone else's."[52] Given Lott's analysis, the self-conscious gap in identification inherent in a poem like

"The Gospel Singer Testifies" restricts a form of cultural appropriation on the part of the Irish American poet. Many of the nineteenth-century blackface minstrels were Irish American, and I cannot be the only one who can recall as a child watching that iconic Irish American entertainer Bing Crosby apply blackface in the film classic *Holiday Inn* to "sing a song of freedom" in celebration of Lincoln's freeing "the darkies"! The difference in Walsh's "Irish" from this long-standing tradition of minstrelsy is that the poet locates blackness and whiteness as constitutive poles of his self-image, and that identity is announced in the title as being Irish. There is no pretense in the poem, no mask of becoming African American. On the contrary, if anything, the poet applies a whiteface mask to obscure his more fundamental blackness.

This is not the case in "Poem for a Negro Voice," where Walsh clearly intends to affect what is to be taken for African American speech inflections:

> Honey, I've been thinking up a poem for you.
> I've been thinking of them mountains
> Hard and rough and not smooth, just white and far.[53]

As in the poem "Irish," whiteness and blackness are set in binary opposition, though in contrast to "Irish" the poet's mask or vocal affectation of blackness assumes prominence. The tone is intimate, affectionate. Sexual urgency and objectification have shifted to an almost plaintive, pastoral apostrophe. Sheep, sheepdogs, white houses of peasants, the sunset bug "like a beautiful lady / opening a green parasol": all the poem's details serve to undermine the minstrel show stereotype of, again, the "libidinous" African American male as acted out by the blackface performer, which for Eric Lott is nothing short of an appropriation of the black male body.[54] It could be argued that the black voice of this poem, placed alongside "Irish," is far more "civilized" than Walsh's hotblooded white antiself. If, as Lott maintains, the minstrel show permitted whites and in particular working-class Irish Americans to test the boundaries of "racial demarcations," then Walsh's poems accomplish this but in ways that invert the conventions of blackface. At the same time, it appears clear that Walsh assumes his "Negro voice" in order to explore the boundaries of his perceived "blackness," his black Irishness.

The result is an exploration of a racially marked self-image that, however curtailed by the poet's early death, nevertheless constitutes an important and precocious output that foreshadows the identity poetics of our own day.

The poems of Ernest Walsh bring to the surface the kind of "double vision" or "double consciousness" that Paul Gilroy understands to be so essential to black identity, though such double consciousness remains at most inferential in the poems of O'Reilly, Branagan, Roche, Connellan, Donnelly, and McManus. In each, the positive identification with African American figures and experience stands behind the poem as a presumption, with the possible exception of Donnelly's "The Gospel Singer Testifies," in which the reader can feel the divide between the white member of the congregation and the black singer. Such double consciousness lies, I believe, behind Irish American poetry whether in the form of a denial or as a kind of abbreviated though deeply felt identification, as in the poems treated above. The experience of double consciousness found in Walsh's "Irish" is nonetheless akin in its incipient way to that which we find in Richard Wright's work: it is the "double vision" of a "warring soul" confronting issues of identity racially, nationally, and globally conceived.[55] "I have double vision," Eamonn Wall writes in his essay "Irish Voices, American Writing, and Green Cards." "I am doubled in every way."[56] It is a sentiment Ernest Walsh would have shared. Black and white define the boundaries of Walsh's psychic conflict in the poem "Irish." However limited—certainly it does not achieve the kind of power we find in the writings of W. E. B. Du Bois or Richard Wright, nor does it rise to great accomplishment as poetry—Walsh's work is the invisible force that urges the poet to enact the vocal minstrelsy of "Poem for a Negro Voice." Walsh embodies the legacy of the Irish diaspora, as well as its fraught, parallel history with the African diaspora, and his poems are not only expressions of the diasporic imagination but examples of the imaginative convergence of two diasporic histories, Irish and African American.

Reflecting on minstrelsy and its efficacy for whiteness, Toni Morrison speculates that "in minstrelsy, a layer of blackness is applied to the white face that released it from the law. Just as entertainers, through or by association with blackface, could render permissible topics that otherwise would have to be taboo, so American writers were able to employ an imagined Africanist persona to articulate and imaginatively act out the forbidden in American culture."[57] Ralph Ellison amplifies Morrison's observation when he observes, "when the white man steps behind the mask of the [blackface] trickster his freedom is circumscribed by the fear that he is not simply miming a personification of his disorder and chaos but he will become in fact that which he intends only to symbolize.[58] Eric Lott further sees the "mask" of blackface as a convenience "through which to voice class resentments" but whose "primary purpose" is to create a double bind in which "ridicule" paradoxically produces an enviable "aura of blackness."[59]

Each of these conceptions of the blackface mask greatly illuminates our understanding of how minstrelsy operates culturally, especially in the literary realm. It is a vehicle for acting out the libidinously and socially forbidden, a way of personifying the symbol of social chaos, as well as a theatrical ritual that enables members of the dominant culture to translate themselves via the mask into the "Africanist other" marginalized by white America. At the same time, the "black voice" in Walsh's poem, despite its obvious affiliation with the minstrel tradition, differs from that tradition in that it enacts a literary hybrid, a kind of pastoral jazz speech that appears driven to create order more than to symbolize disorder, to express a "bidden" black other hidden behind the poet's mask of whiteness instead of a forbidden other worthy of ridicule. It is as if the poem as fictionalized hybrid voice created the opportunity for the poet to bespeak Morrison's "Africanist other" subjectively, rather than to merely objectify that other as a garish mask, the face of racial domination. In Ernest Walsh's poetry the parallel histories of Irish and African America find a surprising confluence.

Shades, Minstrel and Majestic

Where Ernest Walsh is at best a minor poet whose development was cut short by early death, John Berryman is a leading figure of the middle generation of twentieth-century American poets, and his *The Dream Songs* is a masterwork that places minstrelsy front and center as its defining conceit. At the same time, *The Dream Songs* is nothing if not an epic of consciousness, a kind of fractured, postmodern antinarrative of "the growth of the poet's mind" (or perhaps more aptly its dissolution), though the reader is never quite sure how much of Henry, Berryman's protagonist, is derived from Berryman's own life experience—certainly much of his identity is, though fictionalized. Yet it is more than an epic of consciousness: Berryman's great long poem sequence may be read as a saga of double consciousness, one that exhibits all the characteristics of that term, its association with internal psychic conflict, its affiliation with cultural insecurity, as well as its origin in a deeply felt experience of diaspora. Berryman, through Mary Kanar Smith, his grandmother on his father's side, is a son of the Irish diaspora.[60] He is also the son of the Jim Crow South through his mother and, perhaps most evocatively, through his grandfather Robert Glenn Shaver, a renowned Confederate colonel and a commander of the Ku Klux Klan.[61] It is not a far stretch, then, to see Berryman's poetry—already supremely obsessed with matters of identity—as being shaped in pervasive and subtle ways by this dual heritage, necessarily involving both Irish and African American history.

Berryman announces Henry's double consciousness in the preface to *The Dream Songs* when he writes "the poem . . . whatever its wide cast of characters, is essentially about an imaginary character (not the poet, not me) named Henry, a white American in early middle age sometimes in blackface, who has suffered an irreparable loss and talks about himself sometimes in the first person, sometimes in the third, sometimes even in the second; he has a friend, never named, who addresses him as Mr. Bones and variants thereof." Berryman's conception for his long poem places minstrelsy at the core of the project. Moreover, when Henry's unnamed friend addresses him he does so almost invariably in a verbal version of blackface I would call "black voice." There are moments when Henry himself speaks in black voice; indeed, though Berryman assures us of the individual existence of Henry's friend, it is hard, in this elaborate hall of mirrors, not to see the friend as yet another version of Henry himself. The whole scope of the poem is in fact densely self-inwoven.

Moreover, as in minstrelsy, the importance of the hidden, the invisible whiteness behind the mask, is essential to our understanding of the poem's imaginative economy. The theme is announced in the opening song: "Huffy Henry hid the day, / unappeasable Henry sulked."[62]

The natural tendency is to read these opening lines as an inference to Henry's "irreparable loss" and, in turn, to the suicide of Berryman's father, but the line also refers to the sequence's first epigraph, which is also its first inflection of black voice: "Go in Brack Man, de day's yo own." Hiding the day—and thus metaphorically entering the turbulent realm of his unconscious—the middle-age white man Henry gives voice to his black antiself, and, as such, the "Brack man" emerges as well as a prevailing motif and voice in the poem.

The emergence of Henry's black alter ego in turn introduces another prevailing binary in *The Dream Songs*: the interplay of sex and death, eros and thanatos. That supreme theme for the sequence is likewise figured with an unmistakable reference to blackness—"All the world like a woolen lover / once did seem on Henry's side."[63] Given the poem's intentional use of minstrelsy as metaphor to portray the protagonist's divided self, it is consistent that the first lover mentioned in *The Dream Songs* is also inferred to be an African American through the fetish of her "woolen" hair. In the third song, for example, the whiteness of the new lover must be announced. The song's erotic encounters and innuendoes are likewise racially charged, but always ultimately reflective of Henry's strangely miscegenated psyche. The libidinous aspect of *The Dream Songs* might be said in part to appropriate the unspoken white fear of black men seducing white women by, in the first case, inverting that fear.

Death also enters *The Dream Songs* through the theme of sexual potency. "They took away his crotch," Henry reflects in "Dream Song 8."[64] Still more emphatically in "Dream Song 273" the conversation between Henry and his unnamed African American friend goes to the heart of the matter:

> Survive—exist—who is at others' will
> optionless; may gelded be, be put to stud,
> and were sweating sold;
> was sold.—Mr. Bones, dat slavery still
> is of our former coast.—When they make me, Bud,
> I show my genitals, cold.[65]

Henry's vocal metamorphoses are on startling display here: he shifts from Elizabethan speech to black voice to what sounds like the inflections of a Brooklyn mug. The figural prospect of castration, to be made into a gelding, commingles the loss of sexual prowess with imaginative death and also the loss of freedom for the African male slave. The fact that castration was not an unheard of practice in brutalizing African American men during slavery, in the long period of Jim Crow, and during the Civil Rights Movement only intensifies the exchange.

Similarly, lynching is another horrifying motif from African American history imported imaginatively into *The Dream Songs* to evoke the brutalized and self-brutalized psyche of Henry. The motif is particularly vivid in song 57:

> I recall a 'coon treed,
> flashlights, & barks, and I was in that tree,
> and something can (has) been said for sobriety
> but very little.[66]

Here the memory of the lynched black man by sleight of phrase becomes the figure of Henry himself murdered, as it were, by his own psychic dissolution through alcoholism. The dangling figure of the lynched black man, and the drunken poet, by juxtaposition becomes a figure for the poet's impotence in generating anything vital from his own life:

> How in famished youth
> could I foresee Henry's sweet seed
> unspent across so flying barren ground,
> where would my loves dislimn whose dogs abound?
> I fell out of the tree.[67]

Here again thanatos and eros blend almost into one drive, impotent to save Berryman's protagonist.

This interweaving of love and death propels the sequence forward through its seemingly endless metamorphoses and recurs perhaps most movingly in the figure of Henry's daughter, as in "Dream Song 72," which opens: "Shh! On a twine hung from disastered trees / Henry is swinging his daughter. They seem drunk."[68] Set against the backdrop of "Dream Song 57," which this scene clearly echoes, it is impossible not to see the figure of the daughter in relation to the lynched figure of the black man and drunken Henry himself, particularly when in the next stanza their play in the Supreme Court garden is juxtaposed to the justices, who "lean, negro, out, the trees bend."[69] Berryman wrote this song while living in Washington, DC, across from the Supreme Court Building from late 1963 into the next year, at the height of civil rights protests.[70] Still later in the song Henry confesses his hopes "to break his burnt-cork luck." The appropriation of the African American experience of injustice psychically to his misfortune and reflexively to minstrelsy is unmistakable. "Dream Song 72," in turn, powerfully foreshadows the "heavy daughter" of the final dream song, who is, one could argue, the progeny of Henry's imagination, the living figure of his hope of salvation.

Such allusions to African American history and experience pervade *The Dream Songs*, but most pervasive is Berryman's adoption and adaptation of the minstrel tradition in the voice of Henry and his unnamed friend. At the outset of the sequence, in the second dream song, Henry assumes wholly his blackface persona. "The jane is zoned! No nightspot here, no bar / there. . . . Henry are baffled. . . . Arrive a time when all coons lose dere grip," Henry reflects.[71] By implication, it seems the extreme emotional trauma of Henry's life only can be voiced by donning a minstrel's black mask, implying sympathy with the incomparably larger "irreversible loss" of freedom and nation experienced by African Americans, at once demonstrating Berryman's sympathy with the incomparably larger "irreversible loss" of freedom and nation experienced by African Americans, and risking the appropriation of a monumental instance of cultural and historical suffering for the purpose of expressing a personal trauma.

In "Tongue-Tied in Black and White" notable African American poet Michael S. Harper judges Berryman harshly for his use of blackface idiom. "Only your inner voices spoke such tongues," Harper writes.[72] In contrast, Kevin Young, a rising figure from a younger generation of African American poets and editor of Berryman's selected poems for the American Poets Project, confesses he has "come to admire" the white American poet's adaptation of the minstrel tradition in order to express what Ralph Ellison saw as "a profound doubt in the white man's mind as to the authenticity of his own image of himself."[73] In any case, Berryman's blackface trope dares in the extreme, and it is assumed with full consciousness both of the minstrel tradition and of the traumatic history of African America. The second song, in fact, is dedicated to T. D. "Daddy" Rice, the founder of minstrelsy and theatrical inventor of "Jim Crow," his own black alter ego. As John Haffenden notes, "Berryman's source for information on Daddy Rice and the minstrel tradition was Carl Wittke, *Tambo and Bones*."[74] Henry's mask of Mr. Bones obviously derives from this source, and while, as John Haffenden observes, the duo of Henry and his friend recalls such mock-heroic pairs as Don Quixote and Sancho Panza,[75] one also can hear resounding echoes of Amos and Andy from 1940s radio, two white men affecting black voices for their comic banter, carrying forward the blackface tradition into black voice.

From this perspective Berryman's *The Dream Songs* constitutes the preeminent example in American poetry of cultural mixing between the African American and broader American cultural narratives, and as Eric Lott observes in *Love and Theft,* Daddy Rice saw his own theatrical practice of minstrelsy as "the *completion* of black culture, its professional emergence" (italics in original). Further reflecting on the significance of this cultural intersection in the minstrel tradition, Lott goes on to conclude that both narratives "are riveted by the moment of cultural expropriation, and we should look to them . . . as much for what they do not say as for what they do—for the way they construct, and then sometimes blur, racial boundaries."[76] Berryman's Henry does nothing if not blur racial boundaries, though given the role African American cultural history plays in *The Dream Songs,* both as indelible cultural reference and as trope for dramatizing Henry's ongoing psychic trauma, it does not appear that Berryman's sequence constructs racial boundaries in a manner wholly consistent with the minstrel tradition. Instead, it goes some way in its particular idiom toward breaking them down, and it does so by raising the pervasive but likewise hidden experience of "double consciousness" to consciousness.

In "Dream Song 24," for example, Berryman brings the issue of racial boundaries and domination directly into the poem through Henry's reflection on lecturing (as Berryman did) in India:

> He was Introduced, and then he was Summed-up
> He was put questions on racial bigotry;
> *he* put no questions on racial bigotry
> constantly.[77]

Henry's "summing up" in this introduction raises the issue of identity—as if the complexity of one life could be summed up—with Berryman's wry insight turning immediately to the issue of race, identity, the implied systematic summing up of an entire people.

Berryman addresses the issue of race again directly in "Dream Song 60," now in a black-voice exchange that reflects on integration:

> After eight years, be less dan eight percent,
> distinguish' friend, of coloured wif de whites
> in de School, in de Souf.
> —Is coloured gobs, is coloured officers,
> Mr. Bones. Dat's nuffin? –Uncle Tom,
> Sweep shut yo mouf,
>
> is million blocking from de proper job,
> de fairest houses & de churches eben.[78]

On the one hand, Berryman's use of minstrelsy in *The Dream Songs* challenges the reader to consider just how fundamentally offensive the trope might be, first as a literary reiteration of a theatrical tradition that perpetuates racial bigotry and second as a metaphor that implicitly equates a white man's psychic trauma with the oppression of an entire people. On the other hand, it brings to the surface equally fundamental issues of racial equality in their own right and not merely as manifestations of Berryman's black-voice trope. As Henry meditates in "Dream Song 224": "White is the hue of death and victory,"[79] a sentiment that resonates strongly with James Jeffrey Roche's "The White Wolf's Cry." Moreover, far more than Henry, Henry's unnamed friend exhibits wisdom and insight that undermine minstrelsy's hegemonic valorizing of whiteness over blackness.

In "Dream Song 36," Berryman's black voice approaches the subversive clarity of Lear's fool, though without the cutting irony:

> The high ones die, die. They die. You look up and who's there?
> —Easy, easy, Mr Bones. I is on your side.
> I smell your grief.
> —I sent my grief away. I cannot care

forever. With them all again & again I died
and cried, and I have to live.

—Now there *you* exaggerate, Sah. We hafta *die.*
That is our 'pointed task. Love & die.⁸⁰

In these lines Henry's "fool" sees into the essence of the sequence's psychic alchemy of eros and thanatos, the very mélange that defines Henry's traumatized psyche. If Berryman expropriates black cultural materials through his adaptation of the minstrel tradition in the manner described by Eric Lott, then he does so in a way that likewise permits his black-voice persona to see more incisively into the psychic core of the double consciousness that afflicts Henry—his diaspora from himself.

Inevitably, then, through this voice, *The Dream Songs* turn outward as well as obsessively inward to consider the implications of double consciousness both socially, as in the songs considered above, and metaphysically, as in "Dream Song 220": "If we're not Jews, how can Messiah come? / Praise god, brothers, Who is a coloured man."⁸¹ What could be more subversive to dominant white culture than attributing blackness to divinity? Berryman slyly extends his "re-valuation" of the divine racial economy into expressly metaphysical terrain in "Dream Song 266," in which Henry implores, "Dinch me, dark God, having smoked me out."⁸² What has enabled the dark God of apophatic theology to "smoke out" his latest prodigal son? The "burnt cork" of Henry's blackened face. Berryman's use of the minstrel tradition here moves beyond Morrison's rightful concerns with "black surrogacy" in American literature, as well as with a metaphysics of race that reifies white and black into a fixed hierarchy of difference with white as the essentially dominant figure.⁸³

Indeed, in "Dream Song 220" Berryman's parenthetical remark to his black-voice alter ego subverts not only the unstable hierarchy of *The Dream Songs* but the entire minstrel tradition: "Some time we'll do it again in whiteface."⁸⁴ It perhaps goes without saying that the entire racially inflected history of the United States is likewise subverted here, since to "do it in whiteface" would be to place whiteness in the surrogate position relative to blackness. At this parenthetical moment in *The Dream Songs,* the fictional nature of racial construction reveals itself, and that fiction is what permits Berryman to plumb so deeply the affliction of his protagonist's consciousness, the trauma of his personal loss within the context of America's social and cultural divisions, and the shared human experience of diaspora.

"Something black somewhere in the vistas of the heart, " Henry reflects in "Dream Song 92." In view of Berryman's highly orchestrated trope of minstrelsy in *The Dream Songs,* one must view this passing intuition as more than a commentary on Henry's (and Berryman's) obsession with suicide. Blackness has a double meaning here, enjoining the motifs of double consciousness I raised earlier. Henry's blackness goes deeper than black voice. It penetrates the core of his sense of identity, if there is a core. As such, his blackness has not only an inward significance but also an outward power that shapes action. "Shadow and act, shadow and act," Henry remarks in "Dream Song 119" in a phrase that inspired the title of Ellison's book of essays, "better get white or you'll get whacked, / or keep so-called *black* / and raise new hell."[85] The principal qualifying phrase here is "so-called *black,*" which testifies how conscious Berryman is of the fictional nature of racial categories. Henry's double consciousness is, finally, the presiding presence in the sequence, and that presence—shifting through masks of black and white, first, second, and third persons—transcends race and ethnicity.

Henry's masks make him a postmodern Everyman, and as such his consciousness embodies the cultural expressions of racial difference as well as other personifications. He vocalizes Shakespearean and at times dons a Jewish mask. Henry's identity is not singular, but plural—a fiction about the multifarious fictional nature of identity itself. The sequence is nothing if not performative of such vocal plurality, as John Montague suggests in his essay "John Berryman: Henry in Dublin," in which he recounts actor John Hurt's encounter with Berryman during the filming of *A Man for All Seasons:* "He had never read Berryman then, but he was sure of what he heard, as Berryman dipped and dived through falsetto, innuendo, jive talk, blackface coonery, all the startling range of his new work. 'That man has genius,' said Hurt, listening in astonishment, 'And it's burning him up,' he added prophetically."[86]

That said, the whole movement of *The Dream Songs* aims to converge, finally, on Ireland and on Henry's Irishness as the other principal identification in the poem, the other shaping "ethnicity" of his imagination. There are intimations early on of Henry's Irish affiliations, like his "thatch hair" in "Dream Song 13," though they become explicit in "Dream Song 139":

> Celtic Henry groaned with his shoulder to the door
> which never will close again, nor open enough—
> why did he leave her?[87]

Eros is a dominant obsession for Henry's "Celtic" identity as well as for his black-face self, and those two prevailing attributes of his consciousness converge in "Dream Song 205," in which, instead of black voice, Henry speaks in stage Irish: "I take you in me arms / burnt-cork." In these lines Celtic Henry, now transposed into A. E. Housman, embraces his Dark Lady, his blackface lover. Remarkably, at this moment, the nature of the poet's double consciousness is likewise made explicit. "He was a fork," Henry reflects, "saved by his double genius & certain emendations / All his long life."[88]

With the occasional emendation, both culturally and imaginatively, in *The Dream Songs* Berryman's presiding double geniuses are African American and Irish. Importantly, this conjugation of Irish and black in Berryman's sequence harkens back to the same culturally, socially, and historically significant interactions between Irish and black throughout the nineteenth and twentieth centuries. As Eric Lott reminds us, "even before the vast waves of immigration . . . Irish and black tended to share the same class niche, resulting in conflicts of all kinds, but also in interracial friendships and even marriages."[89] Such friendships form the historical groundwork of Berryman's adaptation of the minstrel tradition and not merely the "libidinal" excesses and other "peccadilloes" the minstrel stage "projected onto blacks" often by its immigrant Irish performers.[90] Likewise, Irish brogues and other ethnic dialects were incorporated into minstrelsy.[91] From this perspective, *The Dream Songs* should be considered a theatrical adaptation of minstrelsy—as well as other literary genres—on a grand scale to the end of reinventing the poetic sequence.

If one traces the manifestations of Henry's black voice through the sequence, one finds, in fact, that black voice dominates in the first six sections, allowing for departures into Berryman's elegies for other poets, particularly Randall Jarrell, Wallace Stevens, and Theodore Roethke, and most movingly the many poems for Delmore Schwartz. With "Dream Song 279," the geographical focus of the sequence shifts from the United States and Henry's sporadic journeys around the globe expressly to Ireland. Indeed, the whole circuitous arc of *The Dream Songs* leads to Ireland, and it is while in Ireland that Henry's black-voice companion goes largely silent. Of the 106 Dream Songs that compose this climactic section of Berryman's epic of consciousness, in only a very few does Henry or his unnamed friend speak in black voice. In "Dream Song 299," now in Dublin, Henry as Mr. Bones replies to his friend's injunction to "offer up prayers": "You offers me this hope. Now I thank you / depressed, down on my knees."[92] We hear the black voice again significantly in songs 353, 364, 366, and 374. When the voice is heard in "Dream Song 353," it is in the context of Henry's reflection on genocide—culture's "true light of savagery"[93]—in which Berryman's protagonist includes the Ibo people along with the Armenians and the Jews.

At times, Berryman color-codes the poems, as in "Dream Song 315," in which his lady, like one of Edmund Spenser's, arrives on a white palfrey "all in green," while Henry as medieval knight dresses in black.[94] Green, white, and black appear in various Dream Songs early and late in the sequence, and within the context of Berryman's awareness of the symbolic manifestations of racial difference, none of this color-coding can be taken as purely decorative, as in "Dream Song 139," which opens: "Green grieves the prince over his girl foregone / in the mists of the Hebrew and Irish past / in the mists of the American past."[95] Berryman's intent with this use of color is to extend his imaginative exploration of history, ethnicity, and identity into wider nuances of voice rather than merely to allegorize them. Nevertheless, that other essential element of the allegory, the motif of the journey, provides *The Dream Songs* with the deep structure of their seemingly occasional arrangement.

At the same the time, the last section of *The Dream Songs* begins with an explicit reversal of the journey's expected end. References to travel, journey, and pilgrimage—literal, literary, legendary, and otherwise—pervade Berryman's sequence. Without this motif the songs would become a collection of brilliant but random pieces held together by the nonce form Berryman invented as a kind of eighteen-line elaboration on the sonnet. By organizing the sequence according to this motif he grounds his psychic epic—what I suggest is an epic of double consciousness—in the tradition of the epic journey that shapes Western literary history from Homer and Virgil through Dante, Spenser, and Wordsworth, and up to our own day. Such journeys, as George DeForest Lord observes, resonate with the "trial of the self" to pursue authentic life.[96]

Berryman's *The Dream Songs* is nothing if not a trial of the self, but a trial that calls into question the self's very integrity through the multifarious and nonlinear nature of its employment of the quest motif. Nevertheless, Henry seeks authentic life, the attainment of which is at once a completion and the ecstatic dissolution of one's conscious identity. It is, whether literally or figuratively, death. As such, the archetypal journey to the West is a journey that follows the path of the setting sun. Consistent with that passage, the Irish *immram,* or journey poem, into the western sea made by such figures as Brendan and Mael Duin provides yet another model for Berryman, one to which he alludes directly in "Dream Song 279":

> Leaving behind the country of the dead
> where he must then return & die himself
> he set his tired face due East
> where the sun rushes up the North Atlantic[97]

Like the opposites black and white, East and West play off of each other throughout the sequence. Here, as *The Dream Songs* makes its final turn, the thematic interplay becomes explicit. The sequence is nothing other than a passage inward as well as outward, tracing the protagonist's psychic, social, artistic, historical, and cultural errancy. More than this, Berryman's use of the motif also constitutes both a conscious reversal of the western passage in the Irish *immram*—a kind of return from the land of the young, or in this case the country of the dead—and a reversal of the emigrant passage out of Ireland. It is, essentially, an answering personal diaspora of return that would redress an original diaspora of departure.

What is the significance of this reverse diaspora for Berryman's sequence, and how does it intersect his use of minstrelsy that so shapes the sequence up to this point of reversal? Berryman's long poem is an epic of consciousness and, more pointedly, of double consciousness. At the root of Henry's psychic conflict are confusions and reversals of opposites, of doublings—love and death, black and white, East and West elaborated and emended through any number of manifestations, but most emphatically in tropes of blackface or black voice and, by the last movement of the sequence, in the full emergence of "Celtic Henry." Likewise, running through the sequence are poems in praise of dead poets, elegies for their imaginative achievements. One such poem, a great elegy for William Carlos Williams, who died in 1963, comes in the Ireland section of the manuscript. In "Dream Song 324," Berryman as Henry praises Williams's excellence as a poet, his "good sound," as well as his generosity and, importantly, his virility as a man who "had so many girls" while loving his "one wife."[98] He also envies especially "the being through." In effect, this powerful Dream Song combines three governing motifs of the sequence: sex, death, and poetry—the act of making even to the extinction of the poet. Here, thanatos, eros, and poesis are joined together as a foreshadowing of Berryman's own completion.

Throughout this Irish section, Henry also praises the masters of "the high Irish style"—Joyce, Swift, O'Casey, Kavanagh, Clarke, and especially Yeats. What Berryman through the hybrid, fictional mask of Henry seeks by turning east from the land of the dead to the land of his own father's forebears is nothing less than an imaginative repatriation that will bring with it renewed erotic energy as well as renewed poetic energy. The erotic is revealed in several poems about an Irish lover, not the least of which is the "excellent lady" of "Dream Song 355." "I am you, / you are your moan, you are your sexy moan, / we are a possum treed," Henry declaims—again the blurring of identity, now gender, and again the allusion to being "treed."[99] Is this an evocation of sex as lynching and death as lovemaking, as in the Shakespearean double entendre? Certainly. The poetic urge finds Berryman's most eloquent and emphatic renewal, famously, in "Dream Song 312":

> I have moved to Dublin to have it out with you,
> majestic Shade, You whom I read so well
> so many years ago,

did I read your lesson right? did I see through
your phases to the real? your heaven, your hell
did I enquire properly into?[100]

As a young man, Berryman's "major ambition in crossing the Atlantic . . . was to meet Yeats," which he did shortly before the great Irish poet's death.[101] There is a more profound significance to this second imagined meeting with the poet, who was Berryman's greatest living master and the shaping imaginative force of his youth. It has only marginally to do, in my view, with vanquishing the master in some Oedipal psychomachia, or perhaps Yeats's flirtations with eugenics and fascism late in his life. Rather, this encounter, one of the high points of *The Dream Songs,* enjoins the "inconsolable loss" that reigns at its real and fictive heart, the death by self-inflicted gunshot of Berryman's father, John Allyn Smith, when Berryman was twelve. "To have it out," to make the hidden revealed, the invisible visible, regardless of the cost and conflict, is the animating spirit behind the dream songs. As Berryman writes in "Dream Song 305," "I sing with infinite slowness finite pain / I have reached into the corner of my brain / to have it out."[102] The figure of Yeats and the figure of Berryman's father stand beside each other at the crossroads of the poet's desire for abundant imaginative and erotic life and his insatiable psychic death wish. Here is the root of Berryman's double consciousness: "to have it out" both imaginatively and psychically.

It is no mistake that *The Dream Songs* have to return to Father Ireland rather than Mother Ireland in order to reach completion. Not surprisingly, these two father figures—Yeats, the father of the imagination, and John Allyn Smith, grandson of Irish immigrants, self-murderer, and father of Berryman's personal diaspora—stand at the antipodes of this last movement of *The Dream Songs.* Here is song 384:

> The marker slants, flowerless, day's almost done,
> I stand above my father's grave with rage,
> often, often before
> I've made this awful pilgrimage to one
> who cannot visit me, who tore this page
> out: I come back for more.[103]

The trope is the same in relationship to both fathers: a journey to origins, an *immram,* a pilgrimage—I come back, I come back—one going away from the country of the dead toward new imaginative life, the other going into the country of the dead. Berryman and Henry have two majestic shades, and both tragically and evocatively double for each other in the poet's life and work. They also have a minstrel shade, the legacy of his mother's Southern ancestry.

Where has the blackface minstrel motif gone with the emergence of Ireland to the climactic forefront of the sequence? It is tempting to see the cultural legacy of Berryman's own mother, a dominant figure who loomed over her son's life until his own death by suicide in 1972, dominating *The Dream Songs* until Henry and Berryman return to the psychic and imaginative fatherland of Ireland, at which point the minstrel figure becomes less prominent. Indeed, in these terms, one could read Berryman's sequence as further divided, further doubled in its consciousness, into sections infused with the Southern cultural legacy of Berryman's mother and a final section organized around the father's legacy, both of imaginative life and of psychic death. That seems too easy, however, and it is the minstrel figure of Henry's unnamed friend who in an Irish pub watching an American baseball game addresses Berryman's protagonist—as if he were the poet's own mask—and the reader in a way that prompts Henry to reveal the hidden purpose of Berryman's entire, polyvocal orchestration:

> —Mr. Bones, you on a trip outside yourself.
> Has you seen a medicine man? You sound will-like,
> a testament & such.
> Is you going?— Oh, I suffer from a strike
> & a strike & three balls. . . .
> . . . .
> These Songs are not meant to be understood, you understand.
> They are only meant to terrify and comfort.[104]

Yeats deemed meditation on a mask the necessary catalyst for self-knowledge and poetic making, and *The Dream Songs* are nothing if not populated with masks, or voices voiced through masks, not the least of which is Berryman's "black voice." Beyond manifesting Berryman's own psychic conflicts and aesthetic obsessions, the purpose of this mask, this voiced other, is to enlighten the conversation across racial and ethnic divides that should bring our common humanity, so often invisible to us, into sharper perspective in a way that likewise permits us to survey our losses from a vantage of shared historical and cultural knowledge.

In "Dream Song 73," Berryman evokes the garden at Ryoan-ji as an image resonant with Yeatsian changelessness—not exactly Sato's sword, but an image that in contrast to Yeats places loss in the forefront of our consideration. "I remembers loss," Henry says at that moment in blackface. In her preface to *Playing in the Dark,* Toni Morrison poses a question that probes the heart of just such loss on the cultural instead of the personal scale: "How do embedded assumptions of racial (not racist) language work in the literary enterprise that hopes and sometimes claims to be humanistic?"[105] Answering this question in the literary context, she believes, "offers an unprecedented opportunity to comprehend the resilience and gravity, the inadequacy and force of the imaginative act."[106] In *The Dream Songs* John Berryman engaged that opportunity with the full force of his art and life experience, his personal as well as cultural history. "Naked the man came forth from his mask to be," he declaims in "Dream Song 370" with visionary clarity.[107] It is an ideal that haunts Irish American poetry from Crispus Attucks to Mr. Bones.

After John Berryman jumped off the Washington Avenue Bridge in Minneapolis in January 1972, he entered, literally and no longer figuratively, the country of the dead to join both his Southern and Irish ancestors, whose own lives were part of a still more encompassing diaspora, East and West, that is not only American history but the history of the one race, which is human. At his funeral Mass, as John Haffenden recounts,[108] a young African American student, barefoot, walked vigorously and conspicuously up the aisle, kissed the casket, turned, and left.

ELEVEN

Over There
Irish American Poets Return

Reversing the Journey, Widening the Net

About the weight and size of a small chapbook, bluish-black, with the gold-embossed faded seal front and center looking more like a Rorschach pattern now than an emblem of Empire, my grandfather's passport rests comfortably in my hand, though every time I lift it from the locked safety box I feel myself drawn into an almost palpable confluence of familiarity and strangeness. Above the seal to the far left, block letters spell out PASSPORT, and below them centered in their silken white niche is the number 57926, his identification. Below the seal in its matching niche near the bottom is my grandfather's signature in neat cursive—*Mr. M. Ruane*. Open the cover, and the clouded pink endorsement pages fold out with their nearly infinitesimal lattice weave, some stained over the years from before it came into my possession, all blank except for one that reads after the prompt "Travelling to" in some unknown clerk's patient script, "U.S. American direct or via Canada," stamped "Foreign Office, 17 Feb 1920." On the lower half of the page the more elaborate stamp of the American Consulate, Dublin, Ireland reads: "Seen, No. 1310, Bearer is to Depart For the United States Between 8 Apr 1920 and 8 May 1920, Date 8 April 1920," and signed, "John F Claffey, Consul." An American Consular Fee Stamp for one dollar is pasted below and dated, blurrily, 8 Mar 1920.

One has to unfold the endorsement pages outward like an art book or a broadside to find the outlined details of passport regulations certified by the Foreign Office, November 1919, and read the "Description of Bearer": Age *20,* Profession (left blank), Place and date of birth *Ireland, 22-3-1895,* Maiden name of widow or married woman traveling singly (left blank), Height, *5* feet *7 3/4* inches, Forehead *Medium,* Eyes *Grey,* Nose *Regular,* Mouth *Large,* Chin *Medium,* Colour of Hair *Fair,* Complexion *Pale,* Face *Regular,* Any special peculiarities (left blank), National Status *British Born Subject*. Underneath one finds his signature again, and below that a "Photograph of Bearer," stamped by the Foreign Office 17 February 1920. Someone erased his true age, twenty-six, at the time of emigration and filled in the second digit with a hampered 0 to make him twenty. Himself? My grandmother? My mother? One of his other children? In the margins there are years in pencil and pen subtracted from each other to determine his age—1895 from 1923, 1895 from 1928, from 1929. For what purpose? There is no "Description of the Wife of Bearer," the section crossed out with a stark pen line, since he and my grandmother met in New York sometime after he arrived in 1920 on the S.S. *Kaisarin Auguste Victoria* out of Liverpool.

From his gray, faded passport photograph—a neat suit and tie, hair brushed back from his forehead, mouth closed—he looks outward widely and away from the reader's gaze, toward a present lost nearly ninety years ago or toward a future that elapsed for him in a nursing home bed more than forty years before I record these few details. To the left, under the passport identification number and the red stamp that notes six pence with an image of the crown, the calligraphy and rhetoric by which the British Empire granted my grandfather rite of passage tumbles floridly down the page:

> We, George Nathaniel Curzon, Earl Curzon of Kedleston, Viscount Scarsdale, Knight of the Most Noble Order of the Garter, a Member of His Britannic Majesty's Most Honorable Privy Council, Knight Grand Commander of the Most Exalted Order of the Star of India, Knight Grand Commander of the Most Eminent Order of the Indian Empire, etc. etc. etc. His Majesty's Principal Secretary of State for Foreign Affairs, Request and require in the Name of His Majesty all those whom it may concern to allow [blank space for the name] to pass

DESCRIPTION OF BEARER.

Age 20   Profession —

Place & date of birth Ireland 22-3-95

Maiden name of widow or married woman travelling singly —

Height 5 feet 7¾ inches

Forehead Medium   Eyes Grey

Nose Regular   Mouth Large

Chin Medium   Colour of Hair Fair

Complexion Pale   Face Regular

Any special peculiarities —

National Status British Born Subject

Martin Ruane

June 8ᵗʰ 95

1924

PHOTOGRAPH OF BEARER.

Foreign Office 17 FEB 1920

SIGNATURE OF BEARER.

Specimen signature of applicant, which will be detached and affixed to the Passport when issued.

Martin Ruane

freely without let or hindrance and to afford *him* every assistance and protection of which *he* may stand in need. Given at the Foreign Office, London the 17th day of February 1920.
Curzon of Kedleston

Into the blank space defined by an Empire's eminent bureaucracy my grandfather compliantly signed his name, *Mr. Martin Ruane,* though even now alongside his signature in a bold stroke of black ink reads an assertive and blithely transgressive gloss *A Brave Man*.

The circumstances that prompted my grandfather to leave rural Ireland alone and without profession were undoubtedly the same for thousands of others who sought to escape the economic and social limitations of remaining home even at this latter end of the Irish diaspora. From my twenty-first-century vantage I can place his passage within the context of so many others who filled in the blank of their Foreign Office passports with their names, as subjects of a nation and empire with which they did not wholly if at all identify—all brave men and women to depart alone or with uncertain prospects in a new country. I can place his passage in the still wider concentric circle of those from other countries who made similar journeys for similar reasons and perhaps far more extreme deprivations, and in the still wider context of a countermovement of Americans heading for Europe. After all, my grandfather made his passage in 1920, just two short years after the end of World War I, with all of its epic, world-transmogrifying destruction and its shiploads of American soldiers making their journey to the trenches to the tune of George M. Cohan's "Over There," one of the Broadway genius's songs of buoyant patriotism that now appears concomitant with America's rapid ascension into a global superpower: "For the Yanks are coming, / the Yanks are coming // and we won't come back till it's over over there." I can place his passage, too, in the still wider and more benign context of American expatriate artists and writers who came into their own "over there" rather than, like my grandfather and so many others, over here—the likes of Hemingway and Pound and Eliot and H. D., and lesser, marginal writers like the doomed poet Ernest Walsh, for whom, as we saw, Irishness was a crisis of identity inherited from an earlier emigration.

Born in 1895, the same year as my grandfather, Walsh died in 1926 having composed a few scattered poems of promise while abroad in Europe seeking his literary fortune among the greater lights of his age. These two figures—my nearly anonymous grandfather with his self-asserted and slightly eponymous identity, *A Brave Man,* making his way in the New World, and the largely forgotten poet Ernest Walsh seeking his artistic identity in the old—exemplify an American Irish, Irish American countercrossing that has persisted and evolved over the last century to the present day. In addition to social and historical pressures, this countercrossing exposes how important it is for some Irish American poets to make the passage over there for the sake of ratifying their artistic as well as their ethnic identities. Though not widely acknowledged on either side of the Atlantic, for those poets in particular who remain over there, the passage and the pursuant expatriate life has an urgency and appeal of aesthetic liberation that fuels their work and that ultimately enjoins still broader questions of identity making and the claiming of origins.

America has long been a proving ground for Irish poets, both those who stay for a time and those who stay permanently or semi-permanently. The "progress from Ireland to the United States," as Eamonn Wall cogently observes in *From the Sin-é Café to the Black Hills,* "is a natural right-of-way which has long been forged by history and practice" for all Irish people as well as writers.[1] Wilde and Yeats made famous tours of the States in the late nineteenth and early twentieth century, respectively, and as the last century wore on, the likes of Padraic Colum, Oliver St. John Gogarty, and Brian Coffey made their extended stays. The growing prominence and renown of Irish poets over the last century has to be attributed in part to their desire not only to "make it there" in the United States but to draw to a greater or lesser extent from a native American tradition counter to the European cosmopolitanism of Eliot, Pound, H. D. and the like.

Montague cut his poetic teeth with visits back to America under the influence of William Carlos Williams. Thomas Kinsella taught for years at Temple University, and while his work does not show the kind of American influences one finds in Montague's, the significance is there in a poem like "The Good Fight," commemorating the death of John F. Kennedy. James Liddy followed Ginsberg and eventually found another kindred poet in John Ashbery. The younger poet Eamonn Wall schooled himself on the poems of Frank O'Hara and James Schuyler, came to study here, and stayed. Greg Delanty likewise found a second home in the United States, and his work broadly reflects that influence. Seamus Heaney, Paul Muldoon, and Eavan Boland, as Eamonn Wall acknowledges, have not only been accepted into the American poetry establishment but lionized, with Boland assuming the directorship of Stanford University's Stegner Creative Writing Program and Muldoon winning the Pulitzer Prize and most recently assuming the poetry editorship of the *New Yorker*. Eamon Grennan also enjoys something of a poetic double life in Ireland and the United States, having won prizes on both sides of the Atlantic while he taught for years at Vassar. Still younger poets like Aidan Rooney and Mary O'Donoghue have found teaching positions in the United States, and those positions have enhanced their status in Ireland and with their Irish publishers, even if they are not, as yet, prominent figures on the American poetry scene.

There is, in short, not only a long-standing desire on the part of Irish poets—coming as Eamonn Wall observes "from the poorer country"—to make it in America, there also has been a desire on the part of the academic establishment (and in a good number of cases the poetry establishment) not only to welcome Irish poets into the scene but, increasingly, to celebrate them. There is a great deal to be gained by American poetry through the migrations of these poets, though one wonders how the pattern will develop now that Ireland, per capita, was for a time a wealthier nation than the United States (until the worldwide economic downturn of 2008). Regardless of national economic fortunes, the counterpassage back to Ireland generally has been a good deal more difficult. For one thing, though Ireland has long been hailed popularly as "a nation of poets," expatriate Americans have traditionally headed to England and to France to broaden their horizons. In addition to Eliot and Pound and company, the most self-consciously American of American poets, Robert Frost, published his first book of poems in England. Though through the middle decades of the last century, before the rise of the Celtic Tiger, Irish literature and poetry thrived (despite a milieu of cultural stagnation and, in the North, the long-festering sore of sectarianism that would flare into the Troubles), few American poets made extended stays or saw Ireland as a land of poetic opportunity.

Jeffers, as we saw, is an exception. He intended his Tor House on California's headlands to be a symbol of poetic aspiration transposed and transfigured from the northern headlands of Antrim's Tor and, of course, Thoor Ballylee. So, likewise, is Berryman an exception; his epic *The Dream Songs* reaches its crescendo in Ireland, where the American poet "has it out" with the majestic shade of Yeats. Lowell's last book, *Day by Day,* also comes under the influence of the North after he left Elizabeth Hardwick for Lady Caroline Blackwood and lived near the end of his life on her estate in the north of Ireland.

While a growing number of Irish American poets have spent a significant amount of time in Ireland, with some moving there permanently, the countercrossing back to Ireland does not carry the same urgency or potential for acknowledgment in the United States. Going over there will not necessarily increase a poet's visibility to an American readership. There are exceptions, of course, like Tess Gallagher, Jean Valentine, and Thomas Lynch, though each of these poets had already begun establishing careers before they traveled to Ireland for any length of time. For poets like Chris Agee, Michael Donaghy, and Julie O'Callaghan, just the opposite is true: they are virtually unknown to the American audience for poetry. Moreover, while the American poetry scene might be inclined in some cases to welcome Irish poets as openly as PBS welcomes Riverdance, the Three Irish Tenors, and Celtic Woman, it is not unreasonable to note that the Irish sometimes look on Irish America with a measure of reticence born of the very history that binds the two nations together in the Irish experience of diaspora. It is a perspective resulting from a complex relationship to home and origin that has not yet entirely been resolved socially, culturally, or artistically. This should not be surprising, given the prominence of what Patrick Ward calls "the stock figure of the emigrant returning from America." That figure has been suffused by sentimental representations and parodies of Irishness that, rather than forging authentic ties between Irish Americans and their envisioned lost homeland, actually has "added to the developing divergence between the interests, needs and self-perception of those now resident in America and those at home in Ireland." As such, from Ward's perspective, Irish Americans "acquiesced in their own misrepresentation."[2]

At the same time, it is fair to say that the Irish tourist industry, as well as Irish cultural self-perception and self-representation, has contributed to that acquiescence and has gained by it in the quality and degree of its confidence. Even in the late nineteenth century, as Ward further observes, though America served as both a "refuge and a threat," in terms of cultural production, the larger nation nonetheless "provided a massive market for art from the Old World and rarely distinguished between works emanating from different traditions within Ireland."[3] The like is certainly true today, both in the realm of popular productions and in more subtly sophisticated ways. Eamonn Wall sums up the situation acutely: "What has happened, of course, is that Irish culture has become so widely disseminated and influential in the United States, and travel has become so easy, that Americans bypass Irish America and come straight to Ireland. Similarly, many of the young Irish who go to America nowadays go straight to the Lower East Side of Manhattan and steer clear of an Irish American world they consider as having ground to a halt, wallowing in a time warp."[4] From this standpoint it would appear very difficult indeed for Irish American poets, and especially those seeking to reestablish some authentic relationship to the cultural inheritance of the perceived homeland, to feel secure and artistically legitimate in making their way over there.

To what extent may one's reception as a poet become warped through the lens of what American expatriate poet Chris Agee has called "shamrockry"?[5] That is, he identifies the tendency of Irish America to romanticize Ireland and the potential for the Irish at once to subsidize those expectations in the popular culture for good business reasons and, rightfully, to resist endorsing Irish and Irish American kitsch in the more serious echelons of literary reception. In short, the artistic and professional context for Irish American poets in Ireland appears to be complicated by long-standing issues of cultural identity, allegiance, and self-parody. Beyond these matters, one needs to have made a life over there to be considered an Irish poet, like Julie O'Callaghan, who is now a member of Aosdana, or Chris Agee, who has been a part of the Northern Irish literary scene for three decades.

On the whole, given the situation, Wall is right in affirming "what is important is that the nets be thrown out widely, and that these poets be allowed to negotiate as freely as possible in both America and Ireland."[6]

At the same time, preparing the net requires some consideration of the deeper, often unconsidered motivations behind a poet's desire and ambition to reverse the journey from the wide and eclectic proving ground of America to the more closely knit and insular confirming ground of Ireland.

Fitting Emblems of Return

For some Irish American poets the impetus to make their way professionally in Ireland rather than in America originates in the same complex conditions emerging from the experience of diaspora that have shaped the Irish and Irish American relations both culturally and historically. For such an Irish American poet who may be one, two, or more generations removed from "the homeland," the desire for an artistic connection to Ireland finds its motivation in an enduring sense of Irish identity that has managed to persevere despite the seemingly irresistible power of Americanization. At the same time, as it is for anyone, the poet's assertion of an original identity—Irishness in this case—is at once motivated and subverted by the historical and cultural gulf born of the experience of migration and its inevitable aftermath. While it is possible for a recent emigrant or exile to affirm a cultural and imaginative connection to some homeland without self-consciousness, such an affirmation is far less assured when a person's immediate physical origin in the homeland cannot be declared.

The dissolution of connection is built into the bureaucracies by which nations articulate and manage their conceptions of citizenship, and Ireland is no exception. Like many other Irish Americans, because I was able to prove my connection through a grandfather's passport, and by tracing forward my relationship to him through birth and marriage certificates in Ireland and America, I have been able to lay claim to Irish citizenship despite being two generations removed from the homeland. The mere possession of an Irish passport, however, cannot heal what Stephanie Rains has called "the rupture of emigration," a rupture that in turn creates a "hunger" to complete a more detailed map of one's extended ancestral identity than can be wholly charted by the "meta-narratives" of emigration and diaspora.[7] Hence the powerful lure of genealogical research.

For the Irish American poet, however, the mapping of a family tree is not enough; the claiming of Irishness requires an imaginative response that circumvents the temptations of nostalgia without denying the powerful attraction of Ireland as a nexus of identity. In contrast, recent Irish poets who have come to America to make their way artistically and professionally have no such experience of being "ruptured" from their Irish roots. The hyphen between Irish and American, if applicable at all in this case, signifies something closer to a commuter highway than a mark of erasure or gulf that needs to be bridged. In short, their negotiation between Ireland and America is somewhat freer of the accrued baggage of diasporic history if only because the connection to the place of Ireland is immediate within their life experience and unmediated by the displacement of history. Rains's recognition of the forces motivating Ireland's lure for Irish Americans is pertinent here: "The negotiation of such Irish Americans' relationship to Ireland therefore becomes one dominated by the concept of a home nation which is not only elsewhere, but which is not directly and personally remembered. It is this moment at which Ireland becomes, for the majority of the world's population who identify themselves as Irish, a home understood through the consumption of narrativized images—principally those of film and tourism—rather than firsthand memory or experience."[8]

In the case of the Irish American poet, the images that compose the narrative of identity through the consumer-driven mechanisms that promote Ireland as an idea to be marketed to Irish Americans (among others) need to be resisted like any instance of nostalgia and cliché—at times outright and at times from the inside. Both Irish America and Ireland have been complicit in the production of such images—the Irish American making his return to an Inishfree of John Ford's making and the Irish Cabaret at Jury's Hotel in Dublin benefit similar productions in Ireland and America, but they do not necessarily benefit a more probing art or its reception, or the more complex engagement with questions of origin that refuses the substitution of stock narratives for those critically tested by experience.

What might be called stage Irish American images and narratives persist, suggesting a cultural interaction and milieu that are not always conducive to poetry that engages Ireland and the experience of being Irish American at a deeper level than received or inherited paradigms.

Over the past twenty years the evolving lure of Ireland for American poets exposes an urge for authenticity lacking in some of American poetry as well as a tendency to revert to the well-established conception of Irishness as a locus for all that is naturally and traditionally poetic.

More than twenty years ago, Ben Howard in *The Pressed Melodeon* confronted the issue and identified "the natural eloquence of Irish writers" as one reason for the allure—an affirmation that at once pays homage to the long tradition of Irish poetry and appears to render "naturalness" and "eloquence" as essential qualities of Irish writing, as though an Irish writer could not help but be "naturally eloquent." Hidden in this affirmation is a reiteration of the kind of tourism narrative that exports an idea of Ireland brimming with the spontaneous loquacity of its people, and that has prompted Aer Lingus to weave into its seats quotable quotations from Ó Bruadair to Eavan Boland. I mean no slight here either to Ben Howard or to the tradition of Irish poetry, or even to Aer Lingus—one can only dream of American Airlines seats interlaced with lines from poems by Walt Whitman and Emily Dickinson! There *is* something deeply alluring, as Howard further remarks, about "an English-speaking country where the idea of the poet is still taken seriously,"[9] and consequently where poets are interviewed regularly on RTE, where even a poet's potentially scandalous behavior can spur nationwide debate.

Howard's insightful recognition of the Irish poet's general fluency and place in the culture finds more stable ground in his insight that the "strongest attraction" comes from "the historical capaciousness of Irish poetry . . . a hunger for images of the self in history, of personal identity in relation to historical process."[10] It goes without saying that for the Irish American poet, "the hunger for images of the self in history" involves Irish history specifically and not merely history as a generic process. Not surprisingly, the desire to confront history fuels the Irish American poet's authentic urge to return to the place where history shaped identity and the experience of diaspora. The authentic urge must find an authentic voice.

According to Howard, for the American poet the place of history and the sense of place have been lost in favor of the latter-day confessional poet's reification of the localized psyche in some state of agitation—a troubling personal memory, for example—or merely in repose, registering its quotidian encounters with the world. To this one may add the more recent tendency of some younger American poets to eschew the personal altogether in favor of antinarrative language play, dissociated parodies in which the question of authenticity is elided altogether, having been ruled out as a legitimate concern from the start. Such can be "the skittery poem of our moment," to use Tony Hoagland's phrase.[11] "The question of choosing an authentic voice," Howard observes, is always more complicated for the Irish poet, who must confront the fracture of a dual tradition, English and Irish.[12] In a sense, it is almost impossible for the Irish poet to turn away from history, while for the American poet any number of prevailing cultural and aesthetic trends may turn the poet inward or simply toward the disembodied realms of signifiers fueled by an untethered and untested irony.

In contrast, the urge toward a more authentic encounter with oneself in the context of history and the place of Ireland may be heard in Howard's poem "The Holy Alls":

> Conceived by staunch Midwestern Methodists
> And reared a Christian in a river town,
> Companioned as a child by fields of corn
> And menaced by a temperamental river,
> Am I forever to be understood
> As but the minted product of those forces,
> Its features formal and indelible,
> Its image fixed as on a wooden nickel?
> That I should venture to define myself
> Against the waters of Liscannor Bay
> Or see the image of my aspirations
> In congeries of megalithic stone
> Is no less plausible, it seems to me,
> Than seeing in a Methodist retreat—
> A basement dinner long on casseroles
> But short on zest and sensuality—
> A fitting emblem of my inmost nature.[13]

In blank verse that resonantly echoes Wordsworth's "The Prelude," these lines sharply articulate the problem of place and identity for the

American poet who would seek to pursue a course contrary to the so-called American grain. Though Howard is not Irish American by birth, his poem defines the fundamental prospect of the Irish American poet as one who locates identity in the offing of a horizon that historically stands behind the place of one's immediate self-definition. The authenticity of the poet's voice rests in the choice to be defined by an Irish sense of place rather than his Midwest American home. Embedded, if not expressly, here is an implicit rejection of the consumerist ethos of America in favor of a social nexus and landscape more amenable to the kind of contemplative, place-centered poetry that has become rarer on this side of the Atlantic over the last quarter century. The Irish parish takes precedence over the American corporate park and its ever-widening sprawl.

In addition to the primacy of defining identity through the choice of place, these lines from "The Holy Alls" suggest that a poet's style—the authentic voice—is likewise a matter of choice and that the choice of place confirms a choice of style. While Howard's poem might be considered comfortably New Formalist in its strict blank verse, it is notable that the poem rejects the American populist strain—cornfield and casseroles— that can inform some iterations of the New Formalist poetic. Howard's "fitting emblems" of identity are Irish by reference and turn away from the American grain. Recognizing this prevailing tendency among some poets, Eamonn Wall intuits that Americans, "tired of the abuse of freedom at home, have looked to Ireland for a more stable use of poetic form."[14] Howard's aesthetic certainly supports Wall's insight, though Wall's own work, like James Liddy's, runs largely counter to the more traditional, formal strains of Irish poetry in favor of the more open aesthetic that is perceived to be the American hallmark.

At the same time, for certain Irish American poets who have chosen to define themselves and their work in Ireland rather than in America, the primacy of place and the attraction of the local prove even more alluring. Janice Fitzpatrick Simmons, wife of the late Belfast poet James Simmons, affirms such countervailing views of America and Ireland in her free-verse poem "Many Waters":

> I grew in a sheltered bay
> of the Western Atlantic, the sea around me

my amniotic waters, a source of life,
salty, caressing, dangerous. From her waters
I pulled wonders, fish that could fly, sharks
that sent my father into a panic,
a panic that rises now in my throat
with my own children.

All my best dreams happen by the Irish Sea,
my home—Portmuck's dark and white rock falling
steeply to the water and the shoulder of a harbour.[15]

While Simmons's lines initially echo Whitman's "Starting from Paumanok," it is significant that when the scene shifts to Ireland the poet calls on the specific place name rather than the more anonymous "sheltered bay of the Western Atlantic," which could be anywhere on the East Coast of the United States. While there appears a greater and easier admission of continuity in Simmons's poem between America and Ireland than in Howard's "The Holy Alls," it is clear that the defining sense of home and place has shifted for the poet in favor of Ireland, though the prenatal, amniotic Atlantic waters find their postnatal equivalent in the protective embrace of Portmuck harbor. Rather than history, a sense of the timeless pervades the lines, as it does in Theodore Deppe's "Midsummer's Night, Cape Clear," in which the poet's enthrallment with a local wedding feast on the island off the coast of County Cork leads to his reverie of place names:

I walk the last two hundred miles of the trip
in my mind. Mizen Head and Sheep's Head,

then Allihies by way of Bantry,
each mountainous peninsula conjured
and let go . . .[16]

As in Simmons's "Many Waters," Deppe's invocation of the local names of places in and around Cape Clear Island and County Cork suggests a way not only of conjuring place but of bespeaking the poet's relationship to place as though the poet has managed to create an identity commensurate with the idea of home itself.

Originally from Indiana, Deppe, like Simmons, has since moved permanently to Ireland. It would be easy to suggest that the invocation of Irish place names generally by expatriate American poets amounts to a nostalgic attachment to an outmoded idea of rural Ireland, but another possible motivation for assuming an Irish passion for the local may have to do, at least in Deppe's case, with the poet's painful confrontation with one of the uglier aspects of American history—racism. Written before he moved to Ireland, "The Gatekeeper" draws an indelible portrait of a woman presiding over visitors at a Klan rally. The poem's conclusion suggests more legitimate motivations than mere nostalgia for seeking one's identity as a poet in a country whose habitations, for the poet, offer a release from the shadow side of Howard's American Midwest:

I take with me an image of home

they want me to see, though not clearly.
So now I have no home, or
have one and can no longer recognize it.
Or else have one that is bound
intricately to evil, and still home.[17]

In "The Gatekeeper" we recognize a scene that offers one of the grimmer aspects of what one might call, adapting Kavanagh's use of the word, the American parish. For Kavanagh, the parish has all the potentially civilizing gravity of a self-validating center and may be distinguished from the provincial, which is a cast of mind that seeks validation outside its own bounds in the metropolis.[18] The shadow side of the parish, as Heaney's *North* attests, is the tribal affiliations that breed xenophobia, sectarianism, racism, and violence. To be "unhappy and at home" in the manner of Heaney's poem "The Tollund Man" underscores the need for a hard-won consciousness that, while celebrating the centering benefits of the parish, likewise remains mindful of its potentially limiting and even brutalizing elements—"the appetites of gravity," as Heaney called them in *North*.[19] To be conscious in this manner is to be mindful of history's interfusion with place and parish, however painful that knowledge may be.

Knute Skinner is one American poet who has made the Irish parish surrounding his adopted home of Killaspuglonane the locus of his imaginative life. For fifty years Skinner has been producing poems that evoke the quotidian life of the fields and townlands on the west coast of Clare between Liscannor and Lahinch. His arrival there in the 1960s foreshadowed the coming of poets like Thomas Lynch and Michael Heffernan to the same West Clare locale. Many of Skinner's poems endow even such "fitting" emblems as Tayto Crisps with a kind of parochial value, though Skinner's poems prospect still more richly into the parish in such poems as "The Beautiful White Cow," in which history and its brutalities become embellished by local folklore:

> They came with empty stomachs, pails in their hands,
> all the peasants in walking distance of Moher.
> You can read about that famine in history books,
> about how the blight-prone lumper potato failed
> while the rest of Ireland's produce was shipped to England.
> Landlords evicted tenants, who dropped by roadsides
> with nettle-stained mouths.
> One third of the people starved or died of typhus,
> but briefly there was milk near the Cliffs of Moher,
> just at the bay's edge—at Kilconnell, Liscannor—
> where the shore rises gradually up to the cliffs.
> For one morning a marvelous cow appeared
> as if in answer to the people's prayers,
> and she gave an inexhaustible supply of milk.
> Perhaps the history books don't tell about her,
> but there stood this cow, day and night,
> for as many to milk as lined the shore with their pails.[20]

In these lines, the immediacy of the diurnal life of the parish breaks open into the depths of history in a way that underscores the role of story and poetry in mere survival—as the poet tells us further on, "I wish this story had a happier ending." At the same time, in a poem like "April–June 1968," the cataclysmic historical events of the King and Kennedy assassinations find their counterpoint in the parish life of neighbors' horses and ploughed fields that enable the poet and his family to dig "their grief into the open soil."[21] In this poem the ritual life and natural rhythms of farm work provide a stabilizing center and buffer against a world devolving toward chaos. Similarly, the end of Michael Heffernan's "A Highway Brook in Dingle" underscores the presence of history verging on timeless in the Irish experience of place:

> The water rattling from above us
> purled and winked and murmured underneath. Below,
> the ocean spoke in tones oceans use.
> Old gods might be staring from behind the light
> at this intersection of known worlds,
> where the human roadway rose to carry us.[22]

While Heffernan spends only part of the year in Ireland, Tennessee-born poet Richard Tillinghast has moved there permanently, like Skinner, Simmons, and Deppe. Both Heffernan and Tillinghast are poets with prominent careers in America, though for each Ireland provides a sense of place that appears lacking in the American context. That other attribute of Ireland's allure is a different sense of time, both in the ritualized pace of the rural day and in that day's permeability to the past, as these lines from Tillinghast's "A Quiet Pint in Kinvara" demonstrate:

> From farms down lanes the meat and milk of pasture,
> Root crops and loads of hay,
> By hoof or wagon, come down to Kinvara quay.
>
> And so do I—to drink in the presence
> Of these presences, these ideas given substance
> Solid as your father's signature
> On a letter you unfold sometimes from a quiet drawer,
> Yet semi-detached, half free,
> Like the road that follows the sea down from Galway,
>
> Curving like a decorated S
> Drizzled through a monk's quill plucked from the goose,
> Spelling *Sanctus* onto vellum. . . .[23]

Tillinghast's poem refuses the loss of presence taken for granted by so much postmodern poetry and affirms instead a vision of Ireland as an avatar of the veritable real presence of things, their substance and endurance over time through generations. The poet's quiet pint is nothing less than a sacramental act that allows him "to drink in the presence / of these presences." The double entendre of being present and ingesting these hosts of village life in a kind of semi-secular communion spurs, in turn, the poem's backward acceleration into past time—eventually to "a cell where the soul's damp candle flared" and finally "the weather's roofless inundations." By the end of Tillinghast's poem, present and past interfuse in a moment of expansive insight that renders them nearly coterminus. The rendering of time here is antithetical to the American "futurist" bias, and it may be antithetical to an Ireland that has rapidly transformed itself from a small country on the western edge of Europe to a member of the European Union, the realization of John Boyle O'Reilly's prophetic insight in his poem "Crispus Attucks."

Tillinghast himself laments this transformation in *Finding Ireland,* in which he observes that "the boom and bust" of the so-called Celtic Tiger "is transforming the country, in particular the capital city—and not necessarily for the better." While he has no illusions about Ireland's turbulent history, its history of poverty, and the cultural insularity of the country under de Valera, the American poet in Ireland brings an outsider's perspective that enables him to affirm that while "the prosperity is welcome, it is happening too fast." Indeed, coming into Dublin by train from Belfast on a recent trip, I counted some forty or more skyscraping cranes wheeling about the city, and this after the building boom had slowed considerably. This was late February 2008, and all the talk on the radio was of constructing highways through Tara. As Tillinghast muses understatedly, "One has mixed feelings about many of the recent changes. A new, aggressively acquisitive attitude in a country that once saw itself as 'the land of saints and scholars' can be distressing."[24] He does, however, like the smoking ban, which itself suggests that the American influence on Ireland has been pervasive in some ways, if not subtle, despite Ireland's European sense of identity.

The gravitation of such poets as Simmons, Deppe, Skinner, Heffernan, and Tillinghast toward Ireland's parish life, in spite of changes brought on by the Celtic Tiger, optimally provides a unique vantage on both Ireland and America. Though given Ireland's recent transformations, one might ask whether there is something inherently nostalgic in locating oneself and one's art in an idea of Ireland that both conceptually and literally is slipping ever more rapidly toward the antiquarian. Ireland is now, or was until recently, the richest country in Europe. In a 2008 list published in the *New York Times,* three of ten cities from around the world where the average cost of housing is over a million dollars were located in Ireland: Dublin, Galway, and Limerick. Skinner's nearby village of Liscannor has been developed for tourism from a bypass with two pubs to a new town center, and summer homes (many empty after the housing bust and even before the bust) still dot the shoulders of Donegal's bays. In short, while Kavanagh and Heaney could comfortably inhabit parish life in their poetry, it has become harder and harder to evoke without nostalgia the ritual pieties of townlands untouched by postmodernity. Moreover, if "Ireland can no longer be contained within the frontiers of an island," as Richard Kearney observes, then what are we to make of American and Irish American poets turning to Ireland with the hope of spurring their "migrant minds"[25] to new definitions that will, one hopes, broaden the borders of Irish and Irish American poetry?

Parody and Authenticity

The most immediate problem for Irish American poets seeking to establish their careers on the other side of the Atlantic is the problem of negotiating an idea of origin that appears undermined by Ireland's own transformation into a very different country from the homeland most Irish Americans imagine. There is something close to a Platonic notion of remembrance in the way Ireland is conjured in the family stories of emigrants, of life in the parish, and in the portrayals of Ireland marketed by any number of tourist outlets. It is a portrait perhaps less passionately adhered to by emigrants like my grandfather, who never returned, than by second- and third-generation Irish Americans.

Of course, those Irish who are separated from their national origin by a generation or more have only the repetitions of the stories passed on or perhaps only a vague conception of the homeland or a vague need to travel back. In *The Wake of Imagination* Richard Kearney argues that the encounter with the postmodern milieu requires a "critique of origins rather than a return to them."[26] The root of Irish and Irish American nostalgia, as well as the route toward a more authentic understanding of home, finds its own source in Kearney's distinction. Having it out with the majestic shades requires more of the poet than a simple return to a homeland whose very idea has been founded—in part at least—on a self-generating industry of idealizations and simulacra; it requires also an effort at authenticity beyond the need for a more stable relationship to form.

From this perspective, the poet Jean Valentine, who lived for a time with the Irish painter Barrie Cooke and has spent considerable time in Ireland, offers an alternative sense of the relationship to place. Spare, elliptical, and very nearly placeless in their evocations, Valentine's work comes closer to Dickinson's in her tendency to convey emotion and idea by using language to parse the pregnant edges of things. Here is "Long Irish Summer Day":

> A lorry scatters
> hay down the road
> red as blood.
>
> Down by Tommy Flynn's
> a young man is sowing
> in the ten o'clock sunset
>
> sowing salt tears on the road
> —not for the ice, we already have sand.
>
> Sun and moon shine into our glass room,
> two countries, two cities,
> two glass houses:
> a shotgun is hanging on the wall.[27]

The first two stanzas of "Long Irish Summer Day" allow a picture of the parish to develop only to have that picture effaced by the third stanza's disruptive evocation of sadness. The poem's details subvert its evocations of place—hay "red as blood" and why does the poet note ice in a poem about summer? The final stanza compounds dualities and acknowledges the gulf created between them—"two countries, two cities / two glass houses." The poem moves from outward signifiers of the parish to an inward space where the raw psyche is revealed and the experience of being doubled has the feel of a violent abrasion that could flare still more violently.

"Deprived of the concept of origin the imagination itself collapses," so Kearney reflects, at which point the dominant postmodern paradigm of the "labyrinth of mirrors . . . where the image of the self dissolves into self-parody" comes to the fore.[28] Valentine's elusive postmodern identity, however, does not dissolve; it grows harder-edged in its perceptual acuity and its desire to render potentially painful psychic states that expose the gulf at the heart of the return to origin. As such, her work may be seen as contrapuntal to that of someone like Paul Muldoon, whose poem "The Old Country" is a tour de force of the parodic imagination critiquing, with brutal wit, the whole notion of the idealized homeland:

> Where every town was a tidy town
> and every garden a hanging garden.
> A hall could be had for half a crown.
> Every major artery would harden
>
> since every meal was a square meal.[29]

The poem goes on in this vein for thirteen sections of sonnets that form a wickedly twisted crown. Its repetitions completely subvert the integrity of the old country as idealized origin. Having made the postmodern *immram* to a twenty-first-century American Country of the Young, Muldoon's work is antithetical in sensibility to those poets who find in Ireland an alternative to American commodification—though how long Ireland will be able to stave off such commodification in the new twenty-first-century Ireland is hard to say. His work is, by reputation as well as execution, as transnational as Irish American poetry can be, although its directive is fundamentally eccentric and does not orient itself solely according to a backward look to the homeland. "The Old Country" calls into question the validity of any such retrospective turn.

Where poets like Simmons, Deppe, Skinner, and Heffernan are attracted by the lore and rhythms of place—the *dinnseanchas* tradition in Irish poetry—Muldoon finds his imaginative home in the prospect of an ever-unfolding *immram;* Jean Valentine inhabits a shifting interior landscape—a parish of the psyche—at once attentive and restless wherever the eye alights, whether in Ireland or in America.

If the postmodern imagination has taught us anything, it is that retrospectives and prospects are relative, or should be. The assumption that Irish American poets who return to Ireland implicitly make a fetish of a lost homeland betrays its own inclination to read Ireland through the reifying lens of revivalism, the proclivity to envision the true Ireland as the land of Ireland solely, without reference to the diasporic history of its people. From an adjusted standpoint, in which Ireland as origin becomes decentered from such purely revivalist conceptions, Ireland may be reconceived as a frontier relative to those who would seek their identities as poets away from an American nexus that often appears charted more by professional production and "school" affiliation than by artistic authenticity. The aim, ultimately, for such a poet is not to reconnect with one's lost origins but to pursue one's own originality as an artist in a manner that is concomitant with one's surest lights. Such an adjusted desire for originality eschews neither the stability of traditional form nor the more serious applications of parody.

One eccentric voice among those Irish American poets who found their artistic and professional futures in Ireland rather than in America is that of Julie O'Callaghan. Born in Chicago in 1954, O'Callaghan moved to Ireland when she was twenty years old and has since published five books of poems, including a new and selected collection with Bloodaxe Books. Many poems in her first two books are written in speech patterns from her hometown of Chicago translated to the page. It is interesting that these poems written in what might be called "stage-Chicagoan" advance something close to a parody of American speech that offers a counterpoint to that of the stage Irish. Here is the opening of "Chicawgo":

> In Chicawgo da truck drivers
> an da newspapa boys drive
> der trucks and bikes aroun early in da A.M.
> Da doughnut shot has two coppers

sittin in it every morning;
der squad cars parked next ta each udder.
Day like der doughnuts covered
in chocolatey mush. but day don't like

da new Dago or A-rab or whatever da H he is
makin da coffee. . . .[30]

The strategy in writing such a poem is at once to cherish the sound of the language as it is spoken in a particular place and at the same time to emphasize the poem's offhand speech as a performance. Nevertheless, when asked if she used American speech in her poetry as a way of exploring her American identity from the distance of her expatriate life in Ireland, O'Callaghan reflects that she "wasn't deliberately exploring anything," though at the same time she confesses, "it was a huge help to be able to hear my American accent because of being in Ireland and having it pointed out to me."[31]

In Ireland and England O'Callaghan is a noted poet whose work is familiarly included in Poetry Society Recommendations, but one has to wonder whether the dialect speech performed in such a poem as "Chicawgo" would have made its mark as emphatically in an American context. It is an interesting question to ask whether O'Callaghan's early poems in her native "Chicawgoan" would have received something more of a regional reception in America rather than national exposure. Indeed, O'Callaghan observes, "I wonder if I would have been writing at all if I stayed in Chicago. I didn't know anyone interested in poetry in America and had no clue (and still don't) about how to get published there. I obviously made the right decision to leave and came to the right country."[32] More than any literary reason, it is "homesickness," she claims, that motivated the way she has written about Chicago, though she sees herself as neither "an American [nor an] Irish poet." That said, she acknowledges rightly that "poetry is much more important and prominent in Irish life than in American life."[33]

It might be further observed, then, that because of her transnational identity, in Ireland O'Callaghan's poems have the additional import of raising the issue of how America is rendered to an

Irish/European audience. Given their comic effects, the poems often have the ring of parody while at the same time retaining an authentic local American intonation. Still, if such poems could be considered parody, it is parody that accurately stages not only the voice of the poet's local origins but also the inclination of the reader who is willing to hear the poem as unmediated speech rather than a vocal performance. In this context, O'Callaghan's work typically offers shrewd assessments of her own dual identity as both Irish and American, as in the poem "Home," in which she exposes the arbitrariness of the idea of home and therefore the idea of origin:

> The Illinois sunrise demonstrates
> exactly what an alien you are
> in your car on the prairie
> heading north to Chicago
> where some Irish guy
> aimed a hundred years ago.[34]

As the poem suggests, one must be a "simple soul" to call such a region, or any region, home. Moreover, if the Irish American poet living in Ireland finds motivation for that return in an art tainted by sentimental attachments to an idealized homeland, O'Callaghan surely rejects that pose.

That rejection is even more emphatic in "The Great Blasket Island," in which six men born on the island return after twenty-one years to find their old world overgrown and utterly lost:

> One says, "Ten of us, blown to the winds—
> some in England, some in America, some in Dublin.
> Our whole way of life—extinct."
> He blinks back the tears
> and looks across the island
> past the ruined houses, the cliffs
> and out to the horizon.
>
> Listen, mister, most of us cry sooner or later
> over a Great Blasket Island of our own.[35]

Prominent at the end of this poem is an American voice that reproves and places the loss of home in the ever-wider context of transpersonal losses, which extend well beyond the immediate island and well beyond Ireland. In a sense, the Great Blasket Island becomes an analogue for Ireland itself, and the loss felt by its exiles analogous to the millions of emigrants who were forced by circumstance to leave for England or America, like O'Callaghan's own family. The poet's refusal of the stock pose of exile wholly subverts the paradigm of the exile's return, and as such it clears a space for a more openly transnational voice in the poetry of those who would make their way imaginatively and professionally "over there." In true postmodern fashion, the poem levels possible magnitudes of loss into a flat line of losses at once transpersonal in number and personal in scale. As such, to borrow a phrase from Elizabeth Bishop, "The Great Blasket Island" situates its own "art of losing" within the shifting confluence, where parody and authenticity swirl separately together like oil in water.

Repositioning Home

Parody as an artistic strategy best reflective of the postmodern condition derives from the assumption that, in Kearney's terms, everything from "subjective inwardness" to "referential depth, historical time and coherent human expression" has "dissolved into a play of language" that precludes the poet's work from reflecting anything more than the fractured hall of mirrors of which it is a part.[36] There is no return to origin, no home. In such a framework the historical and personal condition of exile—whether construed as forced or necessarily chosen—elides to errancy, a condition of endless wandering among mere surfaces. If, as Kearney reflects, in such a condition "home is something that cannot be taken for granted," then what is the point of artistically identifying in any sense with the lost homeland, short of engaging in hopeless nostalgia? In his essay "Heaney and Homecoming" Kearney answers this question by affirming that "homeland is less a territorial locality than an ontological locus whose universal dimensions forever elude the boundaries of a particular nation."[37]

Kearney's recognition not only illuminates the role of homecoming in Heaney's poetry but reconfigures the significance of home and homecoming for the Irish American poet. Home is ahead, not behind; it is an "advent" as Elmer Andrews has affirmed, not "an event," and surely not a place to which one returns.[38] It is this reconfiguration of the idea of home that allows the potentially nostalgic cast of the diasporic imagination to alter its perspective to become, in turn, transnational in scope. Such a repositioning of home from retrospective origin to prospective original nullifies the hegemony of parody as the artistic mode most conducive to expressing our present condition, precisely because it locates authenticity in the poet's faring forward rather than in an idealized return. The shift in perspective does not simply permit but requires the poet's engagement with the world aesthetically, ethically, and ontologically.

Two Irish American poets who found their aesthetic prospects across the Atlantic and whose work comes vividly into focus in a transnational context are Chris Agee and Michael Donaghy. Unlike Julie O'Callaghan, who made her new home in Dublin, Chris Agee moved from his native New England to Belfast in 1979. Born two years after Julie O'Callaghan, Agee taught for twenty years at the Open University in Belfast before founding one of the premier contemporary European literary journals, *Irish Pages*. In the thirteen years before publishing his first book of poems, Agee lived and worked in Belfast during much of the most turbulent periods of the Troubles, and his work gradually reflects more and more an engagement with place, with history, and with the poet's ethical response to violence and suffering.

Published by Dedalus Press in 1992, Agee's first book of poems, *In the New Hampshire Woods*, literally embodies the dual inheritance of America and Ireland in its binary structure, "North America" and "Ireland." The first section of the book comprises a vivid montage of Agee's indigenous New England landscape accomplished with a naturalist's keen eye and a historian's passion for the hidden stories that shape one's sense of place. In the title sequence the poet arranges a series of short poems about the flora and smaller fauna of his childhood landscape with all of the minute attentions of the biologist who fashions an array of glass representations from lichen to dragonfly, oxalis to hummingbird. Throughout these poems there is the allure of particular places—a fascination and dedication to the parish—of the kind to be found in Kavanagh and, more immediately for Agee, in the work of Michael Longley.

Here is the opening stanza of Agee's "High Summer":

> Meditate on the summer island.
> Marram dunes with wild-rose hips,
> the foggy hollows and morning roads
> fragrant with honey suckle and cool.
> I smell the warm breath of lily ponds
> in the chill of a starry evening,
> bayberry, sweetpea, and apple trees.[39]

Though Agee's poem intends to evoke "the pastoral past of New England" and does so with a perceptive eye and finely tuned ear, one can hear a tonal hint of the Irish sense of place through the diction of the first two lines in particular—those marram dunes could be in Mayo as easily as Massachusetts or Maine. It is as if in the poet's consciousness Ireland and America had been superimposed on each other. The result is a kind of hybrid sensibility and a tone that is more intense, dense, and place-centered than the typical contemporary American poem of the past twenty years or so.

Agee's poems read as though American transcendentalism had been crossbred with Irish parochialism and then commingled with the interfusing contemporary influence of Charles Wright and Seamus Heaney. The result is a remarkable amalgamation in Agee's work of Irish and American tonalities, along with a hybrid Irish and American sense of place. These combinations become emphatic in a poem like "Trim's Pond":

> Argosies of moonshine shimmered on the flowing tide.
> Sea-lavender shook; saltmarsh hay and spikegrass
> rippled in ghostly cowlicks. High moon had risen
>
> like a radiant Omega in the starry ocean:
> a New World Belmont off a tidewater bridge
> in Rhode Island, the dark pox of moonmarks

>   the proscenium Winds, or blowing putto,
>   of Europe's imperial cartography.
>   Or, in a flash, an inkblot projection
>
>   of the gaping mouth and brow-shadowed eyes
>   of a Goya face: its silver Antilles on tidal wash
>   a ghostdance glistening in the saltponds of Norumbega.[40]

Far from merely invoking a scene known to the poet from the American parish of his first world, "Trim's Pond" performs an interfusion of European and American orientations to place. Both visually stunning and sonically textured, Agee's poem encapsulates the history of colonization in a single moment of perception. The "argosies" of moonshine that begin the poem end in a ghostdance on the saltponds of Norumbega, the original name for New England, which is probably of Native American origin. This interfusion of worlds in the poet's consciousness, and hence in the poem, becomes inscribed under the moon's "Omega," a presiding sign that has all the force of an *In Hoc Signo*.

In other poems Agee likewise employs the original and historical names of places—like Manisses, the Narragansett word meaning "island of the little god," now Block Island, or the early Dutch name Blocx Eylandt for the same locale—as a way of reinscribing history through the textures of language. It is rare to find a contemporary American poet who pitches language in this way, who finds in words and names plumb lines into history. In short, as in much Irish poetry, the parish maintains its dimension of depth, both historically and ontologically. Even in his American poems Agee refuses the signage of a malled American landscape.

Not surprisingly, the second part of Agee's first book, "Ireland," conveys similarly vivid evocations of place over there, as though the poet were staking out the particular vantages of his new parish, vantages that chart a relation to place that would transcend history. "Out here, in the dark, among pines, / history ends. We end. Something begins / perhaps simply the chill earthen fragrance / of empty stillness," so Agee reflects in "The Black Kesh."[41] The lines suggest something of a Taoist relationship both to the natural world and to the nature of reality itself.

This ontological obsession in Agee's poems comes to the fore again in his second book, *First Light,* in a poem like "Occam's Rime," in which "All Ireland under hoarfrost" modulates by the poem's end to a glimpse of "vanishing matter." Agee's engagement with Northern Ireland and its turbulent history becomes even more vitally engaged in the poem "Thistledown," written after the Omagh bombing, in which the gnomon of a clock prompts the poet's meditation on "the parallel lives of light and dark / unfolding and folding," and of his own son's freedom in play in counterpoint to "a tumbleweed of souls fleeing from / the child massacre." Beyond Ireland, Agee's poems in *First Light* offer a deeply engaged response to the genocide in Bosnia, Croatia, and Serbia during the dissolution of the former Yugoslavia:

> Towards the burnt houses and rolling uplands
> Where their lives ended,
> Where high hay is aflush with wildflowers and luminescence,
>
> Where sleepers of shadow dapple the road;
> Picking up, on the way back,
> From the clods, a bit of juniper
>
> Blanched like a dishrag's threads; from a thorn
> Near Afrim's mound, a shoelace tied to plastic twine;
> From a few paces, a scrap of sock.[42]

These lines from "Mass Grave, Padalista," reveal once again Agee's ability to evoke place through the most closely observed detail as well as to counterpoint the human proclivity for violence with nature's Zen-like there-ness. The effect is cinematic and moving. To parody such atrocity would be an insult, and indeed the presence of suffering, like the starkly simple presence of the natural world in its pristine details, gives the lie to versions of postmodern poetry that traffic entirely in surface dazzle. Agee's is a different kind of postmodern poetry, one that posits the irreducible otherness of the world and the brutal conditions of history to which the poem should bear witness.

Living with his family for part of the year in Croatia, Agee has come to embrace a sense of place that is more broadly European than the parish-centered poetry of traditional Ireland. Nevertheless, his work remains connected to the American landscape, a commitment to which the prose-poem sequence "Time" bears witness. Agee, moreover, makes still farther-flung pilgrimages to Mexico in "The Sierra de Zacatecas," as well as Russia. The poems of *First Light,* however, are not tourist poems blithely scanning the quotidian; rather they are poems of transnational consciousness that evince a deeply informed historical sensitivity, a passion for place and nature, as well as a use of language that "breaks through the horizontal surface of mirror-images and . . . reintroduces a dimension of depth."[43]

Agee's is both an ethical and a historical imagination, and his goal appears to be to fare forward toward an evolving consciousness of home, even when he turns back toward home. So a contrapuntal orientation may be heard in these lines from "Offing":

That sun, a moon almost: I remember it like a bindi
On the cool brow of a porcelain Buddha, a red spot

In the mist of dusk. That place, that microcosmos,
The clean lines of clapboard, the crimson cupola,

Summers in New England, light in August,
What can I say? What can you say of life?[44]

Here the insight that envisions place as a microcosm in the offing of what is to come binds together all places—New England, Ireland, Bosnia, Croatia, Mexico—in a single prospect. Chris Agee has called Northern Ireland his "destiny," though as "Offing" underscores, it is also a vantage from which to gain a still wider prospect.

We find that prospect embraced in these lines from "Sea-Campion" in Agee's book *Next to Nothing:*

So back
we come, again,

to the eternal
homeland, this time

the morning machair
right at the end

of summer. Harebell,
hawksbit, dead

thistle and its thistledown,
lady's bedstraw,

bird's-foot trefoil,
wild mint, clumps

of *the hungry grass*—
light's windy atmospherics

in the ecosystem
of spirit.[45]

The "eternal homeland" of "Sea-Campion" displaces the notion of homeland from a literal physical space onto a farther prospect of spirit, a prospect that transcends the transnational and verges on the transhuman. In this prospect binaries like "physical" and "spiritual" themselves break down and become part of one ecosystem at the edge of the speakable. All in all, for Irish American poetry and Irish and American poetry generally, Agee's evolving vision offers a welcome model of extension and engagement beyond the limited paradigm of return.

The Transnational Parish

While discussing the figure of Stephen Daedalus as a model for the "migratory artist," Patrick Ward in his *Exile, Emigration, and Irish Writing* advances a dual understanding that includes both literal and metaphorical senses of "migratory." Such artists, he claims, form "a loose, transnational association of highly conscious artists, imposing their own narrative order on culture and experience," and it is this loose association that in turn defines the artistry of the modernist mode.[46] At the same time, within an Irish cultural and historical framework, the departure of the artist from the security of home is more problematic since it entails a psychic conflict: while home presents the attraction of familiarity and security, it also has the potential of incapacitating the artist from achieving originality. That is why Stephen Daedalus confesses in his diary that he fears John Alphonsus Mulrennan,[47] for Mulrennan represents Stephen's shadow, submerged in rather than lifted by the forces of place, tradition, and inherited identity. The lure of origin, in short, can be inimical to the originality of the artist. There is something apt in extending this model of the migratory artist to an Irish American poet like Chris Agee, who departs only to gain a wider vantage on both his American and his Irish homes. The like is true of Michael Donaghy, though in much of Donaghy's poetry the social and communal ties of an Irish American home take precedence over the natural landscape and its encoded histories.

Born in 1954, into the same mid-fifties America that produced Julie O'Callaghan and Chris Agee, and of Catholic Ulster stock, Michael Donaghy grew up in the Bronx. The mixed immigrant neighborhood of his youth finds its way pervasively into the poems. He died, tragically and suddenly, in 2004. Though Donaghy began his doctorate at the University of Chicago, in 1985 he left for London more to follow his British girlfriend (Maddy Paxman, who would become his wife and mother to their son, Ruari) home than to pursue his career as poet, though, as he reiterated in several interviews, he did not find either American academia or the American poetry scene at all amenable to the kind of work he valued or wanted to write.[48]

His decision, though predominantly personal and only incidentally professional, harkens back to moves made by expatriate poets earlier in the twentieth century, particularly since Donaghy did not make a point of "returning" to Ireland but remained based in London (though he certainly made multiple visits to Ireland over the years). Donaghy's model for originality is defined by the pursuit of his own artistic lights, then, rather than following a pattern of return to the "place of origin." The model, in short, is Joyce's now brought home, so to speak, into an Irish American setting. At the same time, Donaghy's Irish American inheritance is everywhere in the poems, not only as subject matter but in his very conception of tradition. His formative models, as he noted to John Wall, were neither American nor British but Irish,[49] and mainly Mahon, MacNeice, and eventually Muldoon even more than Heaney. Notably, these are all Northern Irish poets, so while Donaghy did not return to Ulster physically, he certainly did so imaginatively.

Donaghy's distinctly Irish understanding of tradition likewise stems from his deep knowledge of Irish traditional music. A traditional musician himself—he played the flute—Donaghy envisions the relationship of the poet to the reader in a way that brings Irish American experience directly into the arena of poetics. He makes the point vividly in his lecture on poetry, *Wallflowers*:

> I'd been playing jigs and reels for a *ceilidh,* watching the set dancers spinning and stamping out with wild precision the rhythms of a dance which can be described (accurately) as a feral minuet. Sometime during the course of the evening the music I had for years only heard and played became visible, filled with spinning sweaty couples, as the abstract shape of a whirlpool fills with water, or an equation takes shape as a tetrahedron. Only after the dancers had left the floor did I notice the circular patterns of black scuffs and streaks their heels had made on the polished wood. This pattern, I recognised, was an enormous encoded page of poetry; a kind of manuscript, or more properly a *predescript*.[50]

Most immediately Donaghy's insight suggests something of an Irish American duende in the "wild precision" and "feral minuet" of the dance that is itself resonant with Yeats's famous lines from "Among School Children": "Oh body swayed to music, Oh brightening glance / How can we know the dancer from the dance." More significantly, Donaghy links his idea of the predescript explicitly to the idea of tradition, which in turn provides a clear vantage as to why the poet departed America for an expatriate life in the British Isles.

For Donaghy, the "politicizing" of tradition by academics and intellectuals, its linkage to orthodoxy, exclusivity, and a Eurocentric idea of culture, existed in stark contrast to his own multicultural immigrant experience in the Bronx that influences his understanding of tradition:

> But I grew up among several communities of immigrants in New York city—Italian, Irish, Puerto Rican—who regarded their oral traditions as a covenant with their respective cultures. A player in such a tradition is expected to improvise, to "make it new," and the possibilities for expression within the proscribed forms are infinite. But it's considered absurd to violate the conventions of the form, the "shape" of the dance tune or story, because you leave the community of your audience behind, and you bring the dancers to a standstill. By "traditional form" I mean the shape of the dance, those verbal and rhythmical schemes shared by the living community which link it to the dead and the generations to come.[51]

As these crucial and insightful observations suggest, tradition for Donaghy connects the poet to a "home" community whose artistic and social life stands beside the equally vital communities and artistries of others. This is no ivory tower of literary monuments. For the poet conscious of his or her art, home and tradition are not inherently conservative but ideally allow for the kind of improvisation that paradoxically breeds originality in the fullest prospective sense. As Richard Kearney observes from inside the academic setting in words that resonate with the poet's, "tradition is not just a homogenous totality; it is a multi-layered manuscript with each layer recording some new crisis, rupture or spasm that has altered the course of history."[52] The difference between Donaghy's perspective and Kearney's, however, is that the poet refuses to limit his view to a crises-centered vision of history. Donaghy thus at once owns the experience of immigration, diversity, and separation in the "parish" of his New York neighborhood while recognizing patterns of continuity within the wider predescript of tradition.

Such patterns of continuity, even across gulfs of history and culture, put one in mind, once again, of Michael Coady's idea of presequence—"the knowing return to a seminal moment of the past from its future."[53] Both concepts—Donaghy's predescript and Coady's presequence—liberate the past from a condition of stasis falsely conferred on it by both monumental conceptions of tradition and crises-centered conceptions of tradition. The former tends toward homogeny, thereby narrowing the spectrum of influence, while the latter reifies disruption and rupture, thereby precluding any acknowledgment of subtending continuity. Tradition is more alive and continuous than either polarity can manage critically or theoretically. This insight into the living nature of tradition is what, at heart, enabled Donaghy to depart from the United States to become one of the most original American poets of his generation, however unknown in the land of his birth. In his departure we find the poet as the child of immigrants become emigrant in the country that was not the original home of his family, but in which the potential for genuine poetic improvisation and community appeared most possible for the poet he wanted to become. At the same time, as the work shows, Donaghy leaves nothing behind.

Michael Donaghy's first book of poems, *Shibboleth,* won England's prestigious Whitbread Poetry Prize, an award analogous to the Pulitzer or National Book Award in American literary circles and a ringing confirmation that his decision to pursue his art in what was for him a new frontier was in fact the one best suited to his sensibility. In an early poem like "Machines," for example, he brings the trope of the metaphysical conceit back into currency with visual immediacy and rhythmic elegance: "Dearest, note how these two are alike: / this harpsicord pavane by Purcell / And the racer's twelve-speed bike." The poem as it proceeds matches its conception with an enviable mastery of invention and execution, and incorporates the English literary tradition within its own improvisational aspiration. Donaghy's aspiration in the poem is free of bald-faced parody but filled nonetheless with playful sleights that inevitably suggest his more serious intentions as well as his eclecticism. His work draws from a diverse set of inspirations—from film noir, Noh plays, and circus acts to Irish traditional music and even voodoo.

In Donaghy's second book, *Errata*—a title itself suggestive of departures and travels (from the Latin *erratus,* wandering)—his Irish American identity assumes a more central focus. "City of God," for example, recounts the return of a seminarian back home to the Bronx of his youth. It vividly portrays both religious obsession and immigrant life while at the same time conveying a profoundly human sense of loss. The failed seminarian is obsessed with a memory system perfected by the Dominicans in the Renaissance that permitted them to recollect almost anything, particularly prayers. In this he resembles Borges' "Funes the Memorious." Memory is, in fact, the presiding directive in the poem—to remember everything as God, ideally, remembers everything and everyone. To do so, as the ex-seminarian's mania suggests, would be to permit the "carrying over" (*tradere*) of memory or tradition to measure up to the "canon" (*kana*) in a perfectly idealized and realized duende of divine imitation—the world preserved and transmogrified in all of its multifarious influences. Of course, his memory is not up to the universe-and-beyond wide web of God, and as such he must return:

> I walked him back one evening as the snow
> hushed the precincts of his vast invisible temple.
> Here was Bruno Street where Bernadette
> collapsed, bleeding through her skirt
> and died, he had heard, in a state of mortal sin;
> here, the site of the bakery fire where Peter stood
> screaming on the red-hot fire escape,
> his bare feel blistering before he jumped;
> and here the storefront voodoo church beneath the el
> where the Cuban *bruja* bought black candles,
> its window strange with plaster saints and seashells.[54]

In addition to its metaphysical resonance, "City of God" is likewise a poem that owes everything to Donaghy's multicultural and, indeed, transnational parish. Like other poems in *Errata,* it evinces a distinctly Irish American perspective that is unflinching in its portrayal of Irish American life within an urban emigrant milieu.

Similarly "A Repertoire" evokes South Bronx Irish American bar life in the Blarney Stone and juxtaposes the love of Irish music alongside a neighbor's Tito Puente tapes. The owner sells the bar to Puerto Ricans to pay his debts and retain enough "to fly his body home" to Ireland, though the bar, as Donaghy tells us, "still rises from South Bronx ash." Other poems like "The Hunter's Purse" and "A Reprieve" equally conjure Irish American life as well as life in the Ireland of Kilrush and Connaught. There is a profound respect in all of these poems for the poet's call to memorialize the tribe—"Who can name them?" he asks in "The Classics." "Where lie their bones and armor?" The poet names them, as well as "their bones and armor" in poems of fierce, worldly openness and patient formal invention.

One of the most important Irish and Irish American figures in Donaghy's poems is his father, who died young and whose fate of dying young would become sadly the poet's own. The centrality of the father for Donaghy's work may be found vividly in "Caliban's Books," from the poet's third collection, *Conjure*. Here is the first stanza:

> Hair oil, boiled sweets, chalk dust, squid's ink. . .
> Bear with me. I'm trying to conjure my father,
> age fourteen, as Caliban—picked by Mr. Quinn
> for the role he was born to play because
> "I was the handsomest boy in school"
> he'll say, straight-faced, at fifty.
> This isn't easy. I've only half the spell,
> and I won't be born for twenty years.
> I'm trying for rainlight on Belfast Lough
> and listening for a small, blunt accent
> barking over the hiss of a stove getting louder like surf.
> But how can I read when the schoolroom's gone
> black as the hold of a shop. Start again.[55]

Donaghy's father as Caliban is at once the son's muse and a reminder that his Irish father as a boy is a colonial subject, a brilliant interfusion of art and historical reality combined with deeply felt personal longing. It is the poet's ability to be imaginatively present to all these nuances that makes him the Prospero of his own poem—the poet as conjuror and assembling intelligence: a wild precision.

Donaghy's improvisational mastery, his knack for interweaving "dance" moves from the American, British, and Irish traditions, likewise shapes his final, posthumous collection, *Safest*. One poem that would have been a major performance and that exists only as a fragment is "Irish Folk Music: A Fascinating Hobby with Some Account of Related Subjects, by Police Chief Francis O'Neil, Chicago, 1910." It would have developed an obsession begun in "A Reprieve." The most startlingly inventive improvisation of the fragment is Donaghy's playful incorporation of "riffs" from the Old Irish "Alphabet Calendar of Amergin" throughout a piece whose travel motif likewise echoes Wallace Stevens's "The Comedian as the Letter C": "Steering roughly / north by the stern bearings of the Southern Cross—the islands are high and the clouds hover over them." Stevens's poem is something of an ecstatic journey in the mode of Shelley's "Alastor," but Donaghy gives the genre a decidedly Irish spin when the Irish music of the title conjures the chief's inner shaman:

> I am a stag for swiftness, says the chief
> I am a fort for shelter
> I am a remedy for flatulence. "Tell her
> I am" the true wind.
> I am a loyal servant
> of the Democratic Administration of this city.
> I am a pocket watch.[56]

In *Wallflowers* Donaghy uses the figure of a pocket watch to exemplify the idea of the spatial and temporal frame that poems make as they hypnotize the reader into the world of the poem: "Chironomy again. With such modest gestures the poet opens the little world for the poem."[57] The watch is a talisman for the poems' power to shape a world in which our world is remade and yet magically remains itself—something akin to a Cornell box.

Donaghy's fragment, had he time to shape it, might have been his most sustained *ars poetica*. Instead, in "Exile's End," the book's penultimate poem, he provides us with a poet's homecoming otherwise conceived at once away from origin and wholly original in its consciousness of being simultaneously inside the death experience and outside of it:

> You will do the very last thing.
> Wait then for a noise in the chest,
> between depth charge and gong,
> like the seadoors slamming on the car deck.
> Wait for the white noise and then the cold astern.
>
> Gaze down over the rim of the enormous lamp.
> Observe the skilled frenzy of the physicians,
> a nurse's bald patch, blood. These will blur
> as sure as you've forgotten the voices
> of your childhood friends, or your toys.

> Or, you may note with mild surprise,
> your name. For the face they now cover
> is a stranger's and it always has been.
> Turn away. We commend you to the light,
> where all reliable accounts conclude.[58]

In addition to being the final journey, the final departure for the exile, death is also the supreme homecoming in which the veritable strangeness of one's own life—the condition of being irreducibly *unheimlich*—is that which makes one most oneself and most like everyone simultaneously. We are, all of us, exiles. And as Edward Said observed, "exile is the unhealable rift forced between a human being and a native place, between the self and its true home."[59] In Donaghy's poem the rift is healed, not in a native land of origin, but in the always original nativity of death.

In his introduction to *The New North,* an anthology of Northern Irish poets born after 1955, Chris Agee reflects that it is "one of the true glories of the Irish cultural 'space' that, over the past half century, it has made an enormous contribution to poetry in particular and world literature in general." Agee bases his judgment in part on the "density" of Ireland's cultural space—"as of many small European nations with an ancient pedigree," Ireland is small in size, but its cultural space is big. One thinks of Hamlet's infinity bound in a nutshell. For Irish American poets like Agee who moved from America to Ireland, or in Donaghy's case to London with easy access to his roots in Northern Ireland and the Republic, the greater substance of the allure is the sense of creative connection to Ireland's more intimate "frontier," with its cultural density as well as the immediacy of its felt history. Relative to America, all of Ireland is a parish. Relative to Ireland and Northern Ireland, in Agee's assessment, London and England reflect the bigger "psycho-spatial" territory of a "metropolitan culture," a culture that for all of its expansiveness may be found wanting in the intensity of "personal, generational, cultural, formal, intellectual, [and] ancestral" energy that can spur smaller cultures to produce great art and thought.[60] Relative to America, however, even England appears parochial with its long and largely centered literary tradition.

One can see that for a certain creative temperament shaped by personal, communal, historical, generational, artistic ties, as well as the fragile but deeply felt ties of diaspora, the extended parishes of Ireland and Britain might well offer an alternative to the sprawling mall of America, with its teeming conflux of influences, scenes, and schools. Ireland and England, of course, are not without their establishments, and on the positive side America's breadth is great enough to become inclusive of the emigrant poet from more than a few nations—Charles Simic has made a life here as well as Paul Muldoon and many others. At the same time, a poet like Paul Muldoon maintains his stature in both Ireland and the United States, and not only because of the amplitude of his achievement. Unlike the early part of the last century, America has largely come to ignore its expatriate poets, to forget that there are American poets who move within alternative traditions without having wholly dispensed with their ties to the country of their birth. Perhaps, one hopes, this will change for those whose bodies of work will prove prescient for a world whose own boundaries are becoming ever more permeable and whose interchanges of cultures and people are becoming ever more transnational in scope and scale. Within that scope and within that scale, it is always the individual poet's quest that improvises originality out of the inheritance of evolving traditions. Dedication to that quest is, after all, the poet's only true passport, the only way of traveling bravely in the art.

A GREEN ROAD IN CLARE

The Burren Way

Homesick for more than home, here, astride the sea's genius,
    I long to dissolve in a limestone landscape—
These terraced beds imprinted with grikes, the pillowed clints
    Interleaved with hollows where for eons rainwater's
Patient nibs scribed the chronicles of absence into karst,
    And still do, lines plumbing sidewise underground,
Forming a web of secret caves like halls in a dream house
    I dreamed of in my parents' house long ago.
I cannot go there, but follow the tracks soft laneway out
    Past stile and waymarking deeper into *boireann,*
The "Place of Rocks," ocean's crushed shells and skeletons formed
    To a horizon risen from the ancient sea.
"Neither tree to hang someone, nor soil enough to bury him,"
    Cromwell lamented, having reached this graven edge,
Though had he looked he'd have seen graves enough: tombs, raths
    Recalling playthings in a Land of Make Believe,
Now this lost Famine village still deserted and brooding
    Where a surface river tumbles from the shale,
Its roofless walls a thriving quarter of dens and fuchsia.
    My green road itself is like a path through loss
Where Famine roads splintered, directionless, to nowhere,
    For the hungry their work a Relief without relief,
While underneath me it flows on—water's flawless love
    Honing the inner spaces, invisibly, constantly,
So along the outer faults the barren world flourishes—
    Cinquefoil, silverweed, cranesbill, gentian, orchid,
Saxifrage splitting the rocks' dappled stencils of bone.
    Rockroses burst beside the ephemeral lakes.
It's not all death, I think, this double cemetery of earth
    And thought with its sunken city off the coast,
With its "green hole" by the harbor the locals call Hell,
    And its cliffs rising from the head of the past

A GREEN ROAD IN CLARE

At the spirit's base—"Who is my father in this world?"
    Or my mother, *Moher, Mothair,* that silent "T"
My central, empty cross? What was it I meant to find
    Here, now, nowhere, raging in the pitch-pipe wind:
An answer, human, out of the sublime? To be whole again?
    Song mastering the wake of everything gone?
You are this longing, the iron in the wish for origin.
    It sounds you, shapes you, water under stone.

IV

The Wake of Everything Gone

TWELVE

Soundings and Erasures
An Irish American Poet Digs Up His Past

Bridge

Atop the bookshelf across from the desk in my study I've propped an old postcard of the Verrazano-Narrows Bridge a friend sent me several years ago, a thoughtful gesture to modestly commemorate my Brooklyn origins. The photograph, taken at night, is a time exposure, so the bridge appears vaguely hieratic with its hazy coronas of streetlamps outlining the tousled shadows of trees along the Belt and its oddly deserted parkway, its bike path curving along the wall and breakwaters where New York Harbor churns into Gravesend Bay. In the near distance Staten Island is an unbroken swatch of hills, rough-edged charcoal that highlights the Narrows shimmering below those vaulting towers with their cables hung like strings of pearls across the sky. The sky itself appears something out of Magritte—bright against a world incongruously dark. The whole effect recalls the scene at the end of *Close Encounters of the Third Kind,* in which the aliens, our lost cosmic brethren, descend in the lightshow crescendo of their mother ship to inaugurate a new dawn of global oneness and universal knowledge, all portended by their sounding, solving, harmonious passage here. Though not exactly in the spirit of Steven Spielberg, I picture the advent of the Verrazano in my book-length sequence of poems, *The Narrows,* with what I hope is a similar if less atmospheric sense of wonder, recollected in "Bridge View" through the lens of adolescence:

> The grandeur of the tower was nothing at first
> but our surmise at what it would become,
> gleaned from rumors; though before long
> we watched the stanchions' gradual ascent
> above Shore Road's distant stand of trees
> where Third narrowed to its vanishing point.[1]

Other memorabilia crowd the shelf: among the knickknacks, Mass cards, shells, and idiosyncratically meaningful schlock are a birthday card from my brother, a Tibetan Buddhist, depicting a mandala of Vajrabhairava, the destroyer of death, and a card in which a man pushes his car down a seemingly endless road past a sign that reads "Next Gas 250 miles." Beside it is the crest of three oak leaves and its caption describing the Tobin family name and history, bought in a Dublin tourist shop for my parents during their first and only visit to Ireland before they died, with the family motto "Do Not Touch Me" ("Noli Me Tangere," the words of Jesus spoken to Mary Magdalene after his resurrection) inscribed below the name. Nearby is the antique marriage photograph of my mother's parents, Nora and Martin, who met in the New World townlands of urban Brooklyn.

An anthropologist coming on this peculiar mélange of personal affiliations, commemoratives, and bric-a-brac might construct a convincing exegesis from this panoply of non sequiturs, assuming she thought it worth the trouble, though what she could not do is orchestrate the narrative that binds together my unlikely archive through the complex personal, familial, cultural, and historical interrelationships and choices that brought them together on a dusty bookshelf in Dorchester, Massachusetts. Everyone, I suspect, accumulates such uniquely eccentric materials in their lives—markers, traces of the elusive plot line that formed them and of which they are a part. On a grander scale, cultures may be understood in kind, engendering through selection, shaping and keeping eidolons of self-definition, in order to know what and who they are and to puzzle over that knowledge. What if we all were like the student "cyborg" interviewed recently on *Scientific American Frontiers*, who strapped a digital camera to his back to record everywhere he had been, or would be, each day downloading his unfolding retrospective to a mainframe for eternal preservation? But the real substance of memory is selection, as it is with culture and history. "We all drink from a leaking cup," William Matthews reflected in his poem "Memory," and in "The Wolf of Gubbio," "art remembers a few things by forgetting many."[2]

Matthews's latter observation goes to the heart of the matter, particularly for the poet who would venture to plumb the historical and not only the personal. So much of history that might spark a poet's compositional fire needs to find its imaginative and dramatic focus, its native intensity, above and beyond the poet's will to witness before it can find new life in the poem—the vital life of art, which is something bound but not reducible to the facts themselves. The poem based on historical as well as personal memory, like memory itself, is a construction, though it is a construction built against the relief of what is no longer there. That is where imagination asserts its necessary pressure. Seeing the height of a man being built in the rising towers of the bridge, the retrospective speaker of "Bridge View" realizes, "It was we who gave that image to the air." For me, the huge structure built in my lifetime above the Narrows is at once a reminder and an embodiment of the shaping relationship between personal memory, historical memory, and the inevitable gulfs surrounding them, as well as a symbol of the poet's imperative to bridge the flood of things seriously, sadly passing away.

Cinema

In the opening lines of *The Bridge*—Hart Crane's brilliant epic riff on Whitman's native grand opera of America—a seagull pivots cinematically above New York Harbor, and it is suddenly as though we were seeing the panorama of "how many dawns," "chained bay waters," and finally the Statue of Liberty from the simultaneously orienting and disorienting perspective of a camera fastened to the bird's breast. Or perhaps the reader's consciousness, like a shaman's, has fused through the poet's orchestration of detail and line into that of the seagull, so we see as the bird sees with the same sweeping aerodynamic movement until the camera lens refocuses into the eye of an office worker, and time telescopes again, and we are plummeted downward by elevator with the other teeming multitudes into a movie theater where we all bend toward some flashing scene.

This remarkable opening performs the guiding method and metaphor of Crane's extraordinarily ambitious work—it is the trope of cinema, from the Greek *kine,* "to move," and *kinema,* "motion," through which the poet is able to capture history and the American continent as well as his own multifarious projection through both in a kind of dynamic suspension. Crane's poem would have us become aware of our movement not only through space and time but through that infinitely more complex and surprising medium of the physicists, space-time. The seagull curves away from our forsaken eyes, while the multitudes bend to the screen and the Brooklyn Bridge in its "curveship" lends "a myth to God," suggesting in no uncertain terms that Crane's ambitious poem would join physics to metaphysics. Just as significantly, however, *The Bridge* is a journey through history and place, and this journey not only is, as ideally it must be in art, an exercise in abstract principles but must be made humanly important. Crane's book-length poem communicates the inescapable fact that we are embedded in history, as well as creatures of the places we are from; moreover, we are literally as well as figuratively the bearers of history, the embodiments of an epic passage over incalculable dawns.

In *The Bridge,* Crane's cinematically tutored imagination gives us a version and a vision of the American sublime communicated in and through the sweep of history. Historical figures from Columbus to Pocahontas and literary figures from Whitman to Poe, as well as individuals from train-jumping hobos to Indiana housewives, populate the poem in lines whose cadences run the gamut from Elizabethan locutions to ad copy. Such is the panorama, both visually and acoustically, that Crane's seagull would have us recognize—a recognition that ultimately associates high and low. When I think of Crane's film-worthy seagull with its dipping wide-angle shot above New York Harbor, I am put in mind of the widening scope of Martin Scorsese's camerawork at the end of the opening sequence of *Gangs of New York,* after Bill the Butcher, head of the Nativists, has slaughtered Priest Vallon, belated chieftain of the emigrant Irish Dead Rabbits. The camera starts from a close-up on the small lives of the bloodied, the living and the dead, the preening victors and dispirited losers of this thin slice of history, and the emotional and human toll history is bound to take on the inheritors, including Priest Vallon's son, who takes up his father's knife. It then moves away and accelerates broadly from the scene of brutality to include the notorious, ramshackle Five Points, with its maelstrom of immigrants; then the surrounding streets; and finally to Manhattan itself as it appeared in the 1840s—a cauldron of conflicting historical narratives portending the Civil War and the Draft Riots—over which the viewer imaginatively superimposes the present-day city, the way Scorsese does at the end of the film, a crystal palace of skyscrapers "morphing" before our eyes out of the tribal town and against a foreground of weathering headstones.

I want to adjust the sight of my own mental camera now, so that it is following the circular path of the Calder mobile above the terminal mall inside the General Mitchell International Airport in Milwaukee, Wisconsin—the brightly colored metal rings floating like hammered lily pads below the skylight, under which my wife and I pass as we make our way through to Security. It is early morning on September 18, 2001, and the esplanade is uncharacteristically empty even for this moderate-size Midwest American city—no crowds milling about or travelers reading the *Journal-Sentinel* in the mock leather chairs; no one perusing sweatshirts or local delicacies in the gift shop; no one surveying the window of the Native American Spirit Shop or paging through the gently used volumes in the Renaissance Bookstore. It will be this way as we file through the security checkpoint with its unfamiliar soldiers and their weapons, as we wait at the gate, and during our nearly empty flight: only a few of us kept our reservations without canceling after the hijacked planes crashed, suicidally brutal and deeply into the American psyche, its sense of history, and not only the physical, monumental building. Only when we pass through Customs in Toronto does the mill of people thicken to have their passports checked as my wife and I make our way to catch our connection to St. John, New Brunswick, and my research at the Irish Canadian Cultural Association.

There was something strangely urgent and galvanizing about traveling to St. John a short, brutal week after the planes struck the Pentagon and the Towers—the Towers I watched being built, like the Narrows Bridge, from my apartment house roof; the Towers where my father worked after he had left the docks; the Towers where my uncle, a Port Authority locksmith, was killed in the first attack in February 1993. Walking through the deserted airport in Milwaukee and the packed stiles of Canadian customs in Toronto, then flying into the small airport beside the Bay of Fundy, I had the feeling of being taken up in a kind of personal wormhole, or a trip through a historical looking glass in which my own family's insignificant stream had found something of a portended assignation. I remember in the archive hallway the newspaper photograph of the Towers, the smoldering, apocalyptic bars of the remnant façade. I remember walking around the dull gray faces of the old wards where my family lived, unskilled emigrant laborers from far-off townlands among other unwelcome transplants to this largely Loyalist community in the Canadian Maritimes. I remember staring out at Partridge Island across the breakwater in the tidal bay where the coffin ships docked and the refugees who did not die of smallpox or cholera were processed, and finally standing at the edge of the plot in St. Mary's Cemetery, at the edge of a huge refinery on the outskirts of town. Under my boot-soles, as Whitman might say: not the poet's elusive presence, but a spread of unmown grass and acid rain, the mass grave where my father's great-grandfather is buried with the other immigrant poor who lived and died in this town at the northern edge of the North American continent.

Archive

The research trip to St. John was not the first, nor the last, in my seventeen-year effort to compose a book-length historical poem that would take as its subject my own family's experience of the Irish diaspora and its aftermath. I had in fact begun thinking about such a poem eight years earlier, shortly after I had graduated from college. Having grown up in Bay Ridge, Brooklyn, a few blocks from where New York Harbor opens into Gravesend Bay, I knew instinctively the place from which the poem would take its shape and its name—the Narrows. I also knew that it would be a very large undertaking, though with my incipient ambition far exceeding my material, intellectual, and imaginative reach, the project went underground very quickly. Any really urgent subject for poetry, however, invariably exerts a pressure from under, even when the writer's intentions may appear to be directed toward other more immediate ends. So I found myself in 1988 sketching an outline in my poetry notebook for a sequence called "The Narrows," a sketch that had very little resemblance to the book that appeared in 2005, but it was a start, a way to begin to focus over time. It was a small step forward out of a rather inchoate desire to make "a big poem" in the manner of Crane or Whitman, and toward an increasingly more directed and surprising engagement with history, poetry, and the purpose of both through my family's journey, like millions of others, to life on these shores.

Though the genre of historical fiction has been prominent on bookstore shelves for sometime, during the period I was working to compose and structure *The Narrows* there seemed little interest in historical poetry. Yet, as T. S. Eliot knew, the historical sense is essential for any poet who would write beyond the age of twenty-five. History is pervasive, not only in archives and museums but in the moment of our living it, however removed or inattentive we may be or appear to be to its unfolding. Elizabeth Alexander in her essay "The Negro Digs Up Her Past: 'Amistad,'" in which she recounts the circumstances and motivations behind the composition of her sequence of poems titled "Amistad," makes a similarly challenging point. While the materials and records of the slave ship famous for the revolt may be housed at the New Haven Historical Society near where she lives, it takes the poet's imaginative engagement to fully inhabit all of the questions history raises, both for the lives we see only dimly if at all in retrospect and for our own lives. As she observes, having been prompted by the archive to explore "the basic material questions about time, place, and the people," she nonetheless concludes, "A poem felt like the only way to explore all of [the] questions simultaneously." Even more perspicaciously, Alexander gives her own take on Eliot's historical sense when she affirms that "Poetry is always implicitly enacting 'I don't want to forget this,' which in the end works the same as the grander 'This must be remembered.'"[3] Prompting her remarks is something more than a passing discovery in an archive near her home; it is the urgent need to bear witness to a distant event deeply felt by and challenging to the poet and her art.

Elizabeth Alexander's imperative to remember that which she could not physically have witnessed herself gains still greater impetus, as well as definition, from her reading of the 1925 essay "The Negro Digs Up His Past" by collector Arthur Schomburg. Against the backdrop of slavery's enduring social damage, Schomburg understatedly affirms in the essay, "a true historical sense develops slowly and with difficulty under such circumstances."⁴ His aim in developing "a true historical sense" is to call to mind the cruel history of African America and its deleterious effect on the nation as a whole. Certainly, two generations later, Alexander's remarks embody Schomburg's historical sense, as well as the further insight that in the history poem "imagination . . . can take up where written history stops."⁵ It is this added dimension, this further amplitude of imagination, that offers the poet the greatest challenge and opportunity. And that is how it must be if the poem is going to have any life at all beyond the received material of the archive's compendium of notices, witness accounts, logs, and miscellanies. Historical writing at its best can make the past come alive with narrative vitality and authority. Historical poetry has to do something more. It needs to have the dramatic clarity and formal presence of any successful work of art.

Reading Elizabeth Alexander's essay and her sequence of poems after *The Narrows* appeared in print was a gratifying confirmation that what I sought for in my own work was not a belated attempt at the modernist long poem but a venture that maybe had some currency. At the same time, unlike "Amistad," *The Narrows* means to be a poem of personal and familial history. More accurately, I wanted a long poem that would explore the complex intersections of history as it is made and written and history as it is lived, as it always is, personally through the life of each person. "The self is interesting only as an example," Patrick Kavanagh observed, a credo to which Seamus Heaney subscribes in his preface to *Preoccupations* and which has always had the ring of truth to me.⁶ The challenge to *The Narrows*—whether I knew it or not when I looked out over the actual body of water with its endlessly passing ships, the old ferry pier jutting into the waves at the foot of Bay Ridge Avenue, and the new bridge arcing over the famous strait—was how to skirt the pitfalls of the merely confessional in order to achieve something fictively vital: the self as example.

The Wards

On our first morning in St. John I was thinking of nothing so theoretical, but rather of the excitement and challenges of digging into the genealogical records that were the last traces of my ancestors who emigrated from Cork to this maritime seaport town sometime, it turns out, between 1850 and 1852, and to feel those records in my hands, or view them on a screen—to be present before them. I had called months before, and spoken with Mary Kilfoil McDevitt at the St. John Parish Registry, having followed a lead given by my father's older sister, who recalled before she died that the Tobins came through Canada—as it turned out, the wrong St. John. From narrative threads I had pieced together over the years from family stories, the genealogist I had consulted in Newfoundland could tell that there were no matching records, but suggested St. John, New Brunswick. Within a minute of providing Mary McDevitt with the ancestral names—James Tobin married to Catherine ni Donovan—she had found the records in her computerized database. They had lived in King's Ward; my great-great-grandfather was, as I would come to see myself, "a Labourer of this City." I could look through the records and search further through the registries of lumber boats that unloaded their cargo in Queenstown, Cork, and secured ballast for the journey back by filling their holds with poor Irish, like my own ancestors, escaping the Famine. Such lists were spotty, and I could find no record of their marriage in St. John, nor any record of their marriage in Ireland—I had already checked for that. Perhaps they had been married en route on their way to the quarantine station on Partridge Island, a mile into the Bay of Fundy off St. John. How appropriate that would have been.

Partridge Island, I would learn from Mary McDevitt, predated Grosse Isle as a way station for emigrants and like Grosse Isle welcomed the coffin ships and lumber boats with their often starving and diseased human cargo, bearing cholera, smallpox—the common maladies. The island now is a ruin, an insular cemetery divided into ethnically sectioned graves with a high cross commemorating those who died there. It is inaccessible except by hired boat, or walking out a mile into the rapidly rising tides of the Bay of Fundy, the strongest tides in the world, on a stone breakwater reachable just below a World War II gun emplacement at Sand Point on the southern edge of town across the St. John River. If you walk across the breakwater to the island, you had better time your return well or be prepared to swim back to shore. Discovering such stories, the history of places, naturally exerts a powerful gravitational force on the imagination.

Genealogical records—those few traces left of my own family, for example— likewise call for an imaginative response precisely because they can only point across a vast narrative gulf of time and space toward the lives that were lived. The lists, data cards, and streams are merely signifiers and as such point at least as much toward the absence of the personal narrative as to the tattered record of the people who lived in this place at this time. All are names only—poor, past facts, to adapt Lowell's phrase from his poem "Epilogue." It is the poet's task to transform the mere information and *prima materia* of records into the reality and mystery of lives having been. The poet's work in composing the historical poem is to transfigure such material signifiers of lost presence into the symbolizing textures and patterns of art.

Of course, to say as much is not to diminish or slight the crucial and necessary work of keeping the record, the work of preservation that enables us to be mindful not only of the past but of the essential doubleness of the past—its simultaneous absence, being as it is no longer for us, and presence, being as it is the very fabric of time and space of which we are made. Mary Kilfoil McDevitt's book, *We Hardly Knew Ye,* provides an invaluable account of the Irish Catholic culture of St. John's in the nineteenth century and more specifically of the St. Mary's Cemetery and its history. St. Mary's is the segregated Irish Catholic graveyard just outside St. John, where James Tobin would be buried before the family left Canada for a tenement in Brooklyn. Here is her short account of life for Irish Catholics in St. John during the time my ancestors lived there:

> The most populous ward in the city, King's Ward, was also the poorest, and it was here that the largest proportion of the St. Mary's families lived. Historian William Baker claims that though Irish Catholics "were extensively distributed throughout the city," constituting "at least a quarter of the residents in all wards of the metropolitan area," undoubtedly, the ward with the greatest concentration of Irish Catholics was King's Ward, and in particular York Point—Mill Pond vicinity.... York Point was an area of waterfront slums, where pestilential, crowded tenements hung over filthy narrow streets. There was no clean water-supply, and two thirds of the houses lacked even basic sanitation facilities. The Mill Pond served as a kind of huge cesspool, where waste from animals, humans, and the city's slaughterhouses was dumped, so that it was "continuously surrounded with an accumulation of putrid and noxious filth." A particularly offensive area known

as Flagor's Alley was eventually boarded up by the St. John Board of Health as being unfit for human habitation.[7]

Such was the quality, as far as historical accountings can give, of the life my ancestors lived in St. John, having been recorded in the 1853 census as living in King's Ward, York Point. James Tobin and Catherine Tobin ni Donovan would continue to live in St. John, eventually graduating to Duke's Ward, until James Tobin's death, after which, in 1882, Edward Tobin took his mother and family out of St. John to Brooklyn, where they lived, the New York census records show, first at 502 Schenk Avenue in East New York and eventually in Red Hook, where my father grew up, still in a tenement with nine siblings, the progeny of William Tobin and Ruth Dotson, herself a daughter of southern wealth who was disowned for marrying an Irish Catholic. From my father's stories of growing up, his first world of Red Hook poverty, street life, bars, docks, and local ethnic gangsters would have made strong subject matter for a sequel to Scorsese's *Gangs of New York*.

Today, as Mary McDevitt further recounts in her history, the old rabidly pestilent York Point is, ironically, like so many areas of historical poverty and squalor, the most coveted address in St. John, with a new high-rise hotel and nicely trimmed lawns and gardens. Similarly, Red Hook Brooklyn's factories and walk-ups are fast becoming converted into artist's lofts and gentrified condos, all below the shadow of the housing projects that replaced the tenements on Henry Street, where my father and his siblings first lived beside the confluence of the East River and the Hudson River across from lower Manhattan, above which might have pivoted Crane's spiraling seagull. In light of these shifting locations, how can a poem successfully evoke at once the elusive presences and particulars of lives long gone and the magnitude of their erasure, not just of my own ancestors through the shards and traces of their story but of those like them, those who live in passing, which is all of us?

These Shores

In my view there are two requisite obligations to which the poet must remain faithful if she or he is going to take on the challenge of composing a historical poem, and perhaps especially a poem that involves family or personal history. The first is the obligation to make oneself present. To make oneself present is not simply to exert an act of will to pursue material such as historical accounts, census lists, museum pieces, relics, potentially resonant technical lingo, and the like. It is to place oneself in an attitude of witness before them as though they actually embodied the lives to which they minimally gesture. In the genealogical case, they are the outward sign of an inward embodiment, the historical remnant of the code of your own making that remains whole inside you. That code, quite literally, contains not only your own immediate ancestry but the whole genomic human passage, and beyond that the whole ontological history of the earth and, beyond that, the cosmos in the uniquely unrepeatable physical presence of your own being. To make oneself present before the objects, or to read historical accounts of locales like King's Ward and the conditions in which people lived, is to become negatively capable, in Keats's understanding, of being able to remain in uncertainty and doubt and mystery without reaching after the kind of summation only fact and reason can satisfy. To make oneself present in this sense is to manifest "a desire for the invisible," to use a phrase from the Jewish philosopher Emmanuel Lévinas.[8] Such a desire can never be satisfied because it originates always from the surplus of our relationships, out of the past retrospectively and prospectively into the future.

Implicitly if not explicitly, then, as in Hart Crane's myth of America, the historical poem bridges metaphysical concerns. To make one self present before one's subject through the physical material of genealogical research was, for me, to take a stand against the idea of genealogical research as merely an assertion of one's own identity or pedigree. Beyond any relationship to the poet's past, historical poems should be what Lévinas calls manifestations of a "metaphysical desire." "The metaphysical desire," Lévinas observes, "does not long to return, for it is desire for a land not of our birth, for a land foreign to every nature, which has not been our fatherland and to which we shall never betake ourselves" and which "does not rest upon any prior kinship."[9] Locating their interest in the self in the self's broadest context, that is, in relation to others, poems of history and genealogy inevitably, if successful, envision the self as something other than a ruminating ego bestowing its exemplary story. Instead, the self "as example" must inevitably be made other to itself in the always partial yet textured and dramatically vital narrative of an unfinishable quest.

One crucial aspect of embarking on such a quest is to make oneself physically present in the surroundings, to embark literally and not just imaginatively and to make pilgrimage to the place that, however humble or transformed by history, is nonetheless charged with significance for the poem. During my few days in St. John I walked the old wards or what was left of them, queued through maritime museums, noted the customs of the city's Loyalist history present still in Union Jack flags and painted curbs the same as in Derry or Belfast, wandered through the gun emplacements on my way to the breakwater leading to Partridge Island, and watched the estranging sight of the Reverse Falls, where every afternoon when the tide comes in, the St. John River flows backwards from the Bay. Most powerfully for me, I stood before the unmarked mass grave in St. Mary's Cemetery where my ancestor, James Tobin, was buried with the others left to the erasures of softening wood, crumbling tablets, and the swells of grass.

The poem that came from this pilgrimage at a contemporary moment of historical erasure is "St. John," and its attempt is to gather the weight of those gone lives into its own cadences of tides moving in a kind of ritual of incantation raised against the forces of loss. The poem envisions the shores, the old city with its modern bridges, the gorge with its back-flowing falls and tourists, the lost shipyards and wards with their "shovel-fisted" Irish—"the remnants of gutted townlands"—and the island with its quarantine stations and coffin ships, and ends where such journeys always end: in the eerie, ineluctable presence of that which is gone:

>   On these shores
> where tombstones recede into earth like shells
>   below the tide,
> I riffle through remains of dig books
>   to find my own past,
>   then drive with my love to the bare knoll's crest,
>   the stone gateposts gateless,
>   no walls, no boundary,
> and walk among the footstones, lost avenues,
>   currents of grass, still ponds
>   of moss
>   fast rising to erase the names.

>   On these shores
> I kneel inside the empty townland of the dead
>   for James and the others,
>   travelers
> who left no trace but this code in my bones,
>   an unmarked grave, the tern's trail
>   of history,
> and the tide coming in with a screech of seabirds
>   on these shores.[10]

The accumulated reserves of imagination obtained from material research and my journey to the actual place where my family first arrived and lived "on these shores" was crucial to the composition of "St. John," but just as important if not more so was my reading of Louis MacNeice's poem, "The Hebrides." MacNeice's poem begins "On those islands / The west wind drops its message of indolence, / No one hurries, the Gulf Stream warms the gnarled / Ramparts of gneiss"[11] and carries on from there with a propulsive cadence—the mind's vocal ruminations about a place foreign to its native inclinations but nonetheless deeply responsive to the physical scene. The at once lulling and profluent echo of the phrase "on those islands" throughout MacNeice's poem, a meditative lyric of some hundred twenty or so lines, underscores the poet's apprehension of the ongoingness of the place, the customs of those who inhabit it, as well as the ritual effluence of the sea endlessly breaking on the land.

Whether by an inheritance lodged in the ear's innate attraction to the sound of certain words and how they are put together by the poet, or by some measure of chosen inheritance, when I read "The Hebrides" aloud to myself, I was able to hear something of the cadence that I wanted to inform my own poem—a poem that while echoing MacNeice's lyrical meditation also exists in thematic counterpoint to it. Where the Hebrides in their rugged beauty and enduring customs welcome the traveling poet with an evocation of "those who lived as their fathers lived," "St. John" aims to evoke the world of those who can no longer live within the immediacy of such traditions. The experience of diaspora in "St. John" is imagined with a historical inflection that is distinctly Irish, but my hope is that it is not narrowly so. The refrain "On these shores" intends not only a counterpoint to MacNeice's

"On those islands" but a kind of subliminal allusion to Robert Hayden's phrase from his great poem "Middle Passage": "Voyage through death / to life upon these shores."[12] The point, as with any allusion that pays homage to a work worthy of deep admiration, is not to appropriate the poet's experience but to enlarge the scope of the composition at hand. Without the artistic template, the records such as they are would remain a compendium of mere information, compelling but lacking the transformational human urgency of art.

The influence of MacNeice's "The Hebrides" on "St. John" brings me to the second requisite obligation for the poet who would write a historical poem, though it is an obligation that really pertains to any poet serious about practicing the art. In the same way that the poet of history is obliged to take accounting of— and ultimately make accounting to—the ancestors, she or he must also be listening for the shaping standards of the predecessors. Elizabeth Alexander's thoughts on the historical poem are apropos here as well: she considers that "the word ancestor has a heft to it, an unassailable *gravitas,* a stentorian demand."[13] Alexander's awareness of the heft and gravity of the ancestor, along with her acknowledgment of the importance of Robert Hayden's "Middle Passage" for her own poem, "Amistad," communicates her awareness of the importance of tradition—the idea that for the poet the historical sense has not only a historical but an unconditional, aesthetic demand.

Invisible History

For the poet who would write such a poem, the historical sense requires not only the curiosity, patience, and dedication of the researcher but also an evolving knowledge of literary and artistic relevance, and the powers of discernment required to tell what precedents actually have currency for her or his own task. Beyond this requirement, Alexander goes on to say that in her poem she wanted "to explore the past in the face of the aggressive a-historicity that plagues and misnames this nation and is a tool for misleading the people."[14] Is there anything more one could ask of a historical poem? By her own design, Alexander's intent is to write a poem of historical redress as well as a political corrective to prevailing narratives of national identity. Again, Arthur Schomburg's observation—"A true historical sense develops slowly and with difficulty under such circumstances"[15]—references explicitly the social damage slavery perpetrated, not only on past generations of African Americans but on the generation of his own time. As noted in chapter 10, Frederick Douglass's observation that Irish (and hence Irish American) poverty does not equal the injustice of slavery remains vividly relevant.

Though the social damage experienced by Irish Americans does not collectively come near to the magnitude of that which shaped the history of African America, the trauma of famine and subsequent social curtailments endured by Irish Americans during the nineteenth century limited the comprehensive development of the historical sense. This slow development has been particularly slow in the art of poetry. The burgeoning of Irish American poetry from the middle of the twentieth century onward touches on the world-defining experience of famine and exile only marginally, despite (or perhaps because of) the advantages most Irish Americans gradually accrued as European immigrants, however ostracized initially from the wider American culture. How strange that an essential American author like Henry David Thoreau can reflect movingly if only in passing on the human loss of an America-bound coffin ship, while no Irish American poet of note makes reference to their plight before Brendan Galvin in his poem "1847," written well into the twentieth century. As my own historical sense grew and developed, I wanted to find my own way of redressing the relative poverty of responses to the legacy of which my own family history was a part.

Growing up in Brooklyn at "the mouth of the Hudson," as Robert Lowell called it in the opening poem of *For the Union Dead*, I found myself compelled early on by the rhythms of movement as well as the glittering, liminal passage that is the Narrows from a majestic river to an expansive ocean. One of my earliest memories is of taking the ferry across to Staten Island before Robert Moses built the Narrows Bridge—the largest in the world at the time—where the Ambrose Lightship used to signal tankers, container boats, and ocean liners into and out of the harbor. Packed in the car with my mother, father, brother, and maternal grandmother, taking the ferry felt as if we were riding the rippling skin of an enormous snake roiling ponderously down along the Manhattan skyline and out into the Atlantic.

When late in adolescence I somehow got it in my head to write poems (ours was a working-class apartment with few books and no art other than my father's prints of steamships from the United States Lines where he worked), I knew there was something about the Narrows that drew me to it and held my fascination. When I first read Lowell's "The Mouth of the Hudson," I was grateful someone had found something of my first world compelling enough to want to write a poem, though Lowell's occasional piece struck me even then as the masterful musing of an outsider, the Brahmin poet's daytrip beyond the rarified air of Cambridge, Beverly Farms, and Mattapoisett. Here the air hinted vaguely of refineries in Elizabeth and Linden and smelled of coffee. No one living near the Narrows calls it "the mouth of the Hudson," and Elizabeth and Linden, like Todt Hill and the Kill van Kull, go unnamed in Lowell's poem. Unlike the Public Garden and the Boston Common, with its monumental statue of Colonel Shaw and his "bronze Negro legion," the Narrows and its history of immigrant crossings remain unfathomed by this major American poet, who took rightfully as his birthright the mainstream of American cultural and historical identity. Nor a century earlier is there in Whitman's inexhaustible catalogue and democratic vista of America much in the way of envisaging the immigrant sea-road that came before the open road of the continent but that nonetheless constitutes an essential part of the "native grand opera" he saw orchestrating itself on these shores.

 I first began thinking in earnest about a poem that would include what at least in my view had been excluded even by Lowell's imaginative birthright and Whitman's all-encompassing vista shortly after I graduated from college, shortly after I started seriously thinking of trying to be a poet—whatever that meant— since at the time I was in near total ignorance of the poet's craft. I knew the place from which the poem had to originate, from which it had to take shape: the Narrows, four blocks down the ridge from the apartment building where I grew up. For years I wrote poems of family, my neighborhood, and, very sporadically, Ireland, with the larger project in the back of my mind, though with no sense of how, which, or if any of the poems might fit together. Beyond the success of individual pieces the ambition was to make a book—really a single work and not just a sequence or collection—in which family, history, place, and the passage from place to place would figure together to compose a complex orchestration, a coherent movement, if not epic then at once symphonic and novelistic in scope. It would have to include narrative and lyric modes as well as formal variation and multiple perspectives and, over the long haul, embody a dramatic arc that would create a sense of closure for the poem without closing the poem down. Though I didn't fully articulate it over the course of all those years, I wanted to make an associative, "postmodern" poem that would retain the modernist attachment to subtending coherence and yet be assessable though vigorously textured and complexly layered. I also wanted it to incorporate tradition in the richest adaptive sense without being derivative or resorting to prevalent modes of irony and parody.

The other pressing imaginative spur for *The Narrows* is the directive to raise to consciousness an invisible history. As historian Stephanie Rains reflects, "not only were the original emigrant founders of most diaspora families, generally speaking, members of largely undocumented and unconsidered working classes, but the fact of their migrations meant that their life histories could not (or would not) be encompassed within the frame work of one national history. This would appear to be particularly true in the Irish and American examples."[16] As a poem that finds its material in genealogical and historical sources as well as geographical migration, *The Narrows* is an effort to make visible the loss of such life histories through the story of my own family while at the same time going some way toward transfiguring the loss through the ordering pressures of art. What and how much of what is "handed over" by tradition should the historical poem assume so that it might "measure up" to its appointed task? Poems are made out of other poems, and traditions find themselves extended even in the process of being contested. Perhaps, I thought, the poet engaged in the difficulties of writing the historical should speak more of traditions than tradition—to prospect across multiple boundaries—and to employ a multitude of the formal and imaginative resources available and discoverable in order to fashion as complex and involving a vision as possible.

Road and Ring

In *Preoccupations,* Seamus Heaney observes that poetry begins to take hold and gather strength when "one's roots are crossed with one's reading,"[17] though in the case of *The Narrows* it would be just as apt to transpose the homonym "routes" for "roots." "St. John," for example, found its cadence by my having traced my roots through the route of my father's line into Canada and then crossing that route with my reading of MacNeice's "The Hebrides." "The Dock Road," one of the last individual poems to find its way into *The Narrows,* came to light unexpectedly after a visit to Liverpool for an academic conference. Attendees could sign up for an afternoon tour of emigration sites around the city. For centuries Liverpool was the most important center in a constant flood of world migration, where emigrant Irish escaping famine or other political hardships of empire mixed with other Europeans en route from their homes along with a myriad of Asian exiles and other emigrants as well. It was also the center of the African slave trade through which millions were "processed" to the New World. My own grandfather, on my mother's side, shipped out of Liverpool and arrived on April 8, 1920, in New York on the SS *Kaiserin Auguste Victoria,* a belated sojourner through the docks of this rugged port city famous for shipping and the Beatles and where, as Nathaniel Hawthorne wrote, the Irish "were thick as maggots in cheese."[18]

The Dock Road is the road along the Mersey, where millions of emigrants walked toward their futures. Along the tour, a site commemorates the Irish Famine dead with stone quarried from the Mourne Mountains in County Down. The final station, on Hope Street around the corner from the university where the conference was being held, was an innocuous plaque identifying the site of a mass grave where hundreds of emigrant Irish had been buried. Their bodies had been transported again to an undisclosed site in order to raise the present office building. The poem, written in off-rhyme terza rima, I composed in the voice of a guide whose authority allows him to say things the poet's voice cannot say for fear of sounding strident. The emigrants it portrays constitute crucial and essential chapters of what Arthur Schomburg called "the full story of human collaboration and interdependence."[19] In "The Dock Road" the poet's unnamed Virgilian guide through contemporary Liverpool encourages his own version of Schomburg's encyclopedic historical sense:

> This city mortared with the blood of slaves
>   manufactured wealth for old world and new

> on the backs of the oppressed. Every race
> walked the dock road, or nearly: Irish and Jew,
>   Chinese, African, German, Italian;
>   though to say *race* is wrong: there is one queue
> only, and we're all in it until it ends.[20]

The Narrows, by facing up to the intractable and often ugly issue of race in more than a few of its poems, places its family story inside the still more multitudinous passage of those "that came with the others here, with those who left / or had to leave,"[21] as the poem "A Coat" reflects. Other poems like "An Island" seek to open a blind on the intimacies of racial prejudice, while a poem like "Lost Garden Elegies," with its racially mixed childhood friendship, offers a more hopeful vantage. In its form and progression the poem pays homage to Robert Hayden's "Elegies for Paradise Valley."

Carrying forward themes of identity and ethnicity from "A Coat" and other poems, "The Ring" in turn seeks to project the recognition of a multitudinous passage still further back. Written earlier after visiting Cobh (formerly Queenstown) in County Cork, one of the major sites of embarkation for Irish escaping famine or simply emigrating, like my mother's mother, after their American wakes, "The Ring" pursues the reverse horizon backward to the source, or rather the absence of one:

>   What was The Ring
> but another station, happened on by chance
> or seeming grace? so why not trace further
> through lost Norman crests, or track DNA
> to nomadic tribes six thousand years gone
> from the banks of the Ganges; or further back
> through each human cell to African Eve,
> her grunts our shibboleth tuning savannahs?[22]

The Ring, *An Rinn,* is an area of Waterford on the Irish Sea, the only *gaeltacht* remaining on the eastern side of Ireland. The Tobins—the name derives from the town of St. Aubyn in France—arrived in Ireland during the Norman Invasions of the eleventh and twelfth centuries and first settled there to become, proverbially, more Irish than the Irish themselves. Nevertheless, the poem's retrospective intends a more embracing conception of lineage, and to that end its blank-verse line also looks prospectively into its rearview horizon.

The choice of blank verse for "The Ring," as with other poems in *The Narrows,* reflects an effort to underscore the narrative nature of the quest, though it is an inherently broken narrative. Other poems such as "Ballsbridge, Dark Night" and the sequence of mostly blank sonnets, "Bay Ridge," make formal nods to literary predecessors—in the first case John Berryman and in the second Robert Lowell. Similarly, the sequence "Pearl Court" borrows formally from Yeats's "Ancestral Houses" in "Meditations in Time of Civil War," as a way of responding to the great Irish poet and his fetish for the Big House tradition in Irish culture by looking at the world inside a Brooklyn apartment building. To answer back in this way is not to rehearse some Oedipal conflict in the manner of Harold Bloom's "misprision," his conception of how poets make their way into the canon by seeking to best their literary fathers. Rather, it is a way of paying homage to artistic achievements while at the same time recognizing the potentially political and social limitations of those achievements. It is a way, artistically, of discerning the baby from the bathwater, the genuinely artistic from the mere "point of view," a vantage Yeats identified with rhetoric rather than poetry.

In the case of Emily Dickinson one finds an especially remarkable crossing of historical fact and literary precedence. At times, the historical archive and the literary archive find marvelous confluence, as in the case of the pallbearers at her funeral, who, it turns out, were Irish emigrants who worked in the Dickinson family garden and who found themselves unknowingly in the living midst of the American literary tradition. "Pallbearers at Emily Dickinson's Funeral" formally juxtaposes the knowledge of their journey, their *immram* west from Ireland, to her final journey into the true West she was facing at sunset when she died:

> She died at sunset facing west,
> her own society
> this room—her soul—its offing
> a vastness like the sea
>
> this six endured on coffin ships,
> her bark their burden now.[23]

The *immram* or journey motif from Irish history and legend has a long-standing resonance in Irish literature and culture. In *The Voyage of Máel Dúin,* the protagonist's directive to his mates as they are about to depart from Ireland—"Leave the boat at rest without rowing and wherever it shall please God to bring it, he will bring it"—presages their entrance into "the great, limitless ocean."[24] It is the same ocean into which Bran and Brendan entered in other Irish voyage narratives.

These voyages echo Odysseus's wanderings after the Trojan War and foreshadow the real-life peregrinations of Irish monks during the medieval period as well as centuries of exiles and emigrants from Ireland well into the twentieth century. Beyond any specifically Irish experience, it should not be surprising that the journey motif ought to have psychic resonance for a species whose evolution depends on an ongoing passage out and whose very physical existence encodes the whole history of the planet's evolution. Such narratives are conveyors of what Whitman called "the similitudes of the past and those of the future," which is what Hart Crane knew deeply and implicitly when he envisioned the Brooklyn Bridge as "One arc synoptic of all tides below— / Their labyrinthine mouths of history / Pouring reply."[25] The formal, linguistic, and operatic cinema of *The Bridge* harkens back recursively to these earlier narrative *kine,* and I wanted *The Narrows* to trace a similar embarkation through its own formal organization and idiom into the limitless.

At the same time, in addition to the *immram,* a contrary motif shapes Irish literature that is at least as prevalent and as old—the *dinnseanchas,* or poems that celebrate and encode the lore of place. Where the *immram* is centrifugal in its imaginative force and effect, the place poem exerts its attraction centripetally. If the first invites routes, the second demands roots. Though it might be overstating the case, it is hard not to venture that the shaping frisson between these two poles may be found throughout Irish poetry, and modern Irish poetry in particular, where it lodges at times as an unconsidered but generative tension in the poet's work. That tension is brilliantly at work in John Montague's *The Rough Field,* for example, which is where the lore of place poem finds expression and a kind of local completion in postmodernist montage.

Like Crane's *The Bridge, The Rough Field* begins in motion, with the poet riding a bus back to his ancestral home in County Tyrone—with all his "circling a failure to return."²⁶ The orchestration that follows amounts to a psychic and cultural burrowing into the historical cauldron soil of Garvaghey, the rough field that is at once name, place, and embodiment of a traumatically conflicted history. Composed over the course of some eleven years through an orchestration of individual poems, *The Rough Field* is a book-length poem that simultaneously begins centripetally to enter the lore of place and ends centrifugally with the home place's transformation through time into "what is already going / going / GONE."²⁷

That cinematic sense of movement, of things going, I associate almost primordially with the Narrows. Unlike Montague's Garvaghey, the Narrows I grew up beside, with its ships passing in and out of the harbor, its endless churning, its confluence between a vast continent and a still vaster ocean, evokes more a world of routes than of roots. As a body of water it is Janus-faced, looking backward toward a sea of emigrant crossings—my own people among them—and ahead into a continent forever changed by those endless arrivals. The Narrows is a threshold, physically marked by the enormous bridge that spans it, itself ultimately a gateway to the West and the far coast with its own vast ocean—an interstate in every sense, at once a retrospect and prospect. Where New York Harbor empties into Gravesend Bay—the Narrows—the centripetal attraction of roots fuses with the centrifugal motion of routes in a single confluence of time and space and stored consciousness.

Lives Indwelling

In a scene at the beginning of John Sayles's film *The Brother from Another Planet,* the mute alien palms the walls of a dilapidated Ellis Island and hears the voices of all the immigrants who walked through those halls—a vast cacophony. It is a brilliant scene, an extraordinary metaphor for what any artist working with history would have to tune into, and especially the poet. The blanched wall admitting the alien's hand to its vocal mysteries, the ultimate synesthesia, might have been the very wall where Edward Lanning's mural hung with its visual panorama of urban immigrants making their way across the American continent, the very mural I found translated to the Kings County Courthouse in downtown

Brooklyn, preserved from Ellis Island's languishment into ruin as well as its subsequent resurrection into a monument of American self-identity.

In fact, it was not until I came on the idea of organizing *The Narrows* as a mural in verse that the book made any genuine progress in its admittedly ambitious orchestration. A mural can and should be viewed as a broad expanse, though each section of a mural should be viewed as a single, panoramic composition, *E pluribus unum:* the one with the many and through the many. There is also something cinematic about a mural, the way the eye is prompted to move along the panorama to follow the sweep of the whole while at the same time, unlike cinema, the individual images draw against that unfolding motion. The poem "The Narrows" is the first long piece in the book of the same name, and the iterative nature of titles says something about how both the individual poem and the collection-as-long-poem is organized—through repetition and recursive movement backward and forward in time and place, present and past, family history and wider history across nations and oceans. I began putting the individual poem on paper during a stint at the Vermont Studio Center in 1998.

The first line of the poem, "The way Lanning painted it, Benton, Rivera—bright panels,"[28] announces the mural as organizational metaphor, though in the early drafts it read, "As Lanning did it, or Rivera— bright / panels," which was intended as a direct allusion to Ashbery's "Self Portrait in a Convex Mirror," though one driven by a contrary aesthetic: the socialist/populist mural of the WPA rather than Vasari's self-inwoven trope of the artist's narcissism made strange in the poem as well as the mirror. The allusion is there still, but more deeply embedded and directed by the poem's first words, "The way," which intend to announce the theme of passage as well as the idea of the poem as passage with its many references to cars and boats and trains and passing people. Then there is, wider still, the passage of *The Narrows,* the collection, as a whole, with its focus on one family's path through history and immigration within the context of other innumerable passages, like my maternal grandmother's through Ellis Island:

> It is as if the *throughother* of her familiar fields
> had changed in a dream she only now awakens to,

> the manifest tag pinned to her lapel,
> a gripped inspection card, barked commands
> from the uniform at the gate, from the uniform on the stairs.
> She stiffens as she's handled, so many hands, her eyelids
> twisted back with a buttonhook, the man ahead marked
> with chalk, a brusque X on his coat
>   before he's shuffled away.
> What's your name? Where are you going? What's your trade?
> Have you a job? Can you read this?
>
>   —"Let my sentence come forth from thy presence;
>   let thine eyes behold the things that are equal."—
>
> Then the shower, a baptism, the old world washed free.[29]

"The Narrows" also announces the centrality of movement, of cinema both in the physical and in the historical sense but also in the musical sense. The book *The Narrows,* poem by poem, section by section, is composed of cinematically orchestrated movements that dovetail into a single recursive arc, a "curveship" to use Crane's term, that is at once self-inwoven and progressive. The way forward is the way back, and the way back brings us forward, or as the poem "Outerbridge Crossing" pictures it, with its car speeding toward the bridge, "the past ahead of us in the mirror's vision."[30]

The next important discovery in drafting "The Narrows," the individual poem, was exploding its initial blank verse, which quickly became too constraining. The model for that break, as well as for the individual poem's structure, was Ezra Pound's "Near Perigord," which is a kind of scholarly inquiry in verse in which the poet seeks to discover the truth about the life of troubadour Betrans de Born, his own artistic progenitor. At the beginning of the second section Pound states, "End fact. Try fiction,"[31] which suggests that the whole poem is an orchestration of failed attempts to find the source. I was able to move forward with "The Narrows" when I realized I could use Pound's poem as a model, albeit, as with Ashbery's "Self-Portrait," from a contrary aesthetic. As in "Near Perigord," there are three sections to "The Narrows," each one offering a different door into the family history: the place that is the Narrows in the New World, the archive holding millions of family histories including those of other immigrant families and, finally, the townland and house that propose to be the native place, the source, in Ireland. The return, as in Pound's poem, is a failure:

> It is like our standing present now
> before this ancestral house
>   passed to unfamiliar hands,
> its thatch removed years ago, a modern extension
> jutting out back from whitewashed clay walls.
>   No one home.
> And as we peer through the window,
>   the hearth inscribes its arc
> halfway up the wall, its border painted brightly,
>   an old-time kettle at the center—
>   Winnie dead, Tommy dead,
> a line of unknown faces trailing back,
>   fanning forward,
> our own to be among them,
> as if now were the space between facing mirrors,
> life's after-life of lives indwelling.[32]

At the same time, the poem refuses Pound's denouement, "the broken bundle of mirrors" at the end of "Near Perigord," which defeats the quest and pitches the poet into self-accusatory narcissism. "The Narrows," both as individual poem and collection—as a symphonic mural (to risk conjuring the awkward synesthesia of a Heritage Center diorama)—aims to turn from the mirror to place the self-portrait between two horizons, one behind and one ahead, along the way to the recognition of what is "gone" to that which is "ongoing."

Poems of course must gain relevance beyond the unspoken affiliations that compose the shelf lives of personal archives. Three archival sources inform "The Narrows," and this is likewise true of the book as a whole. The first is the archive of tradition, in which a poem as different in sensibility to one's own as Pound's "Near Perigord" may exert its influence. The second might be called the archive of place. The geographical country is instinct with signs, Heaney muses of his Northern Irish home in "The Sense of Place." The like is true of the Narrows and, indeed, the names of locales continually signify historical realities emptied, or nearly emptied, of their Native American contexts: Mohegan, Mohonk, Chappaqua, Napanoch. They nonetheless have the force of recitations:

> Whippany, Hope, Netcong, Sparta, Swartzwood—
> The names fled past on the new interstate
> Into signs on roads of diminished light.[33]

These lines from "The Country," written as an elegy to an uncle who was killed in the first World Trade Center bombing in 1993, pursue their route through history to my uncle's unlikely enshrinement as a newsworthy casualty of war. Again, as "The Country" suggests, unlike John Montague's *The Rough Field*, *The Narrows* is self-consciously more a poem of routes, though routes that lead inevitably back to that from which all routes emerge and ahead into which all converge.

The third archival field at work in "The Narrows" is the archive understood in its literal sense, like the archive in St. John, New Brunswick. The second section of the poem dramatizes this archival work in the New York City Bureau of Records on Hudson Street in Manhattan. "The way" of "The Narrows," both the individual poem and the book, is no less a journey into the past through the limited present of microfiche machines, files, and tomes of registries, in which the long dead have had their names inscribed, among them, eventually, one's own, than it is a passage through geographical spaces:

> The rules are strict inside the archive—no food, no bags,
> no talking beyond this point.
>   And don't forget
> to take a number, line up for instruction
> from the stern administrator, who, it turns out,
> is politer than he looks, directing me patiently
> in how to use the volumes of categories and codes,
> as if these tomes were history's phone books,
> as if each of us could dial our origins.[34]

On the one hand, the archive is imagination's prompt, its triggering point to adapt Richard Hugo's idea of the "triggering town." It is a place to begin or extend the poem's quest for embodiment as well as the inscription of imagination's limit: because the past is gone, it is never finished. On the other hand, it is a place in its own right, not merely a vehicle for research but a dramatic locus. I availed myself of a number of archives over the years, seeking, among the materials, genealogical information and senses of place that would help me locate my family's history in the wider historical context of an endless human migration, a passage forced by circumstance or sought and not always endured or wholly recorded.

Further West

To broach the subject of the unrecorded is to confront the circumstance that, to borrow Eavan Boland's apothegm, the vast sum of human experience remains "outside history." At the same time the seemingly inexhaustible engine of cyberspace provides an apparently infinite potential to record one's opinions, musings, and escapades, and even one's most private thoughts, obsessions, delusions, and perversions, in an endless array of blogs, websites, My Space portals, Facebook pages, and constantly flowing digital streams. With the exception of the occasional "found poem," to record is not to make art. Art requires selection, shaping, and the transfiguration of the roiling strata of accidence of which our lives are a part into purposefulness discernable in the completed work. At the same time, the kind of artfulness required by the historical poem must never lose sight of the fundamental incompleteness of narrative experience, which is inexhaustible. Absence, the "not-there-ness" of most of reality, like dark matter or energy presiding in the white spaces between lines and words and stanzas, must be incorporated into the poem. And not only on the margins but within the cumulative, searching attentions of the work as it "betakes" its direction toward closure.

Something of this kind of artistic dedication to the unrecorded or forgotten in relation to a comprehensive sense of existence's ultimate direction may be found in Henry David Thoreau's description of the wreckage of an Irish coffin ship off the Massachusetts coast in "The Shipwreck." Despite Thoreau's less than sympathetic inclination toward the Irish and their culture—"But alas, the culture of an Irishman is an enterprise to be undertaken with a sort of moral bog hoe"[35]—he nonetheless captures brilliantly both the historical reality of what was endured and the insight that whatever the historical record or whatever lies outside the historical record, both must be placed under a still more primary directive:

> The brig St. John, from Galway, Ireland, laden with emigrants, was wrecked on Sunday morning. . . . Why care for these dead bodies? They really have no friends but the worms or fishes. Their owners were coming to the New World, as Columbus and the Pilgrims did,—they were within a mile of its shores; but, before they could reach it, they emigrated to a newer world than ever Columbus dreamed of . . . not merely mariners' tales and some paltry driftwood and sea-weed, but a continual drift and instinct to all our shores. I saw their empty hulks that came to land; but they themselves, meanwhile, were cast upon some shore yet further west, toward which we are all tending.[36]

Thoreau's brief account of the disaster performs nothing short of an act of transfiguration. In it the dead facts of history are reanimated by moral and metaphysical analogy into the human story, and ultimately the cosmic story itself. Everything is emigrating. Everything is migratory by virtue of that subtending, figural westwardness of which everything is a part.

Between the abject wreckage of history and Thoreau's "further shore," however, are those who made it to this shore, like my own family, by whatever convergence of chance and means. One can witness the further historical passage in retrospect, even while we are living it, by making one's way to places like St. John, New Brunswick. Or one can visit the Lower East Side Tenement Museum in New York City, where the very wallpaper is suggestive of the layers of experience, the palimpsest of lives from all parts of the world that struggled and succeeded or struggled and failed here, where Jacob Riis pictured how the other half lives. It is Scorsese territory to be sure. Or one can look and listen outside an apartment building in Brooklyn and hear the latest migration calling up the ancient querulous boundary between sameness and difference, a single voice that, I hope, resonates beyond the narrator of "A Mosque in Brooklyn":

> There is no prayer that can abolish history,
> though in this basement mosque the muezzin's history
>
> gathers in his throat like a tenor's aria
> and he calls to God to put an end to history.
>
> From my courtyard room I hear his song ascending,
> the divine name whirling its rebuke to history—
>
> *Allah, Allah*—above the crowded rowhouse roofs.
> Their rusted antennas, stalled arrows of history,
>
> would transmit a daily riot of talk and news,
> the world boxed inside a glowing square of history.
>
> I've seen them on the street, the faithful in their robes
> walking along store-fronts, a different history
>
> clothing them, like me, in our separate skins,
> though here we are at the scope end of history.[37]

Written two years before 9/11, "A Mosque in Brooklyn" seeks to engage the historical moment by tuning into the tension between the inevitability of history and the desire to transcend it. On the positive side, the poem seeks to redress the history that is the sum of our deeply flawed origins and relations; at the same time it recognizes that this very desire to transcend history creates the legacies by which humans construct boundaries and pursue violence, of whatever kind: "Goodness is timeless, the great English poet wrote / and not just for himself—the crime is history."[38] The English poet is W. H. Auden, but the form of this poem—not English in origin but an adaptation of the Persian *ghazal*—would embody the inclination of art as means to bridge such boundaries, and in its final image of the Sufi congregation of birds "flourishing into the One / without division, without names, without history," it would offer a more beneficent, hoped-for space commensurate with Thoreau's "further shore toward which we all are tending."

The tension appears also in the family poems of *The Narrows,* as in "At the Tree of Many, One," a riff on Wordsworth's "Ode, Intimations of Immortality," where the belated miscarriage of a sister places history—"the drag of created things"[39]—in fraught dialogue with the emptiness of apophatic contemplation. It appears again in the epistolary "Thinking of Meade Mountain," a counterpoint address to the brother who lived and whose Buddhism stands as rebuke to the speaker's attachment to the world. The attraction to the forces of absence, its presiding energies, is most strongly present in "The Book of Ruth," which wants to affirm that the lost diary of my paternal grandmother, along with the names of the generations and even the poem itself, will be "preserved in the emptiness." Or as the fugal "The Book of Ruth" begins:

> In the beginning: everything *in medias res.*
> And the past? Most of it dark matter
> winnowed from diminished stars, an absence
> necessary, the sustaining emptiness.[40]

As a form, the fugue moves recursively, at once backwards and forwards like the reversing falls of the St. John River where it opens into the Bay of Fundy. *The Narrows,* as a single arc composed of the many arcs intersecting of its individual poems, moves similarly.

Looking back, the structure of the book's recursive movement through its twelve sections strikes me as an effort to negotiate the terms of a quotation from Victor Hugo that I keep on my desk, a quotation like the postcard of the Narrows Bridge, a small but important gift given by a friend: "The horizon is the line of reality; the vertical, the line of prayer." I do not know from where my friend took Hugo's words, but they remain essential to my way of understanding both poetry and the world. The horizontal line and the vertical line are ideally wedded in recursive motion, which is fundamental to the motion of poetry. Poetry is grounded in reality and takes flight in measure and pattern. The cutting of a line is an act of imposing, of affirming, the vertical dimension.

Poetry's lineage harkens back to prayer, and so *The Narrows* in poems like "A Mosque in Brooklyn" and "At the Tree of Many, One" juxtaposes the horizontal line of history, with its multifarious lineages, alongside the vertical line that can be fully attained (if at all) only through the horizon of time, space, and the chaotic exigencies of history. *The Narrows* pursues the horizontal line—the westward direction in Thoreau's analogical as well as literal sense—in order to double back.

It is the same westward way the father in "Twentieth Century Limited" travels when he comes back from war—"so far east / he has come back west, only to press east again,"[41] and shadowed across the American continent by his son, who, from the vantage of the future, bears witness to the father's intersections with history: the desert burned to a green glass by the first atomic bomb test, the letters "Nagasaki" forming the shape of his father's tie clip, the lost city of Cahokia in the American bottom. I hoped to press that same continental crossing in the opposite direction earlier in the book, near the end of the poem "The Narrows," in service of begging the question of what it means to be an American—"discovering yourself in the distances?"[42] To do so is not only to make the journey across, through "the hypnotic emptiness of wheat fields and cornfields," for the traveler to arrive at headlands "like visible waves of light" above another Narrows with its other monumental bridge, but to discover that

> there is no end
> just these waves of water waves of land
> flung together,
> feeling on his face the rush of wind,
> and inside him the growing thought that anywhere
> might be home,
> since home has become nowhere.[43]

These lines resonate, at least in my mind, with the purely matter-of-fact historical observation Mary Kilfoil McDevitt makes in her description of St. Mary's Cemetery, that resting place of so many forgotten emigrant Irish, outside St. John, New Brunswick: "St. Mary's is located at the crest of a windswept knoll, on the south side of Lock Lomond Road, in East Saint-John. There are no markers or fences to define its actual parameters."[44]

Indeed, there are no parameters for the dead, no boundaries. Which is why the last poem of *The Narrows,* the long, recursive "Outerbridge Crossing," moves forth and back in time and space across historical, geographical, familial, and personal boundaries as it recounts its passage to Resurrection Cemetery in Staten Island, where my parents—the most recent in a line of ancestors—are buried:

> Now, in Resurrection their names are carved in stone,
> as if stone itself were not slowly lifting off
> into dark energy, or whatever motion
>
> wheels the nano-second of each life inside its course;
> for Gregory of Nyssa a forwarding and return,
> *apokatastasis,* the soul's volta back
>
> into the uncreated, our true home a furtherance—[45]

Gregory of Nyssa, a contemplative and saint of the Eastern rite, was brought up on charges of heresy for his doctrine of *apokatastasis*—the idea that all must be gathered into the salvation before time ends, even the damned. By the poem's end, the speaker and the figure of the beloved, who has shadowed him over the course of the book, follow their own furtherance on the horizontal line of the reality in which they exist. That line includes not only themselves but all the past, all the present, and the open road that is the future. For them, appropriately, the significance of their journey turns into a return across the threshold of the Narrows Bridge and the liminal flow below it:

> Here, in the shadow of the Outerbridge,
> I almost feel names lifting from these stones
> like particles of light somewhere becoming waves;
>
> though we'll drive back, love, over the Narrows
> into our own lives, our unborn still asleep
> in the womb of our choice, and Gravesend
>
> below, lustral in its self-emptying,
> as though it rode a current deeper than history,
> the sky bodied in its waters, bright and ongoing.[46]

Gravesend

To have been. The way. Gone. Ongoing. The first phrase opens "Double Life," the poem that constitutes the threshold of *The Narrows*. The second phrase opens "The Narrows"—the poem within the poem of the book's title—and the third, "Gone," ends that poem. The last word, "ongoing," announces itself the final word in the arc of the whole, the whole movement. To link these together might be to make a short, dense, haiku-like poem instead of a long interwoven montage, a kind of gloss on the completed design at once an epigraph and an epitaph.

> To have been:
> The way, gone—
> Ongoing. . .

Such is the postcompositional seed "cinema" of *The Narrows,* and the linkage of these phrases, along with their compression into this gloss, constitutes something akin to a singularity, the dense imaginative point of its beginning and end. Beyond its own unique expansion and configuration in *The Narrows,* such a point would ideally also constitute a nexus of all potential journeys and not merely the journey of one life or lineage. It would be a point, impossible, of infinite connection in which the disparate frequencies of our broadly singular passages resonate together beyond earshot of our hearing.

THE LINE

Now fall quickens
To margin-less sky,

And these wild geese
Arrowing the Narrows

Could be Zeno's
Imaginary line,

Each moment's point
A fractal integer

Perpetually halved
Until the passage

Brightens the mark
As the mark recedes

Infinitely away,
The way the dead

Make passage
Inside, each life

With their lives
Riding outwards

Like Mael Duin,
Brendan, Bran

Into the limitless
That seems to pause

In the Great Going,
Each hastening span

A well feeding
The annals of loss,

And each life a gloss
From the scribe's nib

Justified
In the needle's eye.

Notes

CHAPTER ONE   Dinner at the Café Marliave

1. A. G. Evans, *Fanatic Heart: A Life of John Boyle O'Reilly 1844–1890* (Boston: Northeastern University Press, 1999).
2. Ibid., 220–21.
3. Ibid., 222, 177, 223.
4. Ibid., 224.
5. Thomas Kinsella, *The Dual Tradition: An Essay on Poetry and Politics in Ireland* (Manchester, UK: Carcanet, 1995), 47.
6. Ibid., 49–51.
7. Edward W. Said, *Culture and Imperialism* (New York: Alfred Knopf, 1993), 336.
8. Declan Kiberd, *The Irish Writer and the World* (Cambridge, UK: Cambridge University Press, 2005), 74.
9. See Daniel Tobin, ed., *The Book of Irish American Poetry from the Eighteenth Century to the Present* (Notre Dame, IN: University of Notre Dame Press, 2007), 43.
10. Stephanie Rains, "Irish Roots: Genealogy and the Performance of Irishness" in *The Irish in Us: Irishness, Performativity and Popular Culture,* ed. Diane Negra (Durham, NC: Duke University Press, 2006), 138.
11. Kinsella, *The Dual Tradition,* 3.
12. Quoted in Evans, *Fanatic Heart,* 228.
13. See Charles Fanning, *The Irish Voice in America: Irish-American Fiction from the 1760s to the 1980s* (Lexington: University Press of Kentucky, 1990), 4.
14. Kinsella, *The Dual Tradition,* 61–62.
15. W. B. Yeats, *Essays and Introductions* (New York: Macmillan, 1961), 521.
16. Kinsella, *The Dual Tradition,* 61.
17. Kiberd, *The Irish Writer,* 55ff.
18. Kinsella, *The Dual Tradition,* 4, 87.
19. Quoted in Kiberd, *The Irish Writer,* 55.
20. See Kiberd, *The Irish Writer,* 35; Richard Kearney, *Navigations* (Syracuse, NY: Syracuse University Press, 2006), 21.

21. Patrick Ward, *Exile, Emigration, and Irish Writing* (Dublin: Irish Academic Press, 2002), 3.

22. Kiberd, *The Irish Writer*, 52.

23. See Tobin, *Irish American Poetry*, 91.

24. Quoted in Ward, *Exile, Emigration*, 243.

25. See Tobin, *Irish American Poetry*, 144.

26. Ward, *Exile, Emigration*, 238.

27. Ibid.

28. Eamonn Wall, *Refuge at DeSoto Bend* (Cliffs of Moher, Ireland: Salmon Publishing, 2004), 25.

29. James Byrne, "Paddy Beyond the Pale: A Cultural Theory of Transnational Irish American Identity" (lecture, Emerson College, Boston, November 12, 2008).

30. Eamonn Wall, *From the Sin-é Café to the Black Hills* (Madison: University of Wisconsin Press, 1999), 108.

31. Ibid., 72.

32. Ibid.

33. Wall, *Refuge*, 56.

34. Greg Delanty, *Collected Poems 1986–2006*, Oxford Poets (Manchester, UK: Carcanet, 2006), 47.

35. Ibid., 109.

36. Wall, *Sin-é*, 57.

37. Ward, *Exile, Emigration*, 241.

38. Michael Coady, "The Sea-Divided Silence," *Poetry Ireland Review* 46 (Summer 1995): 5, 1.

39. Eavan Boland, *Collected Poems* (Manchester, UK: Carcanet, 1995), 129.

40. Wall, *Sin-é*, 57.

41. Kiberd, *The Irish Writer*, 156.

42. Kearney, *Navigations*, 30.

43. Daniel Tobin, "Irish American Poetry and the Question of Tradition," in *Irish American Poetry*, xliv.

44. Kearney, *Navigations*, 31.

45. T. S. Eliot, "Tradition and the Individual Talent," in *Selected Prose of T. S. Eliot*, ed. Frank Kermode (New York: Harcourt, Brace, 1975), 38.

46. Ibid., 39 (my italics).

47. James McMichael, *Capacity* (New York: Farrar, Straus and Giroux, 2006), 46.

48. Brendan Galvin, *Habitat: New and Selected Poems, 1965–2005* (Baton Rouge: Louisiana State University Press, 2005), 220.

49. Ibid.

50. Arthur A. Cohen, *The Tremendum: A Theological Interpretation of the Holocaust* (New York: Crossroad, 1981), 10.

51. Alan Shapiro, *After the Digging* (Chicago: University of Chicago Press, 1981), 4.

52. Ibid., 12.

53. Ibid., 20.

54. Ibid., 22.

55. Ibid.

56. See Wall, *Sin-é*, 6.

57. Ibid., 120.

58. Seamus Heaney, *Preoccupations: Selected Prose, 1968–1978* (New York: Farrar, Straus, Giroux, 1980), 132.

59. Kinsella, *The Dual Tradition*, 12, 36.

60. Ibid., 62, 92, 93.

61. W. B. Yeats, *The Poems* (New York: Macmillan, 1983), 127.

62. Ward, *Exile, Emigration*, 234–35.

63. Seamus Heaney, *Place and Displacement: Recent Poetry of Northern Ireland—The Pete Laver Memorial Lecture* (Cumbria: Frank Peters, 1984), 3.

64. Ibid.

65. Heaney, *Preoccupations*, 132.

66. Fanning, *The Irish Voice in America*, 4.

67. Marianne Moore, *The Poems of Marianne Moore*, ed. Grace Schulman (New York: Viking, 2003), 245.

68. Ibid., 246.

69. Ibid.

70. Ward, *Exile, Emigration*, 83.

71. Robinson Jeffers, *The Selected Poems of Robinson Jeffers* (Berkeley: University of California Press, 2001), 181.

72. James Karman, *Robinson Jeffers: Poet of California* (Brownsville, OR: Story Line Press, 1994), 87.

73. Ibid., 50–51.

74. Ibid., 120.

75. Ibid., 6.

76. Ibid., 21.

77. Ibid., 3.

78. John Montague, ed., *The Book of Irish Verse: An Anthology of Irish Poetry from the Sixth Century to the Present* (New York: Macmillan, 1974), 255.

79. Una Jeffers, *Visits to Ireland* (San Francisco: Ward Ritchie Press, 1954), 44.

80. Jeffers, *Selected Poems*, 676.

81. Louis MacNeice, *Selected Poems* (Winston-Salem, NC: Wake Forest University Press, 1990), 41.

82. Heaney, *Preoccupations*, 143.

83. Jeffers, *Selected Poems*, 362.

84. Ibid.

85. Ibid., 365.

86. Jeffers, *Visits to Ireland*, 33–34.

87. Jeffers, *Selected Poems*, 365.

88. See Tobin, *Irish American Poetry*, 60–61.

89. Ibid., 58.

90. Ibid., 165.

91. Ibid.

92. Galvin, *Habitat*, 152.

93. Ibid.

94. Ibid., 150.

95. Ibid., 151.

96. Ibid., 16.

97. Ibid., 11.

98. Said, *Culture and Imperialism*, 46.

99. Rains, "Irish Roots," 138.

100. Seamus Heaney, *The Redress of Poetry* (New York: Farrar, Straus and Giroux, 1995), 199–200.

CHAPTER TWO   Modernism, Leftism, and the Spirit

This essay first appeared in slightly different form in *New Hibernia Review* 8, no. 3 (Autumn 2004): 65–85.

1. Peter Quartermain, "Lola Ridge," in *The Dictionary of Literary Biography*, vol. 54 (Detroit: Gale, 1986), 354.

2. Ibid.

3. Robert McAlmon, *Being Geniuses Together, 1920–1930*, rev. and with supplementary chapters by Kay Boyle (New York: Doubleday, 1968), 16.

4. Katherine Anne Porter, *The Never-Ending Wrong* (Boston: Little, Brown, 1977), 23.

5. Horace Gregory and Marina Zaturenska, *A History of American Poetry, 1900–1940* (New York: Gordian Press, 1969), 444, 445.

6. Lola Ridge, *The Ghetto and Other Poems* (New York: W. B. Huebsch, 1918), 101.

7. Lola Ridge, *Red Flag* (New York: Viking, 1927), 73.

8. Padraic Pearse, *Plays, Stories, Poems* (Dublin: Talbot Press, 1966), 340.

9. Kay Boyle in McAlmon, *Being Geniuses Together*, 16–17.

10. Ibid., 53.

11. William Carlos Williams, *The Autobiography of William Carlos Williams* (New York: New Directions, 1951), 135.

12. Boyle in McAlmon, *Being Geniuses Together*, 15, 25.

13. Williams, *Autobiography*, 135.

14. Matthew Josephson, *Life Among the Surrealists* (New York: Holt, Rinehart, and Winston, 1962), 246.

15. Harold Loeb, *The Way It Was* (New York: Criterion Books, 1959), 103.

16. McAlmon, *Being Geniuses Together*, 140.

17. T. S. Eliot, *Selected Prose of T. S. Eliot*, ed. Frank Kermode (New York: Harcourt, Brace, 1975), 64.

18. Ezra Pound, *Selected Poems* (New York: J. Laughlin, 1957), 63.

19. Josephson, *Life Among the Surrealists*, 246.

20. Loeb, *The Way It Was*, 123.

21. Ridge, *The Ghetto*, iii.

22. Lola Ridge, "Kreymborg's Marionettes," *Dial* 66 (Jan. 11, 1919): 29–31.

23. Lola Ridge, "The Georgians at Home," *New Republic* 17 (Jan. 11, 1919): 316–17.

24. Ridge, "Marionettes," 29–31.

25. Lola Ridge, "Salt Water," *New Masses* 3 (September 1927): 27.

26. Ridge, *The Ghetto*, 3.

27. Ibid., 4.

28. Ibid., 4–5.

29. T. S. Eliot, *Complete Poems and Plays* (New York: Harcourt, Brace, 1950), 39.

30. Ridge, *The Ghetto*, 14.

31. Ibid., 15.

32. Ibid., 16–17.

33. Ibid., 19–20.

34. Ibid., 22, 25.

35. Ibid., 26 (italics in original).

36. Gerard Manley Hopkins, *The Poems of Gerard Manley Hopkins*, ed. W. H. Gardner and N. H. MacKenzie (New York: Oxford University Press, 1967), 90.

37. Josephson, *Life Among the Surrealists*, 231.

38. Loeb, *The Way It Was*, 122.

39. Josephson, *Life Among the Surrealists*, 246.

40. Ibid., 230.
41. Ridge, *The Ghetto*, 33–34.
42. Ibid., 42.
43. Ibid., 43.
44. Lola Ridge, *Sun-Up and Other Poems* (New York: W. B. Huebsch, 1920), 79.
45. Ridge, *The Ghetto*, 23.
46. Dorothy Day, *The Long Loneliness* (New York: Harper & Row, 1952), 131, 171, 39.
47. Simone Weil, *The Simone Weil Reader*, ed. George Panikas (New York: David McKay, 1977), 60.
48. Ridge, *The Ghetto*, 61.
49. Hart Crane, *The Complete Poems and Selected Letters and Prose of Hart Crane* (New York: Doubleday, 1966), 202.
50. Ridge, "Frank Little at Calvary," in *The Ghetto*, 56.
51. Ibid., 49.
52. Ridge, *Sun-Up*, 87.
53. Quartermain, "Lola Ridge," 359.
54. Ridge, *Red Flag*, 18.
55. Gregory and Zaturenska, *American Poetry*, 445.
56. Day, *The Long Loneliness*, 147.
57. Lola Ridge, *Firehead* (New York: Payson and Clarke, 1929), 25, 20, 17.
58. Quartermain, "Lola Ridge," 359.
59. Ridge, *Firehead*, 113.
60. Ibid., 115.
61. Ibid.
62. Ibid., 122.
63. Lola Ridge, *Dance of Fire* (New York: Harrison Smith and Robert Haas, 1933), 56.
64. Day, *The Long Loneliness*, 120.
65. Weil, *Reader*, 69.

CHAPTER THREE The Westwardness of Everything

1. Wallace Stevens, *The Necessary Angel* (New York: Random House, 1951), 31.
2. W. B. Yeats, *Essays and Introductions* (New York: Macmillan, 1961), 161–62.
3. James Longenbach, *Wallace Stevens: The Plain Sense of Things* (New York: Oxford University Press, 1991), 14.

4. Wallace Stevens, *The Collected Poems of Wallace Stevens* (New York: Knopf, 1955), 326.

5. Harold Bloom, *Wallace Stevens: The Poems of Our Climate* (Ithaca, NY: Cornell University Press, 1977), 70, 115–20.

6. Wallace Stevens, *Opus Posthumous,* ed. Milton J. Bates, rev., enl., corr. ed. (New York: Knopf, 1989), 126.

7. Bloom, *Wallace Stevens,* 130.

8. Ibid., 20.

9. Stevens, *Opus Posthumous,* 17.

10. Stevens, *Necessary Angel,* 81.

11. Ibid.

12. Stevens, *Collected Poems,* 65.

13. Bloom, *Wallace Stevens,* 20.

14. Ibid., 86, 189.

15. Stevens, *Collected Poems,* 325.

16. Ibid.

17. Stevens, *Necessary Angel,* 150.

18. Wallace Stevens, *Letters of Wallace Stevens,* ed. Holly Stevens (New York: Knopf, 1966), 448–49.

19. Stevens, *Collected Poems,* 380.

20. Bloom, *Wallace Stevens,* 189.

21. Stevens, *Collected Poems,* 387.

22. Stevens, *Letters,* 434.

23. Bloom, *Wallace Stevens,* 189.

24. Stevens, *Letters,* 564.

25. Mario Rossi, *Pilgrimage in the West,* trans. J. M. Hone (Dublin: Cuala Press, 1933), 14.

26. Ibid., 16.

27. Ibid., 50.

28. Peter Brazeau, "The Irish Connection: Peter Brazeau and Thomas McGreevy," *Southern Review* 17 (1981): 533.

29. Lee Jenkins, "Thomas McGreevy and the Pressure of Reality," *Wallace Stevens Journal* 18, no. 2 (Fall 1994): 146–47.

30. Stevens, *Letters,* 541.

31. Ibid., 586.

32. Ibid., 610.

33. Ibid., 617.

34. Mary Joan Egan, "Thomas McGreevy and Wallace Stevens: A Correspondence," *Wallace Stevens Journal* 18, no. 2 (Fall 1994): 130.

35. Brazeau, "The Irish Connection," 538.

36. Stevens, *Letters,* 613.

37. Ibid., 537.
38. Ibid., 652.
39. See Brazeau, "The Irish Connection," 535–36; Jenkins, "Thomas McGreevy," 149–51; and Egan, "Thomas McGreevy and Wallace Stevens," 126–27.
40. Stevens, *Collected Poems*, 454.
41. Lawrence Kramer, "A Completely New Set of Objects: The Spirit of Place in Wallace Stevens and Charles Ives" in *Critical Essays on Wallace Stevens*, ed. Stephen Gould Axelrod and Helen Deese, Critical Essays on American Literature (Boston: G. K. Hall, 1988), 226.
42. Stevens, *Letters*, 596.
43. Stevens, *Collected Poems*, 454.
44. Ibid., 454.
45. Quoted in Brazeau, "The Irish Connection," 535–36.
46. Stevens, *Collected Poems*, 455.
47. Ibid.
48. Stevens, *Letters*, 611.
49. Ibid., 691, 632.
50. Bloom, *Wallace Stevens*, 219.
51. Stevens, *Letters*, 292.
52. Ibid., 393.
53. Stevens, *Necessary Angel*, 100.
54. Ibid., 171.
55. Ibid., 100.
56. Stevens, *Letters*, 448, 597.
57. See David M. LaGuardia, *Advance of Chaos: The Sanctifying Imagination of Wallace Stevens* (Hanover, NH: University Press of New England, 1983), 156.
58. Stevens, *Letters*, 611.
59. Stevens, *Necessary Angel*, 169.
60. Ibid., 20.
61. See Paul Gilroy, *The Black Atlantic: Modernity and Double-Consciousness* (Cambridge, MA: Harvard University Press, 1993).
62. Stevens, *Collected Poems*, 455.
63. Stevens, *Letters*, 619.
64. Stevens, *Collected Poems*, 65.
65. Ibid., 137.
66. Ibid., 380.
67. Ibid., 222.
68. See J. E. Cirlot, *A Dictionary of Symbols*, trans. Jack Sage (New York, Philosophical Library, 1962), 233.
69. Stevens, *Collected Poems*, 135.

70. Luke Gibbons, *Transformations in Irish Culture,* Critical Conditions 2 (Notre Dame, IN: University of Notre Dame Press, 1996), 13.

71. Stevens, *Collected Poems,* 455.

72. Ibid., 469.

73. Kramer, "A Completely New Set of Objects," 226.

74. Stevens, *Necessary Angel,* 27.

75. Ralph J. Mills, "Wallace Stevens: The Image of the Rock," in *Wallace Stevens: A Collection of Critical Essays,* ed. Marie Borroff (Englewood Cliffs, NJ: Prentice-Hall, 193), 98.

76. Stevens, *Letters,* 760.

77. Stevens, *Collected Poems,* 501.

78. LaGuardia, *Advance on Chaos,* 157.

79. Stevens, *Collected Poems,* 501.

80. Ibid.

81. Ibid., 502.

82. Ibid., 524.

83. Ibid., 506.

84. Ibid., 528.

85. Walt Whitman, *Leaves of Grass: Authoritative Texts, Prefaces, Whitman on His Art, Criticism,* ed. Sculley Bradley and Harold W. Blodgett (New York: W. W. Norton, 1965), 160.

86. Stevens, *Letters,* 669.

87. Stevens, *Collected Poems,* 526.

88. Stevens, *Letters,* 877.

CHAPTER FOUR   Lines of Leaving, Lines of Returning

An earlier version of this essay appeared in the excellent *Well Dreams: Essays on John Montague,* ed. Thomas Dillon Redshaw (Omaha: Creighton University Press, 2006).

1. John Montague, *Born in Brooklyn: John Montague's America,* ed. David Lampe (Fredonia, NY: White Pine Press, 1991), 34.

2. Ibid., 23.

3. Robert Garratt, "John Montague and the Poetry of History," *Irish University Review* 19, no. 1 (Spring 1989): 94.

4. Elizabeth Grubgeld, "Topography, Memory, and John Montague's *The Rough Field,*" *Canadian Journal of Irish Studies* 14, no. 2 (January 1989): 26, 27.

5. Thomas Dillon Redshaw, "Appreciation," *Eire-Ireland* 11, no. 4 (1976): 124.

6. Gerald Dawe, "Invocation of Powers," in *The Chosen Ground*, ed. Neil Corcoran (Bridgend: Seren Books, 1992), 29.

7. Montague, *Born in Brooklyn*, 34.

8. W. B. Yeats, *A Vision* (New York: Macmillan, 1966), 25.

9. W. B. Yeats, *Essays and Introductions* (New York: Macmillan, 1981), 508.

10. Adrian Frazier, "John Montague's Language of the Tribe," *Canadian Journal of Irish Studies* 9, no. 2 (December 1983): 59, 74.

11. Seamus Heaney, *Preoccupations* (New York: Farrar, Straus, and Giroux, 1980), 143–44.

12. Dawe, "Invocation of Powers," 29 (my italics).

13. John Montague, *The Figure in the Cave* (Syracuse, NY: Syracuse University Press, 1989), 8.

14. John Montague, *Collected Poems* (Loughcrew: Galley Press, 1995), 5.

15. Thomas Dillon Redshaw, "The Bounding Line: John Montague's *The New Siege*," *Canadian Journal of Irish Studies* 13, no. 1 (June 1987): 82.

16. Montague, *Collected Poems*, 201.

17. See George O'Brien, "The Muse of Exile: Estrangement and Renewal in Modern Irish Literature," in *Exile in Literature*, ed. Maria-Ines Lagos-Pope (Lewisburg, PA: Bucknell University Press, 1988), 99.

18. Montague, *Collected Poems*, 196.

19. Ibid., 201.

20. Ibid., 40.

21. Simone Weil, *The Need for Roots* (London: Ark, 1987), 41.

22. Edward Said, "Reflections on Exile," in *Out There: Marginalization and Contemporary Cultures*, ed. Russell Ferguson, Martha Gever, Trinh T. Minh-ha, and Cornel West, Documentary Sources in Contemporary Art, vol. 4 (New York: New Museum of Contemporary Art; Cambridge, MA: MIT Press, 1990), 363.

23. See A. K. Weatherhead, "John Montague: Exiled from Order," *Concerning Poetry* 14, no. 2 (Fall 1982): 97.

24. See Kerby Miller, *Emigrants and Exiles* (London: Oxford University Press, 1985), 131–40.

25. See John Montague, *Figure in the Cave*, 2.

26. Montague, *Collected Poems*, 182.

27. Ibid., 173.

28. Ibid., 44.

29. Ibid., 42.

30. Ibid., 181.

31. Homi K. Bhabha, "DissemiNation: Time, Narrative, and the Margins of the Modern Nation," in *Nation and Narration*, ed. Homi K. Bhabha (New York: Routledge, 1990), 295.

32. Homi K. Bhabha, "Introduction: Narrating the Nation," in Bhabha, *Nation and Narration,* 2.

33. Anindyo Roy, "Postcoloniality and the Politics of Identity in the Diaspora: Figuring 'Home,' Locating Histories," in *Postcolonial Discourse and Changing Cultural Contexts: Theory and Criticism,* ed. Gita Rajan and Radhika Mohanram (Westport, CT: Greenwood Press, 1995), 102.

34. Montague, *Collected Poems,* 206.

35. Ibid., 165.

36. Quoted in Harry Marten, "Memory Defying Cruelty: The Poetry of John Montague," *New England Review* 5, nos. 1–2 (Autumn–Winter 1982): 255.

37. For an excellent discussion of Montague's mythmaking, see Thomas Dillon Redshaw, "Longing for Home: Two Motifs in *The Rough Field,*" *Études irlandaises* 6 (December 1981): 73–86.

38. Bhabha, "DissemiNation," 295.

39. Bruce Robbins, "Homelessness and Worldliness," *Diacritics* 13, no. 3 (Fall 1983): 69.

40. Montague, *Figure in the Cave,* 18.

41. Robert Edwards, "Exile, Self, and Society," in Lagos-Pope, *Exile in Literature,* 16.

42. See Thomas Dillon Redshaw, "Location as Vocation: John Montague's 'The Northern Gate,'" *Canadian Journal of Irish Studies* 5, no. 2 (1972): 46.

43. Edwards, "Exile, Self, and Society," 21.

44. Montague, *Collected Poems,* 294.

45. Ibid., 283.

46. Ibid., 43.

47. Ibid., 166; italics in original.

48. Ibid., 307.

49. Ibid., 46–47.

50. Said, "Reflections on Exile," 359.

51. Thomas Dillon Redshaw, "That Surviving Sign: John Montague's *The Bread God* (1968)," *Eire-Ireland* 17, no. 2 (Summer 1982): 80.

52. Terrence Browne, "*The Dead Kingdom:* A Reading," *Irish University Review* 19, no. 1 (Spring 1989): 105.

53. Montague, *Collected Poems,* 307.

54. Ibid., 166.

55. Ibid., 124.

56. Ibid., 132.

57. Ibid., 285.

58. John Montague, "The Unpartitioned Intellect," in *Irish Writers and Society at Large,* ed. Masaru Sekine, Irish Literary Studies 22 (Totowa, NJ: Barnes and Noble, 1985), 167.

59. Said, "Reflections on Exile," 366.

60. Montague, *Collected Poems*, 73.

61. Ibid., 349.

62. Ibid., 124.

63. See Redshaw, "Two Motifs," 76.

64. Redshaw, "Location as Vocation," 41.

65. Montague, *Collected Poems*, 68.

66. Ibid., 172.

67. See "Elegiac Cheer: A Conversation with John Montague," *Literary Review* 31 (Fall 1987): 28.

68. Marten, "Memory Defying Cruelty," 247.

69. Stephen Arkin, "An Interview with John Montague: Deaths in the Summer," *New England Review* 5, no. 1–2 (Autumn–Winter 1982): 235.

70. For an excellent discussion of Montague's fusion of lyric and epic, see Sidney B. Poger, "Crane and Montague: The Pattern History Weaves," *Eire-Ireland* 16, no. 4 (Winter 1981): 114–24.

71. Quoted in John Montague, "Exile and Prophecy: A Study of Goldsmith's Poetry," in *Goldsmith, the Gentle Master,* ed. Seán Lucy, The Thomas Davis Lectures (Cork, Ireland: Cork University Press, 1984), 56–57 (emphasis in original).

72. John Montague, "In the Irish Grain," in *The Book of Irish Verse: An Anthology of Irish Poetry from the Sixth Century to the Present* (New York: Macmillan, 1974), 37.

73. John Montague, "American Pegasus," *Studies* 48, no. 190 (Summer 1959): 183.

74. "Global Regionalism: Interview with John Montague," *Literary Review* 22, no. 1 (1979): 154.

75. Eamonn Wall, "Exile, Attitude, and the Sin-é Café: Notes on the New Irish," *Eire-Ireland* 30, no. 4 (Winter 1996): 11.

76. Montague, *Figure in the Cave,* 87.

77. "Global Regionalism," 157.

78. Wallace Stevens, *The Necessary Angel* (New York: Vintage, 1951), 36.

CHAPTER FIVE   Starting from Wexford, Ending in the Sublime

An earlier version of the first section of this essay first appeared as "Starting from Wexford: James Liddy and Walt Whitman," *North Dakota Quarterly* 64, no. 2 (Spring 1997): 116–24. An earlier version of the second section first appeared as "Figures in the Set: James Liddy and the Sublime," *An Sionnach* 1, no. 1 (Spring 2005): 57–65.

1. Thomas McGonigle, "An Interview with James Liddy," *Adrift* (Spring 1983): 10.

2. Walt Whitman, *Leaves of Grass: Authoritative Texts, Prefaces, Whitman on His Art, Criticism,* ed. Sculley Bradley and Harold W. Blodgett (New York: Norton, 1973), 712, 566.

3. James Liddy, *The Doctor's House* (Galway: Arlen House, 2008), 54.

4. Ibid., 82.

5. Eamonn Wall, "James Liddy: Editor and Poet," *An Sionnach* 1, no. 1 (Spring 2005): 34–35.

6. Liddy, *Doctor's House,* 109, 110.

7. Wall, "Liddy," 34.

8. Liddy, *Doctor's House,* 77.

9. James Liddy, *Collected Poems* (Omaha: Creighton University Press, 1994), 330.

10. Brian Arkins, *James Liddy: A Critical Study* (Galway: Arlen House, 2000), 13.

11. Ibid., 29.

12. Ibid. (italics in original).

13. Whitman, *Leaves of Grass,* 15.

14. Liddy, *Collected Poems,* 169.

15. Ibid., 171.

16. Ibid., 173.

17. Walt Whitman, *Poetry and Prose,* ed. Louis Untermeyer, Inner Sanctum ed. (New York: Simon and Schuster, 1949), 518.

18. Liddy, *Collected Poems,* 163.

19. Arkins, *James Liddy,* 13.

20. Liddy, *Collected Poems,* 355.

21. Ibid., 70.

22. Ibid., 82.

23. Ibid., 90.

24. Ibid., 96.

25. Ibid., 26.

26. Ibid., 155.

27. Ibid., 108.

28. Ibid., 111.

29. Whitman, *Leaves of Grass,* 49, 50.

30. Ibid., 91–93.

31. Ibid., 847.

32. Liddy, *Collected Poems,* 136.

33. Karl Shapiro, "The First White Aboriginal," in Whitman, *Leaves of Grass,* 951.

34. Havelock Ellis, "Whitman," in Whitman, *Leaves of Grass,* 810.

35. Liddy, *Collected Poems,* 24.

36. Ibid., 142.

37. Whitman, *Leaves of Grass*, 82.
38. Liddy, *Collected Poems*, 252.
39. Ibid., 228.
40. Ibid., 225.
41. Kenneth Rexroth, "Walt Whitman," in Whitman, *Leaves of Grass*, 978.
42. Denis Donoghue, "Walt Whitman" in Whitman, *Leaves of Grass*, 968.
43. Whitman, *Leaves of Grass*, 717.
44. Liddy, *Collected Poems*, 188.
45. Thomas Weiskel, *The Romantic Sublime* (Baltimore: Johns Hopkins University Press, 1976), 3.
46. Liddy, *Collected Poems*, 71.
47. Schiller, quoted in *The Romantic Sublime*, 3.
48. Weiskel, *The Romantic Sublime*, 3.
49. Longinus, "On the Sublime," in *The Critical Tradition*, ed. David Richter (New York: St. Martin's Press, 1989), 78–108.
50. Wallace Stevens, *The Collected Poems of Wallace Stevens* (New York: Knopf, 1955), 131.
51. Ibid.
52. Robert Lowell, *Collected Poems* (New York: Farrar, Straus and Giroux, 2003), 386.
53. Samuel Taylor Coleridge, *Selected Poetry and Prose*, ed. Donald A. Staufer (New York: Random House, 1951), 249.
54. Liddy, *Collected Poems*, 35.
55. Ibid., 143.
56. Ibid.
57. Ibid., 146.
58. Ibid., 142.
59. James Liddy, *Gold Set Dancing* (Cliffs of Moher, Ireland: Salmon Publishing, 2000), 25.
60. Edmund Burke, "From 'A Philosophical Inquiry into the Origin of Our Ideas of the Sublime and the Beautiful,'" in *Critical Theory Since Plato*, ed. Hazard Adams (New York: Wadsworth, 1983), 311.
61. Liddy, *Collected Poems*, 173.
62. Stevens, *Collected Poems*, 501.
63. Liddy, *Gold Set Dancing*, 13.
64. Liddy, *Collected Poems*, 254.
65. Liddy, *Gold Set Dancing*, 72.
66. Ibid.
67. Ibid.
68. Ibid., 71.
69. Ibid., 58.

70. Ibid., 4.
71. Ibid., 52.

CHAPTER SIX   Two for the Road

1. Hardy Drew, "No One as Irish as Barack OBama," One Eyed Parrot Dance Club, n.d., http://www.oneeyedparrot.org/obama.html.
2. Ibid.
3. Eamonn Wall, *From the Sin-é Café to the Black Hills* (Madison: University of Wisconsin Press, 1999), 6.
4. Ibid., 10.
5. Eamonn Wall, "James Liddy: Editor and Poet," *An Sionnach* 1, no. 1 (Spring 2005): 37.
6. Ibid., 56.
7. Wall, *Sin-é Café,* 9.
8. Ibid., 9, 11.
9. Eamonn Wall, *Dyckman 200th Street* (Cliffs of Moher, Ireland: Salmon Publishing, 1994), 3.
10. Ibid.
11. Ibid., 4.
12. Hart Crane, *Collected Poems and Prose* (Washington, DC: Library of America, 2008), 37.
13. Wall, *Dyckman 200th Street,* 14.
14. Ibid., 41.
15. Wall, *Sin-é Café,* 118.
16. Eamonn Wall, *The Crosses* (Cliffs of Moher, Ireland: Salmon Publishing, 2000), 56.
17. Wall, *Sin-é Café,* 113, 116.
18. Eamonn Wall, *Iron Mountain Road* (Cliffs of Moher, Ireland: Salmon Publishing, 1997), 26.
19. Ibid.
20. Wall, *Dyckman 200th Street,* 46.
21. Eamonn Wall, *A Tour of Your Country* (Cliffs of Moher, Ireland: Salmon Publishing, 2008), 41.
22. Wall, *The Crosses,* 7.
23. Ibid., 8.
24. Ibid., 26.
25. Ibid., 32.
26. Eamonn Wall, *Refuge at DeSoto Bend* (Cliffs of Moher, Ireland: Salmon Publishing, 2004), 71.

27. Ibid., 16.
28. Ibid.
29. Wall, *Tour of Your City,* 49.
30. Wall, *Refuge,* 76.
31. Wall, *Tour of Your City,* 15.
32. Ibid.
33. Ibid., 27.
34. Ibid.
35. Ibid., 55.
36. Ibid.
37. Ibid., 57.
38. Greg Delanty, *Collected Poems* (Manchester, UK: Carcanet, 2008), 14.
39. Ibid., 35.
40. Ibid., 6.
41. Ibid., 23.
42. Ibid., 39.
43. Ibid., 49.
44. Ibid. 45.
45. Ibid., 59.
46. Ibid., 109.
47. Ibid., 102.
48. Ibid., 104.
49. Ibid., 115.
50. Ibid.
51. Ibid., 118.
52. Ibid., 157.
53. Ibid., 156, 159.
54. Ibid., 126.
55. Ibid., 143.
56. Ibid., 165.
57. Ibid., 195.
58. Ibid., 194.
59. Ibid., 167.
60. Ibid., 234.

CHAPTER SEVEN   The Parish and Lost America

1. Patrick Kavanagh, *Collected Poems* (New York: Devin-Adair, 1964), 153.
2. Michael Coady, "A Local Habitation," *The Opened Mind,* RTE Radio lecture, 2000.

3. Ibid.
4. Ibid.
5. Michael Coady, *All Souls* (Loughcrew, Ireland: Gallery Press, 1997), 16.
6. Paul Tillich, *Dynamics of Faith* (New York: Harper, 1957), 1.
7. Coady, *All Souls,* 50.
8. Ibid., 54.
9. Michael Coady, *One Another* (Loughcrew, Ireland: Gallery Press, 2003), 13–14 (italics in original).
10. Ibid., 44–45.
11. Michael Coady, *Full Tide: A Miscellany* (Nenagh, Ireland: Relay Books, 1999), 36, 11.
12. Coady, *One Another,* 24–25.
13. Coady, *Full Tide,* 19–20.
14. Ibid., 52.
15. Ibid., 158.
16. Coady, *One Another,* 119.
17. Coady, *Full Tide,* 14.
18. Michael Coady, "The Sea-Divided Silence," *Poetry Ireland Review* 46 (Summer 1995): 1.
19. Ibid., 2–3.
20. Coady, *All Souls,* 84.
21. Ibid., 88.
22. Ibid., 88, 89, 90.
23. Ibid., 133.
24. Ibid., 92.
25. Ibid., 101.
26. Eavan Boland, *Outside History: Selected Poems 1980–1990* (New York: Norton, 1990), 108.
27. Coady, *One Another,* 174.

CHAPTER EIGHT   Back Through Distance

1. Eugene O'Neill, "The Lay of the Singer's Fall," *New London Telegraph,* November 27, 1912, http://www.poetry-archive.com/o/the_lay_of_the_singers_fall.html.
2. Ibid.
3. Marianne Moore, "Compactness Compacted," in *Critical Essays on Louise Bogan,* ed. Martha Collins (Boston: G. K. Hall, 1984), 61.
4. Elizabeth Frank, *Louise Bogan: A Portrait* (New York: Columbia University Press, 1986), 55.

5. See ibid., 6; Louise Bogan, *A Poet's Prose* (Athens: Ohio University Press, 2005), 74.

6. Frank, *Louise Bogan,* 7.

7. Ibid., 4.

8. Bogan, *Poet's Prose,* 74, 80.

9. Louise Bogan, "The Situation in American Writing," in Collins, *Critical Essays on Louise Bogan,* 52.

10. Bogan, *Poet's Prose,* 161.

11. Frank, *Louise Bogan,* 26.

12. Ibid., 47.

13. Bogan, *Poet's Prose,* 150.

14. Louise Bogan, *The Blue Estuaries* (New York: Ecco Press, 1968), 4.

15. Deborah Pope, "Music in the Granite Hill: The Poetry of Louise Bogan" in Collins, *Critical Essays on Louise Bogan,* 153.

16. Quoted in Martha Collins, "Introduction," in Collins, *Critical Essays on Louise Bogan,* 4.

17. Bogan, *Blue Estuaries,* 78.

18. Ibid., 33.

19. Ibid., 19.

20. Theodore Roethke, "The Poetry of Louise Bogan," in *On the Poet and His Craft: Selected Prose,* ed. Ralph J. Mills Jr. (Seattle: University of Washington Press, 1965), 134, 148.

21. Wallace Stevens, *The Necessary Angel* (New York: Vintage, 1951), 22.

22. Roethke, "The Poetry of Louise Bogan," 138.

23. Frank, *Louise Bogan,* 380.

24. Bogan, *Poet's Prose,* 208.

25. Ibid.

26. Ibid., 200.

27. Harold Bloom, "Louise Bogan," in Collins, *Critical Essays on Louise Bogan,* 84.

28. Bogan, *Blue Estuaries,* 21.

29. Ibid., 68.

30. W. B. Yeats, *The Poems,* ed. Richard J. Finneran, new ed. (New York: Macmillan, 1983), 246.

31. Bogan, *Blue Estuaries,* 69.

32. Louise Bogan, "The Pleasure of Formal Poetry," in *The Poet's Work: 29 Masters of 20th Century Poetry on the Origins and Practice of Their Art,* ed. Reginald Gibbons (Boston: Houghton Mifflin, 1979), 246.

33. Bogan, *Poet's Prose,* 156.

34. Ibid., 49.

35. Bogan, *Blue Estuaries,* 118.

36. Frank, *Louise Bogan,* 172.

37. Elizabeth Schmidt, "Where Poetry Begins: Eavan Boland in Conversation," *American Poet* (Spring 1997), http://www.poets.org/viewmedia.php/prmMID/15939.

38. Eavan Boland, *Object Lessons: The Life of the Woman and the Poet in Our Time* (New York: Norton, 1995), 235.

39. Ruth Limmer, "Circumscriptions," in Collins, *Critical Essays on Louise Bogan,* 168–69.

40. Schmidt, "Where Poetry Begins."

41. Frank, *Louise Bogan,* 302.

42. Michael Ryan, "Poetry and the Audience," in *Poets Teaching Poets,* ed. Gregory Orr and Ellen Bryant Voigt (Ann Arbor: University of Michigan Press, 1996), 163.

43. See "Thomas McGrath (1916–1990): Biography," Poetry Foundation, n.d., http://www.poetryfoundation.org/bio/thomas-mcgrath.

44. "An Interview with Thomas McGrath, January 31–February 1, 1987," in *Thomas McGrath: Life and the Poem,* ed. Reginald Gibbons and Terrence Des Pres (Urbana-Champaign: University of Illinois Press, 1992), 44.

45. Quoted in E. P. Thompson, "Homage to Thomas McGrath," in Gibbons and Des Pres, *Thomas McGrath,* 134.

46. "An Interview with Thomas McGrath," 55–56.

47. Terrence Des Pres, "Thomas McGrath," in Gibbons and Des Pres, *Thomas McGrath,* 158.

48. Thompson, "Homage," 106.

49. Des Pres, "Thomas McGrath," 160.

50. Thomas McGrath, *Selected Poems, 1938–1988,* ed. Sam Hamill (Port Townsend, WA: Copper Canyon Press, 1990), 164.

51. Ibid., 12.

52. Ibid., 34.

53. Ibid., 56–57.

54. Reginald Gibbons, "Preface," in Gibbons and Des Pres, *Thomas McGrath,* 2.

55. Sam Hamill, "Preface," in *Letter to an Imaginary Friend: Parts I–IV,* by Thomas McGrath (Port Townsend, WA: Copper Canyon Press, 1997), 1.

56. Ryan, "Poetry and the Audience," 159.

57. Ibid., 181.

58. Thomas McGrath, "Statement to the House Committee on Un-American Activities," *North Dakota Quarterly* (Fall 1982).

59. Dale Jacobson, "Introduction," in *Death Song,* by Thomas McGrath, ed. Sam Hamill (Port Townsend, WA: Copper Canyon Press, 1991), 1.

60. McGrath, *Selected Poems,* 99.

61. "More Questions: An Interview with Thomas McGrath, June 4, 1987," in Gibbons and Des Pres, *Thomas McGrath,* 203.

62. McGrath, *Selected Poems,* 42.

63. Ibid., 107.

64. McGrath, *Death Song,* 30.

65. McGrath, *Letter to an Imaginary Friend,* 185–87.

66. Ibid., 181, 184.

67. Ibid., 189.

68. Ibid., 180.

69. Ryan, "Poetry and the Audience," 161.

70. McGrath, *Letter to an Imaginary Friend,* 364–65.

71. Ibid., 367.

72. Ibid., 369.

73. Ibid., 407.

74. Tim Kendall, *Paul Muldoon* (Chester Springs, PA: Dufour Editions; Bridgend, UK: Seren Books, 1996), 160.

CHAPTER NINE   The Need for Routes

This essay first appeared in *Études irlandaises* 28, no. 2 (Autumn 2003): 51–78.

1. Seamus Heaney, *Opened Ground* (New York: Farrar, Straus and Giroux, 1998), 52.

2. W. B. Yeats, *The Collected Poems of W. B. Yeats: A New Edition,* ed. Richard J. Finneran (London: Macmillan, 1983), 101.

3. Billy Collins, *The Art of Drowning* (Pittsburgh: Pittsburgh University Press, 1995), 95.

4. C. K. Williams, "Poetry and History," in *Conversant Essays: Contemporary Poets on Poetry,* ed. James McCorkle (Detroit: Wayne State, 1990), 394.

5. Simone Weil, *The Need for Roots: Prelude to a Declaration of Duties towards Mankind,* trans. A. F. Wills (London: Ark, 1978), 8.

6. Paul Gilroy, *The Black Atlantic: Modernity and Double Consciousness* (Cambridge, MA: Harvard University Press, 1993), 119.

7. Wallace Stevens, *The Collected Poems of Wallace Stevens* (New York: Knopf, 1954), 291–92.

8. Williams, "Poetry and History," 391.

9. Ibid., 389.

10. Eavan Boland, *Object Lessons: The Life of the Woman and the Poet in Our Time* (New York: Norton, 1995), 9. For Rogers's discusssion, see James S. Rogers, "Flowering Absences: Recent Irish Writers and Genealogical Dead Ends," *New Approaches to Family History, Genealogy and Irish-American Studies* by Janet

Nolan and James Rogers (Ft. Lauderdale, FL: Dept. of Liberal Arts, Nova Southeastern University, 2002), 6–16.

11. Allen Grossman, *Of the Great House: A Book of Poems* (New York: New Directions, 1982), 5.

12. Gilroy, *The Black Atlantic*, 39.

13. Lawrence McCaffrey, *The Irish Diaspora in America* (Washington, DC: Catholic University Press of America, 1984), 52.

14. Toni Morrison, *Playing in the Dark: Whiteness and the Literary Imagination* (Cambridge, MA: Harvard University Press, 1992), 9.

15. Sarah Helen Whitman, "Don Isle," in *The Book of Irish American Poetry from the Eighteenth Century to the Present*, ed. Daniel Tobin (Notre Dame, IN: University of Notre Dame Press, 2007), 72.

16. Ibid.

17. Seamus Heaney, *Preoccupations* (New York: Farrar, Straus and Giroux, 1980), 20–21.

18. John Montague, *Collected Poems* (Loughcrew, Ireland: Gallery Press, 1995), 286.

19. Billy Collins, "My Grandfather's Tackle Box: The Limits of Memory-Driven Poetry," in *After Confession: Poetry as Autobiography*, ed. Kate Sontag and David Graham (St. Paul: Graywolf Press, 2001), 81.

20. Ibid., 84–85, 88.

21. Brendan Galvin, "The Contemporary Poet and the Natural World," in Sontag and Graham, *After Confession*, 199.

22. Robinson Jeffers, *The Selected Poetry of Robinson Jeffers*, ed. Tim Hunt (Stanford, CA: Stanford University Press, 2001), 686.

23. James Karman, *Robinson Jeffers: Poet of California*, rev. ed. (Brownsville, OR: Story Line Press, 1995), 6.

24. Ibid.

25. Stanley Plumly, "Autobiography and Archetype" in Sontag and Graham, *After Confession*, 104–5.

26. Thomas Lynch, *Still Life in Milford: Poems* (New York: Norton, 1998), 52.

27. Ibid., 54–55.

28. Leo Connellan, *The Clear Blue Lobster-Water Country: A Trilogy* (San Diego: Harcourt Brace Jovanovich, 1985), 141.

29. Ibid., 142.

30. Ibid.

31. Susan Donnelly, *Eve Names the Animals*, sel. Anthony Hecht, Morse Poetry Prize 1984 (Boston: Northeastern University Press, 1990), 65.

32. Mary Swander, *Succession* (Athens: University of Georgia Press, 1979), 49.

33. Ibid.

34. Kathryn Stripling Byer, *Wildwood Flower* (Baton Rouge: Louisiana State University Press, 1992), 30.

35. Michael Coady, *All Souls* (Loughcrew, Ireland: Gallery Press, 2001), 91.

36. Ibid., 89.

37. Ibid., 92.

38. Maura Stanton, *Snow on Snow,* Yale Series of Younger Poets, vol. 70 (New Haven, CT: Yale University Press, 1975), 31.

39. Ibid., 31–32.

40. Brendan Galvin, *Great Blue* (Urbana-Champaign: University of Illinois Press, 1990), 154.

41. Brendan Galvin, *Habitat: New and Selected Poems* (Baton Rouge: Louisiana State University Press, 2005), 36.

42. Brendan Galvin, *Sky and Island Light: Poems* (Baton Rouge: Louisiana State University Press, 1996), 29.

43. Gabriel Marcel, *Homo Viator* (New York: Harper & Row, 1962), 71.

44. Williams, "Poetry and History," 395.

CHAPTER TEN   From Crispus Attucks to Mr. Bones

The section of this essay entitled "Shades, Minstrel and Majestic" first appeared in *Affecting Irishness: Negotiating Cultural Identity Within and Beyond the Nation,* ed. James Byrne, Padraig Kirwan, and Michael O'Sullivan (New York: Peter Lang, 2008), 275–90.

1. Gert Van Tonder, Michael J. Lyons, and Yoshimichi Ejima, "Perception Psychology: Visual Structure of a Japanese Zen Garden," *Nature* 419 (Sept. 26, 2002): 359.

2. Toni Morrison, *Playing in the Dark: Whiteness and the Literary Imagination* (Cambridge, MA: Harvard University Press, 1992), xii.

3. Paul Gilroy, *The Black Atlantic: Modernity and Double Consciousness* (Cambridge, MA: Harvard University Press, 1993), 17.

4. Morrison, *Playing in the Dark,* 9, 36–37.

5. Matthew Frye Jacobson, *Special Sorrows: The Diasporic Imagination of Irish, Polish, and Jewish Immigrants in the United States* (Berkeley: University of California Press, 2002), 2, 170.

6. Matthew Frye Jacobson, *Whiteness of a Different Color: European Immigrants and the Alchemy of Race* (Cambridge, MA: Harvard University Press, 1998), 21.

7. Jacobson, *Special Sorrows,* 248.

8. Lawrence J. McCaffrey, *The Irish Diaspora in America* (Washington, DC: Catholic University Press, 1984), 175.

9. Jacobson, *Whiteness*, 2.

10. Luke Gibbons, *Transformations of Irish Culture*, Critical Conditions 2 (Notre Dame, IN: University of Notre Dame Press, 1996), 6.

11. Gilroy, *The Black Atlantic*, 197.

12. James Byrne, "Paddy Beyond the Pale" (lecture, Emerson College, Boston, November 14, 2008).

13. Jacobson, *Special Sorrows*, 5.

14. McCaffrey, *Diaspora*, 175.

15. See also Jacobson, *Whiteness*, 3–10, 53.

16. Gibbons, *Transformations*, 176.

17. Ibid.

18. Ibid.

19. Jacobson, *Whiteness*, 38.

20. Letter from Frederick Douglass to William Lloyd Garrison, *Liberator*, March 27, 1846, reprinted in Philip S. Foner, *Life and Writings of Frederick Douglass*, 5 vols. (New York: International Publishers, 1950), 1:138.

21. Frederick Douglass, *The Complete Autobiographies of Frederick Douglass* (Radford, VA: Wilder Publications, 2008), 254.

22. Eamonn Wall, *Dyckman 200th Street* (Cliffs of Moher, Ireland: Salmon Publishing, 1994), 34.

23. Kerby Miller, *Emigrants and Exiles: Ireland and the Irish Exodus to North America* (New York: Oxford University Press, 1984), 318.

24. Morrison, *Playing in the Dark*, 16.

25. John Boyle O'Reilly, "At Fredericksburg," in *The Book of Irish American Poetry from the Eighteenth Century to the Present*, ed. Daniel Tobin (Notre Dame, IN: University of Notre Dame Press, 2007), 42.

26. Thomas Keneally, *The Great Shame and the Triumph of the Irish in the English-Speaking World* (New York: Anchor Books, 2000), 517.

27. Ibid., 576.

28. Quoted in Keneally, *The Great Shame*, 517.

29. John Boyle O'Reilly, "Crispus Attucks," in Tobin, ed., *The Book of Irish American Poetry*, 46.

30. Morrison, *Playing in the Dark*, 63.

31. Ibid., 47.

32. Paul Laurence Dunbar, "John Boyle O'Reilly," in Tobin, ed., *The Book of Irish American Poetry*, 72.

33. McCaffrey, *The Irish Diaspora*, 112.

34. Ibid., 62.

35. Lawrence J. McCaffrey, *Textures of Irish America*, Irish Studies (Syracuse, NY: Syracuse University Press, 1994), 22.

36. Charles G. Halpine, "Sambo's Right to Be Kilt," in *The Exiles of Erin: Nineteenth-Century Irish-America Fiction,* ed. Charles Fanning, 2nd ed. (Chester Springs, PA: Dufour Editions, 1997), 147.

37. James Jeffrey Roche, *Songs and Satires* (Boston: Tinknor and Fields, 1887), 37.

38. Morrison, *Playing in the Dark,* 47.

39. Thomas Branagan, *Avenia,* in Tobin, *The Book of Irish American Poetry,* 25.

40. Noel Ignatiev, *How the Irish Became White* (New York: Routledge, 1995), 54.

41. Ibid., 55.

42. Leo Connellan, *Provincetown* (Willimantic, CT: Curbstone Press, 1995), 33.

43. Susan Donnelly, *Transit* (Oak Ridge, TN: Iris Press, 2001), 24.

44. Ibid.

45. James McManus, *Great America: Poems* (New York: HarperPerennial, 1993), 57.

46. Gwendolyn Brooks, *Selected Poems* (New York: Harper & Row, 1960), 103.

47. Lee Jenkins, "Black Murphy: Claude McKay and Ireland," *Irish University Review* 33, no. 2 (2003): 279–90.

48. Ernest Walsh, "Irish," in Tobin, *The Book of Irish American Poetry,* 113.

49. Ibid.

50. Ibid.

51. Ibid.

52. Eric Lott, *Love and Theft: Blackface Minstrelsy and the American Working Class* (New York: Oxford University Press, 1993), 92.

53. Ernest Walsh, "Poem for a Negro Voice," in Tobin, *The Book of Irish American Poetry,* 118.

54. Lott, *Love and Theft,* 117, 149.

55. Gilroy, *The Black Atlantic,* 161, 127.

56. Eamonn Wall, *From the Sin-é Café to the Black Hills* (Madison: University of Wisconsin Press, 1999), 72.

57. Morrison, *Playing in the Dark,* 66.

58. Quoted in Lott, *Love and Theft,* 25.

59. Lott, *Love and Theft,* 68, 113.

60. John Haffenden, *The Life of John Berryman* (Boston: Routledge and Keegan Paul, 1982), 11.

61. Ibid., 420–21.

62. John Berryman, *The Dream Songs* (New York: Farrar, Straus and Giroux, 1969), 3.

63. Ibid.
64. Ibid., 10.
65. Ibid., 292.
66. Ibid., 64.
67. Ibid.
68. Ibid., 72.
69. Ibid., 57.
70. John Haffenden, *John Berryman: A Critical Commentary* (New York: New York University Press, 1980), 104.
71. Berryman, *The Dream Songs*, 4.
72. Michael S. Harper, *Songlines in Michaeltree: New and Collected Poems* (Urbana: University of Illinois Press, 2000), 126.
73. Quoted in John Berryman, *Selected Poems,* ed. Kevin Young (Washington, DC: The Library of America, 2004), xxv.
74. Haffenden, *Critical Commentary*, 82.
75. Ibid., 47.
76. Lott, *Love and Theft*, 56.
77. Berryman, *The Dream Songs*, 26.
78. Ibid., 62.
79. Ibid., 237.
80. Ibid., 40.
81. Ibid., 239.
82. Ibid., 266.
83. Morrison, *Playing in the Dark*, 68.
84. Berryman, *The Dream Songs*, 239.
85. Ibid., 136 (italics in original).
86. John Montague, *The Figure in the Cave and Other Essays* (Syracuse, NY: Syracuse University Press, 1989), 205.
87. Berryman, *The Dream Songs*, 156.
88. Ibid., 224.
89. Lott, *Love and Theft*, 95.
90. Ibid., 148.
91. Ibid., 95.
92. Berryman, *The Dream Songs*, 321.
93. Ibid., 375.
94. Ibid., 337.
95. Ibid., 156.
96. See George DeForest Lord, *Trials of the Self: Heroic Ordeals in the Epic Tradition* (Hamden, CT: Archon Books, 1983).
97. Berryman, *The Dream Songs*, 301.

98. Ibid., 346.
99. Ibid., 377.
100. Ibid., 334.
101. Haffenden, *Life of John Berryman,* 88–91.
102. Berryman, *The Dream Songs,* 327.
103. Ibid., 406.
104. Ibid., 388.
105. Morrison, *Playing in the Dark,* xii–xiii.
106. Ibid., xiii.
107. Berryman, *The Dream Songs,* 391.
108. Haffenden, *The Life of John Berryman,* 420.

CHAPTER ELEVEN   Over There

1. Eamonn Wall, *From the Sin-é Café to the Black Hills* (Madison: University of Wisconsin Press, 1999), 56.
2. Patrick Ward, *Exile, Emigration, and Irish Writing* (Dublin: Irish Academic Press, 2001), 169, 135.
3. Ibid., 169.
4. Wall, *From the Sin-é Café,* 57.
5. Author's personal conversation with Chris Agee, March 2008.
6. Wall, *From the Sin-é Café,* 57.
7. Stephanie Rains, "Irish Roots: Genealogy and the Performance of Irishness," in *The Irish in Us: Irishness, Performativity, and Popular Culture,* ed. Diane Negra (Durham, NC: Duke University Press, 2006), 252.
8. Ibid., 141.
9. Ben Howard, *The Pressed Melodeon: Essays on Modern Irish Writing* (Brownsville, OR: Story Line Press, 1996), 26.
10. Ibid., 4.
11. Tony Hoagland, *Real Sofistikashun* (St. Paul: Graywolf Press, 2008), 173.
12. Howard, *The Pressed Melodeon,* 5.
13. Ben Howard, *Dark Pool* (Cliffs of Moher, Ireland: Salmon Publishing, 2004), 74.
14. Wall, *From the Sin-é Café,* 51.
15. Janice Fitzpatrick Simmons, *Starting at Purgatory* (Cliffs of Moher, Ireland: Salmon Publishing, 1999), 28.
16. Theodore Deppe, *Cape Clear: New and Selected Poems* (Cliffs of Moher, Ireland: Salmon Publishing, 2002), 37.

17. Theodore Deppe, *Children of the Air* (Cambridge, UK: Alice James Books, 1990), 29.

18. Patrick Kavanagh, *Collected Prose* (Dublin: Brian and O'Keefe, 1973), 278.

19. Seamus Heaney, *Opened Ground* (New York: Farrar, Straus and Giroux, 1998), 118.

20. Knute Skinner, *The Cold Irish Earth* (Cliffs of Moher, Ireland: Salmon Publishing, 1996), 72.

21. Ibid., 19.

22. Michael Heffernan, *Love's Answer* (Iowa City: University of Iowa Press, 1994), 32.

23. Richard Tillinghast, *A Quiet Pint in Kinvara* (Cliffs of Moher, Ireland: Salmon Publishing, 2001), 10.

24. Richard Tillinghast, *Finding Ireland: A Poet's Exploration of Irish Literature and Culture* (Notre Dame, IN: University of Notre Dame Press, 2008), 37, 47.

25. Quoted in Wall, *From the Sin-é Café*, 51.

26. Richard Kearney, *The Wake of Imagination* (Minneapolis: University of Minnesota Press, 1988), 51.

27. Jean Valentine, *Door in the Mountain: New and Collected Poems* (Middletown, CT: Wesleyan University Press, 2004), 229–30.

28. Kearney, *Wake*, 292.

29. Paul Muldoon, *Horse Latitudes* (London: Faber and Faber, 2006), 38.

30. Julie O'Callaghan, *Tell Me This Is Normal: New and Selected Poems* (Northumberland: Bloodaxe Books, 2008), 33.

31. E-mail correspondence from Julie O'Callaghan to the author, February 2009.

32. Ibid.

33. Ibid.

34. O'Callaghan, *Tell Me*, 79.

35. Ibid., 65.

36. Kearney, *Wake*, 359.

37. Richard Kearney, *Navigations* (Syracuse, NY: Syracuse University Press, 2006), 221.

38. Elmer Andrews, ed., *The Poetry of Seamus Heaney*, Columbia Critical Guides (New York: Columbia University Press, 1998), 58.

39. Chris Agee, *In the New Hampshire Woods* (Dublin: Dedalus Press, 1992), 13.

40. Ibid., 39.

41. Ibid., 51.

42. Chris Agee, *First Light* (Dublin: Dedalus Press, 2003), 31.

43. Kearney, *Wake*, 361.

44. Agee, *First Light*, 61.

45. Chris Agee, *Next to Nothing* (London: Salt, 2008), 88.

46. Ward, *Exile*, 234.

47. Ibid., 235.

48. Michael Donaghy, *The Shape of the Dance*, ed. Adam O'Riordan and Maddy Paxman (London: Picador, 2009), 141–43.

49. Ibid., 143.

50. Michael Donaghy, *Wallflowers* (Gilford, UK: The Poetry Society, 1999), 9.

51. Ibid., 7.

52. Kearney, *Navigations*, 30.

53. Coady, *All Souls*, 88.

54. Michael Donaghy, *Dances Learned Last Night* (London: Picador, 2000), 70.

55. Michael Donaghy, *Conjure* (London: Picador, 2000), 5.

56. Michael Donaghy, *Safest* (London: Picador, 2005), 28.

57. Donaghy, *Wallflowers*, 33.

58. Donaghy, *Safest*, 46.

59. Quoted in Ward, *Exile*, 17.

60. Chris Agee, ed., *The New North* (Raleigh, NC: Wake Forest University Press, 2008), xxxiv–xxxv.

CHAPTER TWELVE   Soundings and Erasures

1. Daniel Tobin, *The Narrows* (New York: Four Way Books, 2005), 88.

2. William Matthews, *Search Party: Collected Poems* (Boston: Houghton Mifflin, 2004), 222.

3. Elizabeth Alexander, "The Negro Digs Up Her Past: 'Amistad,'" *South Atlantic Quarterly* 104, no. 3 (Summer 2005): 464, 465.

4. Arthur A. Schomburg, "The Negro Digs Up His Past," in *The New Negro*, ed. Alain Locke (New York: Atheneum, 1992), 464.

5. Alexander, "The Negro Digs Up Her Past," 465.

6. Quoted in Seamus Heaney, *Preoccupations* (New York: Farrar, Straus and Giroux, 1980), 1.

7. Mary Kilfoil McDevitt, *We Hardly Knew Ye: St. Mary's Cemetery, an Enduring Presence* (St. John, NB: ICCA, St. John Branch, 1990), 105.

8. Emmanuel Lévinas, *Totality and Infinity: An Essay on Exteriority,* trans. Alphonso Lingis (Pittsburgh: Duquesne University Press, 1969), 34.

9. Ibid., 33–34.

10. Tobin, *The Narrows,* 142.

11. Louis MacNeice, *Selected Poems,* ed. Michael Longley (Winston-Salem, NC: Wake Forest University Press, 1990), 39.

12. Robert Hayden, *Collected Poems* (New York: Liveright, 1985), 48.

13. Alexander, "The Negro Digs Up Her Past," 464.

14. Ibid.

15. Schomburg, "The Negro Digs Up His Past," 231.

16. Stephanie Rains, "Irish Roots: Genealogy and the Performance of Irishness," in *The Irish in Us: Irishness, Performativity and Popular Culture,* ed. Diane Negra (Durham, NC: Duke University Press, 2006), 138.

17. Heaney, *Preoccupations,* 26.

18. See Robert Scally, "Through Liverpool: 'Vistas of Want and Woe,'" in *The Irish in America,* ed. Michael Coffey (New York: Hyperion, 1997), 21.

19. Schomburg, "The Negro Digs Up His Past," 237.

20. Tobin, *The Narrows,* 137.

21. Ibid., 48.

22. Ibid., 145.

23. Ibid., 50.

24. H. P. A. Oskamp, *The Voyage of Máel Dúin: A Study in Early Irish Voyage Literature* (Groningen: Wolters-Noordhoff, 1970), 101.

25. Hart Crane, *Complete Poems and Selected Letters* (Washington, DC: The Library of America, 2006), 73.

26. John Montague, *Collected Poems* (Loughcrew: Gallery Press, 1995), 9.

27. Ibid., 81.

28. Tobin, *The Narrows,* 7.

29. Ibid., 9.

30. Ibid., 170.

31. Ezra Pound, *The Selected Poems of Ezra Pound* (New York: New Directions, 1957), 46.

32. Tobin, *The Narrows,* 17.

33. Ibid., 56.

34. Ibid., 11.

35. Henry David Thoreau, *Walden* (Princeton, NJ: Princeton University Press, 1973), 205–6.

36. Henry David Thoreau, *Cape Cod* (New York: Penguin, 1987), 6–7.

37. Tobin, *The Narrows,* 69–70.

38. Ibid.

39. Ibid., 77.
40. Ibid., 133.
41. Ibid., 123.
42. Ibid., 16.
43. Ibid., 17.
44. McDevitt, *We Hardly Knew Ye,* 24.
45. Tobin, *The Narrows,* 172.
46. Ibid., 173.

Works Cited

Agee, Chris. *First Light*. Dublin: Dedalus Press, 2003.
———. *In the New Hampshire Woods*. Dublin: Dedalus Press, 1992.
———, ed. *The New North: Contemporary Poetry from Northern Ireland*. Winston-Salem, NC: Wake Forest University Press, 2008.
Alexander, Elizabeth. "The Negro Digs Up Her Past: 'Amistad.'" *Southern Atlantic Quarterly* 104 (Summer 2005): 464.
Andrews, Elmer, ed. *The Poetry of Seamus Heaney*. Columbia Critical Guides. New York: Columbia University Press, 1998.
Arkin, Stephen. "An Interview with John Montague: Deaths in the Summer." *New England Review*, 2nd ser., 5 (Autumn–Winter 1982): 235.
Arkins, Brian. *James Liddy: A Critical Study*. Galway: Arlen House, 2001.
Berryman, John. *The Dream Songs*. New York: Farrar, Straus and Giroux, 1969.
———. *Selected Poems*. Edited by Kevin Young. New York: Library of America, 2004.
Bhabha, Homi K. "DissemiNation: Time, Narrative, and the Margins of the Modern Nation." In Bhabha, ed., *Nation and Narration,* 291–322.
———. "Introduction: Narrating the Nation." In Bhabha, ed., *Nation and Narration,* 1–7.
———, ed. *Nation and Narration*. New York: Routledge, 1990.
Bloom, Harold. *Wallace Stevens: The Poems of Our Climate*. Ithaca, NY: Cornell University Press, 1977.
Bogan, Louise. *The Blue Estuaries*. New York: Ecco Press, 1968.
———. "The Pleasures of Formal Poetry." In *The Poet's Work: 29 Masters of 20th Century Poetry on the Origins and Practice of Their Art,* edited by Reginald Gibbons, 203–14. Boston: Houghton Mifflin, 1979.
———. *A Poet's Prose*. Athens: Ohio University Press, 2005.
Boland, Eavan. *Collected Poems*. Manchester, UK: Carcanet, 1995.
———. *Object Lessons: The Life of the Woman and the Poet in Our Time*. New York: Norton, 1995.
———. *Outside History: Selected Poems 1980–1990*. New York: Norton, 1990.
Branagan, Thomas. *Avenia: A Tragical Poem*. Philadelphia: Clime, 1810.

Brazeau, Peter. "The Irish Connection: Peter Brazeau and Thomas McGreevy." *Southern Review* (1981): 533.
Brooks, Gwendolyn. *Selected Poems*. New York: Harper & Row, 1960.
Browne, Terrence. "The Dead Kingdom: A Reading." *Irish University Review* 19 (Spring 1989): 105.
Burke, Edmund. "From 'A Philosophical Inquiry into the Origin of Our Ideas of the Sublime and the Beautiful.'" In *Critical Theory Since Plato*, edited by Hazard Adams, 299–307. New York: Wadsworth, 1983.
Byer, Katherine S. *Wildwood Flower*. Baton Rouge: Louisiana State University Press, 1992.
Byrne, James. "Paddy Beyond the Pale." Lecture, Emerson College, Boston, November 14, 2008.
Cirlot, J. E. *A Dictionary of Symbols*. Translated by Jack Sage. New York: Philosophical Library, 1962.
Coady, Michael. *All Souls*. Loughcrew, Ireland: Gallery Press, 1997.
———. *Full Tide: A Miscellany*. Nenagh, Ireland: Relay Books, 1999.
———. "A Local Habitation." *The Opened Mind*, RTE Radio Lecture, 2000.
———. *One Another*. Loughcrew, Ireland: Gallery Press, 2003.
———. "The Sea-Divided Silence." *Poetry Ireland Review* 46 (Summer 1995): 1–12.
Cohen, Arthur A. *The Tremendum: A Theological Interpretation of the Holocaust*. New York: Crossroad, 1981.
Coleridge, Samuel T. *Selected Poetry and Prose*. Edited by Donald A. Staufer. New York: Random House, 1951.
Collins, Billy. *The Art of Drowning*. Pittsburgh: Pittsburgh University Press, 1995.
———. "My Grandfather's Tackle Box: The Limits of Memory Driven Poetry." In *After Confession: Poetry as Autobiography*, edited by Kate Sontag and David Graham, 81–91. St. Paul: Graywolf Press, 2001.
Collins, Martha, ed. *Critical Essays on Louise Bogan*. Boston: G. K. Hall, 1984.
Connellan, Leo. *The Clear Blue Lobster-Water Country: A Trilogy*. San Diego: Harcourt Brace Jovanovich, 1985.
———. *Provincetown and Other Poems*. Willimantic, CT: Curbstone Press, 1995.
Crane, Hart. *Collected Poems and Prose*. Washington, DC: Library of America, 2008.
———. *The Complete Poems and Selected Letters and Prose of Hart Crane*. New York: Doubleday, 1966.
Dawe, Gerald. "Invocation of Powers." In *The Chosen Ground*, edited by Neil Corcoran, 29. Bridgend: Seren Books, 1992.
Day, Dorothy. *The Long Loneliness*. New York: Harper & Row, 1952.

Delanty, Greg. *Collected Poems 1986–2006*. Oxford Poets. Manchester, UK: Carcanet, 2006.
Deppe, Theodore. *Cape Clear: New and Selected Poems*. Salmon Poetry. Cliffs of Moher, Ireland: Salmon Publishing, 2002.
———. *Children of the Air*. Cambridge, MA: Alice James Books, 1990.
Des Pres, Terrence. "Thomas McGrath." In Gibbons and Des Pres, eds., *Thomas McGrath*, 158–92.
Donaghy, Michael. *Conjure*. London: Picador, 2000.
———. *Dances Learned Last Night*. London: Picador, 2000.
———. *Safest*. London: Picador, 2005.
———. *Wallflowers*. Gilford, UK: The Poetry Society, 1999.
Donnelly, Susan. *Eve Names the Animals*. Selected and introduced by Anthony Hecht. Morse Poetry Prize 1984. Boston: Northeastern University Press, 1990.
———. *Transit*. Oak Ridge, TN: Iris Press, 2001.
Donoghue, Denis. "Walt Whitman." In Whitman, *Leaves of Grass*, 962–71.
Douglass, Frederick. *The Complete Autobiographies of Frederick Douglass*. Radford, VA: Wilder Publications, 2008.
Dunbar, Paul Laurence. "John Boyle O'Reilly." In Tobin, ed., *The Book of Irish American Poetry*, 72.
Edwards, Robert. "Exile, Self, and Society." In *Exile in Literature*, edited by Maria Lagos-Pope, 15–31. Lewisburg, PA: Bucknell University Press, 1988.
Egan, Mary Joan. "Thomas McGreevy and Wallace Stevens: A Correspondence." *Wallace Stevens Journal* 18 (1994): 130.
"Elegiac Cheer: A Conversation with John Montague." *Literary Review* 31 (Fall 1987): 28.
Eliot, T. S. *Complete Poems and Plays*. New York: Harcourt, Brace, 1950.
———. *Selected Prose of T. S. Eliot*. Edited by Frank Kermode. New York: Harcourt, Brace, 1975.
Ellis, Havelock. "Whitman." In Whitman, *Leaves of Grass*, 803–12.
Evans, A. G. *Fanatic Heart: A Life of John Boyle O'Reilly 1844–1890*. Boston: Northeastern University Press, 1999.
Fanning, Charles, ed. *The Exiles of Erin: Nineteenth-Century Irish-American Fiction*. Second edition. Chester Springs, PA: Dufour Editions, 1997.
———. *The Irish Voice in America: Irish-American Fiction from the 1760s to the 1980s*. Lexington: University Press of Kentucky, 1990.
Fitzpatrick-Simmons, Janice. *Starting at Purgatory*. Cliffs of Moher, Ireland: Salmon Publishing, 1999.

Foner, Philip S. *Life and Writings of Frederick Douglass.* 5 volumes. New York: International Publishers, 1950.

Frank, Elizabeth. *Louise Bogan: A Portrait.* New York: Columbia University Press, 1986.

Frazier, Adrian. "John Montague's Language of the Tribe." *Canadian Journal of Irish Studies* 9, no. 2 (December 1983): 57–75.

Galvin, Brendan. "The Contemporary Poet and the Natural World." In *After Confession: Poetry as Autobiography,* edited by Kate Sontag and David Graham, 197–213. St. Paul: Graywolf Press, 2001.

———. *Great Blue.* Urbana-Champaign: University of Illinois Press, 1990.

———. *Habitat: New and Selected Poems, 1965–2005.* Baton Rouge: Louisiana State University Press, 2005.

———. *Sky and Island Light: Poems.* Baton Rouge: Louisiana State University Press, 1996.

Garratt, Robert F. "John Montague and the Poetry of History." *Irish University Review* 19 (1989): 91–102.

Gibbons, Luke. *Transformations in Irish Culture.* Critical Conditions 2. Notre Dame, IN: University of Notre Dame Press, 1996.

Gibbons, Reginald. "Preface." In Gibbons and Des Pres, eds., *Thomas McGrath,* 1–6.

Gibbons, Reginald, and Terrence Des Pres, eds. *Thomas McGrath: Life and the Poem.* Urbana-Champaign: University of Illinois Press, 1992.

Gilroy, Paul. *The Black Atlantic: Modernity and Double Consciousness.* Cambridge, MA: Harvard University Press, 1993.

"Global Regionalism: Interview with John Montague." *Literary Review* 22, no. 1 (1979): 157.

Gregory, Horace, and Marina Zaturenska. *A History of American Poetry, 1900–1940.* New York: Gordian Press, 1969.

Grossman, Allen. *Of the Great House: A Book of Poems.* New York: New Directions, 1982.

Grubgeld, Elizabeth. "Topography, Memory, and John Montague's *The Rough Field.*" *Canadian Journal of Irish Studies* 14 (1989): 26.

Haffenden, John. *John Berryman: A Critical Commentary.* New York: New York University Press, 1980.

———. *The Life of John Berryman.* Boston: Routledge and Kegan Paul, 1982.

Hamill, Sam. "Preface." In McGrath, *Letter to an Imaginary Friend,* i–iii.

Harper, Michael S. *Songlines in Michaeltree: New and Collected Poems.* Urbana: University of Illinois Press, 2000.

Hayden, Robert. *Collected Poems.* New York: Liveright, 1985.

Heaney, Seamus. *Opened Ground*. New York: Farrar, Straus and Giroux, 1998.
———. *Place and Displacement: Recent Poetry of Northern Ireland—The Pete Laver Memorial Lecture*. Cumbria: Frank Peters, 1984.
———. *Preoccupations: Selected Prose, 1968–1978*. New York: Farrar, Straus, Giroux, 1980.
———. *The Redress of Poetry*. New York: Farrar, Straus and Giroux, 1995.
Heffernan, Michael. *Love's Answer*. Iowa City: University of Iowa Press, 1994.
Hoagland, Tony. *Real Sofistikashun*. St. Paul: Graywolf Press, 2008.
Hopkins, Gerard Manley. *The Poems of Gerard Manley Hopkins*. Edited by W. H. Gardner and N. H. MacKenzie. New York: Oxford University Press, 1967.
Howard, Ben. *Dark Pool*. Cliffs of Moher, Ireland: Salmon Publishing, 2004.
———. *The Pressed Melodeon: Essays on Modern Irish Writing*. Brownsville, OR: Story Line Press, 1996.
Ignatiev, Noel. *How the Irish Became White*. New York: Routlege, 1995.
"An Interview with Thomas McGrath, January 31–February 1, 1987." In Gibbons and Des Pres, eds., *Thomas McGrath*, 38–102.
Jacobson, Dale. "Introduction." In McGrath, *Death Song*, 1–6.
Jacobson, Matthew Frye. *Special Sorrows: The Diasporic Imagination of Irish, Polish, and Jewish Immigrants in the United States*. Berkeley: University of California Press, 2002.
———. *Whiteness of a Different Color: European Immigrants and the Alchemy of Race*. Cambridge, MA: Harvard University Press, 1998.
Jeffers, Robinson. *The Selected Poetry of Robinson Jeffers*. Stanford, CA: Stanford University Press, 2001.
Jeffers, Una. *Visits to Ireland*. Los Angeles: Ward Ritchie Press, 1954.
Jenkins, Lee. "Thomas McGreevy and the Pressure of Reality." *Wallace Stevens Journal* 18 (1994): 146.
Josephson, Matthew. *Life Among the Surrealists*. New York: Holt, Rinehart, and Winston, 1962.
Karman, James. *Robinson Jeffers: Poet of California*. Revised edition. Brownsville, OR: Story Line Press, 1995.
Kavanagh, Patrick. *Collected Poems*. New York: Devin-Adair, 1964.
———. *Collected Prose*. Dublin: Brian and O'Keefe, 1973.
Kearney, Richard. *Navigations*. Syracuse, NY: Syracuse University Press, 2006.
———. *The Wake of Immigration*. Minneapolis: University of Minnesota Press, 1988.
Kendall, Tim. *Paul Muldoon*. Chester Springs, PA: Dufour Editions; Bridgend, UK: Seren Books, 1996.

Keneally, Thomas. *The Great Shame and the Triumph of the Irish in the English-Speaking World.* New York: Anchor Books, 2000.

Kiberd, Declan. *The Irish Writer and the World.* Cambridge, UK: Cambridge University Press, 2005.

Kinsella, Thomas. *The Dual Tradition: An Essay on Poetry and Politics in Ireland.* Manchester, UK: Carcanet, 1995.

Kramer, Lawrence. "A Completely New Set of Objects: The Spirit of Place in Wallace Stevens and Charles Ives." In *Critical Essays on Wallace Stevens,* edited by Steven Gould Axelrod and Helen Deese, 213–30. Critical Essays on American Literature. Boston: G. K. Hall, 1988.

LaGuardia, David M. *Advance of Chaos: The Sanctifying Imagination of Wallace Stevens.* Hanover, NH: University Press of New England, 1983.

Lévinas, Emmanuel. *Totality and Infinity: An Essay on Exteriority.* Translated by Alphonso Lingis. Pittsburgh: Duquesne University Press, 1969.

Liddy, James. *Collected Poems.* Omaha: Creighton University Press, 1994.

———. *The Doctor's House.* Galway: Arlen House, 2008.

———. *Gold Set Dancing.* Cliffs of Moher, Ireland: Salmon Publishing, 2000.

Loeb, Harold. *The Way It Was.* New York: Criterion Books, 1959.

Longenbach, James. *Wallace Stevens: The Plain Sense of Things.* New York: Oxford University Press, 1991.

Longinus. "On the Sublime." In *The Critical Tradition,* edited by David H. Richter, 78–98. New York: St. Martin's Press, 1989.

Lord, George DeForest. *Trials of the Self: Heroic Ordeals in the Epic Tradition.* Hamden, CT: Archon Books, 1983.

Lott, Eric. *Love and Theft: Blackface Minstrelsy and the American Working Class.* New York: Oxford University Press, 1993.

Lowell, Robert. *Collected Poems.* New York: Farrar, Straus and Giroux, 2003.

Lynch, Thomas. *Still Life in Milford: Poems.* New York: Norton, 1998.

MacNeice, Louis. *Selected Poems of Louis MacNeice.* Edited by Michael Longley. Winston-Salem, NC: Wake Forest University Press, 1990.

Marcel, Gabriel. *Homo Viator: Introduction to a Metaphysic of Hope.* Translated by Emma Craufurd. New York: Harper & Row, 1962.

Marten, Harry. "Memory Defying Cruelty: The Poetry of John Montague." *New England Review,* 2nd ser., 5 (1982): 255.

Matthews, William. *Search Party: Collected Poems of William Matthews.* Edited by Sebastian Matthews and Stanley Plumly. Boston: Houghton Mifflin, 2004.

McAlmon, Robert. *Being Geniuses Together, 1920–1930.* Revised and with supplementary chapters by Kay Boyle. New York: Doubleday, 1968.

McCaffrey, Lawrence J. *The Irish Diaspora in America.* Washington, DC: Catholic University of America Press, 1984.

———. *Textures of Irish America*. Irish Studies. Syracuse, NY: Syracuse University Press, 1994.
McDevitt, Mary Kilfoil. *We Hardly Knew Ye: St. Mary's Cemetery, an Enduring Presence*. St. John, NB: ICCA, St. John's Branch, 1990.
McGonigle, Thomas. "An Interview with James Liddy." *Adrift* (Spring 1983): 10–12.
McGrath, Thomas. *Death Song*. Edited by Sam Hamill. Port Townsend, WA: Copper Canyon Press, 1991.
———. *Letter to an Imaginary Friend: Parts I–IV*. Port Townsend, WA: Copper Canyon Press, 1997.
———. *Selected Poems, 1938–1988*. Edited by Sam Hamill. Port Townsend, WA: Copper Canyon Press, 1990.
———. "Statement to the House Committee on Un-American Activities." *North Dakota Quarterly* (Fall 1982).
McManus, James. *Great America: Poems*. New York: HarperPerennial, 1993.
McMichael, James. *Capacity*. New York: Farrar, Straus and Giroux, 2006.
Miller, Kerby. *Emigrants and Exiles: Ireland and the Irish Exodus to North America*. New York: Oxford University Press, 1984.
Mills, Ralph J. "Wallace Stevens: The Image of the Rock." In *Wallace Stevens: A Collection of Critical Essays,* edited by Marie Borroff, 86–110. A Spectrum Book: Twentieth Century Views. Englewood, NJ: Prentice-Hall, 1963.
Montague, John. "American Pegasus." *Studies* 48 (1959): 183.
———, ed. *The Book of Irish Verse: An Anthology of Irish Poetry from the Sixth Century to the Present*. New York: Macmillan, 1974.
———. *Born in Brooklyn: John Montague's America*. Edited by David Lampe. Fredonia, NY: White Pine Press, 1991.
———. *Collected Poems*. Loughcrew, Ireland: Gallery Press, 1995.
———. "Exile and Prophecy: A Study of Goldsmith's Poetry." In *Goldsmith, the Gentle Master,* edited by Seán Lucy, 61–77. The Thomas Davis Lectures. Cork, Ireland: Cork University Press, 1984.
———. *The Figure in the Cave and Other Essays*. Edited by Antoinette Quinn. Irish Studies. Syracuse, NY: Syracuse University Press, 1989.
———. "In the Irish Grain." In *The Figure in the Cave,* 110–26.
———. "The Unpartitioned Intellect." In *Irish Writers and Society at Large,* edited by Masaru Sekine, 163–68. Irish Literary Studies 22. Totowa, NJ: Barnes and Noble, 1985.
Moore, Marianne. "Compactness Compacted." In *Critical Essays on Louise Bogan,* edited by Martha Collins, 61–63. Boston: G. K. Hall, 1984.
———. *The Poems of Marianne Moore*. Edited by Grace Schulman. New York: Viking, 2003.

"More Questions: An Interview with Thomas McGrath, June 4, 1987." In Gibbons and Des Pres, eds., *Thomas McGrath,* 193–210.

Morrison, Toni. *Playing in the Dark: Whiteness and the Literary Imagination.* Cambridge, MA: Harvard University Press, 1992.

Muldoon, Paul. *Horse Latitudes.* London: Faber and Faber; New York; Farrar, Straus and Giroux, 2006.

O'Brien, George. "The Muse of Exile: Estrangement and Renewal in Modern Irish Literature." In *Exile in Literature,* edited by Maria Lagos-Pope, 82–101. Lewisburg, PA: Bucknell University Press, 1988.

O'Callaghan, Julie. *Tell Me This Is Normal: New and Selected Poems.* Tarset, Northumberland, UK: Bloodaxe Books, 2008.

Olson, Charles. *Collected Poems.* Berkeley: University of California Press.

O'Neill, Eugene. "The Lay of the Singer's Fall." *New London Telegraph,* November 27, 1912. http://www.poetry-archive.com/o/the_lay_of_the_singers_fall.html.

O'Reilly, John Boyle. *Selected Poems.* New York: P. J. Kennedy and Sons, 1913.

Orr, Gregory, and Ellen Bryant Voigt, eds. *Poets Teaching Poets: Self and the World.* Ann Arbor: University of Michigan Press, 1996.

Oskamp, H. P. A. *The Voyage of Máel Dúin: A Study in Early Irish Voyage Literature.* Groningen: Wolters-Noordhoff, 1970.

Pearse, Padraic. *Plays, Stories, Poems.* Dublin: Talbot Press, 1966.

Plumly, Stanley. "Autobiography and Archetype." In *After Confession: Poetry as Autobiography,* edited by Kate Sontag and David Graham, 104–13. St. Paul: Graywolf Press, 2001.

Poger, Sidney B. "Crane and Montague: The Pattern History Weaves." *Eire-Ireland* 16, no. 4 (Winter 1981): 114–24.

Porter, Katherine Anne. *The Never-Ending Wrong.* Boston: Little, Brown, 1977.

Pound, Ezra. *Selected Poems.* New edition. New York: J. Laughlin, 1957.

Quartermain, Peter. "Lola Ridge." In *The Dictionary of Literary Biography,* vol. 54, 354–58. Detroit: Gale, 1986.

Rains, Stephanie. "Irish Roots: Genealogy and the Performance of Irishness." In *The Irish in Us: Irishness, Performativity and Popular Culture,* edited by Diane Negra, 131–60. Durham, NC: Duke University Press, 2006.

Redshaw, Thomas D. "Appreciation." *Eire-Ireland* 11 (1976): 124.

———. "The Bounding Line: John Montague's *The New Siege.*" *Canadian Journal of Irish Studies* 13 (1987): 82.

———. "Location as Vocation: John Montague's 'The Northern Gate.'" *Canadian Journal of Irish Studies* 5 (1972): 46.

———. "Longing for Home: Two Motifs in *The Rough Field.*" *Études irlandaises* 6 (December 1981): 73–86.

———. "That Surviving Sign: John Montague's *The Bread God* (1968)." *Eire-Ireland* 17 (Summer 1982): 80.
Rexroth, Kenneth. "Walt Whitman." In Whitman, *Leaves of Grass,* 976–78.
Ridge, Lola. *Dance of Fire.* New York: Harrison Smith and Robert Haas, 1933.
———. *Firehead.* New York: Payson and Clarke, 1929.
———. "The Georgians at Home." *New Republic* 17 (Jan. 11, 1919): 29–31.
———. *The Ghetto and Other Poems.* New York: W. B. Huebsch, 1918.
———. "Kreymborg's Marionettes." *Dial* 66 (Jan. 11, 1919): 29–31.
———. *Red Flag.* New York: Viking, 1927.
———. "Salt Water." *New Masses* (1927): 27.
———. *Sun-Up and Other Poems.* New York: W. B. Huebsch, 1952.
Robbins, Bruce. "Homelessness and Worldliness." *Diacritics* 13 (Fall 1983): 69.
Roche, James Jeffrey. *Songs and Satires.* Boston: Tinknor and Fields, 1887.
Roethke, Theodore. "The Poetry of Louise Bogan." In *On the Poet and His Craft: Selected Prose,* edited by Ralph J. Mills Jr., 133–48. Seattle: University of Washington Press, 1965.
Rossi, Mario. *Pilgrimage in the West.* Translated by J. M. Hone. Dublin: Cuala Press, 1933.
Roy, Anindyo. "Postcoloniality and the Politics of Identity in the Diaspora: Figuring 'Home,' Locating Histories." In *Postcolonial Discourse and Changing Cultural Contexts: Theory and Criticism,* edited by Gita Rajan and Radhika Mohanram, 101–16. Westport, CT: Greenwood Press, 1995.
Ryan, Michael. "Poetry and the Audience." In Orr and Voigt, eds., *Poets Teaching Poets,* 159–81.
Said, Edward W. *Culture and Imperialism.* New York: Knopf, 1993.
———. "Reflections on Exile." In *Out There: Marginalization and Contemporary Cultures,* edited by Russell Ferguson, Martha Gever, Trinh T. Minh-ha, and Cornel West, 357–66. Documentary Sources in Contemporary Art, vol. 4. New York: New Museum of Contemporary Art; Cambridge, MA: MIT Press, 1990.
Scally, Robert. "Through Liverpool: 'Vistas of Want and Woe.'" In *The Irish in America,* edited by Michael Coffey, 18–26. New York: Hyperion, 1997.
Schmidt, Elizabeth. "Where Poetry Begins: Eavan Boland in Conversation." *American Poet* (Spring 1997). http://www.poets.org/viewmedia.php/prmMID/15939.
Schomburg, Arthur A. "The Negro Digs Up His Past." In *The New Negro,* edited by Alain Locke, 464–65. New York: Atheneum, 1992.
Shapiro, Alan. *After the Digging.* Chicago: University of Chicago Press, 1981.
Shapiro, Karl. "The First White Aboriginal." In Whitman, *Leaves of Grass,* 941–52.

Skinner, Knute. *The Cold Irish Earth*. Cliffs of Moher, Ireland: Salmon Publishing, 1996.

Stanton, Maura. *Snow on Snow*. Yale Series of Younger Poets, vol. 70. New Haven, CT: Yale University Press, 1975.

Stevens, Wallace. *The Collected Poems of Wallace Stevens*. New York: Knopf, 1954.

———. *Letters of Wallace Stevens*. Edited by Holly Stevens. New York: Knopf, 1966.

———. *The Necessary Angel*. New York: Random House, 1951.

———. *Opus Posthumous*. Edited by Milton J. Bates. Revised, enlarged, and corrected edition. New York: Knopf, 1989.

Swander, Martha. *Succession*. Athens: University of Georgia Press, 1979.

"Thomas McGrath (1916–1990): Biography." Poetry Foundation, n.d. http://www.poetryfoundation.org/bio/thomas-mcgrath.

Thompson, E. P. "Homage to Thomas McGrath." In Gibbons and Des Pres, eds., *Thomas McGrath,* 106–57.

Thoreau, Henry David. *Cape Cod*. New York: Penguin, 1987.

———. *Walden*. Princeton, NJ: Princeton University Press, 1973.

Tillich, Paul. *Dynamics of Faith*. New York: Harper, 1957.

Tillinghast, Richard. *Finding Ireland: A Poet's Explorations of Irish Literature and Culture*. Notre Dame, IN: University of Notre Dame Press, 2008.

———. *A Quiet Pint in Kinvara*. Cliffs of Moher, Ireland: Salmon Publishing, 2001.

Tobin, Daniel, ed. *The Book of Irish American Poetry: From the Eighteenth Century to the Present*. Notre Dame, IN: University of Notre Dame Press, 2007.

———. *The Narrows: Poems*. New York: Four Way Books, 2005.

Tonder, Gert Van, Michael J. Lyons, and Yoshimichi Ejima. "Perception Psychology: Visual Structure of a Japanese Zen Garden." *Nature* 419 (Sept. 26, 2002): 359–60.

Valentine, Jean. *Door in the Mountain: New and Collected Poems*. Middletown, CT: Wesleyan University Press, 2004.

Wall, Eamonn. *The Crosses*. Cliffs of Moher, Ireland: Salmon Publishing, 2000.

———. *Dyckman 200th Street*. Cliffs of Moher, Ireland: Salmon Publishing, 1994.

———. "Exile, Attitude, and the Sin-é Café: Notes on the New Irish." *Eire-Ireland* 30 (Fall 1996): 11.

———. *From the Sin-é Café to the Black Hills: Notes on the New Irish*. Madison: University of Wisconsin Press, 1999.

———. *Iron Mountain Road*. Cliffs of Moher, Ireland: Salmon Publishing, 1997.

———. "James Liddy: Editor and Poet." *An Sionnach* 1, no. 1 (Spring 2005): 37.

———. *Refuge at DeSoto Bend*. Cliffs of Moher, Ireland: Salmon Publishing, 2004.

———. *A Tour of Your Country*. Cliffs of Moher, Ireland: Salmon Publishing, 2008.

Walsh, Ernest. *Poems and Sonnets*. New York: Harcourt, Brace, 1934.

Ward, Patrick. *Exile, Emigration, and Irish Writing*. Dublin: Irish Academic Press, 2002.

Weatherhead, A. K. "John Montague: Exiled from Order." *Concerning Poetry* 14 (1982): 42.

Weil, Simone. *The Need for Roots: Prelude to a Declaration of Duties towards Mankind*. Translated by A. F. Wills. London: Ark, 1987.

———. *The Simone Weil Reader*. Edited by George Panikas. New York: David McKay, 1977.

Weiskel, Thomas. *The Romantic Sublime*. Baltimore: Johns Hopkins University Press, 1976.

Whitman, Walt. *Leaves of Grass: Authoritative Texts, Prefaces, Whitman on His Art, Criticism*. Edited by Sculley Bradley and Harold W. Blodgett. New York: Norton, 1973.

———. *Poetry and Prose*. Edited by Louis Untermeyer. Inner Sanctum edition. New York: Simon and Schuster, 1949.

Williams, C. K. "Poetry and History." In *Conversant Essays: Contemporary Poets on Poetry*, edited by James McCorkle, 388–98. Detroit: Wayne State University Press, 1990.

Williams, William Carlos. *The Autobiography of William Carlos Williams*. New York: New Directions, 1951.

Yeats, W. B. *The Collected Poems of W. B. Yeats: A New Edition*. Edited by Richard J. Finneran. London: Macmillan, 1983.

———. *Essays and Introductions*. New York: Macmillan, 1961.

———. *The Poems*. Edited by Richard J. Finneran. New edition. New York: Macmillan, 1983.

———. *A Vision*. New York: Macmillan, 1966.

Index

Adrift, 136
Aer Lingus, 332
African Americans
   Berryman depiction of, 307–21
   Branagan depiction of, 294–95
   Irish American relationship to, 259, 281–82, 287, 288, 300
   Irish experience compared to, 259, 283–85, 286, 382
   Irish racism against, 282, 293–94, 296
   Moore depiction of, 286
   music of, 296–99, 301
   O'Reilly depiction of, 287–92
   poetry of, 256, 258
   and slavery, 256, 258, 280, 282, 284, 294–95
   Stevens depiction of, 95
   Walsh depiction of, 301–5
Agee, Chris, 50, 328, 329, 347–52
   "The Black Kesh," 349
   First Light, 350–51
   "High Summer," 348
   In the New Hampshire Woods, 347–48
   "Mass Grave, Padalista," 350
   The New North introduction, 360
   Next to Nothing, 351–52
   "Occam's Rime," 350
   "Offing," 351
   "Sea-Campion," 351–52
   "The Sierra de Zacatecas," 351
   "Trim's Pond," 348–49
Alexander, Elizabeth
   "Amistad," 381
   "The Negro Digs Up Her Past: 'Amistad,'" 373
Allingham, William, 6
"The Alphabet Calendar of Amergin," 175, 358
Amergin, 184, 230
Amistad, 373
Ammons, A. R., 40
Anderson, Maxwell, 222
Andrews, Elmer, 347
anti-Irish prejudice, 221–22, 284, 293
anti-Semitism, 72, 286
apokatastasis, 399
Arena, 137
Arkins, Brian, 139
Ashbery, John, 20, 161, 326–27
   "Self Portrait in a Convex Mirror," 390, 391
assimilation, 19, 20, 38, 98, 281, 283
   Kinsella on, 23, 34
Attucks, Crispus, 289–90
Auden, W. H., 229, 231, 396

Barry, Kevin, 63
baseball, 20, 51, 189
Baudelaire, Charles
   Les Fleurs du Mal, 144

Beat generation, 138, 148, 154
Beckett, Samuel, 11, 134
Benet, Stephen Vincent, 83
Benet, William Rose, 83
Berkman, Alexander, 85
Berryman, John, 132, 387
　on immigrant crossings, 50, 328
　on sexuality, 308–9, 315, 318–19
　suicide of, 320, 321
　works
　—*The Dream Songs,* 50, 108, 269, 307–21, 328
Bhabha, Homi, 121
Billings, Warren K., 85
bird motif, 131
Bishop, Elizabeth, 230, 346
　"Filling Station," 202
blackface, 303–6
　Berryman on, 307, 310–11, 312–13, 315, 320, 321
Blackwood, Lady Caroline, 328
Blake, William
　"Proverbs of Hell," 143–44
Bloom, Harold, 88, 90, 93, 102, 227, 387
Bogan, Louise, 219–32
　biographical information, 219–21
　formal poetry of, 228–29, 235
　McGrath compared to, 240, 243–44
　and women's poetry, 230–31, 232
　works
　—*The Blue Estuaries, Poems 1923–1968,* 231
　—*Body of This Death,* 223
　—"Cassandra," 225
　—"The Greatest Poet Writing in English Today," 226
　—"Hypocrite Swift," 228
　—"Medusa," 223–24
　—"The Pleasures of Formal Poetry," 228–29
　—*Poems and New Poems,* 231
　—"The Sleeping Fury," 224–25
　—"Stanza," 227–28
　—"Train Tune," 229–30
Boland, Eavan, 162, 197, 230–31, 327, 332, 394
　as feminist, 230
　on genealogy, 257, 258
　works
　—"The Emigrant Irish," 21, 215
　—"Famine Road," 27
　—*Object Lessons,* 230, 257
Bolger, Dermot, 21
Borges, Jorge Luis
　"Funes the Memorius," 356
Boston, Mass., 1–2, 5, 282
Boston Pilot, 288, 294
Bourke, Eva, 23
Boyle, Kay, 61, 86, 222
　and Ridge, 62, 64–66, 65
　works
　—*Being Geniuses Together,* 66
Branagan, Thomas, 305
　Avenia, 294–95, 296
Brazeau, Peter, 95
Bronte, Emily, 162
Brooks, Gwendolyn
　"Bronzeville Woman in a Red Hat," 299–300
Broom, 65–66, 68, 75
The Brother from Another Planet, 389
Browne, Terrence, 126
Burke, Edmund, 153
Burke, Kenneth, 65, 78
Byer, Kathryn Stripling
　"Lineage," 270, 271–72
Byrne, James, 15, 283
Byron, Lord
　"Manfred," 149

Carnevali, Emanuel, 67
Carson, Ciaran, 216
Catholic Worker, 78, 86
Cavanagh, David, 189
Celtic Tiger, 14, 327, 339–40
Celtic Women, 328
Children of Chernobyl, 193
Church, Barbara, 96, 97
Church, Henry, 92
Civil Rights Movement, 300
Clarke, Austin, 318
Clifton, Lucille, 162
Close Encounters of the Third Kind, 367
Coady, Michael, 199–216, 355
   on genealogy and imagination, 213–14, 272–73
   journey trope in, 202–3, 204
   on parochial and provincial, 203, 209
   on religion, 201–2, 208–9
   works
   —"All Souls," 202–4
   —"Assembling the Parts," 210
   —"The Blind Arch," 201
   —"Checkpoint," 206–7, 209
   —"Epic," 211
   —"Extra-Corporeal Circulation," 209
   —"Five Airs from an Older Music," 209
   —*Full Tide: A Miscellany,* 199, 206, 208, 211
   —"The Gift of Tongues," 209–10
   —"Home Abroad," 211
   —"The Letter," 22, 212–13, 215, 272
   —"A Local Habitation," 200, 212
   —"Munster Aisling," 215
   —"Nightdress," 205
   —*One Another,* 199, 206, 208, 209–10, 215
   —"One Another," 204–5
   —"On the Record," 210, 211
   —*Oven Lane,* 199, 212
   —"Recycling the Universe," 208–9
   —"The Sea-Divided Silence," 22, 212
   —"The Things They Say," 209
   —"Three Men Standing at the Met," 210
   —*Two for a Woman, Three for a Man,* 199
   —"The Use of Memory," 22, 211, 212, 213–15, 272–73
Cobh Heritage Center, 183
Coffey, Brian, 11, 17, 326
   "Missouri Sequence," 12, 14, 21, 33
   "Nightfall, Midwinter, Missouri," 12–13
Cohan, George M., 325
Cohen, Arthur, 30
Coleridge, Samuel Taylor, 150
Collins, Billy, 254, 266
   "My Grandfather's Tackle Box," 262–63, 273
   "Some Final Words," 251
Coltrane, John, 297
Colum, Padraic, 17, 222, 230, 326
   "A Rann of Exile," 11–12
Connellan, Leo, 305
   The Clear Blue Lobster-Water Country, 267–68, 269–70
   "Jazz," 296–97, 301
Cooke, Barrie, 341
Cowley, Malcolm, 65–66, 78
Crane, Hart, 39, 66, 77, 137, 148, 206
   and Ridge, 78, 79, 81, 82
   Wall on, 167
   works
   —*The Bridge,* 85, 369–70, 388
   —review of *The Ghetto,* 79

Cronin, Anthony, 137
Croppy Boys, 49
Crosby, Bing, 304

Dadists, 62
Dante Alighieri, 72, 112, 257, 317
Dario, Ruben, 238, 239
Davis, Miles, 296–97
Davis, Thomas, 6
Dawe, Gerald, 115
Day, Dorothy, 78, 79, 83, 86
death motif
  in Berryman, 309, 317, 318
  in Connellan, 269
  in Jeffers, 46, 267
  in Liddy, 145–46, 151, 155
  in Stevens, 108, 109
  in Whitman, 139, 146
Delanty, Greg, 177–95, 327
  biographical information, 178
  dual literary inheritance of, 178–79, 195
  emigrant motif in, 17–20, 183, 191–92, 194–95
  as New Irish poet, 160, 178, 183, 194–95, 215
  Wall compared, 20, 183–84, 186
  works
  —"According to the Nepalese," 192–93
  —"Aceldama," 193–94
  —"The Alien," 191–92
  —"America," 17–19, 182
  —*American Wake,* 181–84
  —"The Arrival," 192
  —"Bad Impression," 187
  —"Behold the Brahmany Kite," 190–91
  —*The Blind Stitch,* 188–91
  —"The Blind Stitch," 190
  —"The Broken Type," 185
  —*Cast in the Fire,* 178
  —"The Children of Lir," 185
  —"The Coronation," 192
  —"The Emigrant's Apology," 179–80
  —"Epistle from a Room in Winston-Salem, North Carolina," 180
  —"The Fable of Swans," 180
  —"The Fifth Province," 181–82
  —"The God of Drymouths," 192
  —"The Hellbox," 187–88
  —*The Hellbox,* 185–88, 189
  —"The Heritage Center, Cobh 1993," 28, 182, 183
  —"Homage to the God of Pollution in Brooklyn," 190
  —"Home from Home," 181
  —"In the Land of the Eagle," 183–84
  —"Leavetaking," 179
  —"Ligature," 186
  —"The Lost Way," 187
  —"The Loudest Sound," 180
  —"The Master Printer," 181
  —"The Memory Quilt," 189, 190
  —"Nightmare," 180–81, 182
  —"Observation by a Pond at Dusk in Gainesville, Florida," 180
  —"On the Renovation of Ellis Island," 182–83
  —"The Printer's Devil," 185
  —*The Ship of Birth,* 188, 191–94
  —"The Shrinking World," 184
  —*Southward,* 178
  —"The Speakeasy Oath," 189, 190
  —"The Splinters," 184–85
  —"Striped Ink," 187

—"Tagging the Stealer," 20, 189
—"To My Mother, Eileen," 190
—"Tracks of the Ancestors," 184
—"We Will Not Play the Harp Backward Now, No," 19, 185–86
—"The Yank," 183
de Paor, Louis, 184
Deppe, Theodore, 343
   "The Gatekeeper," 336
   "Midsummer's Night, Cape Clear," 335
Des Pres, Terrence, 234, 241
Devlin, Denis, 134
Dickey, William, 161
Dickinson, Emily, 177, 220, 243, 244, 387
displacement, 36, 283, 331
   Coady on, 204
   Galvin on, 52, 53–54, 204
   Heaney on, 35, 39
   Kavanagh on, 198
   Montague on, 123, 204
   Moore on, 37, 38
Donaghy, Michael, 50, 328, 347, 353–60
   "Calliban's Books," 358
   "City of God," 356, 357
   "The Classics," 357
   Conjure, 358
   Errata, 356–57
   "Exile's End," 359–60
   "The Hunter's Purse," 357
   "Irish Folk Music," 358
   "Machines," 356
   "A Repertoire," 357
   "A Reprieve," 357, 358
   Safest, 358
   Shibboleth, 356
   Wallflowers, 354–55, 359

Donnelly, Susan, 305
   "The Gospel Singer Testifies," 297–98, 303–4, 350
   "The House of My Birth," 270, 271
Donoghue, Denis, 148
Dos Passos, John, 61, 66
double consciousness and vision, 333
   in Berryman, 307, 311, 313–15, 317, 318, 319
   in Delanty, 17, 192
   in Kinsella, 9, 10–11, 16, 21, 23, 114, 203
   in Montague, 114, 115, 123, 130, 132, 135
   in O'Callaghan, 345
   in Stevens, 102, 105
   in Wall, 15–16, 168, 305
   in Walsh, 305
Douglass, Frederick, 284–85, 382
Dove, Rita
   Thomas and Beulah, 256–57
Draft Riots (1863), 282, 293
Drew, Hardy
   "No One as Irish as Barack OBama," 158–59, 160
Drogheda Arms, 3
Dublin, 33, 137, 161
   Bogan on, 222–23, 224
   Stevens on, 96–97
   U.S. simulacra of, 16, 117, 138
Du Bois, W. E. B., 305
Dunbar, Paul Lawrence, 291–92, 293

East and West, 88
Easter Rising, 63, 64
Edwards, Jonathan, 256
Edwards, Robert
   "Exile, Self and Society," 123–24
Egan, Mary Joan, 97

Eliot, T. S., 62, 72, 327, 373
   on tradition and modernity, 24–26, 67, 68
   works
   —"Burnt Norton," 211
   —"Four Quartets," 175
   —"Gerontion," 73
   —"The Love Song of J. Alfred Prufrock," 71
   —*The Waste Land,* 68, 72
Ellis Island, 183
Ellison, Ralph, 306, 310
   Invisible Man, 287
Emerson, Ralph Waldo, 5, 280, 284
emigration and exile, 10, 21–22, 55, 330
   and assimilation, 19, 20, 23, 24, 281, 283
   as Berryman theme, 317–18
   as Coady theme, 22, 212, 214–15, 272–73
   as Coffey theme, 14, 21
   as Colum theme, 11–12
   as Delanty theme, 17–20, 183, 191–92, 194–95
   and Great Famine, 39, 211, 258–59
   of Irish artists and writers, 326–27
   Irish compared to other groups, 259, 283–85, 286, 382
   as Jeffers theme, 263–66, 269–70
   as Montague theme, 21, 97, 117, 118, 128, 134
   New Irish, 160, 161–62, 173, 177, 286
   and nostalgia, 34–35, 116, 117, 167, 346
   as O'Reilly theme, 7–8, 22, 291
   reasons for emigrating, 160, 325
   reverse emigration, 317–18, 328, 330, 343
   Said on, 6, 55, 118, 130, 360
   as Stevens theme, 96–98, 105–6
   view in Ireland of, 11, 328
   as Wall theme, 15–17, 171–72, 192, 285–86
   as Ward theme, 11, 13, 352–53
Enniscorthy, 49, 168, 170, 173
Evans, A. G.
   Fanatic Heart, 3, 4, 5
feminism, 230
Ferguson, Samuel, 6
The Field Day Anthology of Irish Writing, 21–22
Ford, John, 331
Frank, Elizabeth, 220, 222, 226
Freud, Sigmund, 121, 122, 223
Friedrich, Caspar David, 148, 149
Frost, Robert, 134, 327
Funge, Paul, 137, 161
futurism, 68, 69, 339

Gallagher, Tess, 328
Galvin, Brendan, 263
   sense of place in, 50–54, 275–77
   works
   —"Against Genealogy," 277
   —"Blackthorn and Ash," 53
   —"Dogs of Truro," 54
   —"Donegal," 52–53
   —"1847," 29–30, 382
   —"The Gang from Ballyloskey," 275, 276
   —"Hearing Irish Spoken," 50–52
   —"Inventing Ballygalvin," 275–76
   —*Saints in Their Ox-Hide Boat,* 50
   —*Wampanoag Traveler,* 50
Gangs of New York, 370–71, 377
Gardner, John, 182
Garratt, Robert, 114

Garrison, William Lloyd, 284
Gerald, Earl, 19, 38–39, 186
Gibbons, Luke, 283
   Transformations in Irish Culture, 108
Gibbons, Reginald, 233, 234, 236
Gilroy, Paul, 105, 258, 283, 305
   The Black Atlantic, 24, 253, 280
Ginsberg, Allen, 20, 137, 154, 326
Gogarty, Oliver St. John, 326
Goldman, Emma, 61, 85
Goldsmith, Oliver
   "The Deserted Village," 133
Gorey Arts Centre and Festival, 137–38, 161
Great Famine, 27–33, 385
   and Irish diaspora, 27, 39, 211, 258–59, 283
Gregory, Horace, 63, 64, 82–83, 86
Gregory of Nyssa, 399
Grennan, Eamon, 20, 21, 327
Grossman, Allen
   "Of the Great House," 258
Grubgeld, Elizabeth, 114
Guiney, Louise Imogen, 5, 47–48, 49–50, 51, 229, 296
   "Gloucester Harbor," 48
   "In Leinster," 47–48
Gurr, Andrew, 12

Haffenden, John, 311, 321
Haicead, Padraigin
   "The Emigrant's Love for Ireland," 21
Hall, Donald
   "The Impossible Marriage," 243
Halpine, Charles G.
   "Sambo's Right to Be Kilt," 293–94
Hardwick, Elizabeth, 328
Harlem Renaissance, 300

Harper, Michael S.
   "Tongue-Tied in Black and White," 310
Hartnett, Michael, 137, 203
Hawthorne, Nathaniel, 256
Hayden, Robert, 301
   "Beginnings," 256
   "Elegies for Paradise Alley," 386
   "Middle Passage," 295, 381
Heaney, Seamus, 162, 327, 340, 348
   and Delanty, 180, 187
   on home and homecoming, 347, 393
   Kearney on, 346–47
   sense of place in, 34, 35–36, 44, 115, 250, 261
   works
   —"At a Potato Digging," 27–28
   —"Exposure," 39
   —"For the Commander of the 'Eliza,'" 27, 29
   —"Mossbawn," 260
   —*North,* 102, 336
   —"Place and Displacement," 35–36
   —*Preoccupations,* 374, 384
   —"Requiem for the Croppies," 49
   —"The Sense of Place," 44, 48, 115, 393
   —"Station Island," 204
   —"The Tollund Man," 336
Heffernan, Michael, 50, 337, 343
   "A Highway Brook in Dingle," 338
Hendrix, Jimi, 298
heritage, 126, 193, 219, 226
   Bogan on, 222, 227–28, 229, 232, 244
   dual, 134, 230, 231, 243–44, 307
   McGrath on, 233, 234, 239, 241, 242, 244

heritage (cont.)
   Montague on, 44, 114, 115
   See also double consciousness and vision; Irishness
Hirsch, Edward
   "Ancient Signs," 258
   "Fever," 258
historical poems, 176, 372, 376, 377–78, 381, 394
Hoagland, Tony, 333
Holiday Inn, 304
Holmes, Oliver Wendell, 5
home motif, 10–20, 335–36, 341
   in Agee, 351
   in Daedalus, 353
   in Delanty, 19, 181, 185
   in Heaney, 347
   in Montague, 115–16, 121–23, 125, 126, 128–29, 262
   in O'Callaghan, 345–46
   in Wall, 172–73
Homer, 317
Hopkins, Gerard Manley
   "As Kingfishers Catch Fire," 75
House Un-American Activities Committee (HUAC), 237
Howard, Ben
   "The Holy Alls," 333–34
   The Pressed Melodeon, 332–33
Howells, William Dean, 5
Hugo, Richard, 110
Hugo, Victor, 397
Human Genome Project, 253
humanism, 92, 93, 95
Humphries, Rolfe, 232
Hurt, John, 314

Ignatiev, Noel
   How the Irish Became White, 259, 295
individualism, 108, 131

Ireland
   and American commodification, 342
   as Celtic Tiger, 14, 327, 339–40
   cultural space of, 360
   as divided nation, 129–30
   reasons for emigrating from, 160, 325
   Rebellion of 1798, 49
   reverse emigration to, 317–18, 328
   romanticization of, 329, 332
   traveling tradition in, 24
   U.S. artists and writers in, 327–29
   See also double consciousness and vision; emigration and exile
Irish Famine. *See* Great Famine
Irish language, 9, 10, 52, 203, 209–10
Irishness, 11, 13, 33, 331
   and assimilation, 23
   Berryman on, 314–15
   Bogan on, 221–22
   Coffey on, 15
   Galvin on, 53–54
   McGrath on, 233, 240–41
   Moore on, 39
   and national origin, 340–41, 343
   Stevens on, 87, 90, 94, 98, 104, 112
   Walsh on, 301–2, 325
Irish Pages, 347
irony, 182, 211, 225, 251–52, 263, 294, 384

Jacobson, Dale, 237–38
Jacobson, Matthew Frye, 283, 284
   Special Sorrows, 281
   Whiteness of a Different Color, 281
Jarrell, Randall, 315
jazz, 296–97, 301
Jeffers, Robinson, 39–47, 235
   biographical information, 40–41

on genealogical imagination,
  263–66, 269–70
Irish identity of, 37, 47, 296, 328
journey motif in, 44, 266
Ridge on, 65, 85–86
sense of place in, 40, 49–50
works
—"Antrim," 42, 47
—"At Ossian's Grave," 44–45, 47
—"The Broadstone," 45
—"Carmel Point," 43, 44
—*Descent to the Dead,* 42
—"Patronymic," 263–66, 269–70
—preface to *Visits to Ireland,* 41
—"Shane O'Neill's Cairn," 45–46
—"Tor House," 40
Jeffers, Una, 41, 42, 46
Jews, 286
  genocide against, 211, 258
Josephson, Matthew, 67, 68, 75,
  76, 77
  Life Among the Surrealists, 66
journey motif, 388
  in Berryman, 316–17
  in Coady, 202, 204
  in Donaghy, 358
  in Jeffers, 44
  in Montague, 121–22
  in Stevens, 91, 95
  See also emigration and exile
Joyce, James, 11, 34, 134, 318
  "The Dead," 202, 265–66
Jung, Carl, 35, 223

Karman, John, 41
Kavanagh, Patrick, 197–99, 340, 374
  on American parish, 54–55, 198,
    216, 336
  influence on Irish American poets,
    137, 179, 180, 197, 198, 200, 318

on parochial and provincial, 33,
    134, 197
works
—"The Great Hunger," 27,
    268–69
—"The Hospital," 198, 199, 202
—"In Memory of My Mother,"
    179
—*A Soul for Sale,* 198
Kavanagh's Weekly, 137
Kearney, Richard, 10, 340, 342
  on tradition, 24–25, 355
works
—"Heaney and Homecoming,"
    346–47
—*Navigations,* 20
—*The Wake of Imagination,* 341
Keats, John, 150, 153
Kendall, Tim, 243
Keneally, Thomas
  The Great Shame, 288–89
Kerouac, Jack, 137, 138, 154
Kerrigan, Anthony, 137
Kiberd, Declan, 6–7, 9, 10, 11, 24
King, Martin Luther, Jr., 300
Kinnell, Galway
  "The Avenue Bearing the Initial of
    Christ into the New World," 81
Kinsella, Thomas, 10, 34, 37, 162
  and dual tradition, 8–9, 11, 55,
    114, 123, 203
  on Irish language and tradition, 6,
    8, 9
works
—"The Divided Mind," 9–10
—*The Dual Tradition,* 8–9
—"The Good Fight," 326
—"Nightwalker," 204
—*Oxford Anthology of Irish Verse,* 22
Kirwan, Larry, 161–62

Kramer, Lawrence, 98
Kreymborg, Alfred, 61, 65, 70

Lady Gregory, 95
Larkin, James, 63
Lawrence, D. H., 137, 145, 148
Lawson, David, 66
Ledwidge, Francis, 64
Lennon, John, 165
Lévinas, Emmanuel, 73, 378
Liddy, James, 136–57, 161, 215, 242
  biographical information, 20, 140, 146
  poetic influences on, 140–41, 326–27
  on sex and sexuality, 141–46
  sublime in, 150–54, 156
  works
  —"The Apparitions," 155
  —"Art Is Not for Grown-Ups," 147, 148, 155
  —*Baudelaire's Bar Flowers,* 144, 145–46
  —"Cantico," 139, 146
  —"Casey's Light," 155–56
  —"Coolgreany," 150–51
  —*Corca Bascinn,* 143
  —"Dear Anima, Show These Words," 144
  —"Delphine and Hippolyta," 145
  —*The Doctor's House,* 138
  —"Epithalamion," 141–42, 153
  —"For Jeff, 1978," 156
  —*Gold Set Dancing,* 152, 154–55, 156
  —"Gold Set Dancing," 157
  —"In a Blue Smoke," 146
  —"Katherine Young," 143
  —"A Keening," 156
  —"Last Light in Clare's Mind," 147
  —"Mac Liammoir's Moonlight Is Mine," 155
  —"My Neighbor's Two Brothers," 142–43
  —"Omos do Seán Ó Ríordáin," 155
  —"Our Party Art on Earth," 152–53
  —"Personal Odyssey," 140, 141
  —"Poem for My Sister Nora, at the Reading," 141
  —"Prayer of a Pagan," 144–45
  —"The Sea Is Great," 156
  —"Sitting on a Waterbed at Knute's and Edna's," 154
  —"The Sound of a Moment at Scariff," 151–52
  —"To the Memory of Sylvia Plath: A Personal Note," 144
  —"Tribal City," 155
  —"Venice Poem for Nora's and Tom's Return," 156
  —"Voyage to Cytherea," 144
  —"A White Thought in a White Shade," 152
Limmer, Ruth, 230, 232
Loeb, Harold, 61, 65, 66, 67, 68, 75
Longfellow, Henry Wadsworth, 5
Longley, Michael, 197, 348
Lord, George DeForest, 317
loss, 118, 379
  Coady on, 204–5, 210–11
  Donaghy on, 356
  Guiney on, 48
  Montague on, 127, 128
  O'Callaghan on, 346
  O'Reilly on, 7–8
  Stanton on, 275
  Wall on, 15, 176

Lott, Eric
  Love and Theft, 303–4, 306, 311, 313, 315
Lowell, Amy, 254
Lowell, James Russell, 254
Lowell, Robert, 77, 132, 150, 387
  genealogical sense in, 254–55, 256
  works
  —*Day by Day,* 328
  —"Epilogue," 376
  —*For the Union Dead,* 382
  —"The Mouth of the Hudson," 383
Loy, Mina, 66
Luxemburg, Rosa, 85
Lynch, Thomas, 50, 328, 337
  "The Moveen Notebook," 266–67, 269–70
lynching, 309–10, 318

MacGreevy, Thomas
  Stevens and, 95–96, 98–102, 103, 108, 254
  works
  —"Homage to Hieronymous Bosch," 98
  —"Recessional," 98, 100
MacNeice, Louis, 184, 354
  "The Hebrides," 43–44, 380–81, 385
  "Last Before America," 22
MacPherson, James, 44–45
MacSwiney, Terrance, 64
Mahon, Derek, 137, 162, 354
  "A Disused Shed in County Wexford," 102
  "Glengormley," 197–98
  "The Hudson Letter," 198
A Man for All Seasons, 314

Mangan, James Clarence
  "Dark Rosaleen," 6
  "The Nameless One," 6
  "Siberia," 6
Marcel, Gabriel
  "The Mystery of the Family," 277
Marliave, Henry, 2
Marten, Harry, 122, 132
Marxism, 232–33, 235, 240
Mather, Cotton, 256
Matthews, William, 301
  "Memory," 369
  "The Wolf of Gubbio," 369
McAlmon, Robert, 65, 66, 67
McCaffrey, Lawrence, 258–59, 282, 293
McCarthyism, 82, 237
McDevitt, Mary Kilfoil, 375
  We Hardly Knew Ye, 376–77, 398
McGrath, Thomas, 232–44
  biographical information, 232
  and Bogan, 243–44
  carnivalesque approach of, 241, 242, 243
  Irishness of, 233, 240–41, 242
  leftist politics of, 232–33, 235, 236–37, 238–39, 240
  and Native Americans, 235, 241
  populism of, 242, 243
  Whitman influence on, 234, 235
  works
  —"Blues for Jimmy," 236
  —*Death Song,* 237
  —"The End of the World," 238
  —*Letter to an Imaginary Friend,* 234–35, 239–43
  —"Ode for the American Dead in Asia," 236
  —"Offering," 234

McGrath, Thomas (*cont.*)
—"The Topography of History," 235
—"A Visit to the House of the Poet," 239
—"A Warrant for Pablo Neruda," 239
McHenry, James
"The Haunts of Larne," 260, 261
McKay, Claude, 300
McLarin, Kim, 159–60
McManus, James, 305
"Two Songs for Hendrix," 298–99, 301
McMichael, James
"The Begotten," 28–29, 30
The Measure, 222
Melville, Herman, 280
memory, 173, 369
  ancestral, 262–63, 275
  Coady on, 204–5, 211–15
  Donaghy on, 356–57
  and imagination, 98, 263
  poetry driven by, 262–63, 266
Mills, Ralph, 110
Mingus, Charles, 301
modernism, 37, 75, 95, 219
  and antimodernism, 62, 67, 69, 71, 85
  Ridge and, 61, 62, 67, 69, 71, 73, 82
Montague, John, 21, 23, 113–35, 137, 204, 210
  double vision of, 114, 115, 123, 130, 132, 135
  genealogical sense of, 261–62, 269–70
  Liddy contrasted to, 148
  literary influences, 162, 326
  sense of place in, 44
  works

—"All Legendary Obstacles," 21, 113
—"American Pegasus," 134
—*The Book of Irish Poetry,* 47
—"Border Sick Call," 130
—"The Bread God," 126, 131
—"Bus Stop, Nevada," 121–22
—"The Cage," 119, 122
—"A Christmas Card," 119–20
—"The Complex Fate of Being Irish-American," 113
—"The Country Fiddler," 129
—*The Dead Kingdom,* 21, 113, 119, 120, 125, 128, 133
—"Emigrants," 117
—"Exile and Prophecy," 133
—"The Figure in the Cave," 118–19, 123, 135
—"A Flowering Absence," 120–21, 262
—*Forms of Exile,* 131
—"A Grafted Tongue," 187
—"A Graveyard in Queens," 129, 130, 131, 261–62, 269–70
—*The Great Cloak,* 130, 133
—"In the Irish Grain," 134
—introduction to *The Book of Irish Verse,* 134
—"John Berryman: Henry in Dublin," 314
—"The Last Sheaf," 125–26
—"The Locket," 119, 120, 122
—"Molly Bawn," 122
—"Mother Cat," 124–25
—"Mount Eagle," 131
—"A Muddy Cap," 125, 127–28
—"A New Siege," 116, 117
—"The Northern Gate," 131
—"Ó Riada's Farewell," 124, 131
—"Patriotic Suite," 131

—*The Rough Field,* 113, 114, 116, 118, 129, 131, 133, 388–89, 393
—"The Rough Field," 204
—"The Same Fault," 120
—"The Sean Bhean Bhocht," 125
—"Sheela na Gig," 126, 128
—"Soliloquy on a Southern Strand," 117
—"Stele for a Northern Irish Republican," 117
—"What a View," 132
—"The Wild Dog Rose," 123
Montez, Lola, 62
Mooney, Tom, 78, 85
Moore, Marianne, 36–39, 44, 66, 86, 286, 296
  and Bogan, 222, 229
  and Jeffers, 43
  works
  —"The Fish," 37
  —"The Jerboa," 37
  —"The Pangolin," 37
  —"Spenser's Ireland," 19, 37–39, 185, 285, 286
Moore, Thomas, 6
Morrison, Toni, 259, 289–90, 294, 305
  Beloved, 295
  Playing in the Dark, 280, 287, 321
Moses, Robert, 382
Muldoon, Paul, 178, 204, 243, 327, 361
  biographical information, 20
  literary influence, 198, 354
  works
  —"Madoc," 243
  —*Moy Sand and Gravel,* 20
  —"The Old Country," 342
multiculturalism, 24, 198, 354, 357
music, Irish traditional, 354, 357

"Na Pratai Dubha," 209
Nast, Thomas, 284
nationalism, 126
  Irish, 94, 116
Native Americans, 18, 46, 165, 235, 326, 393
  Irish Americans and, 166, 241, 288
Nelson, Marilyn, 301
Neruda, Pablo, 238, 239
New Formalism, 334
New School poetics, 179
New Yorker, 327
New York Times, 340
Nietzsche, Friedrich, 93
nostalgia, 34–35, 201, 331, 336, 340
  Kearny on, 341, 346
  in Montague, 116, 117–18
  in Wall, 167

Obama, Barack, 159, 160
objectivism, 75, 132
O'Brien, Kate, 103
Ó Bruadair, Dáibhí, 8, 332
O'Callaghan, Julie, 50, 328, 329, 343–46, 347
  "Chicawgo," 343–44
  "The Great Blasket Island," 345–46
  "Home," 345
O'Casey, Sean, 318
O'Connell, Daniel, 292
O'Connor, Joseph, 21
O'Connor, Liam, 137
O'Donoghue, Mary, 327
Ogham, 234–35, 240
O'Hara, Frank, 17, 137, 162, 327
  "The Day Lady Died," 163
  Lunch Hour Poems, 163
O'Heigeartaigh, Padraig
  "My Sorrow, Donncha," 22

Óisin, 44, 45, 88, 91
O'Leary, John, 159
Olson, Charles, 49–50, 75, 193
　"Enniscorthy Suite," 48–49
O'Muirthile, Liam, 190
O'Neill, Eugene, 218–19, 244
　"The Lay of the Singer's Fall," 218
　A Long Day's Journey into Night, 244
　"Submarine," 218
Oppen, George, 75
Ó Rathaille, Aogán, 8
O'Reilly, John Boyle, 2–10, 17, 35, 51, 136, 159, 305
　and bardic tradition, 6–7, 8, 55, 243
　biographical information, 2–4
　on race, 287–93, 296
　works
　—"America," 5
　—"At Fredericksburg," 5, 22, 288
　—"Crispus Attucks," 5, 289–91, 292, 293, 339
　—"The Exile of the Gael," 7–8
Ó Riada, Sean, 131
Orr, James
　"Song, Composed on the Banks of Newfoundland," 21
Otto, Rudolf, 30

Parnell, Charles Stewart, 289
parody, 343, 345, 346–47, 384
Pearse, Padraic, 64, 75
Phillips, Wendell, 289
place, sense of, 33–47, 49–50, 338, 392–93
　in Coady, 200, 206
　in Galvin, 50, 51, 275
　in Guiney, 48, 49–50
　in Heaney, 34, 35–36, 44, 115
　in Jeffers, 40, 49–50
　in McHenry, 260, 261
　in Montague, 44, 261–62
　in Stevens and Wallace, 96–98
　in Wall, 171–72
Plath, Sylvia, 225, 230, 231
Plumly, Stanley
　"Autobiography and Archetype," 266
Pope, Deborah, 224
Porter, Katherine Anne, 63
Pound, Ezra, 73, 134, 327
　antimodernism of, 62, 67, 69, 71
　works
　—*The Cantos,* 73
　—*Hugh Selwyn Mauberley,* 67, 71, 88
　—"Near Perigord," 391, 392
　—"Pisan Cantos," 81

Quartermain, Peter, 81, 82, 83

race signifiers, 280, 281, 290
racism, 252, 296
　and anti-Irish prejudice, 221–22, 284, 293
　by Irish, 282, 293–94, 296
　by writers and poets, 95, 126, 284, 292
　See also blackface
Rahner, Karl, 74
Rains, Stephanie, 55, 330, 331, 384
Redshaw, Thomas Dillon, 114, 117
return motif, 330–40
　in Berryman, 317
　in Galvin, 53, 54
　and homecoming, 122–23, 347, 360
　in Jeffers, 47, 49–50
　in Montague, 122–23, 128
revivalism, 24, 34, 94, 159, 343
Rice, T. D. "Daddy," 311
Rich, Adrienne Cecile, 225, 230, 231

Ridge, Lola, 22, 61–86
  biographical information, 61
  and Bogan, 222, 229
  and *Broom,* 65–66, 68, 75
  leftist politics of, 61–62, 63–64, 68–69, 73–74, 80–82, 238
  and modernism, 61, 62, 67, 69, 71, 73, 82
  works
  —"Crucible," 65, 85, 86
  —*Dance of Fire,* 81, 85
  —"Death Ray," 82–83
  —"East River," 81
  —"Electrocution," 82
  —"Faces," 76
  —*Firehead,* 64, 81, 83–84
  —"Flotsam," 76
  —"Fuel," 78–79
  —*The Ghetto,* 69, 76, 77, 79, 81
  —"The Ghetto," 65, 70–75, 77, 81
  —"He," 83
  —"Incompatibility," 64
  —"Jaguar," 81
  —"Kelvin Barry," 82
  —"The Living Flame of Love," 85
  —*The Long Loneliness,* 78
  —"Lullaby," 65, 77
  —"Mo-Ti," 82
  —*Red Flag,* 64, 82
  —"Red Flag," 82
  —"Reveille," 80, 81
  —"The Song of Iron," 79–80
  —"Sons of Belial," 76, 77, 81
  —"Stone Face," 85
  —"Street Accident," 82
  —*Sun-Up,* 80, 81
  —"The Tidings," 64
  —"To the American People," 69–70
  —"Wall Street at Night," 81

Riefenstahl, Leni, 149
Riis, Jacob, 395
Rilke, Rainer Maria, 229
Riverdance, 159, 328
Robinson, Edward Arlington, 66, 296
Roche, James Jeffrey, 5, 296, 305
  "The White Wolf's Cry," 294, 312
Roethke, Theodore, 132, 225–26, 231, 315
  "The Lost Son," 81
Rogers, James, 257
Rooney, Aidan, 327
Rossi, Mario
  Pilgrimage to the West, 94–95
Roy, Anindyo, 121
Ryan, Michael, 232, 237, 240

Sacco and Vanzetti, 63, 83
Said, Edward, 34, 122, 126
  on exile, 6, 55, 118, 130, 360
Sayles, John, 389
Schiller, Friedrich, 149
Schomburg, Arthur, 373–74, 381–82, 385
Schuyler, James, 17, 162, 163, 327
Schwartz, Delmore, 315–16
Scorsese, Martin, 370–71, 377, 395
sectarianism, 125, 126, 129, 327, 336
September 11, 2001, 371
sex and sexuality
  Berryman on, 308–9, 315, 318–19
  Liddy and Whitman on, 141–46
  Montague on, 128
  and sublime, 153
  Walsh on, 302–3
Sexton, Anne, 225
Shapiro, Alan
  "After the Digging," 30–33
Shawn, William, 230

Shelley, Mary
  Frankenstein, 149
Shelley, Percy, 82
  "Alastor," 88, 149, 359
Simic, Charles, 361
Simmons, Janice Fitzpatrick, 343
  "Many Waters," 334–35
Skinner, Knute, 337, 343
  "April–June 1968," 337–38
  "The Beautiful White Cow," 337
slavery, 256, 258, 280, 282, 284, 294–95
  and Middle Passage, 283, 291, 295
Smith, Robert Jerome, 122
Snyder, Gary, 137
Spenser, Edmund, 284, 317
Spicer, Jack, 137
Stafford, William, 162
Stanton, Maura
  "Elegy for Snow," 274–75
Stein, Gertrude, 65–66, 75
Stevens, Holly, 88, 89, 96
Stevens, Wallace, 37, 87–112, 291, 315
  genealogy in, 253–54
  Irishness as trope for, 87, 90, 94, 98, 104, 112
  and MacGreevy, 95–96, 98–102, 103, 108, 254
  on "pressure of reality," 135, 226
  sense of place in, 96–98
  sublime in, 89, 104, 105, 106, 108–9, 111
  on westwardness, 106–7, 108–9, 111, 167, 202, 254
  works
  —"The American Sublime," 108, 149–50, 151
  —"Blanche McCarthy," 88–90, 91
—"The Comedian as the Letter C," 88, 104, 107, 358–59
—"Credences of Summer," 107–8
—"Dutch Graves in Bucks County," 102–3, 254
—"Esthetique du Mal," 91
—"Evening Without Angels," 107
—"Farewell to Florida," 88
—"The Figure of the Youth as Virile Poet," 89
—"Final Soliloquy of the Interior Paramour," 111
—"Hermitage at the Center," 111
—"The Idea of Order at Key West," 90, 95
—"Imagination as Value," 91
—"The Irish Cliffs of Moher," 110, 111, 112, 154
—"Le Monocle de Mon Oncle," 109, 110
—"Like Decorations in a Nigger Cemetery," 95
—*The Necessary Angel,* 103, 104
—"The Noble Rider and the Sound of Words," 87
—"Notes Toward a Supreme Fiction," 92–93, 107, 241
—"Of Mere Being," 90, 91, 106
—"An Ordinary Evening in New Haven," 109
—"Our Stars Come from Ireland," 98, 99, 100, 101–2, 103, 105–6, 107, 109, 110, 111, 202–3, 254
—*The Palm at the End of the Mind,* 88, 91, 106
—"The Relation between Poetry and Painting," 104
—*The Rock,* 109, 110
—"The Rock," 111–12

—"The Sense of the Sleight-of-
  Hand Man," 107
—"Sunday Morning," 91
—"Tea at the Palaz of Hoon," 107
sublime, 149, 155
  in Liddy, 150–54, 156
  in Stevens, 89, 104, 105, 106,
    108–9, 111
Swander, Mary
  "Succession," 270–71, 272
Swift, Jonathan, 318

Teilhard de Chardin, Pierre, 147–48
Thomas, R. S., 177
Thompson, E. P., 234
Thoreau, Henry David, 382, 394–95
Three Irish Tenors, 328
Tillich, Paul, 202
Tillinghast, Richard
  Finding Ireland, 339
  "A Quiet Pint in Kinvara," 338
time motif, 338, 339, 376
  in Coady, 197, 210, 213, 214
  in Galvin, 277
  in Kavanagh, 198–99
  in Liddy, 150–51
  in Lynch, 267
  in Montague, 210
  in Wall, 172, 173
Tir na nÓg, 108
Tobin, Daniel
  family history, 282–83, 322–25,
    375, 377, 385
  works
  —"At the Tree of Many, One,"
    397, 398
  —"Ballsbridge, Dark Night," 387
  —"Bay Ridge," 387
  —"The Book of Ruth," 397
  —"Bridge View," 367–68

—"A Coat," 386
—"The Country," 393
—"Crossings," 245
—"The Dock Road," 385–86
—"Double Life," xv
—"A Green Road in Clare,"
  363–64
—"Irish American Poetry and the
  Question of Tradition," 24
—"An Island," 386
—"The Line," 401–2
—"Lost Garden Elegies," 386
—"A Mosque in Brooklyn,"
  396–97, 398
—*The Narrows,* 367, 372–73, 374,
  384–94, 397–98, 400
—"The Narrows," 390, 391–94,
  398, 400
—"Near Hag's Head," 57
—"Outerbridge Crossing," 391,
  399
—"Pallbearers at Emily
  Dickinson's Funeral," 387–88
—"Pearl Court," 387
—"The Ring," 386–87
—"St. John," 379–81, 385
—"Thinking of Meade
  Mountain," 397
Tóibín, Colm
  Brooklyn, 215
Toomer, Jean, 66
transcendentalism, 104, 348
trauma
  cultural, 283
  of displacement, 36
  historical, 37, 211, 261, 281, 285,
    286
  individual and collective, 35
  psychic, 10, 311
Trevelyan, Charles, 27, 30

Untermeyer, Louis, 224

Valentine, Jean, 328, 343
    "Long Irish Summer Day," 341–42
Verdi, Giuseppe
    La Forza del Destino, 210
Verrazano-Narrows Bridge, 367, 382, 399–400
Virgil, 317
Voigt, Ellen Bryant
    "Short Story," 257–58
The Voyage of Máel Dúin, 388

Walcott, Derek, 177
Waldman, Anne, 162
Wall, Eamonn, 13–17, 21, 160–77, 194–95, 327
    biographical information, 13–14, 160–61
    Delanty compared to, 20, 183–84, 186
    on dissemination of Irish culture, 23, 329, 334
    emigrant motif in, 15, 16, 171–72, 192, 285–86
    and Liddy, 138, 162
    as New Irish poet, 160, 161–62, 183, 194–95, 215, 286
    on parochial and provincial, 34, 134
    works
    —"All the Worshippers," 173–74
    —"The Art of Forgetting," 172
    —"Ballagh," 174
    —"The Black Hills, the Gorey Road and Object Lessons," 168–69
    —"A Christmas Card from Ireland," 166
    —"The Class of 1845," 28, 285–86
    —*The Crosses,* 162, 164, 169
    —"The Crosses," 170–71
    —"Dawn in Pennsylvania," 174
    —*Dyckman 200th Street,* 161, 162, 163, 166, 170
    —"Election Day," 164
    —"Four Stern Faces/South Dakota," 164–66, 183
    —"From St. Louis, Missouri," 14–15
    —*From the Sin-é Café to the Black Hills,* 15–16, 160, 164, 326
    —"The Grassy Garbage of Inwood," 163–64
    —"Hart Crane's Bridge," 167, 168, 186
    —"Helsinki Sequence," 170
    —"Homeland Security," 164
    —"Homework with Her Cat," 169
    —"How You Leave," 172
    —"Irish Voices, American Writing, and Green Cards," 305
    —*Iron Mountain Road,* 162, 164–65
    —"Junk Food," 164, 183
    —"Know Your Place," 171–72
    —"Leaving Boise," 16–17, 176–77
    —"Lewis and Clarke: Omaha, Nebraska," 175–76
    —"Midsummer's Eve," 174–75
    —"Mother and Daughter Aubade," 169
    —"Of Multitude," 175, 176
    —"Outside the Tall Building: Federal Plaza," 166–67
    —"A Radio Foretold: Green Card," 166–67
    —*Refuge at DeSoto Bend,* 14, 162, 164, 171, 172, 174
    —"Revelation," 172–73
    —"A Rose in Coyoacan," 170

—"A Route to Dunbrody," 173, 174
—"Song at Lake Michigan," 167–68, 183
—*A Tour of Your Country,* 162, 164, 169, 170, 172, 173, 174, 176, 177
—"Two Stops on the River," 166–67
—"The Westward Journey," 170, 172
—"The Wexford Container Tragedy," 14, 33
—"Winter Thoughts from Nebraska," 169
Wallace, Mike, 138
Walsh, Ernest, 65–66, 301, 326
  "Irish," 301–3, 305
  "Poem for a Negro Voice," 301, 304–5
Ward, Patrick, 13, 34, 39, 55, 328
  Exile, Emigration, and Irish Writing, 11, 352–53
Weil, Simone, 79, 86
  "Factory Work," 78
  The Need for Roots, 117–18, 252
Weiskel, Thomas, 149
Wescott, Glenway, 66
westwardness, 87, 105, 395
  as Stevens theme, 106–7, 108–9, 111, 167, 202, 254
  as Wall theme, 170–71
Whitman, Sarah Helen
  "Don Isle," 259–60, 261, 262
Whitman, Walt, 140, 148, 243, 244, 388
  on America as open road, 102, 108, 255, 273
  Delanty and, 186
  on genealogy, 259–60, 261, 262
  Liddy and, 138, 142–43

McGrath and, 234, 235
Ridge and, 70
on sex and sexuality, 142, 143, 145, 146
works
—*Leaves of Grass,* 137, 139, 141, 142, 186
—"Out of the Cradle Endlessly Rocking," 145
—"Song of Myself," 112, 142, 145
—"Starting from Paumanok," 139, 141, 335
—"When Lilacs Last in the Dooryard Bloomed," 145
Whittier, John Greenleaf, 5
Wilde, Oscar, 5, 326
Williams, C. K., 251, 277–78
  "The Poet and History," 255–56
Williams, William Carlos, 37, 66, 137, 148
  Berryman elegy to, 318
  as futurist, 67–68, 69
  and Montague, 132, 326
  on objectivism, 75
  works
—*Autobiography,* 66
—*In the American Grain,* 134
Wilson, Edmund, 222–23
Wittke, Carl
  Tambo and Bones, 311
women, 67
  poetry by, 225, 230, 232
Woods, Macdara, 137
Wood-Smith, Cecil
  The Great Hunger, 30
Wordsworth, William, 149, 177, 317
  "Ode, Intimations of Immortality," 397
  The Prelude, 35, 92
  "The Prelude," 239, 333

Wright, Charles, 348
Wright, Richard, 305

Yeats, Elizabeth, 94
Yeats, William Butler, 9, 87, 88, 264, 326
  on genealogy and ancestry, 250–51, 253
  as influence on Bogan, 220, 226–27, 229
  mask idea of, 223, 320
  poetic influence of, 41, 94–95, 318, 319
  on unity of being, 114–15
  works
  —"Among School Children," 354
  —"Ancestral Houses," 387
  —bird songs, 90–91
  —"General Introduction to My Work," 25
  —"Meditations in Time of Civil War," 236, 387
  —"Pardon, Old Fathers," 251, 252, 273
  —"September 1919," 159
  —"To Be Carved on a Stone at Thoor Ballylee," 41
Young, Kevin, 310

DANIEL TOBIN
is professor and interim dean of the School of Arts
at Emerson College. He is the author and editor
of a number of books, including
The Book of Irish American Poetry from the Eighteenth Century to the Present
(University of Notre Dame Press, 2008).

www.ingramcontent.com/pod-product-compliance
Lightning Source LLC
Chambersburg PA
CBHW020117240426

43673CB00038B/516